7th Workshop on Sign Language Translation and Avatar Technology: The Junction of the Visual & the Textual Challenges and Perspectives (SLTAT 7)

Held at LREC 2022

Marseille, France
24 June 2022

Editors:

Eleni Efthimiou
Stavroula-Evita Fotinea
Thomas Hanke
John C. McDonald
Dimitar Shterionov
Rosalee Wolfe

ISBN: 978-1-7138-6139-3

Printed from e-media with permission by:

Curran Associates, Inc.
57 Morehouse Lane
Red Hook, NY 12571

Some format issues inherent in the e-media version may also appear in this print version.

Association for Computational Linguistics
209 N. Eighth Street
Stroudsburg, Pennsylvania 18360

Phone: 1-570-476-8006
Fax: 1-570-476-0860

acl@aclweb.org

Additional copies of this publication are available from:

Curran Associates, Inc.
57 Morehouse Lane
Red Hook, NY 12571 USA
Phone: 845-758-0400
Fax: 845-758-2633
Email: curran@proceedings.com
Web: www.proceedings.com

LREC 2022 Workshop
Language Resources and Evaluation Conference
24 June 2022

7th Workshop on Sign Language Translation and Avatar Technology: The Junction of the Visual & the Textual Challenges and Perspectives (SLTAT 7)

PROCEEDINGS

Editors:
Eleni Efthimiou, Stavroula-Evita Fotinea, Thomas Hanke,
John C. McDonald, Dimitar Shterionov, Rosalee Wolfe

Proceedings of the LREC 2022 7th Workshop on Sign Language Translation and Avatar Technology: The Junction of the Visual & the Textual Challenges and Perspectives (SLTAT 7)

Edited by:
Eleni Efthimiou, Stavroula-Evita Fotinea, Thomas Hanke,
John C. McDonald, Dimitar Shterionov, Rosalee Wolfe

For more information:
European Language Resources Association (ELRA)
9 rue des Cordelières
75013, Paris
France
http://www.elra.info
Email: lrec@elda.org

Preface

This volume documents the Proceedings of the 7th Workshop on Sign Language Translation and Avatar Technology, held on June 24, 2022 as part of the LREC 2022 conference (International Conference on Language Resources and Evaluation).

Sign language translation and avatar technologies have the potential to improve communication between Deaf and hearing communities. In this seventh edition of the SLTAT workshop there is encouraging evidence that the dream of automated translation between signed and spoken languages is coming closer to reality. Coupled with the 10th Workshop on the Representation and Processing of Sign Languages, this meeting offers a forum for researchers focusing on building connections between the diverse and beautiful signed and spoken languages of the world.

Part and parcel of this research specialty are two of this year's Hot Topics: Multilingualism and Language Technology for All and Machine Learning and Multimodality. The editors are pleased to report that several of the papers address these on point.

The papers in these proceedings appear in alphabetical order by the first author. An author index provides an easy means of accessing papers written by a particular author.

Many thanks to our exemplary program committee who were a tremendous help in providing substantive and constructive feedback to authors in a very short time frame.

Organizers

Eleni Efthimiou, Institute for Language and Speech Processing, Athens, Greece
Stavroula-Evita Fotinea, Institute for Language and Speech Processing, Athens, Greece
Thomas Hanke, Institute of German Sign Language, University of Hamburg, Germany
John C. McDonald, School of Computing, DePaul University, Chicago, USA
Dimitar Shterionov, University of Tilburg, The Netherlands
Rosalee Wolfe, Institute for Language and Speech Processing, Athens, Greece

Program Committee:

Nicoletta Adamo-Villani, West Lafayette US
Souad Baowidan, Jedda, SA
Josep Blat, Barcelona ES
Richard Bowden, Guildford UK
Penny Boyes Braem, Zürich, CH
Annelies Braffort, Orsay FR
Onno Crasborn, Nijmegen NL
Mathieu de Coster, Ghent BE
Mirella De Sisto, Tilburg NL
Connie de Vos, Tilburg University, NL
Sarah Ebling, Zürich CH
Michael Filhol, Orsay FR
Neil Fox, London, UK
Sylvie Gibet, Vannes FR
Alexis Heloir, Valenciennes FR
Matt Huenerfauth, Rochester US
Giacomo Inches, Lugano CH
Amy Isard, Hamburg DE
Hernisa Kacorri, College Park US
Reiner Konrad, Hamburg DE
Kevin Lee, Seoul KR
Robyn Moncrief, Chicago US
Carol Neidle, Boston US
Fabrizio Nunnari, Saarbrücken DE
Floris Roelofsen, Amsterdam NL
Ellen Rushe, Dublin IE
Marc Schulder, Hamburg DE
Lynette Van Zijl, Stellenbosch ZA
Anthony Ventresque, Dublin IE

Table of Contents

Proceedings of the 7th International Workshop on Sign Language Translation and Avatar Technology (SLTAT 7), pages 1–6
Language Resources and Evaluation Conference (LREC 2022), Marseille, 20-25 June 2022

Synthesis for the Kinematic Control of Identity in Sign Language

Félix Bigand, Elise Prigent, Annelies Braffort
Université Paris-Saclay, CNRS, LISN, Orsay, France
{felix.bigand, elise.prigent, annelies.braffort}@lisn.upsaclay.fr

Abstract

Sign Language (SL) animations generated from motion capture (mocap) of real signers convey critical information about their identity. It has been suggested that this information is mostly carried by statistics of the movements kinematics. Manipulating these statistics in the generation of SL movements could allow controlling the identity of the signer, notably to preserve anonymity. This paper tests this hypothesis by presenting a novel synthesis algorithm that manipulates the identity-specific statistics of mocap recordings. The algorithm produced convincing new versions of French Sign Language discourses, which accurately modulated the identity prediction of a machine learning model. These results open up promising perspectives toward the automatic control of identity in the motion animation of virtual signers.

Keywords: Sign Language, Anonymized Content, Identity Conversion, Motion Generation, Machine Learning

1. Introduction

Using motion capture (mocap) systems, the movements of signers can be recorded with high accuracy and be used to produce natural and comprehensible content (Lu and Huenerfauth, 2010; Gibet, 2018). However, this process raises an unexpected problem, related to the human ability to identify individuals from their movements (Troje et al., 2005; Loula et al., 2005; Bläsing and Sauzet, 2018). As for spoken languages in the auditory domain, where voice parameters inform about the identity of a speaker, signers can be identified from their movements (Bigand et al., 2020). We present a synthesis algorithm for controlling the motion features that characterize the identity of a signer. This would allow producing anonymized, non-identifiable, content with virtual signers, which is crucial (e.g., for sharing anonymized testimony) given that Sign Languages (SLs) have no written form (Lee et al., 2021).

In line with prior work on non-SL movements (Troje et al., 2005; Carlson et al., 2020; Zhang and Troje, 2005), our recent studies suggested that identity was mainly inferred from the kinematic aspects of the movements, beyond size, shape or posture of the signers (Bigand et al., 2020; Bigand et al., 2021). Using a machine learning model, we automatically extracted the specific kinematic aspects of motion that carry identity, using time-averaged statistics (Section 2). The present synthesis algorithm was then developed in order to manipulate the identity-specific statistics of original mocap recordings (Section 3). We tested the performance of the synthesis algorithm by modifying the identity attribute of mocap recordings in French Sign Language, and by assessing the identity inferred from the new excerpts (Section 4). This constitutes the first step toward automatically anonymizing the movements of signers in SL animations, in the same way as for the voice of a speaker, which can be anonymized by modifying specific vocal parameters (Section 5).

2. Motion statistics of identity

Mocap recordings were taken from MOCAP1 corpus (Benchiheub et al., 2020). Six signers had freely described the content of 24 pictures using French Sign Language (LSF). From each of the 24 original recordings, one mocap recording unit of 5-seconds duration was extracted from the beginning of the utterance (see examples in Videos 7.1 to 7.6). As shown in Figure 1, the used markers were (L = left, R = right, F = front, B = back): (1) pelvis, (2) stomach, (3) sternum, (4) LB head, (5) LF head, (6) RB head, (7) RF head, (8) L shoulder, (9) L elbow, (10) LB wrist, (11) LF wrist, (12) LB hand, (13) LF hand, (14) R shoulder, (15) R elbow, (16) RB wrist, (17) RF wrist, (18) RB hand, (19) RF hand. The mocap examples were normalized with respect to size, shape and posture of the signers (see Bigand et al. (2021)). The mocap data of the pelvis marker were ignored as it was set as the origin, which leads to zero vectors. Position and velocity of the body markers were used as temporal features. Velocity was estimated by time differentiation of the mocap position coordinates.

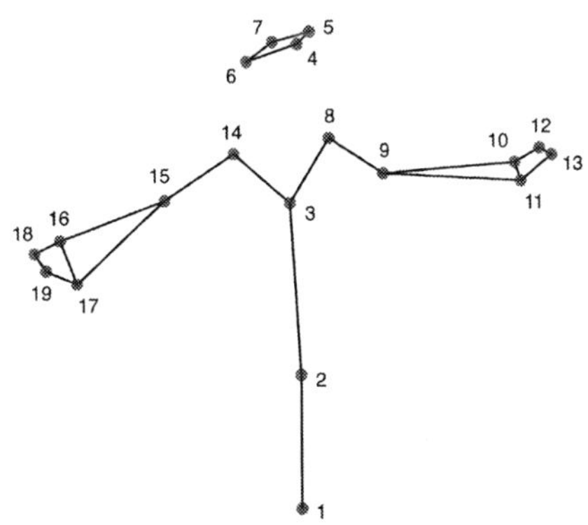

Figure 1: The 19 upper-body markers used in the mocap recordings.

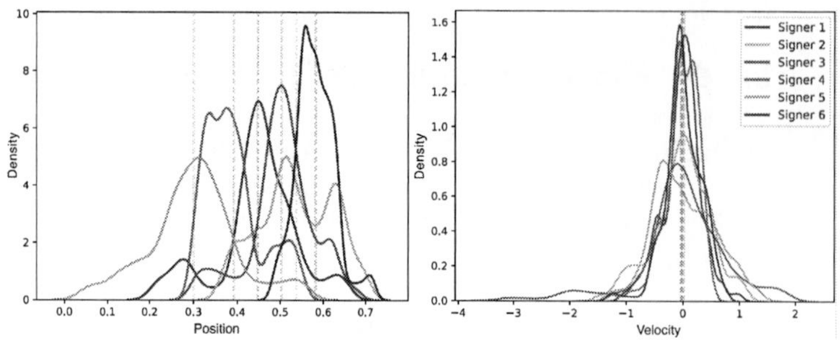

Figure 2: Distributions of position and velocity data of the RF hand marker along the Z axis, for mocap example 24. Dashed vertical lines represent the means.

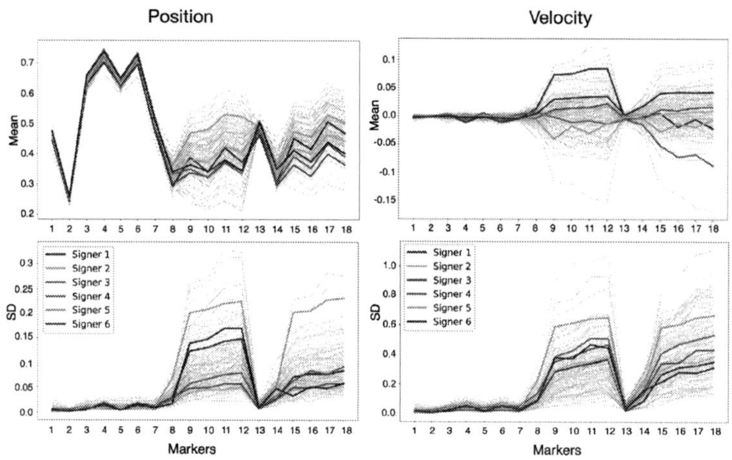

Figure 3: The two moments of the position and velocity data along the Z axis, for all markers and all 144 mocap examples. Thick lines represent the average statistics of each signer across their 24 examples.

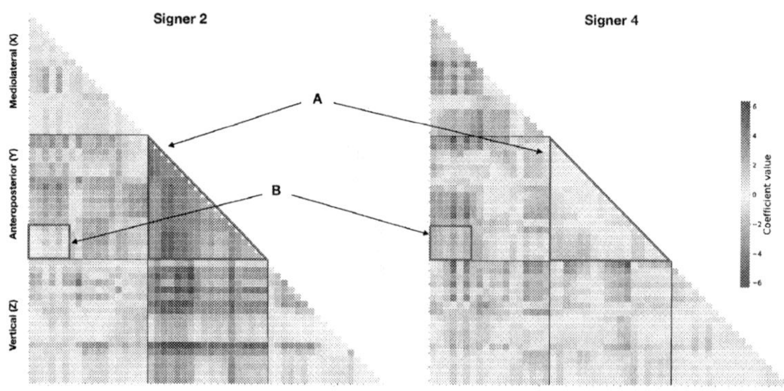

Figure 4: The covariance of velocity between body markers (rows and columns) of Signer 2 and Signer 4 in the three dimensions, for mocap example 24. Markers are sorted from the 1st to the 19th as presented in Bigand et al. (2021), along X, Y and Z axes. Coefficients correspond to the covariance measures centered and standardized across examples and signers. Blue represent positive covariances, while red represent negative ones. (A) covariance between all markers along the Y axis. (B) covariance between the right hand and arm markers along the Y axis, and the trunk and head markers along the X axis.

Statistics of the mocap examples were then computed as follows. Based on previous research investigating the perception of auditory and visual textures (McDermott and Simoncelli, 2011; Portilla and Simoncelli, 2000), we measured the first two moments (i.e., mean and standard deviation (SD)) of position and velocity, and covariances of velocity between body markers. The first two moments of position and velocity described their statistical distributions, which may vary from one individual to another, as shown for expert gesture analysis (Tits, 2018). Moreover, the covariance of velocity allowed for quantifying the extent to which any two markers covaried with each other, in two directions. This latter statistic has been shown to allow for automatic person identification from dance movements (Carlson et al., 2020).

These statistics vary substantially across the mocap data of different signers. For instance, as shown in Figure 2, the position and velocity data of one body marker are distributed differently across signers, for one mocap example (i.e., for comparable content: the description of the same picture in LSF). Distributions of position data differ in location of the peak (captured by the mean) and width (captured by the standard deviation). Figure 3 further supports that the two moments of position and velocity may capture substantial differences across signers.

Furthermore, velocity covariances capture different aspects of motor coordination between the markers in three dimensions, which can differ across signers. Various distinct coordination patterns can be extracted. For instance, for mocap example 24, the movements of Signer 2 show an overall substantial (positive) covariance between body markers along the Y axis, while this covariance is near zero for Signer 4 (Figure 4.A). Inversely, Signer 4 displays an important (negative) covariance of movements of the right arm and hand along the Y axis with the trunk (i.e., stomach and sternum) and head markers along the X axis, while this covariance is less important for Signer 2 (Figure 4.B). Taken together, these examples raise the possibility that the identity of a signer is conveyed by statistical properties of his or her movements.

3. Methods

The automatic signer identification model presented in Bigand et al. (2021) allowed extracting specific kinematic statistics that carry identity information about the signers. A linear classifier was trained to extract the statistics of the mocap data characteristic of identity (i.e., the ones that allow for accurate signer identification).

Then, the aim of the present synthesis algorithm was to manipulate the statistics of an original SL mocap recording (i.e., impose new statistics to the original recording), in order to reduce ($\alpha < 0$) or exaggerate ($\alpha > 0$) the identity attribute, following Equation 1:

$$\tilde{\mathbf{d}}_{\alpha} = \mathbf{d_{orig}} + \alpha \mathbf{d_k} \tag{1}$$

where $\tilde{\mathbf{d}}_{\alpha}$ is a vector containing the new target statistics to be imposed by the synthesis alogrithm, $\mathbf{d_{orig}}$ is a vector containing the original statistics of the mocap example, $\mathbf{d_k}$ is a vector containing the overall statistical patterns characteristic of the identity of Signer k, and α is a scalar related to the amount of reduction ($\alpha < 0$) or exaggeration ($\alpha > 0$) of the identity attribute.

The different steps of the synthesis process are displayed in Figure 5. In summary, the synthesis process consisted of modifying (i.e., "re-synthezing") an existing mocap recording in order to change the identity attribute of the signer, according to the following steps. First, statistics of the original mocap example are measured, while the discriminant statistical kinematic patterns are extracted by the automatic identification model (see Bigand et al. (2021)). Then, the discriminant statistics characteristic of Signer k are either added to ($\alpha > 0$) or subtracted from ($\alpha < 0$) the ones of the original example (see Equation 1). Multiple manipulations can then be done using this technique, depending on the values of k and α. For instance, if the original mocap example relates to Signer 1, reducing the importance of her identity-specific statistics (i.e., $k = 1, \alpha < 0$) would make her less identifiable (i.e., kinematic anonymization). By contrast, increasing the importance of the identity-specific statistics of Signer 2 (i.e., $k = 2, \alpha > 0$) would make this latter signer identifiable while the SL movements were originally executed by Signer 1 (i.e., kinematic identity conversion). Once the target statistics defined, they are imposed to the original mocap signal by the algorithm, which creates a new mocap excerpt.

Target statistics were imposed using an iterative process where a synthesized mocap signal (initialized with the content of the original mocap recording) is modified until its statistics are sufficiently close to the target ones $\tilde{\mathbf{d}}_{\alpha}$. Mathematically, the objective of this process is to minimize the loss function that calculates the mean square of the differences between the target statistics and the statistics of the synthesized movements (see Equation 2). We imposed the first two moments (mean and SD) of position and velocity data and the covariance of velocity between markers, as they were found to be the most important statistics for signer identification (Bigand, 2021). Imposing the mean of position and mean of velocity of the markers was done to maintain consistent motion data when synthesizing (e.g., to avoid the generation of unrealistic, non-biological, movements), although these two statistics had only minor role in the identification.

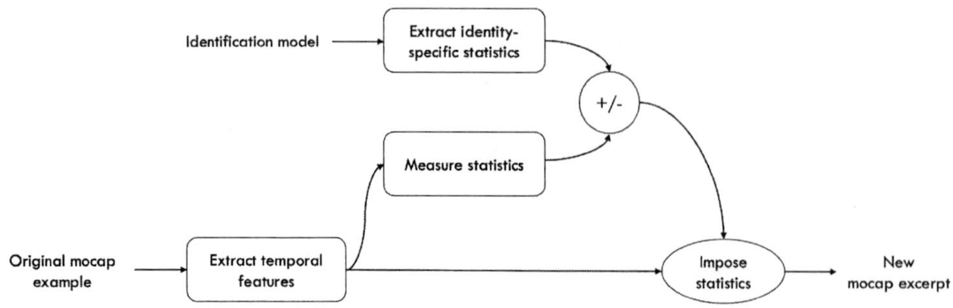

Figure 5: Schematic representation of the steps used in the synthesis algorithm for the kinematic control of identity.

$$\begin{aligned} loss_1 &= \sum_m (\mu_{pos,m,targ} - \mu_{pos,m,synth})^2 \\ loss_2 &= \sum_m (\sigma_{pos,m,targ} - \sigma_{pos,m,synth})^2 \\ loss_3 &= \sum_m (\mu_{vel,m,targ} - \mu_{vel,m,synth})^2 \\ loss_4 &= \sum_m (\sigma_{vel,m,targ} - \sigma_{vel,m,synth})^2 \\ loss_5 &= \sum_{i,j} (C_{i,j,targ} - C_{i,j,synth})^2 \\ loss_{tot} &= \sum_{i=1}^{5} loss_i \end{aligned} \quad (2)$$

where $\mu_{pos,m}$, $\sigma_{pos,m}$, $\mu_{vel,m}$ and $\sigma_{vel,m}$ are the first two moments of position and velocity data of marker m ($m \in [1, 54]$), $C_{i,j}$ is the covariance of velocity between markers i and j. $targ$ and $synth$ subscripts distinguish between target statistics and statistics of the synthesized movements, respectively.

In order to be able to minimize all of the five loss components of Equation 2 despite the differences in ranges of amplitude across statistics, we used a weighted loss function, whose weights then need to be optimized (see Equation 3). The loss function was then minimized using the Adam optimization algorithm for gradient descent. Each iterative step of the gradient descent modified the synthesized mocap signals (i.e., position temporal curves of the 19 markers along the three dimensions) so that they approached the target statistics.

$$loss_{tot} = \sum_{i=1}^{5} w_i loss_i \quad (3)$$

where $loss_i$ is the loss function related to one statistical measure and w_i the optimized weight.

Initially, there was no constraint in the synthesis process that forced the position and velocity signals of the synthesized movements to remain consistent with their initial temporal structure in the original movements. The limitation of this first version of the algorithm is that, although it managed to impose the statistics present in Equation 2, the modifications applied to the new movements seemed to generate noise artifacts rather than changing relevant aspects of the motion of the signer (see Video 10.1). In fact, the imposing algorithm managed to impose the target statistics but by modifying the movements in an undesired manner. First, low-energy segments of the motion were modified in the same way as high-energy ones, which is not relevant as they may not be perceived by observers. Moreover, reaching the target statistics caused very rapid oscillations in the synthesized velocity temporal curves, which are unlikely to be perceived as biological motion by the observers (but rather noisy, wobbling, markers).

In order to modify the movements in proportion to their energy (i.e., modify the aspects of the movement at relevant times of actual, perceptible, motion), we included another target statistic in the imposing algorithm: the correlation of velocity between the original and synthesized movements. The algorithm then aimed to minimize the mean squared error between this correlation and a value of 1, which characterizes two signals that are perfectly positively correlated (see Equation 4). In other words, imposing this additional statistic (Equation 5) allowed forcing the velocity curves of the synthesized movements to be consistent with their initial temporal structure in the original mocap recording (Figure 6).

$$loss_6 = \sum_m (1 - \rho_{vel,m,synth})^2 \quad (4)$$

$$loss_{tot} = \sum_{i=1}^{6} w_i loss_i \quad (5)$$

where $\rho_{vel,m}$ is the correlation of velocity between the original and synthesized movements of marker m ($m \in [1, 54]$). The target correlation value is set to 1 for all markers, in order to preserve the original temporal structure of velocity curves.

4. Results

This synthesis procedure was run on mocap examples of different signers and for different modifications of the identity attribute. In order to visualize how these

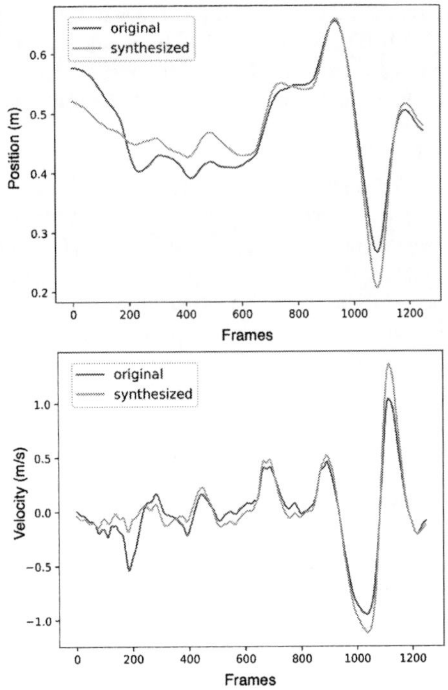

Figure 6: Example of the synthesis results for the identity conversion from Signer 1 to Signer 2 (mocap example 1). Position (up) and velocity (down) data of RF hand marker along the Z axis are shown, for the original mocap recording and synthesized mocap excerpt.

new statistics affected the movements of the SL discourse of Signer 1, the original and synthesized mocap examples can be seen as "point-light" display videos. For instance, the movements of Signer 1 were modified so that the perceived identity was that of Signer 2 (i.e., identity conversion) (see Videos 10.3 and 10.4). Then, they were modified to make Signer 1 not identifiable, without making another signer identifiable specifically (i.e., anonymization) (see Videos 10.5 and 10.6). One further synthesis example of identity conversion (from Signer 2 to Signer 1) can be found in Bigand (2021).

In order to assess the extent to which the novel movements generated by our algorithm could convey a modified identity attribute (e.g., could be anonymized, or identified as movements of another signer), we tested our automatic signer identification model on the synthesized mocap examples. If the identity-specific aspects of the movements are correctly modified by the synthesis algorithm, then automatic identification from these synthesized examples should be compromised.

When converting the identity of Signer 1 into that of Signer 2, the automatic signer identification model identified the synthesized mocap example as that of Signer 2, while it identified the original motion as produced by Signer 1 (see Table 1). Then, when anonymizing the content of Signer 1, the signer identification model did not manage to identify Signer 1 from the synthesized movements (see Table 1). Moreover, the highest identification probability from this excerpt was 0.43, which means that it did not clearly identify any other signer from the anonymized movements.

Table 1: Output of the automatic signer identification model from original and synthesized movements of Signer 1. The synthesized versions consist of identity conversion into Signer 2 and anonymization. Each output number is the probability that the movements were produced by the signer. Bold numbers represent the highest probability across the six signers.

	Original	Synthesized	
		Conversion	Anonymization
Signer 1	**0.99**	0.00	0.05
Signer 2	0.00	**0.99**	0.34
Signer 3	0.00	0.00	0.14
Signer 4	0.00	0.00	0.01
Signer 5	0.00	0.00	0.02
Signer 6	0.00	0.00	**0.43**

5. Discussion

This paper shows that simple statistics of the movements of a signer can be manipulated in order to regenerate mocap recordings with a modified identity attribute. The mocap data of SL discourses can undergo various manipulations, such as kinematic identity conversion or anonymization. Moreover, the synthesis algorithm preserves the original temporal structure of the movements, which is crucial because degrading temporal structure could impair the comprehension of the SL discourse.

Up to now, anonymization methods of SL content were modifying appearance, using virtual signers (Kipp et al., 2011) or modified videos (e.g., face-swapped videos, where the face of the signer is replaced with another face) (Lee et al., 2021; Bragg et al., 2020). Our technique focuses on controlling the identity in the kinematics of the signers, which could interestingly complement prior approaches in order to provide full anonymity, beyond face or body shape manipulations. Moreover, the proposed algorithm has the advantage that it can render the movements of signers as neutral (i.e., not reflecting the identity of any other signer), by contrast with face-swapping techniques.

However, some limitations of the present work should be noted in order to ensure an effective use of these tools in actual applications. First, although we aimed to use SL mocap data as representative as possible of real-life conditions (i.e., spontaneous LSF), the discourses used in the present study were picture descriptions, which may have involved specific linguistic structures more than others (e.g., depicting ones). The different outcomes reported here should be further tested in a wider linguistic context.

Moreover, the present computational findings call for further tests with human participants. Three key problems should be investigated, similarly to prior work on video anonymization (Lee et al., 2021): (1) identifiability, by verifying that the ability of human observers to identify the signers is compromised when showing the synthesized modified movements, as compared to the original ones (e.g., with "point-light" displays like in Bigand et al. (2020) and Troje et al. (2005)); (2) comprehensibility, by evaluating the extent to which the observers still understand the SL content in the modified motion examples; and (3) acceptability, by assessing the deaf user perspective on the virtual signers animated with the modified movements and discussing potential use cases (e.g., with focus groups). Should these three fundamental points be validated, the present work could constitute a first step of interest toward automatically controlling the identity of deaf SL users when expressing themselves via virtual signers. Moreover, as shown for videos (Bragg et al., 2020), preserving anonymity in mocap recordings could increase willingness of SL users to participate in mocap research (e.g., in data collection), which is crucial to develop effective and acceptable technologies.

6. Acknowledgements

This work has been funded by the Bpifrance (`https://www.bpifrance.fr/`) investment project "Grands défis du numerique", as part of the ROSETTA project (RObot for Subtitling and intElligent adapTed TranslAtion).

7. Bibliographical References

Bigand, F., Prigent, E., and Braffort, A. (2020). Person identification based on sign language motion: Insights from human perception and computational modeling. In *Proceedings of the 7th International Conference on Movement and Computing*, pages 1–7.

Bigand, F., Prigent, E., Berret, B., and Braffort, A. (2021). Machine learning of motion statistics reveals the kinematic signature of a person's identity in sign language. *Frontiers in Bioengineering and Biotechnology*, 9:603.

Bigand, F. (2021). *Extracting human characteristics from motion using machine learning : the case of identity in Sign Language*. Theses, Université Paris-Saclay, November.

Bläsing, B. E. and Sauzet, O. (2018). My action, my self: Recognition of self-created but visually unfamiliar dance-like actions from point-light displays. *Frontiers in psychology*, 9:1909.

Bragg, D., Koller, O., Caselli, N., and Thies, W. (2020). Exploring collection of sign language datasets: Privacy, participation, and model performance. In *The 22nd International ACM SIGACCESS Conference on Computers and Accessibility*, pages 1–14.

Carlson, E., Saari, P., Burger, B., and Toiviainen, P. (2020). Dance to your own drum: Identification of musical genre and individual dancer from motion capture using machine learning. *Journal of New Music Research*, pages 1–16.

Gibet, S. (2018). Building french sign language motion capture corpora for signing avatars. In *Workshop on the Representation and Processing of Sign Languages: Involving the Language Community, LREC 2018*.

Kipp, M., Heloir, A., and Nguyen, Q. (2011). Sign language avatars: Animation and comprehensibility. In *International Workshop on Intelligent Virtual Agents*, pages 113–126. Springer.

Lee, S., Glasser, A., Dingman, B., Xia, Z., Metaxas, D., Neidle, C., and Huenerfauth, M. (2021). American sign language video anonymization to support online participation of deaf and hard of hearing users. In *The 23rd International ACM SIGACCESS Conference on Computers and Accessibility*, pages 1–13.

Loula, F., Prasad, S., Harber, K., and Shiffrar, M. (2005). Recognizing people from their movement. *Journal of Experimental Psychology: Human Perception and Performance*, 31(1):210.

Lu, P. and Huenerfauth, M. (2010). Collecting a motion-capture corpus of american sign language for data-driven generation research. In *Proceedings of the NAACL HLT 2010 Workshop on Speech and Language Processing for Assistive Technologies*, pages 89–97.

McDermott, J. H. and Simoncelli, E. P. (2011). Sound texture perception via statistics of the auditory periphery: evidence from sound synthesis. *Neuron*, 71(5):926–940.

Portilla, J. and Simoncelli, E. P. (2000). A parametric texture model based on joint statistics of complex wavelet coefficients. *International journal of computer vision*, 40(1):49–70.

Tits, M. (2018). *Expert Gesture Analysis through Motion Capture using Statistical Modeling and Machine Learning*. Ph.D. thesis, Ph. D. Dissertation.

Troje, N. F., Westhoff, C., and Lavrov, M. (2005). Person identification from biological motion: Effects of structural and kinematic cues. *Perception & Psychophysics*, 67(4):667–675.

Zhang, Z. and Troje, N. F. (2005). View-independent person identification from human gait. *Neurocomputing*, 69(1-3):250–256.

8. Language Resource References

Benchiheub et al. (2020). *MOCAP1 corpus*. distributed via ORTOLANG: `https://hdl.handle.net/11403/mocap1/v1`, v1.

Proceedings of the 7th International Workshop on Sign Language Translation and Avatar Technology (SLTAT 7), pages 7–12
Language Resources and Evaluation Conference (LREC 2022), Marseille, 20-25 June 2022

Analysis of Torso Movement for Signing Avatar Using Deep Learning

Shatabdi Choudhury
School of Computing, DePaul University, 243 S. Wabash Ave, Chicago, IL 60604, USA,
schoud12@depaul.edu

Abstract

Avatars are virtual or on-screen representations of a human used in various roles for sign language display, including translation and educational tools. Though the ability of avatars to portray acceptable sign language with believable human-like motion has improved in recent years, many still lack the naturalness and supporting motions of human signing. Such details are generally not included in the linguistic annotation. Nevertheless, these motions are highly essential to displaying lifelike and communicative animations. This paper presents a deep learning model for use in a signing avatar. The study focuses on coordinating torso movements and other human body parts. The proposed model will automatically compute the torso rotation based on the avatar's wrist positions. The resulting motion can improve the user experience and engagement with the avatar.

Keywords: Sign Language, Avatar, Neural Network, Deep Learning

1. Introduction

Interactive avatars have grown popular as learning tools for spoken languages. Virtual reality has become a new tool to aid deaf or hard-of-hearing learners with specialized guidance in learning core academic concepts, such as mathematics and science (Zirzow, 2015). A signing avatar has been proposed to assist deaf students in a comprehensive educational environment(De Martino et al., 2017). Avatars are evaluated as a potential communication medium to facilitate language learning in babies (Nasihati Gilani et al., 2019).

Avatars are also increasingly popular in social media, personalizing users' contributions to interacting and representing users and their behaviors. People prefer to have an avatar in their profile to secure their visual anonymity or pseudo-anonymity. Anonymity enables them to express and observe opinions they would not necessarily be comfortable with elsewhere while holding personal characteristics (Vasalou et al., 2008). Historically, people have adopted a pen name or alias to express themselves anonymously for several reasons. Deaf experience in signing online is inherently not anonymous. An avatar would help signers who do not want to reveal their identity.

There is a rise of a new generation of AI avatars for speech interaction, such as Amelia, that serves as virtual cognitive assistant (Davenport et al., 2020). Deep learning capacities support her ability to learn human interaction continuously and create an engaging user experience to drive higher business value.

The use of avatars in signing can be equally exciting and has potential benefits over video recordings of a sign. One can see a sign from a different angle or zoom in, or the pace or rhythm of the signing can be customized based on users' needs. The scene's background can also be adapted based on the context or better clarity of the sign (Jaballah and Jemni, 2014). The modeling and animation of signed contents generated once can automatically become reusable software components, which can be re-purposed for novel utterances.

Though the need to make avatars natural is widely recognized in the animation industry, the current quality of signing avatars is still not satisfactory for producing human-like user experiences, making them less acceptable to the Deaf community (Jancso et al., 2016). Since speech is missing in sign language, supporting movements are essential to engage the communication. This research recognizes that torso movements are critical for direct linguistic communication (McDonald et al., July 8 11 2014). However, incorporating the coordination for each movement is a time-consuming process for animators. The avatars driven by linguistic input become robotic because linguistic descriptions lack the subtleties of human motion. Motion capture can automatically incorporate natural torso support but is inflexible for generating new signing that has not been specifically recorded. Furthermore, multiple processes in signing can affect the torso simultaneously, and the effects can be difficult to separate or isolate in such recordings (Filhol et al., 2017).

This paper introduces a novel application of deep learning to predict the torso movement of a signing avatar. The method will build a deep sequential neural network, implement it in the avatar and test it against the source motion capture data for validation.

2. Importance of Torso Motion in Signing

Analyzing and modeling the supportive motions, such as torso movements, is crucial to make the avatar mimic human movements accurately. The motions supported by the torso include reach, balance, emotion, or the turning of the body to assume participants' positions in reported speech or to indicate a side-facing object. The principles of overlapping movements are essential for the avatar to get a natural and believable feel (Burleigh et al., 2018).

The following figures show three illustrations of torso movements during the signing of a scene description. In Figure 1, the signer is twisting her torso to produce a side-facing sign, and in Figure 2, the signer is leaning her torso to the side to balance. In Figure 3, the signer is bending backward to illustrate a scene.

An arm raised outwards and another arm moved across the body impacts how the torso is twisted and should be positioned to look natural. Shoulder, wrist, and hand movements must be carefully considered, especially when transitioning from one type of composition to another. One must

Figure 1: Twisting the torso to depict objects to the side of the signing space

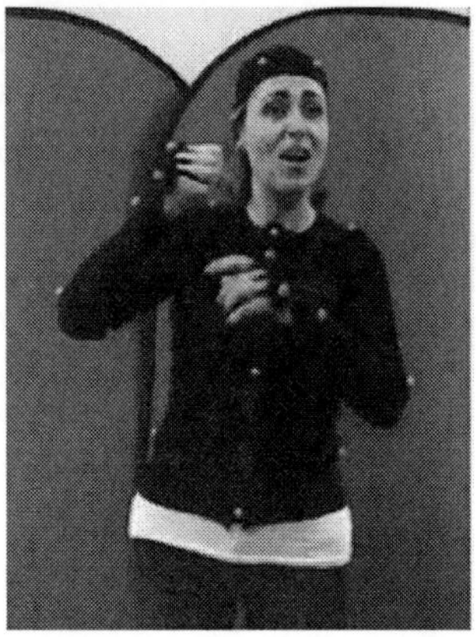

Figure 2: Leaning the torso to the side for balance

consider how much the wrist is bent and how the elbow is raised to orient the palm. All these specific actions can make the avatar more realistic in its movements. Modeling and automating such coordination would result in a practical, accurate, and interactive synthesis. It will elevate the avatar to drive a deeper connection with users.

3. Related Work

Though the natural movements of the spine are captured and can be directly replayed from motion capture data, the segmentation and synthesis of novel discourse from motion capture data is a complicated process that is the focus of ongoing research (Gibet, 2018). Many efforts for sign synthesis focus on describing sign language using a phonetic description called the Hamburg Notation System (Hanke, 2004) (Efthimiou et al., 2010). It subdivides the movements of the signer into a string of individual specifications for the parts of the body. The linguistic descriptions do not encode the motions of the torso unless they have a specific linguistic meaning (Kennaway, 2015).

The Paula avatar uses a heuristic adjustment (McDonald et al., 2016) for the torso position and does not consider other features, such as the neck, shoulder, or wrist orientations. The heuristic model was created based on the artist's proficiency with animating signs and not on data-driven insights. It modeled a precise interaction of the spine and the arms to save the artist time setting up initial poses rather than general movements of the arms and torso. Furthermore, the kind of movements discussed in the last section applies to only the reaching action of the torso. There is no research yet to coordinate torso movement with hand movement in a general way for a signing avatar using a data-driven model. This paper addresses this need by studying a motion capture data set through deep learning.

Neural networks (Bishop, 1994) have been used in sign language synthesis. They are employed to combine motion capture sequences for novel utterances for Japanese Sign Language (Brock et al., 2018). It is also used to classify hand positions for signing avatars (Jaballah and Jemni, 2014). Neural Networks have also been explored for their ability to generate continuous 2D skeletal signing motion based on video (Stoll et al., 2018). However, these have not considered direct 3D models of torso postures driven by the positions of the signers' hands.

Figure 3: Bending the torso to depict objects to the front of the signing space

4. Proposed Solution

This study focuses on the coordination of the torso with other body parts during the signing. The resulting framework predicts the torso movements of a signing avatar. The framework is based on a deep neural network, which learns from large motion capture (Mocap) data sets of human signers. A neural network in this context can learn and detect nonlinear relationships between independent and dependent variables. A sequential neural network model was used since it is the simplest model and can learn without prior application knowledge to find human motions (Baccouche et al., 2011). Implementing the proposed solution on the avatar will produce lifelike natural postures.

Due to the opacity of the neural network for interpretation, a regression model was also trained to compare with the neural network result. This companion model aids the interpretation of the primary relationships computed by the more sophisticated black-box neural network model.

This study is focused on creating a framework that will produce an improved natural movement of the torso in the avatar, which is based solely on the position and orientation of the signer's wrists. The suggested solution must be accurate compared to the actual human signer.

4.1. Data set

The LIMSI, CNRS laboratory collected human motion data for Langue des Signes Française, (LSF) in BVH format. The data were recorded with a mocap system, video, and annotations of signed descriptions of scenes elicited by a picture from human signers (Benchiheub et al., 2016).
The mocap data is recorded with sensors along the spine, neck, head, shoulders, elbow, and wrist orientations. Since the signing consists of descriptions of scenes, it has very few lexical signs in the data that would differ highly from one sign language to another (Baker et al., 2016). So, even though the recorded signing is in LSF, the body postures captured are applicable across sign languages. However, this should not be generalized to all types of signers.
The 3DS Max software package was used to import the motion capture data, convert the data to match the avatar's coordinate system, resolve data issues, such as outliers, derive new variables required for the ML model, and finally save the data to CSV files. Python scripts tested the data, combined all CSV files into a master file, and performed other intermediate tasks.
The data covered four signers, 25 descriptions, 25 frames per second and roughly 800 frames per description in the study. The final data set has 66644 rows and 34 columns. A specific signer was chosen to train the model to avoid confusion with different signing styles because the specific signer's style is highly consistent, while other signers use more excessive body movements.

4.2. Target definition

Three attributes for the spinal movement in the data were the primary targets: the torso's twist, side, and forward motions. The three Twist, Side, and Forward attributes across the spine bones were summed up to a derived variable to simplify the computation. It helped reduce the target or dependent variable set from 12 to only three attributes and gave a better idea of the overall movement of the spine.

Name	Action	Rotation Axis
Twist	Transverse twisting	Z-axis
Side	Lateral bending	X-axis
Forward	Sagittal bending	Y-axis

Table 1: Torso movements

4.3. Linear regression

The primary motivation to start with linear regression is that it is highly interpretable and enables a better understanding of the independent variables' impact on the dependent variable. The linear regression model enabled to match the coordinate systems of the motion capture data, where the data comes from with the signing avatar, where the model is implemented. It helped to calibrate the model. It also served as the baseline model, critical for capturing the evaluation metrics before initiating the deep learning model. The steps followed from start to end are shown in Figure 4.

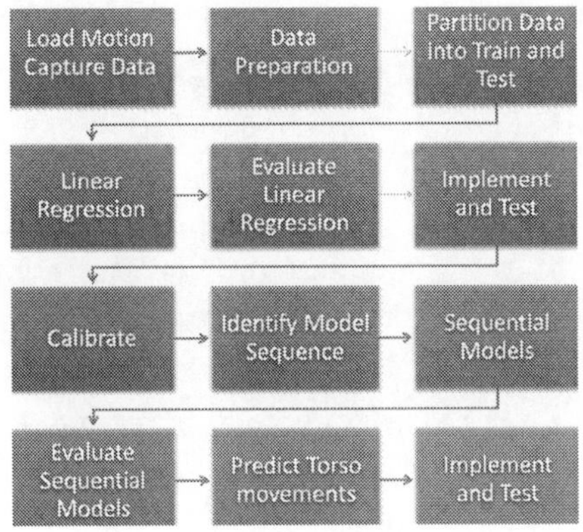

Figure 4: Process diagram

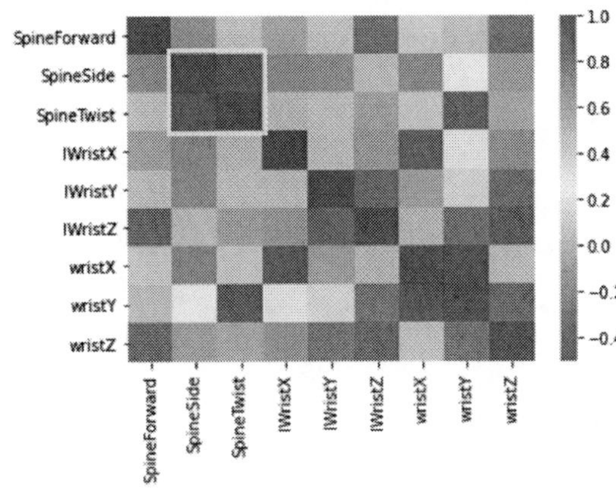

Figure 5: Correlation analysis

The independent variables employed in the study are linear X, Y, and Z positions of the left and right wrists. Based on the exploratory correlation analysis shown in Figure 5 and experiments with linear regression, it was determined that chained regression between the dependent variables was appropriate. The analysis identified a linear sequence to arrange three models. The first model uses all independent variables and predicts spine twist. The second model uses all independent variables and the prediction output from the previous model to predict the spine side rotation, and so on. The chained regression approach increased the predictive power of the model significantly.

High accuracy is the main priority to make the signing avatar natural. However, the evaluation metrics from Linear Regression, such as mean squared error and R-Squared, are not satisfactory. The regression formulas for each of the three movements are displayed in equations (1) - (3).

The equations helped a more intuitive knowledge of the relationship between the independent and dependent variables, such as if wrist X increases, the twist also increases, and so on.

$$
\begin{aligned}
Twist = 0.02 &+ 0.12 * wristX \\
&- 0.20 * wristY \\
&+ 0.04 * wristZ \\
&+ 0.16 * lWristX \\
&+ 0.16 * lWristY \\
&- 0.05 * lWristZ
\end{aligned} \tag{1}
$$

$$
\begin{aligned}
Side = 1.56 &- 0.02 * SpineTwist(Predicted) \\
&- 0.03 * wristX \\
&+ 0.08 * wristY \\
&- 0.14 * wristZ \\
&- 0.05 * lWristX \\
&- 0.04 * lWristY \\
&+ 0.15 * lWristZ
\end{aligned} \tag{2}
$$

$$
\begin{aligned}
Forward = 5.78 &+ 0.45 * SpineTwist(Predicted) \\
&+ 8.57 * SpineSide(Predicted) \\
&+ 0.18 * wristX \\
&- 0.58 * wristY \\
&+ 1.09 * wristZ \\
&+ 0.32 * lWristX \\
&+ 0.25 * lWristY \\
&- 1.22 * lWristZ
\end{aligned} \tag{3}
$$

4.4. Applying the neural network

Deep learning techniques can train the nonlinear representation of data through multiple hidden layers. The deep learning structure can perform feature extraction and transformation without prior knowledge. Keras, an open-source neural network library (Chollet and others, 2015) was used. Keras runs on top of the TensorFlow platform (Bisong, 2019), used to run computations requiring tensors. A tensor can be considered a machine that accepts vectors as inputs and produces another vector as output. The most straightforward way to build a deep learning model in Keras is a sequential model. The sequential model is suitable for a typical stack of layers where each layer has precisely one input tensor and one output tensor. Figure 6 shows the sequential model summary used in the study.

The model used a simple multi-layer perceptron with three layers with the shape of the independent variables (predictors) as a parameter. The first and second layers contain 64 units with rectified linear activation function (ReLU), and the output layer contains just one unit. The network used the "Adam" optimizer, a stochastic gradient descent method for the training model. The 'Mean Squared Error' served as the regression loss function that the model minimized during training. The model was trained on movement information from the descriptions of the first 80% of scenes and held out the rest as a test set. The training sample was used to build a deep learning model and the test sample to evaluate the model. The regression metrics reported are loss, root mean squared error (RMSE), and

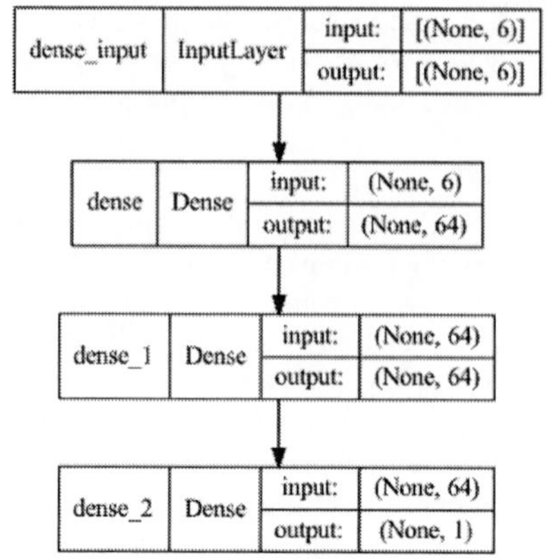

Figure 6: Model summary

R-Squared. The optimal model was chosen based on test RMSE using the smallest value as it also indicates the overall expected error in the predictions.

4.5. Chained regression approach

As indicated by the regression models, the neural network also followed a chained approach. The first model predicts spine twist by using all independent variables. The second model uses all independent variables and the prediction output from the spine twist model to predict the spine side. The third model uses all independent variables, predicted output from the previous two models, and predicts spine forward.

5. Results

The models are evaluated based on the resulting predictive performance on the holdout test data using loss, RMSE, and R- Squared of the test set with 100 epochs. Table 2 shows the performance metrics of three dependent variables.

	Twist	Side	Forward
MSE	1.68	4.82	6.89
RMSE	1.30	2.20	2.63
R^2	0.95	0.70	0.48

Table 2: Performance of the neural network models

The results show that the proposed application significantly improves accuracy over linear regression, the baseline, and the companion model. It also improves accuracy over the heuristic model from (McDonald et al., July 8 11 2014), which currently used on the avatar. The RMSE using the neural network is 1.3, while the RMSE using the heuristic model using identical predictors is 4.60 in spine twist movement. Compared to the heuristic methods, the proposed model resulted in a 72% reduction of RMSE for the twist. Tables 3 to 5 compares the models based on RMSE of the predicted spine angles in degrees. The comparison includes the performance of the regression and heuristic methods.

Model	R-Squared	RMSE
Neural Network	0.95	1.30
Linear Regression	0.86	3.62
Heuristic Model	-	4.60

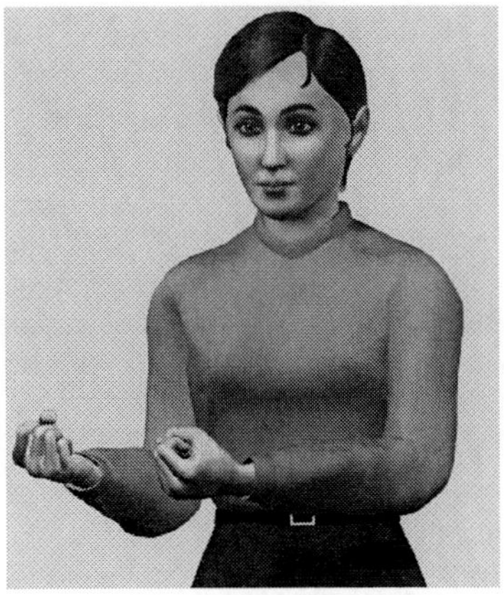

Figure 7: Signing avatar twisting the torso to depict objects

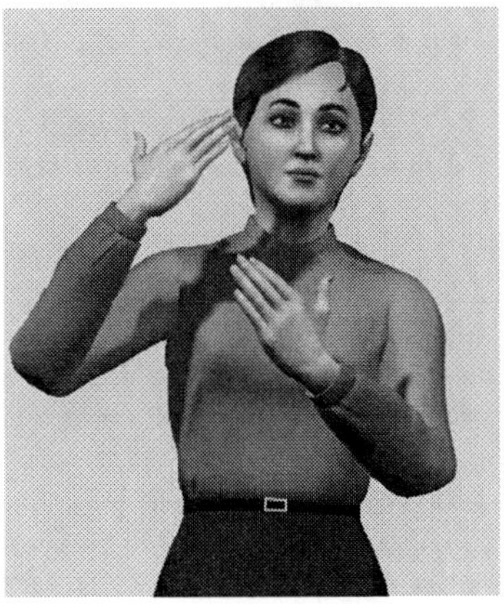

Figure 8: Signing avatar leaning the torso to the side for balance

Table 3: Spine Twist Performance Comparison

Model	R-Squared	RMSE
Neural Network	0.70	2.20
Linear Regression	0.24	11.29
Heuristic Model	-	3.5

Table 4: Spine Side Performance Comparison

Model	R-Squared	RMSE
Neural Network	0.48	2.63
Linear Regression	0.17	21.73
Heuristic Model	-	3.2

Table 5: Spine Forward Performance Comparison

6. Implementation

The model is successfully implemented in the avatar using Python and tested against the original mocap positions. We scaled the torso movements to adapt the morphology of the avatar to that of the skeleton of the captured data. Examples for each of the three key spine movements are displayed in Figures 7 to 9. Naturalness is a piece of subjective information, and there is an effort to figure out how to measure it. A

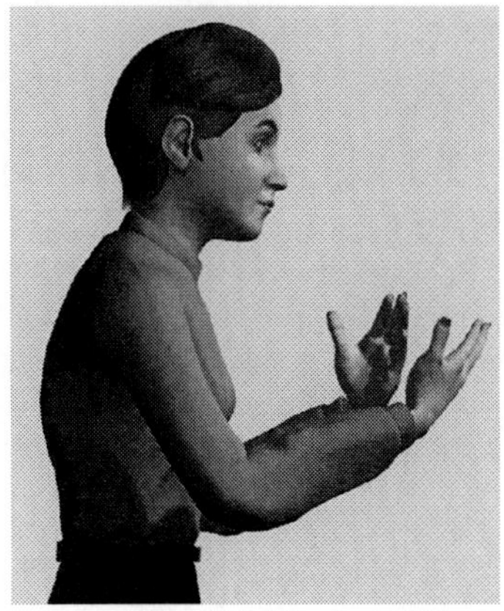

Figure 9: Signing avatar leaning forward the torso to depict objects

user survey from the ASL community, which combines the Deaf community and the experts in the ASL domain, will be requested to compare the avatar with and without the proposed solution. The outcomes of the survey will serve as a measure of naturalness. Currently, the performance is fast enough for the avatar to respond to user interaction in real-time. This framework will be updated once future data is collected, so the model will learn using new data.

7. Conclusions and Future Work

This paper describes the potential power of the proposed model to compute the torso positions of the avatar, which will improve the interaction and engagement of users with the avatar. The proposed model is implemented on an avatar using motion capture data. The initial testing and validation produce satisfactory results. In sign language, signing style varies from person to person. Different signers use the torso in very distinct ways. Some signers like to move more than others. The future effort has started incorporating personal signing styles and refining the models to include additional independent variables and data. Additionally, work is in progress to create a multi-target neural network model to combine the current implementation's three models. The unified model will streamline the implementation process and may deliver better predictions than individual models. Deep neural networks have many parameters, and it is usually prone to overfitting. Since the model will soon include more independent variables, it may have overfitting issues. The companion linear regression model will be leveraged to prevent the overfit. There is a plan to handle overfitting by applying regularization techniques or tuning the neural network parameters. Though the primary focus of the study is sign language avatars, the model can be implemented in any other human animation. There are plans to apply this framework to other sign languages, such as German or Mexican.

8. Acknowledgement

This paper and the study would not have been possible without the outstanding support of Dr. John McDonald. The assistance provided by Dr. McDonald, Dr. Wolfe and the entire ASL team at DePaul University is deeply appreciated.

9. Bibliographical References

Baccouche, M., Mamalet, F., Wolf, C., Garcia, C., and Baskurt, A. (2011). Sequential deep learning for human action recognition. In *International workshop on human behavior understanding*, pages 29–39. Springer.

Baker, A., van den Bogaerde, B., Pfau, R., and Schermer, T. (2016). *The linguistics of sign languages: An introduction*. John Benjamins Publishing Company.

Benchiheub, M., Berret, B., and Braffort, A. (2016). Collecting and analysing a motion-capture corpus of french sign language. In *10th LREC Workshop on the Representation and Processing of Sign Languages: Corpus Mining, ELRA*.

Bishop, C. M. (1994). Neural networks and their applications. *Review of scientific instruments*, 65(6):1803–1832.

Bisong, E. (2019). Tensorflow 2.0 and keras. In *Building Machine Learning and Deep Learning Models on Google Cloud Platform*, pages 347–399. Springer.

Brock, H., Nishina, S., and Nakadai, K. (2018). To animate or anime-te? investigating sign avatar comprehensibility. In *Proceedings of the 18th International Conference on Intelligent Virtual Agents*, pages 331–332.

Burleigh, T. L., Stavropoulos, V., Liew, L. W., Adams, B. L., and Griffiths, M. D. (2018). Depression, internet gaming disorder, and the moderating effect of the gamer-avatar relationship: An exploratory longitudinal study. *International Journal of Mental Health and Addiction*, 16(1):102–124.

Chollet, F. et al. (2015). Keras. `https://github.com/fchollet/keras`.

Davenport, T., Guha, A., Grewal, D., and Bressgott, T. (2020). How artificial intelligence will change the future of marketing. *Journal of the Academy of Marketing Science*, 48(1):24–42.

De Martino, J. M., Silva, I. R., Bolognini, C. Z., Costa, P. D. P., Kumada, K. M. O., Coradine, L. C., Brito, P. H. d. S., do Amaral, W. M., Benetti, Â. B., Poeta, E. T., et al. (2017). Signing avatars: making education more inclusive. *Universal Access in the Information Society*, 16(3):793–808.

Efthimiou, E., Fontinea, S.-E., Hanke, T., Glauert, J., Bowden, R., Braffort, A., Collet, C., Maragos, P., and Goudenove, F. (2010). Dicta-sign–sign language recognition, generation and modelling: a research effort with applications in deaf communication. In *Proceedings of the 4th Workshop on the Representation and Processing of Sign Languages: Corpora and Sign Language Technologies*, pages 80–83.

Filhol, M., McDonald, J., and Wolfe, R. (2017). Synthesizing Sign Language by connecting linguistically structured descriptions to a multi-track animation system. In *11th International Conference on Universal Access in Human-Computer Interaction (UAHCI 2017) Held as Part of HCI International 2017*, volume 10278 of *Universal Access in Human–Computer Interaction. Designing Novel Interactions*, Vancouver, Canada, july. Springer.

Gibet, S. (2018). Building french sign language motion capture corpora for signing avatars. In *Workshop on the Representation and Processing of Sign Languages: Involving the Language Community, LREC 2018*.

Hanke, T. (2004). Lexical sign language resources: synergies between empirical work and automatic language generation. In *Fourth International Conference on Language Resources and Evaluation, LREC*.

Jaballah, K. and Jemni, M. (2014). Hand location classification from 3d signing virtual avatars using neural networks. In *International Conference on Computers for Handicapped Persons*, pages 439–445. Springer.

Jancso, A., Rao, X., Graën, J., and Ebling, S. (2016). A web application for geolocalized signs in synthesized swiss german sign language. In *International Conference on Computers Helping People with Special Needs*, pages 438–445. Springer.

Kennaway, R. (2015). Avatar-independent scripting for real-time gesture animation. *arXiv preprint arXiv:1502.02961*.

McDonald, J., Wolfe, R., Schnepp, J., Hochgesang, J., Jamrozik, D. G., Stumbo, M., Berke, L., Bialek, M., and Thomas, F. (2016). An automated technique for real-time production of lifelike animations of american sign language. *Universal Access in the Information Society*, 15(4):551–566.

McDonald, J. C., Wolfe, R., Moncrief, R., Baowidan, S., and Schnepp, J. (July 8-11, 2014). A kinematic model for constructed dialog in american sign language john c. mcdonald1, rosalee wolfe1, robyn moncrief1, souad baowidan1, jerry schnepp2. In *6th Conference of the International Society for Gesture Studies*. San Diego, CA.

Nasihati Gilani, S., Traum, D., Sortino, R., Gallagher, G., Aaron-Lozano, K., Padilla, C., Shapiro, A., Lamberton, J., and Petitto, L.-A. (2019). Can a signing virtual human engage a baby's attention? In *Proceedings of the 19th ACM International Conference on Intelligent Virtual Agents*, pages 162–169.

Stoll, S., Camgöz, N. C., Hadfield, S., and Bowden, R. (2018). Sign language production using neural machine translation and generative adversarial networks. In *Proceedings of the 29th British Machine Vision Conference (BMVC 2018)*. University of Surrey.

Vasalou, A., Joinson, A., Bänziger, T., Goldie, P., and Pitt, J. (2008). Avatars in social media: Balancing accuracy, playfulness and embodied messages. *International Journal of Human-Computer Studies*, 66(11):801–811.

Zirzow, N. K. (2015). Signing avatars: Using virtual reality to support students with hearing loss. *Rural Special Education Quarterly*, 34(3):33–36.

Proceedings of the 7th International Workshop on Sign Language Translation and Avatar Technology (SLTAT 7), pages 13–20
Language Resources and Evaluation Conference (LREC 2022), Marseille, 20-25 June 2022

Isolated Sign Recognition using ASL Datasets with Consistent Text-based Gloss Labeling and Curriculum Learning

Konstantinos M. Dafnis[*1], **Evgenia Chroni**[*1], **Carol Neidle**[2], **Dimitris N. Metaxas**[1]
[1] Rutgers University, 110 Frelinghuysen Road, Piscataway, NJ 08854 USA
[2] Boston University, Boston University Linguistics, 621 Commonwealth Ave., Boston, MA 02215 USA
kd703@cs.rutgers.edu, etc44@cs.rutgers.edu, carol@bu.edu, dnm@cs.rutgers.edu

Abstract

We present a new approach for isolated sign recognition, which combines a spatial-temporal Graph Convolution Network (GCN) architecture for modeling human skeleton keypoints with late fusion of both the forward and backward video streams, and we explore the use of curriculum learning. We employ a type of curriculum learning that dynamically estimates, during training, the order of difficulty of each input video for sign recognition; this involves learning a new family of *data parameters* that are dynamically updated during training. The research makes use of a large combined video dataset for American Sign Language (ASL), including data from both the American Sign Language Lexicon Video Dataset (ASLLVD) and the Word-Level American Sign Language (WLASL) dataset, with modified gloss labeling of the latter—to ensure 1-1 correspondence between gloss labels and distinct sign productions, as well as consistency in gloss labeling across the two datasets. This is the first time that these two datasets have been used in combination for isolated sign recognition research. We also compare the sign recognition performance on several different subsets of the combined dataset, varying in, e.g., the minimum number of samples per sign (and therefore also in the total number of sign classes and video examples).

Keywords: ASL, Isolated Sign Recognition, Curriculum Learning, ASLLVD, WLASL

1. Introduction

There are >70 million deaf people worldwide, and >200 signed languages (World Federation of the Deaf, 2022). In the US, there are 28 million Deaf or Hard-of-Hearing people (Lin et al., 2011), and ASL is the primary language for an estimated 500,000 (or more) (Mitchell et al., 2006). Signed languages like ASL are full-fledged natural languages, but they are structurally distinct from spoken languages. Language in the visual modality involves movements of the hands and arms, as well as facial expressions and movements of the head and upper body. ASL has no standard written form.

Computer-based research on sign recognition from video will pave the way for technologies to benefit the Deaf community and to improve communication between deaf and hearing individuals, such as ASL-to-English translation, for which sign recognition is a precursor; or educational applications to support ASL learners. It will also enable development of a variety of computational tools for signers, such as Google-like sign search by example over videos on the Web.

However, this is a difficult problem, and research in this area is badly needed. Here we focus on recognition of isolated, citation-form signs. Sign recognition from continuous signing is a related but more complex problem. As with any other natural language, there is considerable variability in the production of signs in ASL, which poses a challenge for sign recognition. Progress in this area requires the availability of large, linguistically annotated, video datasets with consistent gloss labeling of signs, and with representation of many and diverse signers and a sufficient number of samples per sign, to serve as a basis for computer learning.

1.1. Issues related to Data

As observed in Dafnis et al. (2022) Neidle et al. (2022a), and Neidle and Ballard (2022), the Word-Level ASL (WLASL) video dataset (Li et al., 2020)—which is potentially valuable for sign recognition research in that it brings together multiple publicly shared ASL video datasets—is problematic in one critical respect: there is no enforced 1-1 correspondence between gloss labels and sign productions. Figure 1 illustrates the problem with using the WLASL gloss labels as "ground truth" for sign recognition research. Each of the ASL signs shown in this figure—one glossed as "A-LOT," the other as "MANY" in our ASLLRP Sign Bank (Neidle et al., 2022b), `https://dai.cs.rutgers.edu/dai/s/signbank`)—has several different gloss labels within the WLASL dataset, whereas particular gloss labels, such as "a lot" or "numerous," are used for totally different ASL signs.

For this reason, we have created, and shared publicly `http://dev.dai.cs.rutgers.edu/dai/s/aboutwlasl`, a spreadsheet that provides, for a large subset of the WLASL videos, gloss labels consistent with those used for the ASLLRP Sign Bank, where such 1-1 correspondences are enforced. This makes it possible to take advantage of the large and varied set of WLASL video files while ensuring internally consistent gloss labeling; this is precisely what was done in Dafnis et al. (2022).

Moreover, this also makes it possible to combine the WLASL and ASLLRP isolated sign datasets (of which

[*] Equal contribution.

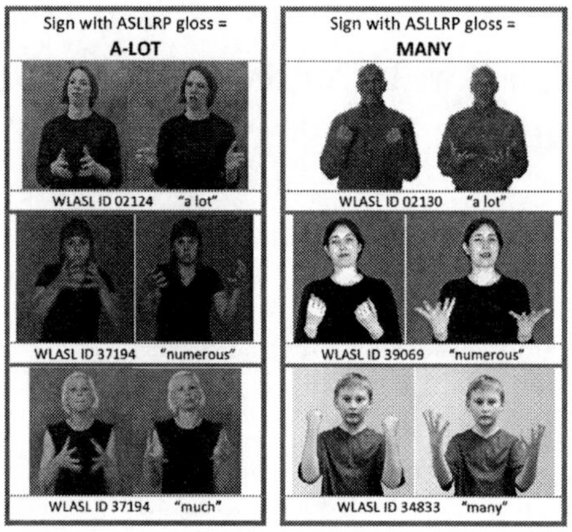

Figure 1: Inconsistent WLASL gloss labels: examples

the American Sign Language Lexicon Video Dataset (ASLLVD) (Athitsos et al., 2010; Neidle et al., 2012) is a part), with consistent gloss labeling across both, giving rise to a combined dataset larger and richer than either of the two. That is what we have done here.

The ASLLRP datasets include, for each sign: gloss labels (main entry plus variant labels); annotations of the linguistic start and end frames; start and end handshapes for each hand (in 1- and 2-handed signs); and sign type categorization (e.g., lexical, fingerspelled, loan sign, classifier, compound, etc.).

The current research relies on using both the ASLLVD and WLASL datasets in combination. In experiments to be reported on below, we used (1) lexical signs merged from both collections for which we had at least 6 or 12 examples per sign; and (2) these same datasets expanded to include not only lexical signs, but also loan signs and compounds, for which we had at least 6 or 12 examples per sign from the merged datasets. Complete details of the datasets used for each of these experiments are available from our website: `http://www.bu.edu/asllrp/signrec.html`.

1.2. Overview of our Approach

Our isolated sign recognition approach uses a spatial-temporal Graph Convolution Network (GCN) architecture for modeling human skeleton keypoints, with late fusion of forward and backward video streams, as in Dafnis et al. (2022). We also explore curriculum learning: dynamic estimation, during training, of the order of the difficulty of input videos for sign recognition; this involves learning a new family of parameters using a differentiable curriculum.

2. Related Work

Early research on isolated sign recognition from video, as well as more recent work (Cooper et al., 2012; Badhe and Kulkarni, 2015; Tamura and Kawasaki, 1988; Xiaohan Nie et al., 2015; Tornay et al., 2020), uses either color thresholding for feature extraction or hand-crafted features, such as hand positions, movement, location, and distances between the hands and specific body parts, in conjunction with classifiers, such as SVMs, KNNs, CRFs and HMMs (Memiş and Albayrak, 2013; Dardas and Georganas, 2011; Yang, 2010; Metaxas et al., 2018; Tornay et al., 2020). However, these features and the distribution assumptions inherent to these approaches result in systems with limited capability for generalization.

2.1. RGB-based Approaches

Over the past decade, most of this research shifted toward end-to-end deep learning methods, spurred by the success for computer vision problems of Convolutional Neural Networks (CNNs) in extracting spatial features and of Recurrent Neural Networks (RNNs) in capturing temporal information. Promising initial results were achieved in the domain of sign language recognition using CNN-based end-to-end deep learning methods, e.g., Pigou et al. (2016), which uses a 2D CNN for sign recognition of Flemish Sign Language (VGT) and Dutch Sign Language (NGT).

Later, many researchers leveraged modified CNNs (3D-CNN) in the context of sign and action recognition. For example, Li et al. (2020), who introduced the WLASL for isolated sign recognition, compare 4 different deep-learning architectures: 2 RGB-based and 2 pose-based approaches. The pose-based networks use body keypoints extracted using OpenPose (Cao et al., 2019; Simon et al., 2017) as input. These methods include a 2D-CNN in conjunction with an RNN, a pose-based RNN, a 3D-CNN, and a pose-based Temporal GCN. The authors show that the 3D-CNN outperforms the other approaches. While the 3D-CNN model performs better than previous approaches in learning short-term memory dependencies, a major drawback is that it restricts the learning of long-term dependencies at the final temporal global average pooling stage.

Recent architectures exploit the self-attention mechanism of Transformers for video understanding (Bertasius et al., 2021). De Coster et al. (2020) use a 2D-CNN and a Video Transformer Network for isolated sign recognition; they use the self-attention encoder layers without masking, while they remove the cross-attention decoder, and their results are promising.

2.2. Skeleton-based Approaches

Instead of using RGB frames as input, some methods, such as those mentioned in Li et al. (2020), use body keypoints to focus the learning procedure on the relevant information. When the off-the-shelf pretrained human pose estimation systems are robust, these methods show good performance in both learning and recognition, as the recognition models are not affected by irrelevant information from the background.

Early research on action and sign recognition used pose-based CNNs, followed by an RNN for the relevant temporal information (Soo Kim and Reiter, 2017; Liu et al., 2017). However, a disadvantage of these models is that they cannot encode information about keypoint interactions in both space and time. In order to overcome this disadvantage, Yan et al. (2018) proposed a Spatial-Temporal Graph Convolutional Network (ST-GCN) and showed the effectiveness of GCNs for learning spatiotemporal skeleton dynamics. Shi et al. (2019b) exploited a 2-stream approach using both keypoints and bone information, while Shi et al. (2020) proposed a 4-stream approach in which bones and the motion of keypoints are added. Their approach resulted in improved action recognition. de Amorim et al. (2019) used an extension of the ST-GCN model for isolated sign recognition and achieved close to 60% accuracy on a vocabulary of 20 signs. Jiang et al. (2021) used a pose-based GCN approach, as in Shi et al. (2020), in conjunction with other modalities, such as RGB frames, optical flow, and depth video. Their proposed GCN was the first successful attempt to tackle isolated sign recognition using body skeleton graphs.

In Dafnis et al. (2022), we follow a similar GCN approach, with the addition of forward and backward data streams and use of the acceleration of keypoints and bones. This improved isolated sign recognition on 1,449 lexical signs from the WLASL dataset, with glosses modified as discussed in Section 1.2.

2.3. Curriculum Learning Approaches

Curriculum learning is a "strategy that trains a machine learning model from easier data to harder data, which imitates the meaningful learning order in human curricula" (Wang et al., 2021). Curriculum learning was introduced by Bengio et al. (2009), who proved that training a neural network starting with easy examples and gradually increasing the difficulty of the data provides significant improvement to the overall accuracy and convergence of the model. The inspiration was derived from the way humans learn best: starting with easier concepts and gradually increasing complexity, rather than randomly learning different concepts.

However, deciding which samples to categorize as easy or hard is not trivial. Much research has been conducted on how to define which data samples to consider easy or difficult (e.g., Hacohen and Weinshall (2019), Weinshall et al. (2018), Wu et al. (2020), Zhou et al. (2020)). In this work, the order of difficulty is defined before training; the most common techniques are 1) to use pretrained models on the examined dataset; and 2) to create annotations, which could be time-consuming. Those techniques are task-specific and non generalizable. As a result, curriculum learning research later focused on finding a way to estimate the importance (or weight) of each sample directly during training, based on the observation that easy and hard samples behave differently and can therefore be separated.

The first step in this direction was taken by Kumar et al. (2010), who proposed a dynamic way to apply curriculum learning using the idea of self-paced learning. Instead of using a predefined order of difficulty of the samples, this method dynamically determines this order by feedback from the learner itself. Inspired by this idea, many classification tasks were further improved, since curriculum learning provided a quicker and better convergence (Cascante-Bonilla et al., 2020; Pi et al., 2016; Zhao et al., 2015; Saxena et al., 2019).

3. Technical Approach

The key aspects of our approach include a spatial-temporal GCN architecture for modeling the skeleton keypoints; dynamic estimation during training of the order of difficulty of each input video for sign recognition by learning a new family of data parameters using a differentiable curriculum; and a late ensemble method that fuses both the forward and backward video streams, as in Dafnis et al. (2022).

Section 3.1 presents our deep-learning model for isolated sign recognition based on skeleton keypoints. Our ensemble data fusion method is explained in 3.2. Section 3.3 then introduces the data parameters that we use for learning a differentiable curriculum and the training strategy we follow based on curriculum learning.

3.1. Sign Recognition Model

As mentioned in Section 2, previous studies on isolated sign recognition have revealed that spatial-temporal graph architectures, in conjunction with a self-attention mechanism, can boost recognition accuracy. Hence, we use a spatial-temporal GCN model similar to Jiang et al. (2021) and Dafnis et al. (2022) for isolated sign recognition on the reported dataset, as presented below.

GCN for human skeleton keypoints. Our adopted spatial-temporal GCN learning approach consists of 10 basic GCN blocks; see Figure 2. Each basic block consists of a sequence of Decoupled Spatial Graph Convolutional layers (Decoupled SGCNs) (Cheng et al., 2020), a cascaded spatial-temporal-channel attention mechanism (Shi et al., 2020), and a Temporal Convolutional layer (TCN). The Decoupled SGCN helps our GCN model boost its capacity with no extra cost. In addition, a DropGraph layer as in Cheng et al. (2020) is added. This module helps to avoid overfitting. At the end, we apply a global average pooling on both the spatial dimensions (within a skeleton) and the temporal dimensions (across skeletons), along with a dropout before a fully-connected layer for recognition.

Spatial-Temporal Graph Convolution. We first present the spatial convolution operations within a skeleton graph. To define the graph convolution in the spatial dimension for our human skeleton graph, we follow Yan et al. (2018). The implementation of the spatial part of the GCN is expressed as follows:

$$u_{out} = D^{-\frac{1}{2}}(I + A)D^{-\frac{1}{2}}u_{in}W, \qquad (1)$$

where matrices A and I represent the intra-body and self-connections respectively. D is the diagonal matrix of (I+A), while W represents the weight matrix of the convolutions. In practice, the spatial graph convolution operation is implemented by performing standard 2D convolution and then multiplying the outcome by $D^{-\frac{1}{2}}(I + A)D^{-\frac{1}{2}}$.

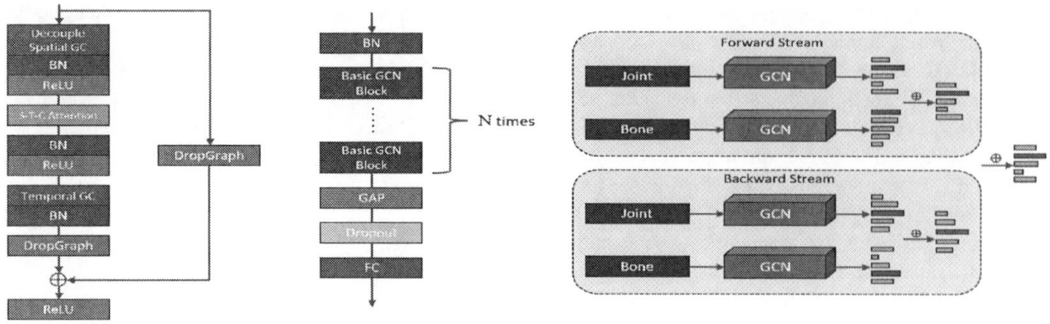

(a) Basic GCN Block (b) Network Architecture (c) Multi-stream Architecture

Figure 2: Illustration of the GCN pipeline: (a) Basic GCN block architecture; (b) GCN architecture. There are 10 basic GCN blocks in all. GAP represents the global average pooling layer and FC the fully connected layer. (c) The overall architecture of the Multi-stream GCN. The forward and backward scores are fused using weighted summation to obtain the final prediction.

To capture the temporal relationships among skeleton graphs in consecutive frames, we use temporal convolutions. These temporal graph convolution operations can be also expressed as a standard 2D convolution using a kernel size k_t×1, where k_t is the reception field. In practice, the human skeleton keypoints are connected to themselves in the temporal dimension. Thus, the traditional 2D convolution formulation is modified to a 1-dimensional convolution.

Spatial Graph Construction. To construct the skeleton graph, we extract 2D skeleton keypoints using Alphapose (Fang et al., 2017), a pretrained model that extracts 136 face and body keypoints from a given video frame. However, using all 136 keypoints for isolated sign recognition reduces the recognition rate. This is because the upper body keypoints are more informative than those of the lower body for sign recognition. In addition, because of blurriness during hand movements, it can be hard for the 2D skeleton extractor to detect the hand keypoints accurately. To overcome these issues, following Jiang et al. (2021) and Dafnis et al. (2022), we reduce the number of skeleton keypoints used for skeleton graph construction. Our graph consists of 27 nodes corresponding to 10 keypoints for each hand and 7 upper body keypoints: nose, eyes, shoulders, elbows. The 10 hand keypoints correspond to the base and tip of each finger. Given the variability in lexically related mouthing, and our current sample sizes, we did not include keypoints around the mouth on the graph. We found that including them did not increase accuracy, but we hope to incorporate this in the future. Each node on our graph has a (x, y, c) vector, where (x, y) are the 2D coordinates of the corresponding keypoints and c is the keypoint detection confidence score.

Forward and Backward Sign Recognition. Following Dafnis et al. (2022), we use both the forward and backward directions of the video data for isolated sign recognition. In each direction, we use two types of data streams as input: the human skeleton keypoint (joint) coordinates, and the bone vector (distance between keypoints). As demonstrated in Dafnis et al. (2022), these two streams are the most informative for isolated sign recognition since, because of noise in the estimation of joint locations, the joint velocities and acceleration vectors are not reliable.

We generate the bone vectors for our graph by setting the nose as the root keypoint on the skeleton graph. Let two ordered connected keypoints $v^K_{i,t}$, $v^K_{j,t}$ at frame t, with coordinates $v^K_{i,t} = (x_{i,t}, y_{i,t}, c_{i,t})$ and $v^K_{j,t} = (x_{j,t}, y_{j,t}, c_{j,t})$ respectively. Then the bone vector is computed as:

$$v^B_{j,t} = v^K_{j,t} - v^K_{i,t},$$

$$v^B_{j,t} = (x_{j,t} - x_{i,t}, y_{j,t} - y_{i,t}, c_{j,t} - c_{i,t})\ \forall (i, j) \in V, \quad (2)$$

where V contains all skeleton keypoint connections.

3.2. Score Fusion

In both the forward and backward directions, our framework uses multiple streams of information (i.e., joints and bones) to make aggregate predictions for each direction. We first fuse the prediction scores from all streams in each direction. We use the respective *softmax* scores in each stream (Shi et al., 2019b; Shi et al., 2019a; Shi et al., 2020; Cai et al., 2021; Dafnis et al., 2022) to compute an optimized weighted summation of the scores for each direction. We then fuse the prediction softmax scores for each direction by computing an optimized weighted summation that produces a prediction of the sign labels.

3.3. Curriculum Learning

To further enhance our recognition accuracy, we use a type of curriculum learning introduced in Saxena et al. (2019), which dynamically estimates during training the order of difficulty of each input video for sign recognition by using a new family of trainable parameters for deep neural networks called *data parameters*. Each sign class and each sign instance are assigned *data parameters*, which are updated after every iteration during training. The respective learning process determines which sign samples and classes need more attention compared to the others to improve sign recognition automatically, as follows: We define

$$\{(x^i, y^i)\}^N_{n=1}, \quad (3)$$

where x^i is a data sample (a video of a sign) that is input to the neural network, y^i is the label of x^i, and N represents the number of input samples. The neural network is defined as f_θ, and the logits are z^i, i.e., $f_\theta(x^i) = z^i$. We also define the data parameter ϕ_i^* as the sum of the instance and class parameters as follows:

$$\phi_i^* = \phi_{y_i}^{class} + \phi_i^{instance} \tag{4}$$

We use the cross entropy loss as the loss function, where the logits are scaled using the data parameter ϕ_i^*:

$$L^i = -log(p_{y^i}^i), \tag{5}$$

where

$$p_{y^i}^i = \frac{exp(z_{y^i}^i/\phi_i^*)}{\Sigma_j exp(z_j^i/\phi_i^*)}). \tag{6}$$

L^i is the cross entropy, ϕ_i^* is the data parameter, $z_{y^i}^i$ is the logit and $p_{y^i}^i$ is the probability of the target class y^i for sample x_i. In order to estimate the sign class given an instance we need to minimize L^i:

$$\min_{\theta,\phi^*} \frac{1}{N}\Sigma_{i=1}^N L^i \tag{7}$$

During training, the class parameters, $\phi_{y_i}^{class}$, take into account the average of the gradients from all the class samples in each mini-batch, while instance parameters, $\phi_i^{instance}$, aggregate the gradients from each individual sample. This process has the following advantages:

1) Some videos in our dataset are of low resolution and, as a consequence, those samples are blurry and noisy. This makes learning from those data difficult, and so they need to be ignored. Using the learnable instance parameters, the algorithm can learn which samples help the recognition part of the model and which samples should be ignored or paid less attention.

2) If, during training, the data samples of a class are correctly classified, the corresponding data parameter of this class is decreased, resulting in the acceleration of the learning process (the loss function is decreased). However, if they are misclassified, then the class parameter is increased, which results in the deceleration of the learning process (the loss function is increased).

In the above curriculum learning method, we use 3 optimizers: 1 for training the model, 1 for training the class parameters, and 1 for training the instance parameters. The optimizers for the class and instance parameters are used only during training, since we do not have the data parameters ϕ^* for the test set.

This method is simple and effective, and it boosts the accuracy of sign recognition, as demonstrated in Section 4. Using those parameters, the algorithm can automatically learn to ignore noisy samples. In addition, it accelerates the learning of easier classes, while it decelerates and focuses on the learning of harder classes.

4. Experiments

The adopted GCN-based framework is tested for isolated sign recognition on the combined WLASL and ASLLVD isolated sign dataset (with consistent gloss labeling). Our training and testing protocol for both the forward and backward directions is described in Section 4.1. Section 4.2 explains the fusion of the forward and backward streams and the evaluation of the use of *data parameters* for curriculum learning.

Set ID	Sign Types	Min. # samples per sign	Total # class labels	Total # examples
LEX-6	Lexical	6	1,480	22,853
LEX-12	Lexical	12	983	18,362
ALL-6	All	6	1,502	23,016
ALL-12	All	12	990	18,482

Table 1: Dataset Statistics. *All* includes lexical signs, loan signs, and compounds

4.1. Training and Testing Protocol

4.1.1. Dataset Preprocessing

As described in (Dafnis et al., 2022), we modified the WLASL (Li et al., 2020) gloss labeling to make it consistent with the conventions of the ASLLRP datasets (which includes the ASLLVD), thereby also enforcing consistency of gloss labeling for the WLASL videos. As explained in Section 1.1, we merge the WLASL and ASLLVD isolated sign datasets (resulting in a set of 23,017 videos for 1,502 signs), and we use either lexical signs, or lexical plus loan signs and compounds; and we further restrict these sets to signs with at least either 6 or 12 examples. Increasing the minimum number of samples per sign also decreases the total number of available videos. Table 1 presents the numbers of sign classes and total videos for each set.

We split this dataset following (Li et al., 2020) into training, validation, and testing sets using a ratio of 4:1:1 for each sign. To evaluate the recognition performance, we use the mean scores of the *Top-K* recognition accuracy with $K = 1, 5$ over all sign instances.

4.1.2. Keypoint Extraction & Data Preprocessing

We use the pretrained Alphapose model of Fang et al. (2017), which estimates 136 keypoints of the whole body from single RGB images, and construct our skeleton graph of 27 nodes. To construct the graph, we first normalize the keypoint coordinates to [-1,1], and then apply random sampling, mirroring, rotation, scaling, and shifting as data augmentation techniques. Since the videos differ in total number of frames, the length of all videos is aligned to 200 frames. If a video has more than 200 frames, the first 200 are extracted from the video. However, given the length of the signs in our datasets, no information was lost as a result of this operation. If a video has fewer than 200, we repeat the frame sequence until the video length is 200 frames.

4.1.3. Training Details

To speed up and improve the training, we use a GCN model with pretrained weights from the AUTSL dataset (Sincan and Keles, 2020). The GCN models are implemented in PyTorch. All experiments were conducted using PyTorch 1.7.0 and an NVIDIA Quadro RTX8000s. To train the GCN model, the Stochastic Gradient Descent (SGD) with Nesterov Momentum

Streams	**LEX-6**				**LEX-12**				**ALL-6**				**ALL-12**			
	Forward		**Backward**		**Forward**		**Backward**		**Forward**		**Backward**		**Forward**		**Backward**	
	Top-1	*Top-5*	*Top-1*	*Top-5*	*Top-1*	*Top-5*	*Top-1*	*Top-5*	*Top-1*	*Top-5*	*Top-1*	*Top-5*	*Top-1*	*Top-5*	*Top-1*	*Top-5*
Joint	74.05	91.60	73.67	91.38	79.00	94.38	78.24	94.01	72.96	91.42	74.19	91.14	79.18	94.09	78.24	93.78
Bones	71.35	91.12	71.02	90.86	75.87	93.59	75.69	93.56	72.63	91.47	72.09	91.09	76.31	93.51	76.49	93.30
Multi-stream	77.35	94.08	77.54	93.70	82.95	96.08	82.22	95.87	77.58	94.21	77.65	94.24	83.07	95.87	82.26	95.87
Forward Multi-stream w/CL	**77.73**	**93.70**			**83.20**	**95.69**			**77.63**	**94.34**			**82.59**	**96.23**		
	Top-1		*Top-5*		*Top-1*		*Top-5*		*Top-1*		*Top-5*		*Top-1*		*Top-5*	
Fusion (no CL)	**78.54**		**94.72**		**84.23**		**96.69**		**78.70**		**94.79**		**84.70**		**96.56**	

Table 2: Recognition accuracy for all subsets.

(0.9) is selected as the optimization algorithm. The Cross-Entropy loss function is used, and the weight decay is set to 10^{-4}. The batch size for both the training and testing processes is set to 64, while the total number of epochs used for training our models is 300. In addition, the learning rate is initially set to 0.1 and divided by 10 when 150 and 200 epochs are reached.

4.2. GCN Performance

Table 2 shows the *Top-1* and *Top-5* recognition performance of the forward and backward stream directions. Of the streams for which there is both the forward and backward direction, the keypoint stream provides the best accuracy. The score fusion approach for the forward and backward directions further improves overall recognition accuracy in all the test cases. Table 2 shows recognition accuracy for all signs with at least 6 and 12 samples. We observe that using more samples per sign with fewer total sign classes—resulting in a more balanced dataset—increases the recognition rate by 5%.

4.3. GCN Performance with CL

Table 2 also shows the contribution of using curriculum learning (CL) over just using fusion of the forward streams. The current results are inconclusive; we will explore varying the CL parameters in the future, in particular to adapt CL for imbalanced datasets. After optimizing the parameters, we will add CL to the backward as well as the forward stream prior to fusion, to assess the extent to which CL may improve overall results.

4.4. Overall Results

Figure 3 summarizes the recognition accuracy for the subsets of the combined dataset that included all sign types (lexical, loan signs, compounds) using signs for which we had a minimum number of samples per sign of either 6 or 12, showing our fusion results (without incorporation of improvements from curriculum learning) for top-1, top-2, top-3, top-4, and top-5.

Table 2 shows little difference in recognition accuracy for datasets restricted to lexical signs, in part because lexical signs still predominate in the larger datasets, but also because we have not yet incorporated into our approach methods tailored to the specificity of linguistic properties of lexical signs, as we have done in previous research (Thangali et al., 2011; Dilsizian et al., 2014).

5. Discussion and Conclusions

We presented a new GCN-based approach to isolated sign recognition. It is distinctive in these respects:

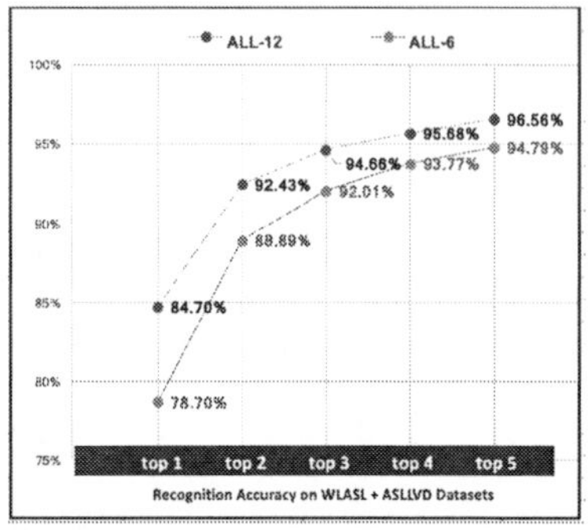

Figure 3: Summary of Sign Recognition Results: Based on Fusion (without curriculum learning)

1) Our method uses late fusion of forward and backward streams of joints and bones (following Dafnis et al. (2022)), not typically used in sign recognition.
2) This is the first time that ASL sign recognition research has been conducted by combining the ASLLVD and WLASL datasets, which gives rise to a large, rich, and diverse set of videos. This was made possible by our modifications to gloss labeling for WLASL videos, to enforce consistency of gloss labeling across these datasets, thereby also providing internally consistent gloss labels for the WLASL (not otherwise available).
3) This represents, to our knowledge, the first exploration of use of curriculum learning in sign recognition, by attending to the sign classes most difficult to learn, although our preliminary findings as to its promise for improving sign recognition accuracy are inconclusive.

To further improve recognition accuracy, in future research: 1) We will develop new curriculum learning methods to improve the estimation of difficult-to-recognize input signs, and integrate them with transformers. 2) We will further expand our dataset to include other data collections shared by the American Sign Language Linguistic Research Project (also with consistent gloss labeling). 3) We will conduct new machine learning research on extraction of 3D models from 2D video, with explicit integration of handshape recognition and incorporation of statistical information about the dataset that reflects linguistic constraints on the internal structure of signs.

6. Acknowledgments

We thank Matt Huenerfauth, Augustine Opoku, Carey Ballard, Indya-loreal Oliver, Lutece Dekker, Qilong Zhangli, Gregory Dimitriadis & Douglas Motto for assistance. We also gratefully acknowledge Stan

Sclaroff, Ashwin Thangali, Vassilis Athitsos, Joan Nash, Ben Bahan, Rachel Benedict, Naomi Caselli, Elizabeth Cassidy, Lana Cook, Braden Painter, Tyler Richard, Tory Sampson & Dana Schlang for collaboration in development of the ASLLVD. This research was supported in part by NSF grants 2040638, 1763486, 1763523 & 1763569. Any opinions, findings, or conclusions expressed here are those of the authors and do not necessarily reflect the views of the NSF.

7. Bibliographical References

Athitsos, V., Neidle, C., Sclaroff, S., Nash, J., Stefan, A., Thangali, A., Wang, H., and Yuan, Q. (2010). Large Lexicon Project: American Sign Language Video Corpus and Sign Language Indexing/Retrieval Algorithms. In *Workshop on the Representation and Processing of Sign Languages: Corpora and Sign Language Technologies (CSLT)*, volume 2.

Badhe, P. C. and Kulkarni, V. (2015). Indian sign language translator using gesture recognition algorithm. In *2015 IEEE International Conference on Computer Graphics, Vision and Information Security (CGVIS)*, pages 195–200.

Bengio, Y., Louradour, J., Collobert, R., and Weston, J. (2009). Curriculum learning. In *Proceedings of the 26th annual international conference on machine learning*, pages 41–48.

Bertasius, G., Wang, H., and Torresani, L. (2021). Is Space-Time Attention All You Need for Video Understanding? *arXiv preprint arXiv:2102.05095.*

Cai, J., Jiang, N., Han, X., Jia, K., and Lu, J. (2021). JOLO-GCN: mining joint-centered light-weight information for skeleton-based action recognition. In *Proceedings of the IEEE/CVF Winter Conference on Applications of Computer Vision*, pages 2735–2744.

Cao, Z., Hidalgo Martinez, G., Simon, T., Wei, S., and Sheikh, Y. A. (2019). OpenPose: Realtime Multi-Person 2D Pose Estimation using Part Affinity Fields. *IEEE Transactions on Pattern Analysis and Machine Intelligence.*

Cascante-Bonilla, P., Tan, F., Qi, Y., and Ordonez, V. (2020). Curriculum labeling: Revisiting pseudo-labeling for semi-supervised learning. *arXiv preprint arXiv:2001.06001.*

Cheng, K., Zhang, Y., Cao, C., Shi, L., Cheng, J., and Lu, H. (2020). Decoupling GCN with DropGraph Module for Skeleton-Based Action Recognition. In *Computer Vision–ECCV 2020: 16th European Conference, Glasgow, UK, August 23–28, 2020, Proceedings, Part XXIV 16*, pages 536–553. Springer.

Cooper, H., Ong, E.-J., Pugeault, N., and Bowden, R. (2012). Sign language recognition using sub-units. *JMLR*, 13:2205–2231.

Dafnis, K. M., Chroni, E., Neidle, C., and Metaxas, D. N. (2022). Bidirectional Skeleton-Based Isolated Sign Recognition using Graph Convolution Networks. In *13th International Conference on Language Resources and Evaluation, LREC 2022*, Marseille, France, June 2022.

Dardas, N. H. and Georganas, N. D. (2011). Real-time hand gesture detection and recognition using bag-of-features and support vector machine techniques. *IEEE Transactions on Instrumentation and measurement*, 60(11):3592–3607.

de Amorim, C. C., Macêdo, D., and Zanchettin, C. (2019). Spatial-Temporal Graph Convolutional Networks for Sign Language Recognition. In *International Conference on Artificial Neural Networks*, pages 646–657. Springer.

De Coster, M., Van Herreweghe, M., and Dambre, J. (2020). Sign language recognition with transformer networks. In *12th International Conference on Language Resources and Evaluation*, pages 6018–6024.

Dilsizian, M., Yanovich, P., Wang, S., Neidle, C., and Metaxas, D. (2014). A new framework for sign language recognition based on 3D handshape identification and linguistic modeling. In *9th International Conference on Language Resources and Evaluation, LREC 2014*, pages 1924–1929.

Fang, H.-S., Xie, S., Tai, Y.-W., and Lu, C. (2017). RMPE: Regional Multi-person Pose Estimation. In *Proceedings of the IEEE international conference on computer vision*, pages 2334–2343.

Hacohen, G. and Weinshall, D. (2019). On the power of curriculum learning in training deep networks. In *International Conference on Machine Learning*, pages 2535–2544. PMLR.

Jiang, S., Sun, B., Wang, L., Bai, Y., Li, K., and Fu, Y. (2021). Sign Language Recognition via Skeleton-Aware Multi-Model Ensemble. *arXiv e-prints*, pages arXiv–2110.

Kumar, M., Packer, B., and Koller, D. (2010). Self-paced learning for latent variable models. *Advances in neural information processing systems*, 23.

Li, D., Rodriguez, C., Yu, X., and Li, H. (2020). Word-level deep sign language recognition from video: A new large-scale dataset and methods comparison. In *Proceedings of the IEEE/CVF winter conference on applications of computer vision*, pages 1459–1469.

Lin, F. R., Niparko, J. K., and Ferrucci, L. (2011). Hearing loss prevalence in the United States. *Archives of internal medicine*, 171(20):1851–1853.

Liu, H., Tu, J., and Liu, M. (2017). Two-Stream 3D Convolutional Neural Network for Skeleton-Based Action Recognition. *arXiv preprint arXiv:1705.08106.*

Memiş, A. and Albayrak, S. (2013). A kinect based sign language recognition system using spatio-temporal features. In *6th International Conference on Machine Vision (ICMV 2013)*, volume 9067, page 90670X. International Society for Optics and Photonics.

Metaxas, D., Dilsizian, M., and Neidle, C. (2018). Linguistically-driven framework for computationally efficient and scalable sign recognition. In *Pro-*

ceedings of the 11th International Conference on Language Resources and Evaluation (LREC 2018).

Mitchell, R. E., Young, T. A., Bachelda, B., and Karchmer, M. A. (2006). How many people use ASL in the United States? Why estimates need updating. *Sign Language Studies*, 6(3):306–335.

Neidle, C. and Ballard, C. (2022). Why Alternative Gloss Labels Will Increase the Value of the WLASL Dataset. ASLLRP Project Report No. 21. `http://www.bu.edu/asllrp/rpt21/asllrp21.pdf`, Boston, MA: Boston University, March 2022.

Neidle, C., Thangali, A., and Sclaroff, S. (2012). Challenges in Development of the American Sign Language Lexicon Video Dataset (ASLLVD) Corpus. In *5th workshop on the representation and processing of sign languages: interactions between corpus and Lexicon, LREC*.

Neidle, C., Opoku, A., Ballard, C., Dafnis, K. M., Chroni, E., and Metaxas, D. (2022a). Resources for Computer-Based Sign Recognition from Video, and the Criticality of Consistency of Gloss Labeling across Multiple Large ASL Video Corpora. In *10th Workshop on the Representation and Processing of Sign Languages: Multilingual Sign Language Resources*, Marseille, France, June 2022.

Neidle, C., Opoku, A., and Metaxas, D. (2022b). ASL Video Corpora & Sign Bank: Resources Available through the American Sign Language Linguistic Research Project (ASLLRP). https://arxiv.org/abs/2201.07899 .

Pi, T., Li, X., Zhang, Z., Meng, D., Wu, F., Xiao, J., and Zhuang, Y. (2016). Self-paced boost learning for classification. In *IJCAI*, pages 1932–1938.

Pigou, L., Van Herreweghe, M., and Dambre, J. (2016). Sign classification in sign language corpora with deep neural networks. In *International Conference on Language Resources and Evaluation (LREC), Workshop, Proceedings*, pages 175–178.

Saxena, S., Tuzel, O., and DeCoste, D. (2019). Data parameters: A new family of parameters for learning a differentiable curriculum. *Advances in Neural Information Processing Systems*, 32.

Shi, L., Zhang, Y., Cheng, J., and Lu, H. (2019a). Skeleton-based action recognition with directed graph neural networks. In *Proceedings of the IEEE/CVF Conference on Computer Vision and Pattern Recognition*, pages 7912–7921.

Shi, L., Zhang, Y., Cheng, J., and Lu, H. (2019b). Two-stream adaptive graph convolutional networks for skeleton-based action recognition. In *Proceedings of the IEEE/CVF Conference on Computer Vision and Pattern Recognition*, pages 12026–12035.

Shi, L., Zhang, Y., Cheng, J., and Lu, H. (2020). Skeleton-based action recognition with multi-stream adaptive graph convolutional networks. *IEEE Transactions on Image Processing*, 29:9532–9545.

Simon, T., Joo, H., Matthews, I., and Sheikh, Y. (2017). Hand Keypoint Detection in Single Images using Multiview Bootstrapping. In *CVPR*.

Sincan, O. M. and Keles, H. Y. (2020). AUTSL: A Large Scale Multi-modal Turkish Sign Language Dataset and Baseline Methods. *IEEE Access*, 8:181340–181355.

Soo Kim, T. and Reiter, A. (2017). Interpretable 3D Human Action Analysis with Temporal Convolutional Networks. In *Proceedings of the IEEE Conference on Computer Vision and Pattern Recognition Workshops*, pages 20–28.

Tamura, S. and Kawasaki, S. (1988). Recognition of sign language motion images. *Pattern recognition*, 21(4):343–353.

Thangali, A., Nash, J. P., Sclaroff, S., and Neidle, C. (2011). Exploiting phonological constraints for handshape inference in ASL video. In *CVPR 2011*, pages 521–528. IEEE.

Tornay, S., Aran, O., and Doss, M. M. (2020). An HMM Approach with Inherent Model Selection for Sign Language and Gesture Recognition. In *Proceedings of the 12th Language Resources and Evaluation Conference*, pages 6049–6056.

Wang, X., Chen, Y., and Zhu, W. (2021). A survey on curriculum learning. *IEEE Transactions on Pattern Analysis and Machine Intelligence*.

Weinshall, D., Cohen, G., and Amir, D. (2018). Curriculum learning by transfer learning: Theory and experiments with deep networks. In *International Conference on Machine Learning*, pages 5238–5246. PMLR.

World Federation of the Deaf. (2022). `https://wfdeaf.org/our-work/`. Accessed: 2022-04-12.

Wu, X., Dyer, E., and Neyshabur, B. (2020). When do curricula work? *arXiv preprint arXiv:2012.03107*.

Xiaohan Nie, B., Xiong, C., and Zhu, S.-C. (2015). Joint action recognition and pose estimation from video. In *Proceedings of the IEEE Conference on Computer Vision and Pattern Recognition*, pages 1293–1301.

Yan, S., Xiong, Y., and Lin, D. (2018). Spatial Temporal Graph Convolutional Networks for Skeleton-Based Action Recognition. In *Thirty-second AAAI conference on artificial intelligence*.

Yang, Q. (2010). Chinese sign language recognition based on video sequence appearance modeling. In *2010 5th IEEE Conference on Industrial Electronics and Applications*, pages 1537–1542. IEEE.

Zhao, Q., Meng, D., Jiang, L., Xie, Q., Xu, Z., and Hauptmann, A. G. (2015). Self-paced learning for matrix factorization. In *Twenty-ninth AAAI conference on artificial intelligence*.

Zhou, T., Wang, S., and Bilmes, J. (2020). Curriculum learning by dynamic instance hardness. *Advances in Neural Information Processing Systems*, 33:8602–8613.

Proceedings of the 7th International Workshop on Sign Language Translation and Avatar Technology (SLTAT 7), pages 21–28
Language Resources and Evaluation Conference (LREC 2022), Marseille, 20-25 June 2022

Example-based Multilinear Sign Language Generation from a Hierarchical Representation

Boris Dauriac[1], Annelies Braffort[2], Elise Bertin-Lemée[3]
[1]R&D MocapLab, 70 rue du Landy, 93300 Aubervilliers, France, boris.dauriac@mocaplab.com
[2]Université Paris-Saclay, CNRS, LISN, Orsay, France, annelies.braffort@lisn.upsaclay.fr
[3]SYSTRAN, 5 rue Feydeau, Paris, France elise.bertinlemee@systrangroup.com

Abstract

This article presents an original method for automatic generation of sign language (SL) content by means of the animation of an avatar, with the aim of creating animations that respect as much as possible linguistic constraints while keeping bio-realistic properties. This method is based on the use of a domain-specific bilingual corpus richly annotated with timed alignments between SL motion capture data, text and hierarchical expressions from the framework called AZee at subsentential level. Animations representing new SL content are built from blocks of animations present in the corpus and adapted to the context if necessary. A smart blending approach has been designed that allows the concatenation, replacement and adaptation of original animation blocks. This approach has been tested on a tailored testset to show as a proof of concept its potential in comprehensibility and fluidity of the animation, as well as its current limits.

Keywords: Sign Language, avatar animation, motion capture, representation of Sign Language, AZee

1. Introduction

Rosetta[1] is a French project that aimed to study accessibility solutions for audiovisual content. One of the experiments consisted in designing an automatic translation system from text to Sign Language (SL) displayed through animation of a virtual signer.

The three main contributions concerning SL in this project were the constitution of Rosetta-LSF (Dauriac, 2022), an aligned corpus of text and SL captured using a mocap system, a translation system from text to AZee (Bertin-Lemée et al., 2022b), a representation of SL content, and a system allowing to generate virtual signer animations from AZee input.

This article describes the third contribution: the system of generation from AZee to virtual signer animations. After an overview of recent works in the field, we give some indications on the Rosetta-LSF corpus and the way it has been annotated in order to facilitate its use for generation, then we describe the main steps of the generation system. Finally, we give preliminary results and discuss the questions raised for evaluation.

2. Sign Language Generation

Sign language generation consists of creating animations that represent contents in SL, applied to a virtual character. These creations must be guided by a linguistic model of SL. The first section lists the concepts used in this article and the second one provides an overview of representative recent work in the field.

2.1. Avatar Animation

An avatar is made up of a complex 3D mesh that is given a humanoid shape, forming a virtual *skin*. It can be animated thanks to a virtual *skeleton* which is a tree structure composed of rigid segments called *bones* connected by joints. Each joint represent the six degrees of freedom (three rotations and tree translations) of a bone with respect to its parent, also called *3D pose*. A rig makes the link between the skeleton and the skin by defining the deformation of the latter depending on the bones' 3D pose.

An animation is a sequence of avatar poses displayed at a given frequency. Some poses, defined at a given timecode, are called *keyframes*. They act as control points in space and time, and may not be defined at each frame. From the main approaches listed by Naert et al. (2020), one can summarize three main approaches used for animation creation:

- *Hand-crafted*: The specification of keyframes is done manually, possibly assisted by computer and with techniques such as rotoscoping. The transitions between keyframes can be automatically computed using interpolation, resulting in a continuous movement. The quality of such animations relies on the skill level of the animator who select the keyframes. If they are not well chosen, this can result in movements that are robotic and perceived as not bio-realistic.
- *Automatic keyframing*: The principles are almost the same, except that the sequence of keyframes is provided by a representation of the sign structure rather than created by hand. Here also, the animation can be perceived as not good enough, because the computation relies on models that do not always take into account all the properties that allow the synthesis of a bio-realistic movement.
- *Data-driven*: The motion is captured on a human

[1]https://rosettaccess.fr/index.php/home-page-english/

	Generation of basic animation			Generation of final animation	
Name of the project	Hand crafted	Automatic keyframing	Mocap	Simple concat.	Edited concat.
JASigning		x		x	
EMBR		x		x	
Naert's project			x		x
Paula	x	x			x
Rosetta			x		x

Table 1: List of the most recent signing avatar systems.

using a motion capture (mocap) device. This allows for a high level of bio-realism but requires the use of a mocap system, and therefore a post-processing step on the recorded data.

To generate the final content, there are two main approaches:

- *Simple concatenation*: Blocks of animations are concatenated to form the final animation. These animations may have been created using any of the techniques outlined above. A process, called animation blending and described below, must then be implemented to link the blocks so that there is no break between the concatenated animations.
- *Edited concatenation*: There is still concatenation, but, in addition, edition of the blocks of animations is possible, in order to adapt the block to the context or to add realism to the whole animation.

One simple way to use existing data and combine them into new data is to use animation blending. This technique is implemented in different animation softwares like Blender or Motionbuilder. Video games industry relies a lot on blending, for example to generate a transition from running to walking. This is the same idea as a video or sound editing software. One can have several clips of animation on several tracks. Each track controls the 3D pose of a defined set of bones. On a given track, depending on the way clips overlap or not, two methods can be used:

- *Temporal interpolation*: When there is no overlapping between clips, temporal interpolation can be controlled between them.
- *Blend*: When there is overlapping of two clips, a blend is applied to transition from one clip to another. This blend is basically a weighted average of the set of 3D poses in the two clips. A "function of activation" is used to control the fading in and fading our of each clip across time.

2.2. Virtual Signer Animation

The generation of animations for virtual signers is a relatively new and underdeveloped field. Despite this, the different approaches listed above have been tested in research projects or even commercial products on SL. We propose here a synthesis of the most recent ones by positioning them according to these categories, grouped in Table 1.

A first generation of projects have been based on "Automatic keyframing / Simple concatenation" approaches: The first step consists of creating a collection of animations representing isolated lexical units (signs) which are stored in a database and identified by a gloss[2]. These sign animations are automatically keyframed, using a sign-level representation that describes the key poses. The signs are generally described in their citation form, i.e. not inflected by the linguistic context. Some procedural processes sometimes allow to inflect the signs so as to match with their surrounding linguistic context, or to add behaviour activity (e.g. breathing), but generally in a very limited manner. As a second step, SL utterances are built as a sequence of animation blocks. As such they are generally based on a simple concatenative approach. They are extracted from a database and concatenated to form a SL utterance. To date, the two platforms of this kind that have been most used are:

- JASigning: The Java Avatar Signing system is a platform tool for the synthesis of any sign language, freely available for research purposes (Elliott et al., 2008). It has been used for several projects with various SLs (Ebling and Glauert, 2013; Ebling and Glauert, 2016; Efthimiou et al., 2019; Roelofsen et al., 2021). The signs are represented in their citation form using SiGML, which is built on HamNoSys, a transcription system for signs. Sign inflection is possible in a limited manner and only at the sign level.
- EMBR (Embodied Agents Behavior Realizer) (Heloir and Kipp, 2009; Huenerfauth and Kacorri, 2015): The signs are represented in their citation form using k-pose-sequences called EMBRScript, coming with explicit timing information. Sign inflection is not possible.

These approaches have the same drawbacks: they use signs in their citation form with little or no sign inflection capabilities, they do not integrate linguistic structures such as classifiers, and they do not have a very advanced management of temporal aspects, either at the

[2]A gloss is a text label, generally a single word, reflecting the meaning of the sign it stands for.

level of signs or utterances. Moreover, as the animation is built from pure procedural synthesis, the rendering is rather robotic and far from being bio-realistic.
More recent projects aim to overcome these limitations, using edition approaches each with its own specificity:

- Naert's project: This project is based on the use of a mocap database in which movements have been annotated using a linguistic model. Several techniques are used to build new signs and to modify signs regarding the context. These processes are currently limited to phenomena involving the hand location and handshape (Naert, 2020).

- Paula: The DePaul University signing avatar project has been designed first for American Sign Language but is now being used for various SLs (McDonald et al., 2016). Initially designed to support professional animator's work by including a number of automation of current processes for the generation of content in SL, it is based on handcrafted animations. It relies on a multitrack animation engine, allowing for flexible and accurate synchronisation between the various parts of the body to be animated. Several procedural tools allow to increase naturalness, to modify or adapt signs to the context, or to create new ones, including classifiers, thanks to a formal linguistic representation of SL called AZee (McDonald and Filhol, 2021).

The approach we present here, used in the Rosetta project, is based on the use of gold standard motion capture for the constitution of a database of LSF extracts, AZee as the representation that drives the generation of the final animation, and on an edition approach, combining concatenation and procedural techniques.
First of all, we briefly present the corpus produced within the framework of this project.

3. Motion Capture Corpus

In our project we used the first task of the Rosetta-LSF corpus (Dauriac, 2022), downloadable from Ortolang[3]. This consists in richly annotated LSF translations of 194 news in French which are between three and 35 words in length, for instance: *"L'Everest menacé de réchauffement climatique"* (Everest threatened by global warming). More details on this corpus can be found in Bertin-Lemée et al. (2022a). After the motion capture, a 3D avatar with the same body proportions as the signer was created from the marker set. The avatar animations were then implemented into a 3D player to produce a video for each acquisition (see fig. 1), allowing to use an annotation software to annotate the SL content.
While AZee describes the structure and content of the SL utterance, the annotation scheme was designed to provide descriptions at the sign level. The annotations specify articulatory constraints and temporal information relevant for the generation process. Two tracks were used to annotate manual activity of right and left arms and hands. Annotation was carried out in a classical way, by segmenting and annotating manual units, but was not limited to assigning a simple gloss to them (*IdGloss* attribute). We added the different constraints to be applied on these units for any context of use, so as to inform the generation process about the possibilities or needs for modification in a new linguistic context.
For each segment, on each track, four attributes have been specifically defined to help the generation pro-

[3]https://www.ortolang.fr/market/corpora/rosetta-lsf

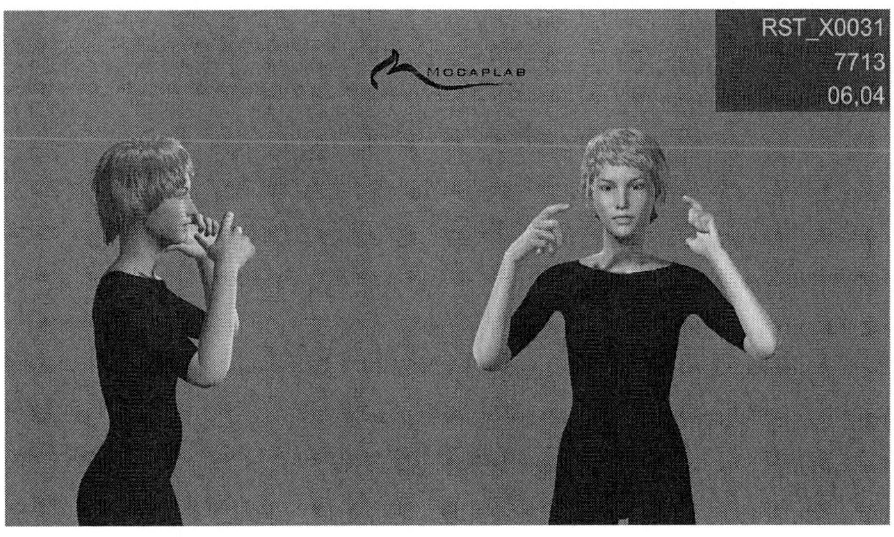

Figure 1: Avatar rendering

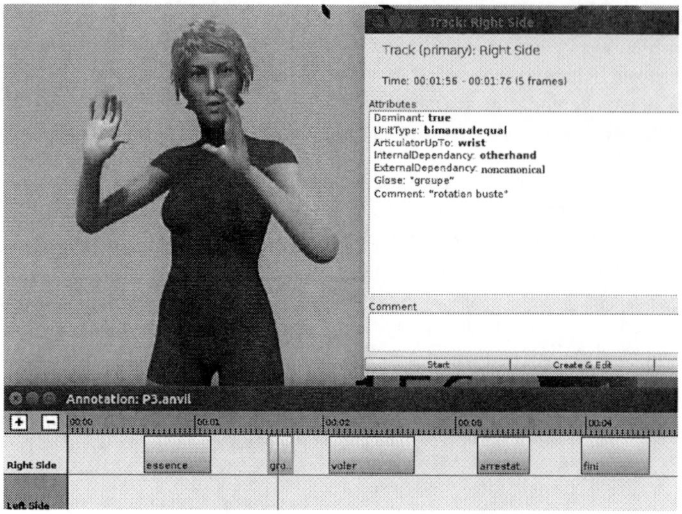

Figure 2: Example of annotation using ANVIL (Kipp, 2014)

cess:

- *UnitType*: This attribute allows to distinguish three categories of unit according to the number of hands involved and the nature of the relationship between the hands. It may have four values: monomanual (unit performed with one hand, this is the default value), bimanualequal (unit performed with both hands where there is no dominance of one hand over the other), bimanualdominant (unit performed with both hands for which there is a relationship of dominance of one hand over the other), and unknown (in case of doubt).
- *ArticulatoryUpTo*: This attribute identifies the articulatory constraints of the unit for the considered side. The aim is to indicate to the generation process the necessary and sufficient constraints, thus leaving the process free to modify the bending of certain joints if needed. This concerns the local constraints of all articulatory segments from the fingers to the shoulder. It is therefore more precise than what is usually called "handshape". This attribute may have six values: no (unconstrained posture), fingers (all the fingers are constrained and not the whole hand), wrist (the whole hand is constrained and not the forearm), elbow (the hand and forearm are constrained and not the arm), other (other cases to be detailed in the comments), and unknown (in case of doubt). No more indication is given (handshape, orientation and location), as this is directly retrievable from the mocap data.
- *InternalDependency*: This attribute describes the constraints between the hand and other parts of the body. The objective is to indicate the necessary and sufficient constraints to satisfy when modifications are applied to certain articulators (e.g. moving a hand, rotating the head, etc.). It may have six values: no (no constraints, default value), otherhand (constraint with respect to the other hand), head (constraint with respect to the head), body (constraint with respect to the torso), other (constraint with respect to another part of the body, to be specified in the comments), and unknown (in case of doubt).
- *ExternalDependency*: This attribute indicates the possibility or existence of constraints of the hand with respect to the signing space. The aim is to indicate if the articulation depends on a spatial context (e.g. modification of hand orientation or location, movement amplitude), so that the generation can be adapted to the spatial context. The possible values are notapplicable (for a sign that cannot be modified), canonical (when it is not modified), non canonical (when modified), and unknown (in case of doubt).

The fig. 2 shows an example of annotation for the sign *"GROUPE"* (GROUP) on the Right track: The *Dominant* attribute value is true (the signer is right-handed), the sign type is *bimanualequal* (no dominance of one hand over the other), and articulatory constraints up to the *wrist* (no constraints on other segments on the right side), with an *otherhand* internal dependency of one hand to the other, and an *noncanonical* external dependency as it is relocated.

To date, all 194 titles in task 1 have been annotated. This corpus was used to generate new utterances. The principles used to create these new animations are described below.

4. Generation Methodology

As for the Paula project, the description of the utterance to be generated is given by an AZee description. AZee is a formal approach to SL discourse representation (Hadjadj et al., 2018; Challant and Filhol, 2022). It allows to define *production rules* that associate forms to be articulated (to generate an animation in SL) and identified meaning. By combining them, one builds tree-structured expressions that generate signed utterances. Each node of the expression hierarchy therefore represents a portion of the utterance by itself, with the root node by definition covering the entire discourse. A "%t" pragma is appended on the AZee source line of nodes, followed by the corresponding text and the video frame numbers identifying the beginning and the end of aligned segment (see fig. 1, top right, second line: 7713), as illustrated in fig. 3. In this example, three nodes are defined: the first one is "*ont vendu leur vaisselle*" (sold their tableware) from frames 1739 to 1967, and it includes 2 sub-nodes: "*vaisselle*" (tableware) from frames 1767 to 1851, and "*vendu*" (sold) from frames 1855 to 1967. Each node with a "%t" is thus associated with a segment of mocap file forming an animation block, which we will call *AZee block* in the following. The smallest AZee block that can be found in the corpus is at the level of the sign.

```
:info-about %F ont vendu leur vaisselle %t 1739-1967
    'topic
    :là
    'info
    :info-about
        'topic
        :all-of %F vaisselle %t 1767-1851
            'items
            list
                :assiette
                :assiette
        'info
        :multiplicity %F vendu %t 1855-1967
            'elt
            :vendre
```

Figure 3: Excerpt from an AZee discourse expression.

Using our corpus, composed of the mocap files, associated annotations and AZee descriptions, we are able to generate a new sentence, by collecting blocks of mocap data, concatenating, and modifying them when needed, with the approach summarized in fig. 4.

The general principle of the smart blending methodology we designed in the Rosetta project is based on the fact that motion is managed synchronously over several animation tracks. Each track corresponds to a set of anatomical parts representing effectors such as the right arm, left arm, trunk, head, facial expressions, eye gaze, and the rest of the body. Thus, using a non linear animation blending tool on this hierarchical skeleton, it becomes then possible to assemble several blocs to generate new sign language sentences while keeping a multi-track approach. This is the main particularity of our proposed approach.

A new sentence to be generated is described within an AZee file: each necessary AZee block is extracted from the database, then, there are two blending cases:

- either a *%fallback* AZee block is mentioned, meaning that no higher-level block have been found to make the link between one sub-block and another ("Fallback" box fig. 4).
- Or a sub-block is replaced inside an AZee block ("Replacement" box fig. 4).

For each case, we have designed one blending methodology which corresponds to the two necessary operations for the creation of the new utterance.

In the first case, the *fallback blending*, one wants to transition from the end of one block to the beginning of the second one. As no information is known on how to put these two pieces together in a seamless sequence, this transition can occur simultaneously on all tracks (including facial expression, eye gaze, etc.) but require some precaution on the duration of such transition. In the corpus, the main end-effectors with the highest dynamics were found to be the wrists and the head. To compute the time allowed for transition between two blocks, i.e. the blending time, 3D position in the global 3D frame of these end-effectors have been used. To ensure the bio-realistic dynamics of the transition and predict the necessary time window, a simple proportional calculation have been used on the distance covered by each end-effector (wrist and head) in high dynamic movements between annotated AZee blocks from the corpora. The maximum of the predicted time windows for the three end-effectors has been used.

In the second case, the *replacement blending*, one wants to change an AZee sub-block inside an AZee block. In the simplest case, one wants to change one sign in a block, a city name for example. In many cases, animation from the arms have to be replaced while the rest of the body must be maintained to preserve the AZee block structure. This replacement may raise several problems:

- The block to be replaced and the one to be inserted don't have the same duration.
- The position of each segment in the global 3D frame are not the same between the replaced and inserted blocks, requiring a blending at the beginning and end.
- The inserted block may not have the same number of tracks as the replaced one.

For the duration offset between replaced and inserted blocks, it has been chosen to keep the inserted block duration. This means that each track where nothing is replaced (head and eye gaze tracks for example) has to be stretched or squeezed to match the inserted block duration. This choice has been made as the majority

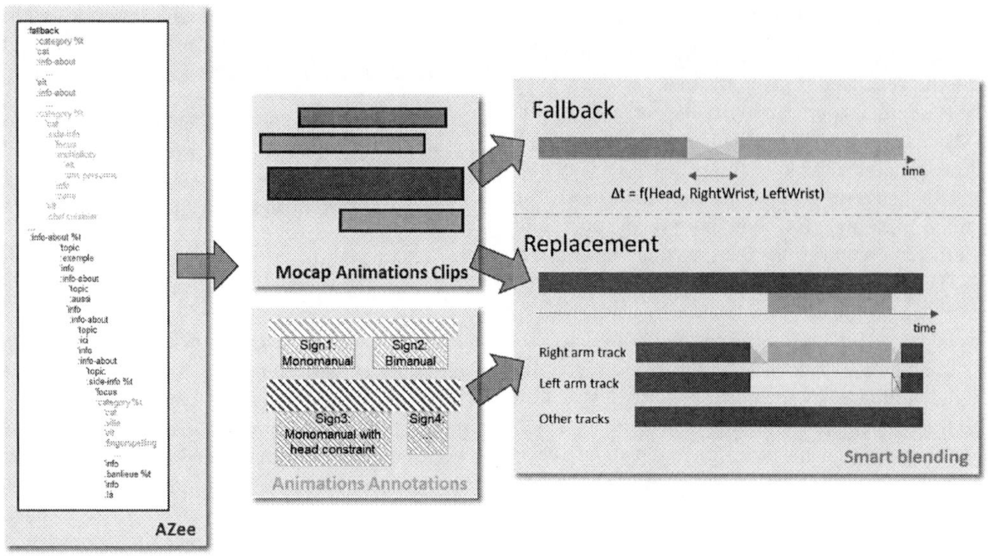

Figure 4: Smart Blending generation approach in Rosetta

of the inserted blocks were longer in duration than the replaced ones.
Blending time between the previous AZee sub-block and the next AZee sub-block is maintained on the replaced tracks.
For track replacements, for example if one takes the smallest AZee sub-block, i.e. a sign, it can be monomanual or bi-manual. When replacing a bimanual sign with a monomanual one, the non dominant arm track needs to be "emptied" and the monomanual animation of the non dominant arm is not used as it is not meaningful. Between the end of the previous AZee sub-block and the replaced sub-block end, the animation on the non dominant arm track is deleted and a blend is performed between the end of the sub-block and the beginning of the next AZee sub-block. When replacing a monomanual sign with a bimanual one, the non dominant arm track is replaced like the dominant one with the inserted sub-block. The same principle was applied to bigger AZee sub-blocks and other track conflicts by searching through the corpora annotations on the articulatory constraints (UnitType and InternalDependency Attributes).
At the end of the procedure, a video of the newly generated sentence has been created with a rendering engine (Unity[4]).
The approach aims at minimizing the edition of recorded movements to leverage the fine-grained precision of motion capture. For Fallback, motion edition only occurs during blending on all tracks. For Replacement, the methodology focused on the two arm tracks and their dependencies with other articulatory tracks. No edition was made to modify originally directional signs, nor on facial expressions as they were not annotated.

5. Tests and Discussion

In order to test the whole translation system from text to SL via the animation of a virtual signer, a testset was built by creating new sentences mixing segments from different newstitles of our corpus. 15 sentences were created and we retained the AZee translation of seven of them to test the functionality of our generation system. For example, we got the AZee description of the following sentence: "*Alsace : de grands chefs ont vendu leur vaisselle pour les plus modestes dans la banlieue de Gerstheim.*" (Alsace: top chefs sold their tableware for households in the lowest income group in the suburbs of Gerstheim.).
The corresponding animation was generated using mocap blocks extracted from the LSF translations of the following three sentences present in the corpus:

- "*Samedi 30 et dimanche 31 mars, de grands chefs ont vendu leur vaisselle en Alsace, à Gerstheim.* (On Saturday 30 and Sunday 31 March, top chefs sold their tableware in Alsace, in Gerstheim.)
- "*Moins de TVA pour les plus modestes: " Il ne faut pas traiter ça par le mépris ",lance Xavier Bertrand au gouvernement*" (Less VAT for households in the lowest income group: "We must not treat this with contempt", says Xavier Bertrand Bertrand to the government.)
- "*Le superéthanol n'est proposé que dans 1 000 stations-service en France, comme ici dans la banlieue de Bordeaux*" (Superethanol is only

[4]https://unity.com/

available at 1,000 service stations in France, like here in the suburbs of Bordeaux.)

From sentence animations, six AZee blocks have been extracted corresponding to *"Alsace"*, *"Gerstheim"*, *"grands chefs"*, *"ont vendu leur vaisselle"*, *"pour les plus modestes"* and *"comme ici dans la banlieue de Bordeaux"*. Fallbacks where used to associate all the AZee blocks, apart from *"comme ici dans la banlieue de Bordeaux"* where *"Bordeaux"* needed to be replaced with *"Gerstheim"* inside the block. The annotation indicated that *"Gerstheim"* AZee block has constraints: both arms are used (UnitType attribute). The fallback methodology allowed to compute a blending time between each AZee block. They lied between 0.19 and 0.49 seconds. The duration of *"Bordeaux"* AZee block was 0.24 seconds whereas the *"Gerstheim"* one took 3.48 seconds (because this proper name is fingerspelled). *"Bordeaux"* AZee block has been slowed down to match *"Gerstheim"* AZee block duration. Then, on the right and left arm tracks, the animation of *"Bordeaux"* AZee block has been replaced with *"Gerstheim"* one. In *"comme ici dans la banlieue de Bordeaux"*, the AZee block before *"Bordeaux"* was *"là"* and the one afterwards was *"banlieue"*. A blend from the end of *"là"* AZee block and the beginning of *"Gerstheim"* AZee block as well as between *"Gerstheim"* AZee block end and *"banlieue"* AZee block beginning was applied according to the given annotation duration.

A video showing the result of the whole system (translation and generation) for the seven sentences can be seen on the project website[5]. The second sentence of the video is the one described here above.

Although a real evaluation could not be carried out on such a limited number of examples, we were able to show them to the advisory board of the project which gave us some qualitative feedback. There were few comments on the multi-track methodology itself, with remarks focusing more on possible translation problems, contextualisation problems with the image added to the left of the avatar, or signing speed problems, as the person we recorded signs quickly. A few negative points were noted related to the appearance of the avatar (we only had a very simplified avatar in this project), the presence of a very local sign and therefore not necessarily known by everyone (the sign representing the Parisian urban transport company: RATP), and an error in the choice of a variant for the sign "là", probably due to a lack of precision during the annotation process. The positive points that were identified concern the fluidity of the animation. A comparison between an animation generated with a classical concatenation method and the method presented here was shown to the advisory board members, who preferred the rendering of the second one. There was no difference in the perception of smoothness between the animations with our method and the animations generated by simply replaying the mocap.

Of course, there are still a number of aspects to be addressed. For example, we have not yet annotated the non-manual elements (mouthing, facial expressions, eye gaze) in the corpus. Once done, there will be no particular difficulty in taking them into account during the animation process because the methodology already allows for this. Another important aspect concerns the management of the signing space. The annotation already provides an indication of whether a sign is in its canonical form or not regarding the spatial context (ExternalDependency attribute). Several strategies can be explored. For example, for a given sign performed in a canonical way, one could generate a non canonical relocated form by combining the handshape(s) with the location of another sign, while respecting the possible internal dependencies.

6. Conclusion and Prospects

We have presented here a new system of automatic generation from AZee (a hierarchical representation of SL) to French Sign Language (LSF), by means of the animation of an avatar, based on smart blending approaches and the use of an aligned corpus of AZee descriptions and mocap data, the Rosetta-LSF corpus. An implementation of the system has been made and has allowed to test its functioning on some examples, thus providing a proof of concept.

The capacities of this system and the size of the corpus still need to be extended before real evaluations can be carried out. But we can already stress that the evaluation of such a system will not be easy.

Metrics for evaluating the quality of translations, such as the ones proposed in the European QT21 project[6], provide a scoring grid for the types of errors produced by the translation system, which makes it possible to highlight the shortcomings of the systems and subsequently prioritise the areas for improvement. This project has proposed Multidimensional Quality Metrics (MQM), which is a framework for describing and defining custom translation quality metrics. It provides a flexible vocabulary of quality issue types, a mechanism for applying them to generate quality scores, and mappings to other metrics.

Some of the error categories, linked to the translation process itself, are called "Accuracy". There is an accuracy error when the target does not accurately reflect the source message. Our generation system does not handle the translation process, which role is to translate between French text into AZee description, and so we cannot use this type of error to analyse the quality of the animation. Another category called "Fluency" allows us to evaluate the quality of an utterance, whether it is the result of a translation or not. These errors can

[5] `https://rosettaccess.fr/index.php/rosettas-final-demonstrator/` - Note that the subtitles were also automatically produced, and therefore may contain errors compared to the spoken French version.

[6] `https://www.qt21.eu/`

be related to grammar, spelling, typography, inconsistency, opacity. In our case, the target is not a text, but an avatar animation, thus some of these categories cannot be used at all, and other should be adapted. For example, it is not necessarily easy to define the types of grammatical errors for SL. Anyway, it would be interesting to study if this kind of evaluation could be adapted to our system. To these categories, we will certainly have to add a category related to "Body Fluency", allowing to evaluate all the aspects linked to the naturalness of the movement and its bio-realistic aspect, making a distinction between linguistic fluency and body fluency.
The establishment of a robust and comprehensive evaluation protocol is clearly a subject of study in its own that needs to be pursued in the near future.

7. Acknowledgements

This work has been funded by the Bpifrance investment project "Grands défis du numérique", as part of the ROSETTA project (RObot for Subtitling and intElligent adapTed TranslAtion).
We thank Noémie Churlet, Raphaël Bouton and Media'Pi! for their commitment to this project, which would not have had the same validity and impact without them.

8. Bibliographical References

Bertin-Lemée, E., Braffort, A., Challant, C., Danet, C., Dauriac, B., Filhol, M., Martinod, E., and Segouat, J. (2022a). Rosetta-LSF: an Aligned Corpus of French Sign Language and French for Text-to-Sign Translation. In *13th International Conference on Language Resources and Evaluation (LREC)*.

Bertin-Lemée, E., Braffort, A., Challant, C., Danet, C., and Filhol, M. (2022b). Example-Based Machine Translation from Text to a Hierarchical Representation of Sign Language. *arXiv preprint arXiv:2205.03314*.

Challant, C. and Filhol, M. (2022). A First Corpus of AZee Discourse Expressions. In *Language Resources and Evaluation Conference (LREC), Representation and Processing of Sign Languages, Marseille, France*.

Ebling, S. and Glauert, J. (2013). Exploiting the full potential of JASigning to build an avatar signing train announcements. In *Third International Symposium on Sign Language Translation and Avatar Technology*.

Ebling, S. and Glauert, J. (2016). Building a Swiss German Sign Language avatar with JASigning and evaluating it among the Deaf community. *Universal Access in the Information Society*, 15:577—587.

Efthimiou, E., Fotinea, S.-E., Goulas, T., Vacalopoulou, A., Vasilaki, K., and Dimou, A.-L. (2019). Sign Language Technologies and the Critical Role of SL Resources in View of Future Internet Accessibility Services. *Technologies*, 7(1).

Elliott, R., Glauert, J., Kennaway, R., Marshall, I., and Safar, E. (2008). Linguistic modelling and language-processing technologies for avatar-based sign language presentation. *Universal Access in the Information Society*, 6:375—391.

Hadjadj, M., Filhol, M., and Braffort, A. (2018). Modeling French Sign Language: a Proposal for a Semantically Compositional System. In *International Conference on Language Resources and Evaluation*.

Heloir, A. and Kipp, M. (2009). EMBR: A realtime animation engine for interactive embodied agents. In *2009 3rd International Conference on Affective Computing and Intelligent Interaction and Workshops*.

Huenerfauth, M. and Kacorri, H. (2015). Augmenting EMBR Virtual Human Animation System with MPEG-4 Controls for Producing ASL Facial Expressions. In *5th International Workshop on Sign Language Translation and Avatar Technology (SLTAT)*.

Kipp, M. (2014). ANVIL: A Universal Video Research Tool. pages 420–436.

McDonald, J. and Filhol, M. (2021). Natural synthesis of productive forms from structured descriptions of sign language. *Machine Translation*, 35(3):363–386.

McDonald, J., Wolfe, R., Schnepp, J., Hochgesang, J., Gorman Jamrozik, D., Stumbo, M., Berke, L., Bialek, M., and Thomas, F. (2016). An automated technique for real-time production of lifelike animations of American Sign Language. *Universal Access in the Information Society*, 15:551—-566.

Naert, L., Larboulette, C., and Gibet, S. (2020). A survey on the animation of signing avatars: From sign representation to utterance synthesis. *Computers Graphics*, 92:76–98.

Naert, L. (2020). *Capture, annotation and synthesis of motions for the data-driven animation of sign language avatars*. Phd thesis in computer science, Université de Bretagne Sud.

Roelofsen, F., Esselink1, L., Mende-Gillings, S., and Smeijers, A. (2021). Sign Language Translation in a Healthcare Setting. In *Translation and Interpreting Technology Online (TRITON)*, pages 110—-124.

9. Language Resource References

Dauriac, B. et al. (2022). *ROSETTA-LSF corpus*. distributed via ORTOLANG: `https://hdl.handle.net/11403/rosetta-lsf/v1`, v1.

Proceedings of the 7th International Workshop on Sign Language Translation and Avatar Technology (SLTAT 7), pages 29–38
Language Resources and Evaluation Conference (LREC 2022), Marseille, 20-25 June 2022

Fine-tuning of Convolutional Neural Networks for the Recognition of Facial Expressions in Sign Language Video Samples

Neha Deshpande[1], **Fabrizio Nunnari**[2], **Eleftherios Avramidis**[3]
[1]Technical University of Berlin,
[2]German Research Center for Artificial Intelligence (DFKI),
Saarland Informatics Campus D3.2, Saarbrücken, Germany
[3]German Research Center for Artificial Intelligence (DFKI), Alt Moabit 91c, Berlin, Germany
nehadeshpande97@gmail.com, fabrizio.nunnari@dfki.de, eleftherios.avramidis@dfki.de

Abstract

In this paper, we investigate the capability of convolutional neural networks to recognize in sign language video frames the six basic Ekman facial expressions for 'fear', 'disgust', 'surprise', 'sadness', 'happiness' and 'anger' along with the 'neutral' class. Given the limited amount of annotated facial expression data for the sign language domain, we started from a model pre-trained on general-purpose facial expression datasets and we applied various machine learning techniques such as fine-tuning, data augmentation, class balancing, as well as image preprocessing to reach a better accuracy. The models were evaluated using K-fold cross-validation to get more accurate conclusions. Through our experiments we demonstrate that fine-tuning a pre-trained model along with data augmentation by horizontally flipping images and image normalization, helps in providing the best accuracy on the sign language dataset. The best setting achieves satisfactory classification accuracy, comparable to state-of-the-art systems in generic facial expression recognition. Experiments were performed using different combinations of the above-mentioned techniques based on two different architectures, namely MobileNet and EfficientNet, and is deemed that both architectures seem equally suitable for the purpose of fine-tuning, whereas class balancing is discouraged.

Keywords: facial expression recognition, sign language

1. Introduction

While people are speaking, their facial expressions convey emotional information. Sign languages are visual languages that relies on movements of hands, body, as well as facial muscles. Thus, facial expressions are already involved in conveying the meaning of a message. To what extent, and how, facial expressions of signers are also involved in the communication of emotions is still an open and under-investigated topic.

This work consists of a focused experimentation which is a preliminary step in the broader research on SL recognition, where we try to understand if a computer can recognize facial expressions from a signer as good as it can already do for the facial expressions of speaking subjects. Since this is one of the first experiments on this topic, and given the lack of more descriptive datasets of appropriate size, we hypothesize on the applicability of deep learning and proceed with specific assumptions: we are based on a shallow labelling of only 6 emotions, we don't consider linguistic content/markers and we focus on the face, ignoring spatial and manual elements.

Facial expressions are culture-specific, due to which most positive emotions are communicated with culture-specific signals, while the negative emotions can be recognized across cultures (Sauter et al., 2010). In this work, we focus on German sign language.

Deep convolutional neural networks (CNN), the state-of-the-art in image recognition, require a large amount of data and a limited amount of facial expressions data is available specifically for the German SL, making it difficult to train a Facial Expression Recognition (FER) model from scratch. Therefore, this work uses fine-tuning of pre-trained models that showed a state-of-the-art accuracy on common facial expression datasets. The pre-trained models used during the experiments follow a lightweight architecture which makes it easier to fine-tune and still provides high accuracy.

For this study, it was hypothesized that fine-tuning a pre-trained FER model (trained on a very large image dataset) helps improve the prediction rate on a SL dataset, annotated with the six basic emotions of 'sad', 'surprise', 'fear', 'angry', 'disgust', and 'happy' along with the 'neutral' and 'none' labels. Apart from fine-tuning, the experiments include various machine learning techniques such as data augmentation, image normalization and class balancing to improve the performance of the fine-tuned model.

The rest of the paper is organized as follows. A survey of related literature is given in Section 2. Section 3 includes a description of the methods used. Section 4 contains details about the experiments. Section 5 presents the results of these experiments followed by Section 6, which concludes the paper.

2. Related Work

As discussed in the previous section, to tackle the complexity of FER, several machine learning (ML) techniques have been used including both conventional as well as deep-learning-based approaches. A review of FER in the past years, including a comparison of several techniques based on certain evaluation metrics, is provided in Ko (2018).

Deep-learning-based approaches such as Convolutional Neural Networks (CNN) and Recurrent Neural Networks (RNN) can perform end-to-end feature extraction, classification as well as recognition tasks with high accuracy (Kim et al., 2019; Chu et al., 2017). However, they need large datasets, computing power, amounts of memory and are time-consuming for both the training and testing phases (Ko, 2018). In the reminder of this section, we introduce related work in the detection of facial expressions using CNNs and how to improve their performance when data is scarce.

2.1. Existing Deep-Learning-Based Models

State-of-the-art techniques involving deep-learning-based approaches used for FER are presented below. Savchenko (2021) presented a simple training pipeline where a model can provide state-of-the-art accuracy using lightweight neural networks in FER trained on images and videos of the AffectNet data-set (Mollahosseini et al., 2019). The high performance, reduced speed and model size of this model is the result of pre-training of facial feature extractor for face identification, which was done by a very large VGGFace2 (Gennaro and Vairo, 2019) data-set. The features extracted by this network can be used with more complex classifiers, and therefore can be explored for FER in the case of SL.

Frame Attention Networks (FAN) can be used to automatically discriminate frames in the network by taking a videos with various image frames as its input and produce a fixed-dimension feature representation which can be then used for FER through a CNN (Meng et al., 2019). This framework provided a high performance on the CK+ (Lucey et al., 2010) and AFEW 8.0 (Kossaifi et al., 2017) datasets (both including seven emotion labels).

Along with deep-learning-based models, models pre-trained with Local Binary Patterns (LBP) to extract facial features and Support Vector Machines (SVM) to classify them were also recently used, although their accuracy on some datasets has been lower than that with a CNN (Ravi et al., 2020).

2.2. Improving CNNs

Data augmentation techniques (O'Mahony et al., 2019), which include geometric transformations such as flipping the training images horizontally, as well as cropping them randomly to increase the training data, are used for improving the performance of a CNN (Savchenko, 2021). In most CV tasks involving image classification, flipping the images horizontally before training is sufficient and helps in improving the overall performance of the CNN (Zheng et al., 2020). Apart from data augmentation, using data pre-processing techniques such as resizing, face detection, cropping, adding noise, data normalization, histogram equalization, etc., also helps in boosting the performance of a CNN trained for recognizing emotions from facial images (Pitaloka et al., 2017).

CNN architectures such as EfficientNet (B0 to B7), MobileNet, ResNet, etc., help in reducing the calculations required making them more lightweight and faster (Tan and Le, 2019; Tan and Le, 2021). Using several optimizers instead of just one also improves the performance and generalization of a CNN (Taqi et al., 2018). Along with the commonly used Adam optimizer, using an additional optimizer such as the Sharpness Aware Minimization (SAM) and Stochastic Gradient Descent (SGD) for the last few epochs boosts the overall performance by providing a better coverage (Savchenko, 2021). Other important parameters that could help boost the performance of a CNN are: appropriate learning rates, choice of the activation function, balancing the imbalanced classes, etc. (Kandel and Castelli, 2020).

Last but not least, transfer learning, i.e., using the parameters learned for a problem as starting values (instead of random values) to train on a new dataset, helps in reducing training time (Akhand et al., 2021; O'Mahony et al., 2019).

3. Methods

This section describes the methods used in the experiments. The methods explained are chosen due to the state-of-the-art accuracy they provided in Facial Expression Recognition models presented by Savchenko (2021).

3.1. Image Preprocessing

Image preprocessing plays a vital role in achieving state-of-the-art results in a CNN, as the raw data does not always produce good accuracy. The improvement in accuracy of a CNN is dependent on the image preprocessing technique being used along with its network architecture. This work uses two image preprocessing techniques: face cropping and image normalization.

Face Cropping is a technique used in CV to extract the area of the image which is required for image recognition or classification tasks. In the case of FER, faces are cropped from the image dataset to remove the unnecessary information from the images and only keep the pixels that constitute the facial information. To crop faces from an image, Savchenko (2021) has proposed the use of a Multi-task Cascaded Convolutional Network (MTCNN), a framework used for face detection and alignment. MTCNN performs three tasks: face classification, bounding box regression, and facial landmark localization (Xiang and Zhu, 2017).

The face is cropped from an image in the following steps: detect and extract the face mesh from images, extract the face bounds, and then crop the images (Emami and Suciu, 2012). Detection and recognition of faces is done using a Haar Cascade (Soo, 2014), an object detection method used to locate an object of interest in images. A Haar-like feature considers neighboring rectangular regions, sums up the pixel intensities in each region, and calculates the difference between these sums, which helps to categorize the image into subsections. We use the implementation of OpenCV, which has shown good performance for face detection (Boyko et al., 2018).

Image Normalization. Studies have shown that for image classification as well as recognition tasks image normalization has helped in enhancing the performance of the CNN (Savchenko, 2021; Koo and Cha, 2017; Heidari et al., 2020).
Image normalization is a technique where the mean along each of the features (dimensions of images) from the training sample is calculated and is subtracted from every image. This results in normalizing the brightness of the whole training set concerning each dimension as shown in the equation below (Pal and Sudeep, 2016):

$$X' = X - \mu \tag{1}$$

where X' is the normalized data, X represents the original data, and μ is the mean vector across all features of X.

3.2. CNN Architectures

CNNs are artificial neural networks that play a significant role in Natural Language Processing (NLP), CV tasks such as image detection, recognition, etc. (Albawi et al., 2017). Several CNN architectures have been developed to solve real-world problems. In this work we use the MobileNet and EfficientNet architectures which are explained below.

The MobileNet Architecture - MobileNet-v1 The MobileNet architecture (Savchenko, 2021) uses depthwise separable convolutions followed by pointwise convolutions where each input channel is filtered separately. This results in a drastic reduction in model size and cost compared to standard convolutions. In comparison to other more efficient architectures, the accuracy obtained with MobileNet reduces as the number of parameters is increased in the model.
The MobileNet v1 architecture has 28 layers wherein each layer is followed by batch normalization and a Rectified Linear Unit (ReLU) (Ioffe and Szegedy, 2015). The architecture starts with a regular 3×3 convolution, followed by 13 depthwise separable convolutional blocks and pointwise convolutions (Michele et al., 2019). The depthwise convolution in MobileNet is the channel-wise spatial convolution (Howard et al., 2017). Whereas the pointwise convolution is 1x1 convolution which is used to change the dimension. These depthwise and pointwise convolutions result in a reduction in model size and computation cost by about 8 to 9 times as compared to the usage of standard convolutions (Sinha and El-Sharkawy, 2019).
The MobileNet v1 architecture has been used for a variety of object detection and image recognition applications such as palm print recognition (Michele et al., 2019), handwriting character recognition (Ghosh et al., 2020), FER (Savchenko, 2021), and more.

The EfficientNet Architecture - EfficientNet-B0 EfficientNet (Tan and Le, 2019) is another neural network architecture that consists of 8 model types, from B0 to B7. The accuracy and the number of model parameters increase with the model number. EfficientNet uses an activation function called Swish instead of the Rectifier Linear Unit (ReLU) of the MobileNet architecture. The main building block for EfficientNet is the inverted bottleneck MBConv, which consists of a layer that first expands and then compresses the channel (Tan and Le, 2019; Sandler et al., 2018). This architecture has in-depth separable convolutions that reduce the calculation by almost k^2 factor compared to traditional layers, where k is the kernel size which denotes the width and height of the 2D convolution window (Sandler et al., 2018). EfficientNet has been recently used for several applications such as plant leaf disease classification (Atila et al., 2021) and automated diagnosis of COVID-19 (Marques et al., 2020).

The EfficientNet architecture is more efficient than MobileNet and has provided state-of-the-art accuracy on several transfer learning datasets as it is easily scalable (Tan and Le, 2019). On the one hand, when used for image classification problems, the EfficientNet architecture scaled up the image size leading to large memory consumption compared to MobileNet. On the other hand, the MobileNet architecture is more lightweight and it works efficiently for a small number of parameters.

3.3. Training

Fine-tuning is the process of initializing a pre-trained classification network and then training it further for a different task (Radenović et al., 2018). It is applied when there is the need to fit a low resource dataset starting from models pre-trained on bigger datasets. One of the motivations for using fine-tuning instead of fully training a model from scratch is that the low-level basic features are common for most images and hence an already trained (pre-trained) model can be useful for classification by just fine-tuning the high-level features.
The proposed FER technique (Akhand et al., 2021; Ngo and Yoon, 2020; Savchenko, 2021) is to use a CNN model pre-trained for image classification, and fine-tune it by replacing the upper layers with the dense layer(s) to make it compatible with the target dataset. These new dense layers are first tuned to the target dataset, followed by training the whole CNN with this same dataset.

Optimization in Neural Networks The aim of a CNN is to learn from the given data by minimizing the loss. The loss function is reduced with the help of an optimization algorithm which is a numerical function performed on the model parameters. A gradient descent algorithm is commonly used in neural networks for optimization as it minimizes the objective function by updating the parameters in the reverse direction of the gradient of the objective function. Here we briefly explain the three optimizers used. In addition to the most popular optimizers (such as Adam and Stocastic Gradient Descent), **Sharpness Aware Minimization (SAM)** is an optimization technique that seeks parameters that lie in neighborhoods having uniformly low loss leading to sub-optimal model quality (Foret et al., 2020). SAM is shown to improve the generalizability of the model across several datasets and to provide robustness to noisy labels and helped achieve a better performance when applied on fine-tuned EfficientNet models pre-trained on ImageNet. Using SAM for optimizing the categorical cross-entropy loss for the last two epochs also provided a state-of-the-art accuracy on fine-tuned EfficientNet models pre-trained on ImageNet (Savchenko, 2021).

Data Augmentation Flipping data horizontally before feeding it to the CNN has been shown to be not only safe but also one of the most common and effective data augmentation technique (Shorten and Khoshgoftaar, 2019). Other augmentation methods, such as rotation and noise disturbance are not used here, because as noted by Zheng et al. (2020), they could have a large impact on the image structure if the images are small in size, resulting in poor performance.

Class Weights The datasets available for FER do not always consist of balanced classes as they have a different number of samples in each class. This can result in incorrect evaluation and a need for balancing these classes to achieve uniform results across classes. An algorithm-based technique used to balance the classes is called class weighting where different weights are used for every class depending on the number of training samples present in a class. As explained by Johnson and Khoshgoftaar (2019), class weights for each class can be calculated as follows:

$$cw = max_i|Ci|min_i|Ci|$$

Here, cw is the class weight for a minority class. Consider that the largest class in the dataset has 100 samples and the smallest class has 10 samples. If the class weight for the majority class is set to 1 then that for the minority class will be set to 10.

4. Experimental Setup

The goal of our experiments is to maximize the classification accuracy of the facial expressions. As baseline and a basic model for fine-tuning we used the models by Savchenko (2021), trained on generic facial expression data, as they provided a state-of-the-art accuracy with the MobileNet and EfficientNet architectures. In our experiments, the baseline model is first fine-tuned to a dataset of facial expressions of signers. Then, various techniques such as data augmentation, image preprocessing, as well as class weight balancing were applied one after the other in different combinations.
For every configuration we measure the overall accuracy, the sensitivity per class, as well as the average sensitivity. The overall accuracy is the ratio of the number of correct predictions to all the predictions, whereas the sensitivity per class gives the ratio of the correct predictions of a class over its number of samples.

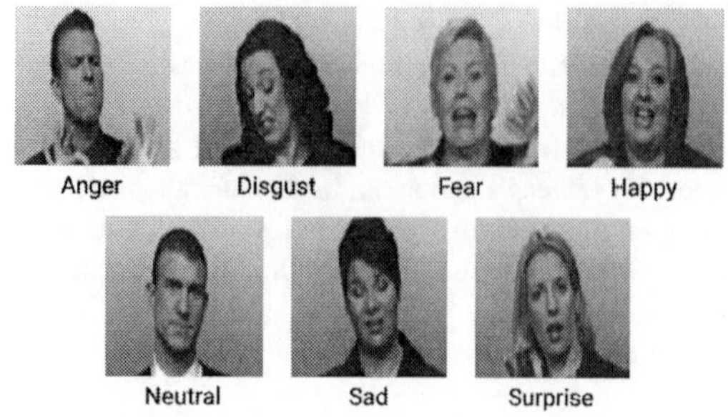

Figure 1: Images from 7 classes in the FePh dataset

4.1. Sign Language Dataset

The fine-tuning was targeted on the Facial Expression Phoenix (FePh) dataset (Alaghband et al., 2021), an annotated sequenced facial expression dataset in the context of the German SL. It comprises over 3,000 facial images extracted from the daily news and weather forecast of the public TV-station PHOENIX. The data was annotated with the six basic Ekman (1999) emotions of 'anger', 'disgust', 'fear', 'sad', 'happy', and 'surprise' along with the 'neutral' class (see figure 1). An aditional 'none of the above' class exists for images where no label could be assigned. Known limitations of this dataset are the size of the dataset, the existence of only 6 shallow labels, the lack of linguistic/content markers and the lack of spatial and manual elements. Since to the best of our knowledge this was the only available dataset suitable for this task, we proceed with using it despite the mentioned concerns in order to confirm our technical hypothesis.

4.2. Data Preparation

The FePh dataset went under three pre-processing steps. The first step consisted of **removing frames** of two types. The first type is the frames labeled as 'none of the above', which did not fall neither under any of the 6 Ekman labels nor 'neutral'. The second type of removed frames were asociated with more than one emotion, and their inclusion would change the ML task to a multi-label classification problem (Huang et al., 2019; Durand et al., 2019). Removing these frames resulted into 2,531 facial images annotated with the 6 Ekman emotions plus 'neutral'.
The second preprocessing step consists of applying a

emotion	data distribution
Anger	18.30%
Disgust	7.72%
Fear	12.43%
Happy	7.92%
Neutral	7.58%
Sad	14.36%
Surprise	31.85%

Table 1: Labels distribution in the training set.

abbr.	technique
FT	Fine-tuning
SGD	Stochastic Gradient Descent optimizer
SAP	Sharpness Aware Minimization
IP	Image preprocessing
HF	Horizontal flip
CW	Class weights

Table 2: Abbreviations used for the techniques used during the experiments

face cropping (Section 3.1) to the images before feeding them to the CNN. This was needed because the images in the FePh dataset include some parts of the upper body. This conforms with the pre-processing applied to the pre-trained models. The data distribution across the different emotion classes in the training set is shown in table 1.

Finally, the FePh sign-language dataset was randomly split in a training (80%, used for fine-tuning the pre-trained models) and a test set (20%, used for evaluation). Images belonging to the same video sequence were kept in the same split. This phase allowed trying 10 configurations on top of the baselines.

The small size of the dataset raises questions on whether the results may generalize in a bigger dataset. For this purpose, we applied a **5-fold cross-validation** test to the two baselines models and to their 4 most promising varied configurations. Across the 5 folds, the average accuracy and sensitivity per class were calculated together with their standard deviation.

4.3. Pre-trained Models for Facial Expression Recognition (FER)

Here we provide details about the pre-trained models available for FER, which aim to recognize the seven basic Ekman emotions on generic datasets. As explained, these pre-trained models were fine-tuned on the SL-specific dataset and several techniques were added. To get the state-of-the-art results, the models presented by Savchenko (2021), which provide a lightweight CNN for the recognition of facial emotions based on two different architectures, were chosen as they achieve state-of-the-art accuracy.

The two models that were further used in the experiments are based on two CNN architectures: (1) MobileNet and (2) EfficientNet (Section 3.2). Both pre-trained models were trained on the AffectNet dataset (Mollahosseini et al., 2017) which includes almost 440k annotated images, having before been pre-trained on the much larger VGGFace2 dataset (Gennaro and Vairo, 2019).

The abbreviations used for the techniques used during the experiments are shown in table 2. All of the experiment configurations are summarized in table 3 and are detailed in the following two sections for the exploratory and the cross-validation phase, respectively.

4.4. Exploratory Phase

This exploration consists of a combination between pre-processing techniques and hyperparameters that were tested on a single 20% FePh data split.

4.4.1. Experiments with MobileNet

No-FT: Baseline Pre-trained Model This experiment was performed to check how the existing pre-trained model performs when tested on the SL data.

FT: Simple Fine-tuning This configuration consists of fine-tuning the pre-trained model with the 80% split of the FePh. A simple fine-tuning approach was used for the MobileNet architecture. In a CNN, the last layer learns the high-level features, and hence the last few layers are sufficient for transfer learning (Tajbakhsh et al., 2016). The last layer of the pre-trained model was first removed and a new dense layer was added to the CNN and all the previous layers of the base net were frozen to train just the last layer. This last layer was then trained on the new dataset including images from the SL (FePh) dataset for 3 epochs. Finally, all the previous frozen layers were unfrozen and the entire CNN was trained on the FePh data for 7 more epochs. The categorical cross-entropy loss was optimized by the Adam optimizer with a learning rate equal to 0.001.

FT-SGD: Fine-tuning with Stochastic Gradient Descent (SGD) In this configuration, following Savchenko (2021), the baseline model was fine-tuned with Adam optimizer for 5 epochs and SGD was used for the last two epochs with learning rate of 0.0001.

FT-SGD + CW: Class Weights for an Imbalanced Fine-tuning Set As explained (section 3.3), CNNs may perform poorly because of an imbalance in the fine-tuning data caused by a significant difference in amount of data in a class compared to the others, resulting in an insufficient representation of the minority classes. To tackle this imbalance across classes, we assign different class weights to each of the classes in the training data. This results in increasing the loss value for the classes that are insufficiently represented. The data distribution across classes in the fine-tuning dataset is shown in table 1.

FT-SGD + HF: Fine-tuning with Data Augmentation We horizontally flip images before feeding them to the CNN, thus doubling the training data.

architecture	configurations exploratory	c/v	description
MobileNet	No-FT	M0	Base model
	FT		Simple fine-tuning of base model with Adam optimizer
	FT-SGD		Fine-tuning of base model with Adam and SGD optimizers
	FT-SGD + CW		FT-SGD + Classes balanced with class weights
	FT-SGD + HF		FT-SGD + Training dataset augmented with images flipped horizontally
	FT-SGD + IP		FT-SGD + Images normalized before training
	FT-SGD + IP + HF + CW	M1	FT-SGD + Image normalization, horizontal flip and class weights
	FT-SGD + IP + HF	M2	FT-SGD + image normalization and horizontal flip
EficientNet	No-FT	E0	Base model
	FT + SAM + HF + CW	E1	Base model fine-tuned with SAM optimizer + horizontal flip + class weights
	FT + SAM + HF	E2	Base model fine-tuned with SAM optimizer + horizontal flip
	FT-SGD + SAM + HF		Base model fine-tuned with SAM and SGD optimizers + horizontal flip

Table 3: Configurations used for the experiments

FT-SGD + IP: Fine-tuning with Image Preprocessing Along with fine-tuning, the images were normalized using the preprocessing function in Keras, where each color channel is zero-centered with respect to the ImageNet dataset (Ketkar, 2017; Savchenko, 2021).

FT-SGD + IP + HF + CW This is a direct replication of the similar experiment performed by Savchenko (2021), but by fine-tuning the pre-trained model with the FePh fine-tuning dataset. Since it had provided a state-of-the-art accuracy, this setting was tested to see if the combined effects of fine-tuning with data augmentation, image preprocessing, and class weights would improve the accuracy also with the FePh dataset compared to the previous settings.

FT-SGD + IP + HF Fine-tuning with data augmentation and image preprocessing. Here, the experiment was repeated with image preprocessing and horizontal flipping but without class weights.

4.4.2. Experiments with EfficientNet

As discussed in Chapter 3, the EfficientNet architecture provides better accuracy on ImageNet than MobileNet, and is considered a powerful tool in CV (Wang and Yu, 2021). Hence, the MobileNet experiments with the higher accuracy were replicated for EfficientNet to allow comparison of the two architectures. Among the EfficientNet variants, the EfficientNet-B0 architecture was chosen, as its default input image size (224x224) is the same as the size of the images in the dataset. Image preprocessing (IP) was not considered for this architecture as it was not suggested for the base models of Savchenko (2021).

No-FT: Pre-trained Model The baseline EfficientNet configuration pre-trained on AffectNet data and tested on the FePh test set.

FT + SAM + HF + CW: Fine-tuning with Sharpness Aware Minimization, Data Augmentation, and Class Weights This experiment is a replica of the pre-trained model provided by Savchenko (2021), but with additional fine-tuning on the FePh dataset. Moreover, this configuration uses the Sharpness Aware Minimization (SAM) optimizer (Foret et al., 2020). Initially, only the last layer is fine-tuned on FePh, for 3 epochs, with a learning rate of 0.001 while freezing all layers in the base net. Finally, all the layers are trained with the SAM optimizer with a learning rate of 0.0001 for 6 epochs as was proposed by Savchenko (2021). This experiment has also used horizontal flip as data augmentation technique and class weighting.

FT + SAM + HF: Fine-tuning with SAM and Data Augmentation This configuration uses fine-tuning with SAM along with horizontal flip. Class weighting was removed to check its contribution.

FT-SGD + SAM + HF: Fine-tuning with SAM and Data Augmentation and SGD This configuration tests the results using Stochastic Gradient Descent as optimizer while fine-tuning, because it was found to give the best results with MobileNet.

4.5. Cross-validation Phase

The best performing configurations from the exploratory phase were further evaluated by performing cross-validation (summarized in table 3 with their abbrevations shown in the 'c/v' column). Their description follows.

No-FT (M0 & E0) As a baseline, two pre-trained models (one for MobileNet and one for EfficientNet) presented by Savchenko (2021) were evaluated each on the 5 test sets obtained after splitting the FePh data into 5 folds. The accuracy and sensitivity per class were calculated and then the average and standard deviation was calculated.

The MobileNet configurations chosen for the cross-validation phase were:

FT-SGD + IP + HF + CW (M1) providing a state-of-the-art accuracy on AffectNet (Savchenko, 2021) and

FT-SGD + IP + HF (M2) showing promising results during the exploratory phase, despite the lack of class weighting, so it was chosen for cross-validation.

Cross-validation was also performed on the EfficientNet architecture with the respective configurations **FT + SAM + HF + CW (E1)** and **FT + SAM + HF (E2)**, which have been described in the previous section.

5. Results

This section showcases the results obtained from experiments conducted with two CNN architectures (MobileNet-v1, EfficientNet-B0) with several data processing techniques in both the exploratory phase the cross-validation phase. As **evaluation metrics** the model accuracy, the sensitivity per class and the average sensitivity are given for every model. As **baseline** we consider the result obtained from the experiment conducted without fine-tuning, and the rest of the experiments are compared against that.

5.1. Exploratory Phase: MobileNet-v1

As shown in table 4, fine-tuning improved the overall accuracy for more than 13%, whereas there was an additional small improvement when the model was optimized with the Adam optimizer for the first few epochs and with the SGD optimizer for the last 3 epochs. It can be also seen that adding class weights alone reduced the overall accuracy, but when class weights were combined with image preprocessing and horizontal flip, it provided the highest average sensitivity of 63.3%. Data augmentation with horizontal flipping did not provide any improvement in the accuracy of the fine-tuned model. Similarly, image normalization did not improve the accuracy. However, when data augmentation was combined with image normalization, the accuracy was increased to 67% providing the best accuracy across all the models trained.
The setting with the best overall accuracy (M0) and the one with the best average sensitivity (M1) are chosen to be further investigated in the cross-validation phase.

5.2. Exploratory Phase: EfficientNet-B0

Table 4 shows that the best accuracy was provided by the configuration wich combines fine tuning with SAM and horizontal flipping. Similar to the MobileNet-v1 architecture, with class weighting from the base model, the accuracy is 2.6% higher. The EfficientNet-B0 models took 25% longer to fine-tune due to SAM as the main optimizer, as compared to the MobileNet-v1 models which use Adam for the most epochs and SGD for the last two epochs (section 3.2).

5.3. Cross-validation Phase

Table 5 shows the results obtained after averaging the accuracies across 5 models trained while performing 5-fold cross-validation, where the average sensitivity and the sensitivity per class were also recorded in a similar way. Since these metrics are averaged on different folds of training sets from the FePh dataset, they are more suitable in drawing overall conclusions, as the ones shown in the exploratory phase.

First, it can be observed that fine-tuning using the best combination of techniques outperforms the model with no fine-tuning (at least by 17%). This **confirms the main hypothesis** that for sign-language FER, fine-tuning a generic pre-trained model on a sign-language-specific dataset helps to improve the performance on this task. Additionally, it should be noted that the achieved overall accuracy of 62.4-62.8% is comparable to the state-of-the-art accuracy of the base models in the generic FER tasks (Savchenko, 2021).
For MobileNet-v1, the configuration that significantly gave the best accuracy was FT-SGD + IP + HF (M2). By comparing this configuration with its variant lacking class-weights, we can see that **class-weights are harmful** in this setting.
For EfficientNet-B0, it was found that the configuration FT + SAM + IP + HF (E2) gave the highest accuracy (62.8%). The difference of this setting with the configuration including class weights is not significant in this case, so one cannot say with confidence whether class weights are improving or harming EfficientNet.
No specific conclusion can be drawn regarding the differences between the MobileNet and EfficientNet architectures **both architectures seem equally suitable for the purpose of fine-tuning**. Nevertheless, one should consider that EfficientNet took slightly longer time to fine-tune, which might be an issue in future works, if larger fine-tuning datasets are considered.
The results based on the average sensitivity as well as the sensitivity per class vary a lot, e.g. one can see that different classes seem to be predicted best with different configurations. Nevertheless, these small sensitivity differences do not allow significant comparisons due to the very large standard deviations, which are attributed to the very small dataset. On the other side, we can confirm that the settings that provide significant accuracy improvements are still the optimal ones, since they do not cause a significant deterioration of the class and average sensitivities.
By comparing the 7 classes, we see that 'fear' has the lowest sensitivity (29.2%), followed by 'disgust' and 'neutral'. The best predicted class is 'happy' (82.7%) followed by 'surprise'.

6. Conclusion and Future Work

Through our experiments, we confirmed the hypothesis that fine-tuning a neural network alreaddy pre-trained to recognize facial expressions, togather with other the preprocessing techniques and optimizers, improves the model performance in classifying facial expressions on a sign language dataset. The achieved accuracy is satisfactorily high, as it is comparable to the state-of-the-art accuracy of the base models in generic FER of prior work. No significant difference was observed between the best configurations of MobileNet and EfficientNet architectures, but the training time for the EfficientNet models was higher than that of MobileNet.
The overall accuracy improved when image normaliza-

	configuration	c/v	acc.	sensitivity per class							avg.
				anger	disgust	fear	happy	neutral	sadness	surprise	sens.
MobileNet	No-FT	M0	52.0	54.5	**74.2**	26.3	15.8	26.2	11.9	79.6	41.0
	FT		65.4	81.1	38.7	45.6	63.1	35.7	50.8	77.8	56.1
	FT-SGD		65.7	**82.6**	58.0	47.4	73.7	33.3	57.6	70.0	60.4
	FT-SGD + CW		54.0	65.2	71.0	**56.1**	78.9	28.6	**61.0**	42.5	57.7
	FT-SGD + HF		64.7	77.3	51.6	50.9	63.2	28.6	55.9	74.3	57.4
	FT-SGD + IP		65.3	**82.6**	35.5	43.9	68.4	28.6	45.8	**80.2**	55.0
	FT-SGD + IP + HF + CW	M1	63.7	75.0	**74.2**	**56.1**	**84.2**	**38.1**	52.5	63.5	**63.3**
	FT-SGD + IP + HF	M2	**67.0**	81.8	61.3	40.4	68.4	33.3	50.8	79.6	59.3
EfficientNet	No-FT	E0	53.5	50.8	67.7	**36.8**	47.4	47.6	18.6	73.1	49.0
	FT + SAM + HF + CW	E1	63.9	62.9	67.7	**36.8**	84.2	**76.2**	66.1	67.1	65.9
	FT + SAM + HF	E2	**66.5**	**68.2**	67.7	31.6	84.2	69.0	**67.8**	**73.7**	**66.1**
	FT-SGD + SAM + HF		63.9	65.2	**71.0**	33.3	**89.5**	59.5	59.3	71.9	64.1

Table 4: The overall accuracy, sensitivity per class, and average sensitivity (in %) obtained for all configurations (described in table 3) of the exploratory phase (i.e., tested on a single fold). The configurations that have an abbreviation in the column 'c/v' are repeated later in the cross-validation phase (table 5).

	acc. (std)	average sensitivity per class (std)							avg. sens. (std)
		anger	disgust	fear	happy	neutral	sadness	surprise	
M0	44.1 (4.7)	44.4 (10.3)	**58.4 (2.4)**	**25.8 (12.4)**	47.3 (19.3)	20.8 (5.7)	17.2 (9.1)	63.8 (6.7)	39.7 (9.4)
M1	51.7 (7.4)	51.3 (21.4)	37.3 (13.8)	11.6 (5.5)	**56.6 (16.4)**	**75.3 (16.7)**	**60.4 (23.5)**	58.2 (12.0)	50.0 (15.6)
M2	**62.4 (3.2)**	**73.7 (5.9)**	41.9 (14.1)	23.6 (9.6)	53.7 (12.2)	50.2 (22.3)	57.2 (16.1)	**82.1 (6.7)**	**54.6 (12.4)**
E0	45.7 (4.7)	42.3 (7.7)	55.6 (3.9)	30.1 (14.4)	53.3 (12.7)	54.6 (16.8)	19.5 (11.3)	59.7 (12.1)	45.0 (11.3)
E1	62.2 (2.4)	**65.3 (9.3)**	**57.5 (12.6)**	**35.8 (13.3)**	72.3 (9.8)	**66.1 (10.0)**	**59.1 (16.8)**	68.5 (6.4)	**60.7 (11.2)**
E2	**62.8 (4.7)**	62.3 (8.6)	45.4 (18.8)	29.2 (16.6)	**82.7 (11.7)**	59 (17.6)	52.7 (22.2)	**79.2 (8.5)**	58.6 (14.9)

Table 5: The overall accuracy, sensitivity per class, and average sensitivity (in %) with the standard deviation (std) obtained for all the MobileNet-v1 and EfficientNet-B0 configurations calculated during the cross-validation phase

tion was used in combination with augmenting training data with horizontally flipped images. Despite the obvious lack of balance between the classes in the dataset, balancing classes with the help of class weights can harm the accuracy.

The best models obtained from the experiments conducted were configured as following: MobileNet-v1 fine-tuned with Stochastic Gradient Descent using tuning data normalized and augmented using horizontally flipped images, and EfficientNet-B0 fine-tuned with Sharpness Aware Minimization using tuning data augmented with horizontally flipped images.

It is obvious through our analysis that further work would require bigger datasets that would allow more robust results, if possible also including spatial and manual elements and offerring better resolution, a broader domain and reacher modalities (e.g., full video sequences). Additionally, one should consider coverage of other sign languages and cultural backgrounds, whereas we are actively working on the adaptation of the labels to include linguistic content/markers and other affective aspects relevant to communication purposes.

7. Acknowledgements

The work was accomplished as a MSc thesis, part of the program ICT Innovation (Technical University of Berlin). The supervision was funded by the project SocialWear (German Ministry of Research and Education; BMBF) and by the EU Horizon 2020 programme within the EASIER project (Grant agreement ID: 101016982).

8. Bibliographical References

Akhand, M., Roy, S., Siddique, N., Kamal, M. A. S., and Shimamura, T. (2021). Facial emotion recognition using transfer learning in the deep cnn. *Electronics*, 10(9):1036.

Albawi, S., Mohammed, T. A., and Al-Zawi, S. (2017). Understanding of a convolutional neural network. In *2017 International Conference on Engineering and Technology (ICET)*, pages 1–6. Ieee.

Atila, Ü., Uçar, M., Akyol, K., and Uçar, E. (2021). Plant leaf disease classification using efficientnet deep learning model. *Ecological Informatics*, 61:101182.

Boyko, N., Basystiuk, O., and Shakhovska, N. (2018). Performance evaluation and comparison of software for face recognition, based on dlib and opencv library. In *2018 IEEE Second International Confer-*

ence on Data Stream Mining & Processing (DSMP), pages 478–482. IEEE.

Chu, W.-S., De la Torre, F., and Cohn, J. F. (2017). Learning spatial and temporal cues for multi-label facial action unit detection. In *12th IEEE International Conference on Automatic Face & Gesture Recognition (FG 2017)*, pages 25–32. IEEE.

Durand, T., Mehrasa, N., and Mori, G. (2019). Learning a deep convnet for multi-label classification with partial labels. In *Proceedings of the IEEE/CVF Conference on Computer Vision and Pattern Recognition*, pages 647–657.

Ekman, P. (1999). Basic emotions. *Handbook of cognition and emotion*, 98(45-60):16.

Emami, S. and Suciu, V. P. (2012). Facial recognition using opencv. *Journal of Mobile, Embedded and Distributed Systems*, 4(1):38–43.

Foret, P., Kleiner, A., Mobahi, H., and Neyshabur, B. (2020). Sharpness-aware minimization for efficiently improving generalization. In *International Conference on Learning Representations*.

Gennaro, C. and Vairo, C. (2019). Improving multiscale face recognition using vggface2. In *New Trends in Image Analysis and Processing–ICIAP 2019: ICIAP International Workshops, BioFor, PatReCH, e-BADLE, DeepRetail, and Industrial Session, Trento, Italy, September 9–10, 2019, Revised Selected Papers*, volume 11808, page 21. Springer Nature.

Ghosh, T., Abedin, M. M.-H.-Z., Chowdhury, S. M., Tasnim, Z., Karim, T., Reza, S. S., Saika, S., and Yousuf, M. A. (2020). Bangla handwritten character recognition using mobilenet v1 architecture. *Bulletin of Electrical Engineering and Informatics*, 9(6):2547–2554.

Heidari, M., Mirniaharikandehei, S., Khuzani, A. Z., Danala, G., Qiu, Y., and Zheng, B. (2020). Improving the performance of cnn to predict the likelihood of covid-19 using chest x-ray images with preprocessing algorithms. *International journal of medical informatics*, 144:104284.

Howard, A. G., Zhu, M., Chen, B., Kalenichenko, D., Wang, W., Weyand, T., Andreetto, M., and Adam, H. (2017). Mobilenets: Efficient convolutional neural networks for mobile vision applications. *arXiv preprint arXiv:1704.04861*.

Huang, J., Qin, F., Zheng, X., Cheng, Z., Yuan, Z., Zhang, W., and Huang, Q. (2019). Improving multi-label classification with missing labels by learning label-specific features. *Information Sciences*, 492:124–146.

Ioffe, S. and Szegedy, C. (2015). Batch normalization: Accelerating deep network training by reducing internal covariate shift. In *International conference on machine learning*, pages 448–456. PMLR.

Johnson, J. M. and Khoshgoftaar, T. M. (2019). Survey on deep learning with class imbalance. *Journal of Big Data*, 6(1):1–54.

Kandel, I. and Castelli, M. (2020). The effect of batch size on the generalizability of the convolutional neural networks on a histopathology dataset. *ICT express*, 6(4):312–315.

Ketkar, N. (2017). Introduction to keras. In *Deep learning with Python*, pages 97–111. Springer.

Kim, D. H., Baddar, W. J., Jang, J., and Ro, Y. M. (2019). Multi-objective based spatio-temporal feature representation learning robust to expression intensity variations for facial expression recognition. *IEEE Transactions on Affective Computing*, 10(2):223–236.

Ko, B. C. (2018). A brief review of facial emotion recognition based on visual information. *sensors*, 18(2):401.

Koo, K.-M. and Cha, E.-Y. (2017). Image recognition performance enhancements using image normalization. *Human-centric Computing and Information Sciences*, 7(1):1–11.

Kossaifi, J., Tzimiropoulos, G., Todorovic, S., and Pantic, M. (2017). Afew-va database for valence and arousal estimation in-the-wild. *Image Vision Comput.*, 65(C):23–36, sep.

Lucey, P., Cohn, J. F., Kanade, T., Saragih, J., Ambadar, Z., and Matthews, I. (2010). The extended cohn-kanade dataset (ck+): A complete dataset for action unit and emotion-specified expression. In *2010 IEEE Computer Society Conference on Computer Vision and Pattern Recognition - Workshops*, pages 94–101.

Marques, G., Agarwal, D., and de la Torre Díez, I. (2020). Automated medical diagnosis of covid-19 through efficientnet convolutional neural network. *Applied soft computing*, 96:106691.

Meng, D., Peng, X., Wang, K., and Qiao, Y. (2019). Frame attention networks for facial expression recognition in videos. In *2019 IEEE International Conference on Image Processing (ICIP)*, pages 3866–3870. IEEE.

Michele, A., Colin, V., and Santika, D. D. (2019). Mobilenet convolutional neural networks and support vector machines for palmprint recognition. *Procedia Computer Science*, 157:110–117.

Mollahosseini, A., Hasani, B., and Mahoor, M. H. (2017). Affectnet: A database for facial expression, valence, and arousal computing in the wild. *IEEE Transactions on Affective Computing*, 10(1):18–31.

Mollahosseini, A., Hasani, B., and Mahoor, M. H. (2019). Affectnet: A database for facial expression, valence, and arousal computing in the wild. *IEEE Transactions on Affective Computing*, 10(1):18–31.

Ngo, Q. T. and Yoon, S. (2020). Facial expression recognition based on weighted-cluster loss and deep transfer learning using a highly imbalanced dataset. *Sensors*, 20(9):2639.

O'Mahony, N., Campbell, S., Carvalho, A., Harapanahalli, S., Hernandez, G. V., Krpalkova, L., Riordan, D., and Walsh, J. (2019). Deep learning vs. traditional computer vision. In *Science and Information Conference*, pages 128–144. Springer.

Pal, K. K. and Sudeep, K. (2016). Preprocessing for image classification by convolutional neural networks. In *2016 IEEE International Conference on Recent Trends in Electronics, Information & Communication Technology (RTEICT)*, pages 1778–1781. IEEE.

Pitaloka, D. A., Wulandari, A., Basaruddin, T., and Liliana, D. Y. (2017). Enhancing cnn with preprocessing stage in automatic emotion recognition. *Procedia computer science*, 116:523–529.

Radenović, F., Tolias, G., and Chum, O. (2018). Fine-tuning cnn image retrieval with no human annotation. *IEEE transactions on pattern analysis and machine intelligence*, 41(7):1655–1668.

Ravi, R., Yadhukrishna, S., et al. (2020). A face expression recognition using cnn & lbp. In *2020 Fourth International Conference on Computing Methodologies and Communication (ICCMC)*, pages 684–689. IEEE.

Sandler, M., Howard, A., Zhu, M., Zhmoginov, A., and Chen, L.-C. (2018). Mobilenetv2: Inverted residuals and linear bottlenecks. In *Proceedings of the IEEE conference on computer vision and pattern recognition*, pages 4510–4520.

Sauter, D. A., Eisner, F., Ekman, P., and Scott, S. K. (2010). Cross-cultural recognition of basic emotions through nonverbal emotional vocalizations. *Proceedings of the National Academy of Sciences*, 107(6):2408–2412.

Savchenko, A. V. (2021). Facial expression and attributes recognition based on multi-task learning of lightweight neural networks. In *2021 IEEE 19th International Symposium on Intelligent Systems and Informatics (SISY)*, pages 119–124.

Shorten, C. and Khoshgoftaar, T. M. (2019). A survey on image data augmentation for deep learning. *Journal of Big Data*, 6(1):1–48.

Sinha, D. and El-Sharkawy, M. (2019). Thin mobilenet: An enhanced mobilenet architecture. In *2019 IEEE 10th Annual Ubiquitous Computing, Electronics & Mobile Communication Conference (UEMCON)*, pages 0280–0285. IEEE.

Soo, S. (2014). Object detection using haar-cascade classifier. *Institute of Computer Science, University of Tartu*, 2(3):1–12.

Tajbakhsh, N., Shin, J. Y., Gurudu, S. R., Hurst, R. T., Kendall, C. B., Gotway, M. B., and Liang, J. (2016). Convolutional neural networks for medical image analysis: Full training or fine tuning? *IEEE transactions on medical imaging*, 35(5):1299–1312.

Tan, M. and Le, Q. (2019). Efficientnet: Rethinking model scaling for convolutional neural networks. In *International Conference on Machine Learning*, pages 6105–6114. PMLR.

Tan, M. and Le, Q. (2021). Efficientnetv2: Smaller models and faster training. In *International Conference on Machine Learning*, pages 10096–10106. PMLR.

Taqi, A. M., Awad, A., Al-Azzo, F., and Milanova, M. (2018). The impact of multi-optimizers and data augmentation on tensorflow convolutional neural network performance. In *2018 IEEE Conference on Multimedia Information Processing and Retrieval (MIPR)*, pages 140–145. IEEE.

Wang, K. and Yu, X. (2021). Mobilenet and efficientnet demonstration on google landmark recognition dataset. *International Core Journal of Engineering*, 7(3):313–319.

Xiang, J. and Zhu, G. (2017). Joint face detection and facial expression recognition with mtcnn. In *2017 4th international conference on information science and control engineering (ICISCE)*, pages 424–427. IEEE.

Zheng, Q., Yang, M., Tian, X., Jiang, N., and Wang, D. (2020). A full stage data augmentation method in deep convolutional neural network for natural image classification. *Discrete Dynamics in Nature and Society*, 2020.

9. Language Resource References

Alaghband, M., Yousefi, N., and Garibay, I. (2021). Facial expression phoenix (feph): An annotated sequenced dataset for facial and emotion-specified expressions in sign language. *International Journal of Electronics and Communication Engineering*, 15(3):131–138.

Proceedings of the 7th International Workshop on Sign Language Translation and Avatar Technology (SLTAT 7), pages 39–44
Language Resources and Evaluation Conference (LREC 2022), Marseille, 20-25 June 2022

Signing Avatar Performance Evaluation within the EASIER Project

Athanasia–Lida Dimou[1], Vassilis Papavassiliou[1], John McDonald [2], Theodoros Goulas[1], Kyriaki Vasilaki[1], Anna Vacalopoulou[1], Stavroula-Evita Fotinea[1], Eleni Efthimiou[1], Rosalee Wolfe [1]

[1] Institute for Language and Speech Processing (ILSP)/ ATHENA R.C.

[2] School of Computing, DePaul University

[1]Artemidos 6 & Epidavrou, 15125 Maroussi, Greece
[2] 243 S. Wabash Ave, Chicago, IL 60604, USA
{ndimou, vpapa, tgoulas, kvasilaki, avacalop, evita, eleni_e, rosalee.wolfe,}@athenarc.gr,
jmcdonald@cs.depaul.edu

Abstract

The direct involvement of deaf users in the development and evaluation of signing avatars is imperative to achieve legibility and raise trust among synthetic signing technology consumers. A paradigm of constructive cooperation between researchers and the deaf community is the EASIER project[1], where user driven design and technology development have already started producing results. One major goal of the project is the direct involvement of sign language (SL) users at every stage of development of the project's signing avatar. As developers wished to consider every parameter of SL articulation including affect and prosody in developing the EASIER SL representation engine, it was necessary to develop a steady communication channel with a wide public of SL users who may act as evaluators and can provide guidance throughout research steps, both during the project's end-user evaluation cycles and beyond. To this end, we have developed a questionnaire-based methodology, which enables researchers to reach signers of different SL communities on-line and collect their guidance and preferences on all aspects of SL avatar animation that are under study. In this paper, we report on the methodology behind the application of the EASIER evaluation framework for end-user guidance in signing avatar development as it is planned to address signers of four SLs -Greek Sign Language (GSL), French Sign Language (LSF), German Sign Language (DGS) and Swiss German Sign Language (DSGS)- during the first project evaluation cycle. We also briefly report on some interesting findings from the pilot implementation of the questionnaire with content from the Greek Sign Language (GSL).

Keywords: signing avatar performance1, on-line questionnaire2, evaluation methodology3, signing avatar rating4, signer involvement5, deaf-friendly interfaces6.

1. Introduction

The use of avatars in signed communication can be implemented in multiple communication contexts permitting a significant degree of freedom in content creation and signer anonymization. Avatars offer the advantage of being flexible to editing changes of the signed content and anonymity of the user. These features enable avatars to serve as agents for various interactive environments and communication platforms. However, currently SL avatars have not yet reached a level of performance that would make them acceptable to their end-users.

To identify how human signers perceive and evaluate the performance of an avatar's synthetic signing, within EASIER project, we have developed a shell environment which incorporates an on-line questionnaire for feedback collection. This allows for easy creation of targeted on-line questionnaires to be addressed to signer groups of different SLs to collect feedback on various aspects of interest regarding research work on synthetic signing technology.

The paper reports on the implementation framework of this user involvement methodology, the goal being the steady improvement of animation regarding legibility and clarity of synthetic signing.

In section 2, we present the on-line questionnaire structure along with the methodological approach adopted to optimize its usability and structural design, aiming to eliminate common and uncommon biases.

Starting from the shell questionnaire design, the goal has been to create an environment which would maintain user-friendly characteristics and respect accessibility requirements of its target audience while guarding against bias. To exemplify application of the adopted methodology, in section 3, we also present results from the questionnaire's first pilot implementation with content from the Greek Sign Language (GSL). Finally, section 4 provides a discussion on our goals and up-to-date experience.

2. The EASIER Questionnaire for Avatar Performance Evaluation

The key performance indicators (KPIs) regarding the EASIER avatar performance are clearly user-centric, identified around perceived naturalness and comprehensibility. To encourage user engagement in the evaluation process, the users themselves participated in the development of the questionnaire format from the state of its design. To further facilitate usability of the questionnaire, comprehensibility is subject to a yes/no response, while naturalness is related to a rating scale from 1 to 5 (various aspects of collecting user feedback with similar focus is also reported in (Kipp et al., 2011) and (Kacorri et al., 2015) among others). It becomes also clear that user involvement from early stages of development

[1] https://www.project-easier.eu/

becomes mandatory, if both these qualities are to be judged positively during an official evaluation procedure (EUD, 2018; WFD, 2018 on user attitude). Here we present the overall rationale as well as those specific parameters which led decision-making regarding the design of the shell questionnaire environment that allows creation of targeted on-line questionnaires for the evaluation of the various aspects of avatar performance under development, making use of language material from different SLs.

2.1 Questionnaire Content Design

While designing the architecture of the shell on-line questionnaires we considered various parameters which allow for generation of the overall layout of each specific questionnaire. Among the issues to be tackled are decisions as to how the questionnaire should be best distributed to its audience along with the profile of those it would be addressed to. This is directly connected also with the need to regularly address end-users while proceeding with different stages of technological development (Wolfe et al., 2021). Thus, decisions on questionnaire content led to focused, short lasting questionnaire implementations.

One of our main concerns was to balance between a reasonable questionnaire duration (maximum 20 minutes) that would not cause discomfort or fatigue to the participants, and adequate content to provide clear data on the intended user preferences for which feedback is requested. By setting up a viable, easily updated on-line survey we opted to engage in a steady dialogue with signers' communities with respect to novel enhancements in the signing avatar technology.

Having the possibility to adapt the survey outline according to the evaluation requirements at each stage of avatar development was a decisive factor that weighed on the survey framework design. We needed to provide options for one item viewing at a time or head-to-head alternative performance presentations so that viewers can express their preference, but also provide scorings associated with each performance. To test content presentation settings and design adequacy regarding collection of user opinions in view of the project evaluation procedures, the pilot application of the on-line questionnaire involved two distinct avatars and was composed of two parts that address a set of evaluation questions from different angles. In this setting, the first questionnaire part presented the two avatars on the same screen in a head-to-head manner, while the second part presented one avatar at a time. In this way, we had the opportunity to gather user feedback regarding the entire range of options for content presentation and rating mechanisms incorporated in the shell-questionnaire environment. The customizable aspect of this shell environment allows for tailored, easy, and fast content integration on targeted questionnaires, independent from language specific characteristics or context induced particularities.

Special care was taken so that in the questionnaire pages in which two different versions of signing avatar performance appear, these are presented in similar body and face dimensions and against a similar background, to minimize bias in display settings.

2.2 Questionnaire Usability and Technical Features

A major concern was to provide a survey shell fully adapted to the three-dimensional language modality. Considering that language is the principal tool for human interaction, we ensured that all questionnaire parts and items can be accessible with the use of sign language only. Hence, in every stage of the questionnaire participants are provided with instructions as to what they are expected to do and how they may interact with the questionnaire environment in the following three ways:

i. Via SL videos recorded by an L1 signer of the addressed SL community,
ii. Via written text available to be viewed if selected, in a text box below each instructive video, and
iii. Via screen capture videos demonstrating the requested action by the user in the form of a visual manual.

An introductory video presents the scope of the questionnaire, the identity of the research team and a brief description of the EASIER project.

Questionnaire pages make use of color code to indicate user selections. Color is also used to notify for missing actions which are required to be completed in a given page before the user is allowed to move to the next page. Checking graphical signals are also used to help visualization of user selections (
Figure **1**).

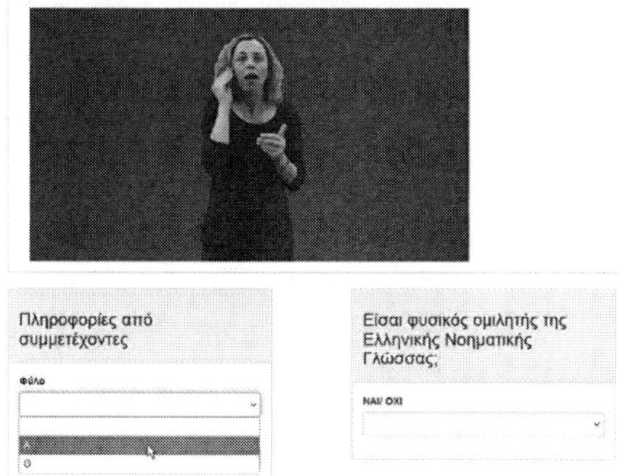

Figure 1: Photo from the screen capture video presenting the instruction module with SL video display and visualizing user selections.

Written text instructions to guide user preference selection have also been subject of extensive study aiming to avoid disorienting the users from the focus point of each questionnaire page.

The pilot implementation of the on-line survey was performed with input from the Greek Sign Language (GSL) and was addressed to GSL signers. Therefore, all instructions were linguistically adapted to the target language.

Each on-line questionnaire is available via a URL in which participants can watch avatar productions in the form of embedded videos. Regarding software technologies, the shell questionnaire is created using the open-source Cascading Style Sheets of the Bootstrap Framework. Bootstrap is a framework that allows the creation of responsive, mobile-first web applications. Thus, web applications created by Bootstrap Framework can be executed by most desktop as well as mobile browsers. However, due to the considerable number of images and videos in the application, participants are encouraged to use Firefox or Chrome for optimum performance. The user interface has been created using HTML5 and JavaScript (jQuery). The database in which participants' answers are stored is MySQL. Php is used to store the data in the database.

3. Aspects of the Pilot Questionnaire Application

For the pilot survey, the questionnaire was divided in two parts, Part A and Part B. Part A targeted GSL user opinion on affect, hand movement, hand, and finger configuration accuracy in isolated signs and in fingerspelling, and Part B targeted smoothness of transition in short phrases. Both parts made use of the EASIER signing avatar "PAULA" (McDonald et al., (2016), (Wolfe et al., 2011) initially developed at DePaul University (http://asl.cs.depaul.edu/), and the Dicta-Sign signing avatar "FRANÇOISE" (Jennings et al., 2010) developed at the University of East Anglia (UEA) (http://vh.cmp.uea.ac.uk).
The linguistic content of the questionnaire was distributed in the following manner:
In Part A the participants were presented with pairs of avatars, head-to-head in randomized order. There were 19 signing instances in all, grouped into 4 categories. For each pair, participants indicated the avatar they preferred and rated the performance quality of both avatars. The four categories were:
(i) Avatar expressivity via inspection of still images of avatar face, in various affect expressions.
(ii) Avatar productions performing signs with varying articulatory formations
(iii) Avatar performance in proper name fingerspelling tasks
(iv) Avatar productions of short phrases composed from previously evaluated isolated signs integrated with signs not yet viewed by participants.
In Part B participants observed one avatar at a time. Each avatar performed a set of signs and short phrases. In this part each of the two avatars displayed different content. The aim here was to lead viewers to focus on specific features of interest in each avatar performance. Tasks included rating each avatar separately in respect to:
(i) Overall hand motion performance,
(ii) Overall body motion performance,
(iii) Head and eyes movement,
(iv) Mouth movement.
The pilot survey has focused on L1 and L2 signers' different preferences of the two avatars. Hence, the sample of the population to which the questionnaire was offered, consisted of L1 and L2 GSL signers, L1 signer group including deaf, hard of hearing or hearing signers that acquired GSL from their immediate family environment from early childhood, and L2 signer group including deaf, hard of hearing or hearing signers that acquired GSL via educational procedures (Costello et al., 2006). L1 signers where not further defined as deaf or codas.
Due to General Data Protection Regulation (GDPR) issues and research ethics guidelines and regulations, responding to the questionnaire was anonymous, while participants personal information was restricted to a minimal set of metadata concerning demographic information on gender, age group, education level and GSL manner of acquisition (L1 vs L2).

Within a three-week period, the questionnaire was distributed among members of the GSL Community including deaf clubs and educational institutions. 91 distinct IP addresses were identified as having visited the questionnaire. However, only 32 participants completed the questionnaire, of which 17 identified themselves as L1 signers and 15 as L2 signers. Thus, only the responses of those 32 participants were considered in the analysis of the results. All participants were adults between 18 and 61 years of age.

3.1 Overview of the Results from the Pilot On-Line Survey

Participants were asked to rate the performance of each avatar in each signing occurrence in a 5-scale rating (Bad / Rather Bad / Average / Good / Very Good). The relative frequency distributions on this 5-scale rating for parts A and B are illustrated in the bubble charts of Figure **2** and Figure **3**, respectively, where the size of each bubble denotes the percentage of responses for a specific rating. In Part A, about 76% of the participants considered PAULA's performance "good" or "very good", while only 6% assign a low rate of "bad" or "rather bad". The relative frequencies for FRANÇOISE were 41% for good/very good ratings and 20% for bad/very bad ratings (Figure **2**).

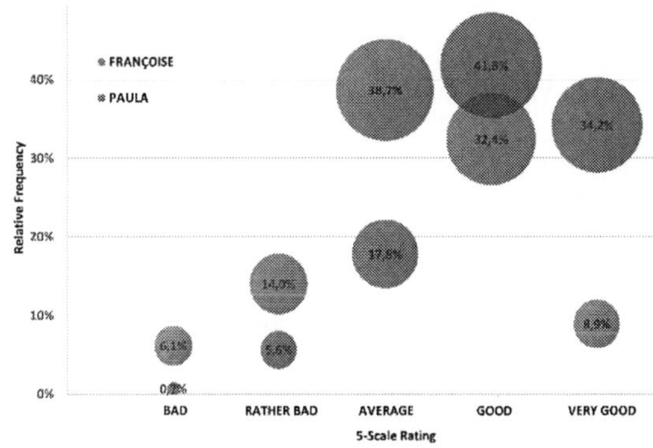

Figure 2: Relative frequency distribution of 5-scale rating for all signing occurrences of Part A.

The frequency distributions of Part B were similar as can be seen in Figure **3**. Obviously, the pairs of bubbles (for FRANÇOISE and PAULA at each rate) are either very close or significantly overlapped. For instance, about 36% and 39% of the rates were at the level "good" for PAULA and FRANÇOISE, respectively. Moreover, the relative frequencies at "rather bad" and "average" are also comparable. This similarity would become apparent if one drew lines that connect the centers of the bubbles for each avatar.
Considering the data from both parts, the descriptive analysis of results shows an overall preference for PAULA avatar performance. However, our goal is to investigate the preferences that the two sub-groups (L1 and L2) expressed towards the two avatars. Even though the collected metadata were based on participants' statements (e.g., they identified themselves as L1 or L2 signers), we strongly believe that nobody would benefit from misleading us given that the evaluation's scope is to strengthen the constructive cooperation between researchers and the deaf community.

In this sense, we considered the L1 and L2 participants two independent groups. It is worth mentioning that we target signers who favor this cooperation such as the volunteers who participated. To this end, we consider the participants a sample of the targeted population. However, we are aware of the random sampling process, and we plan to adopt it in the next evaluation phase when many more participants will be involved.

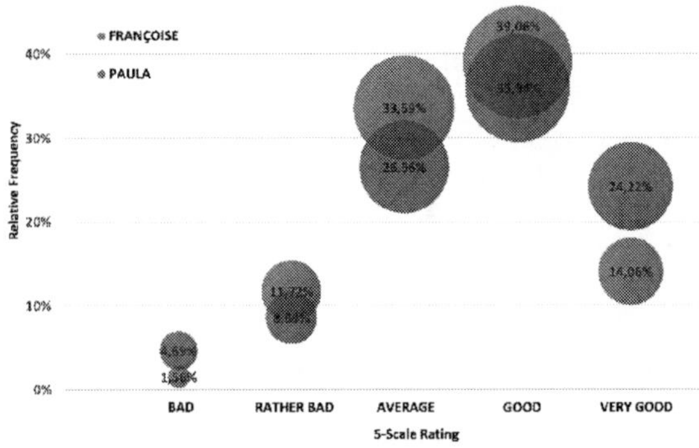

Figure 3: Relative frequency distribution of 5-scale rating for all signing occurrences of Part B.

3.1.1 Preferences Investigation of L1 and L2 Signers

In the light of the above, we hypothesized that the two subgroups expressed the same preferences towards the two avatars (NULL hypothesis). To explore this hypothesis, we conducted Mann Whitney U Tests[2] to test if there is a statistically significant difference in the rating of an avatar between the two groups. We applied the analysis on both PAULA and FRANÇOISE for Part A and Part B.

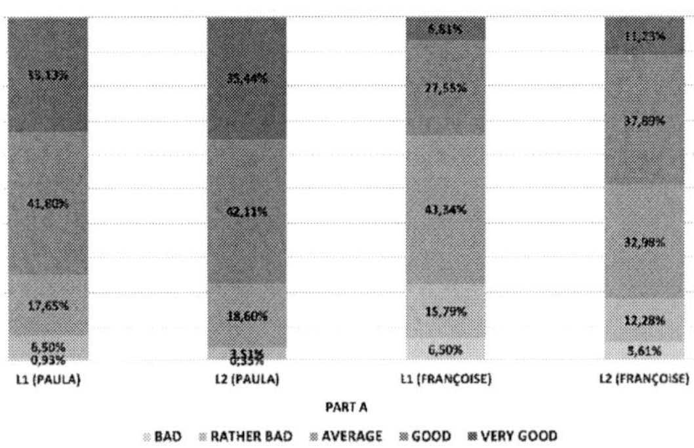

Figure 4: Part A: Distribution of relative frequencies of the 5-scale rating in Part A for both avatars in the two sub-groups (L1 and L2 signers).

The distribution of relative frequencies on the 5-scale rating for both avatars in the context of parts A and B for each group are illustrated in Figure **4** and Figure **5** respectively. Based on these results, one could observe (by comparing the first two columns of Figure **4**) that the results for PAULA in Part A are very similar for both groups of signers. Although it seems that there are differences in the other cases i.e., rates of L1 and L2 groups for FRANÇOISE in Part A (3rd and 4th columns of Figure **4**), and Part B (3rd and 4th columns of Figure **5**), and for PAULA (first two columns of Figure **5**), the statistically significant ones, will be concluded by inferential statistics.

In Part A, the comparison of the two signer sub-groups (L1 vs L2) for both avatars resulted in the following:

PAULA: the resulted p-value was 0.17 > 0.05 (the selected significance level), hence the NULL hypothesis cannot be rejected which can be interpreted that both sub-groups rate PAULA's response similarly.

FRANÇOISE: the resulted p-value was 0.0004 < 0.05 and thus we can accept the alternative hypothesis and state that there is a statistically significant difference between the rates provided by L1 and L2 signers. Given that the median values of rates of each sub-group are equal to "AVERAGE" (i.e., percentages for "BAD", "RATHER BAD" and "AVERAGE" sum up to more than 50% in both groups of green shades), we cannot decide which sub-group provides higher rates to FRANÇOISE. However, by observing the modes of each sub-group (i.e., 43,34% of L1 and 37,89% of L2 rated this avatar of "AVERAGE" and "GOOD" performance respectively) we could say that L2 signers graded FRANÇOISE higher than what L1 signers did.

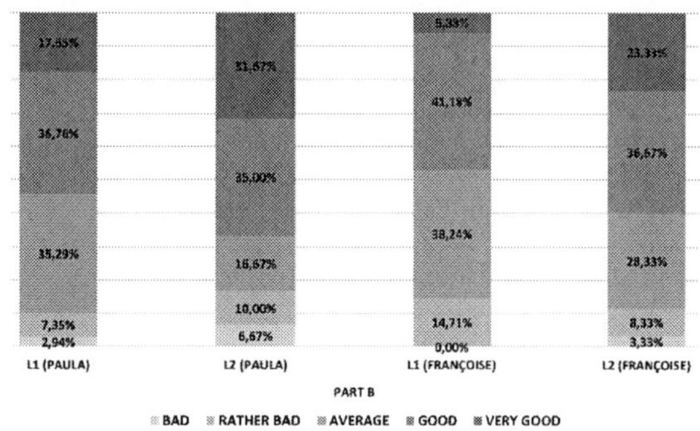

Figure 5: Distribution of relative frequencies of the 5-scale rating in Part B for both avatars in the two sub-groups (L1 and L2 signers).

In Part B, the comparison of the two signer sub-groups in respect to their ratings of the two avatars provides the following results:

PAULA: the resulted p-value was 0.087 > 0.05, hence the NULL hypothesis cannot be rejected which can be interpreted that both sub-groups rate PAULA's response similarly. It is worth mentioning that this conclusion was also conducted for this avatar in Part A.

FRANÇOISE: the resulted p-value was 0.022 < 0.05 and thus we can accept the alternative hypothesis and state that there is a statistically significant difference between the rates provided by L1 and L2 signers. In Part B (see last two columns of Figure **5**), the median values of rates of L1 and L2 signers are "AVERAGE" and "GOOD" respectively (i.e., percentages for "BAD", "RATHER BAD" and

[2] The Mann Whitney U Test is the alternative of the independent t-test. It is a non-parametric test proper for statistical analysis when the data are ordinal and there is no assumption of the distribution of the population and the two groups have unequal sizes.

"AVERAGE" sum up to more than 50% in L1 group, while "GOOD" is required to be included in L2 group), and thus we could say that again the L2 signers sub-group graded FRANÇOISE slightly higher than what L1 signers did.

3.1.2 Interpretation of Results with Respect to End-User Preferences

Regarding the first part (Part A) of the survey and the head-to-head presentation of the two avatars, for which participants were asked to choose the avatar that had a signing performance closer to the performance of a human, results showed that PAULA was the avatar of preference, as shown from the ratings as well as from the responses count from the Head-to-Head comparison; out of the total 608 signing occurrences (19 stimuli of images and videos multiplied by 32 participants), Paula was chosen in 428 of them.

The statistical analysis showed that the most frequent response for the totality of the signing occurrences for PAULA is "Good" and for FRANÇOISE is "Average" (Figure **2**). This finding is consistent with the obtained results from the head-to-head avatar comparison.

Even though a larger amount of data is necessary to safely draw conclusions, the here attempted interpretation of the results simply highlights the general tendency which favors PAULA's signing over FRANÇOISE's one.

In the second part of the questionnaire (Part B), each avatar was individually rated for its signing performance with respect to a compilation of signing occurrences consisting of isolated lemmas and phrases. The overall inspection of the collected data for Part B attests that both avatars performed equally well. An investigation of their performance with respect to the four movement parameters that were evaluated (hand movement, body movement, head and eye movement, mouth movement) led to the following findings: PAULA received higher rankings for hand movement and eyes movement, while FRANÇOISE was preferred over PAULA for her mouth movement. Both avatars were equally evaluated with respect to their body movement. These are important findings that need to be investigated in more signing occurrences, within context as well as in isolated instantiations.

With respect to the preferences comparison of two sub-groups among the GSL signers we comment on the following: In both parts of the questionnaire the two sub-groups expressed the same preferences regarding PAULA. However, the difference between them regarding FRANÇOISE's rating is a finding worth further investigating. Further interpretation of this finding given the collected data yields two additional insights; a good avatar performance is rated similarly by both groups of signers, L1 and L2. However, an average signing performance gives room for varying ratings among signers. In this case L1 signers are shown to be more consistent in their ratings than the group of L2 signers who participated in the survey. To be able to interpret these results it is important to redress this issue in the follow-up surveys.

For this pilot implementation of the on-line survey, the number of participants was sufficient to perform an initial descriptive analysis. However, to further investigate the participants' choices and their respective ratings with respect to different variables (i.e., gender, age, SL manner of acquisition (L1 vs L2), educational status etc), we need to extend our survey aiming at a broader randomly selected pool of participants.

4. Discussion

The reported findings from the pilot on-line survey on avatar performance evaluation provided significant feedback not only with respect to the targeted aspects of avatar performance, but also regarding methodological issues such as the outreach of the survey so that statistical analysis of results is better supported, various distribution issues among participant groups, the size and structure of the survey content and the phrasing of the requested tasks. This feedback is exploited in the user evaluation surveys the design of which is reported here. These will constantly address different SLs in the framework of our strategy of ongoing signer consultation on avatar development as implemented within the EASIER project.

The pilot implementation of the on-line survey has demonstrated a successful user-centered design and incorporates accessibility features of the shell questionnaire environment which may effectively achieve to engage signers in the development of signing avatar technology.

Planned accommodation of content from four SLs (GSL, LSF, DGS and DSGS) will enable a wide application of the questionnaire in the next period, which will provide significant input from the part of users regarding how they perceive the parameters of naturalness and comprehensibility of the synthetic signing and will further guide development of the EASIER avatar.

5. Acknowledgements

The work presented here is supported by the EASIER (Intelligent Automatic Sign Language Translation) Project. EASIER has received funding from the European Union's Horizon 2020 Research and Innovation Programme, Grant Agreement n° 101016982.

6. Bibliographical References

Costello, B., Fernandez, F., & Landa, A. (2006). The non-(existent) native signer: Sign Language research in a small deaf population. In B. Costello, J. Fernández, & A. Landa (Eds.), *Theoretical issues in Sign Language Research (TISLR) 9 Conference*. Florianopolis, Brazil.

European Union of the Deaf. (2018,). Accessibility of information and communication. https://www.eud.eu/about-us/eud-position-paper/accessibility-information-andcommunication [Accessed October 26, 2018]

Jennings, V., Elliott, R., Kennaway, R. and Glauert, J. (2010). Requirements for a signing avatar. In the *Proceedings of the Workshop on Corpora & Sign Language Technologies (CSLT)*, Satellite workshop of the LREC 2010 Conference, Valetta, Malta, p. 33–136.

Kacorri, H., Huenerfauth, M., Ebling, S., Patel, K. & Willard, M. (2015). Demographic and Experiential Factors Influencing Acceptance of Sign Language Animation by Deaf Users. In *Proceedings of the 17th International ACM SIGACCESS Conference on Computers & Accessibility (ASSETS '15)*. Association for Computing Machinery, New York, NY, USA, 147-154.

https://doi.org/10.1145/2700648.2809860

Kipp, K., Nguyen, Q., Heloir, A. & Matthes, S., (2011). Assessing the deaf user perspective on sign language avatars. In The *Proceedings of the 13th International ACM SIGACCESS Conference on Computers and accessibility (ASSETS '11)*. Association for Computing Machinery, New York, NY, USA, p. 107–114. DOI: https://doi.org/10.1145/2049536.2049557

McDonald, J., Wolfe, R., Moncrief, R. and Baowidan, S. (2016). A computational model of role shift to support the synthesis of signed language. In the *Proceedings of the 12th Theoretical Issues in Sign Language Research (TISLR)*, Melbourne, Australia, p. 4–7.

Wolfe, R., McDonald, J. and Schnepp, J. C. (2011). An Avatar to Depict Sign Language: Building from Reusable Hand Animation. In *Proceedings of the International workshop on Sign Language Translation & Avatar Technology Workshop (SLTAT'11)*.

Wolfe, R., McDonald, J., Efthimiou, E., Fontinea, E-S., Picron, F., Van Landuyt, D., Sioen, T., Braffort, A., Filhol, M., Ebling, S., Hanke, T. and Krausneker, V. (2021). The Myth of Signing Avatars (long paper). In the *Proceedings of the 1st International Workshop on Automatic Translation for Signed and Spoken Languages (AT4SSL)*, Shterionov D., Editor, Association for Machine Translation in the Americas (2021). p: 33-42.

World Federation of the Deaf. (2018). WFD and WASLI statement of use of signing avatars. https://wf-deaf.org/news/resources/wfd-wasli-statement-use-signing-avatars/ [Accessed March 14, 2018].

Proceedings of the 7th International Workshop on Sign Language Translation and Avatar Technology (SLTAT 7), pages 45–52
Language Resources and Evaluation Conference (LREC 2022), Marseille, 20-25 June 2022

Improving Signer Independent Sign Language Recognition for Low Resource Languages

Ruth Holmes, Ellen Rushe, Frank Fowley, Anthony Ventresque
School of Computer Science, University College Dublin & SFI Lero
{ruth.holmes,frank.fowley}@ucdconnect.ie, {ellen.rushe,anthony.ventresque}@ucd.ie

Abstract

The reliance of deep learning algorithms on large scale datasets represents a significant challenge when learning from low resource sign language datasets. This challenge is compounded when we consider that, for a model to be effective in the real world, it must not only learn the variations of a given sign, but also learn to be invariant to the person signing. In this paper, we first illustrate the performance gap between signer-independent and signer-dependent models on Irish Sign Language manual hand shape data. We then evaluate the effect of transfer learning, with different levels of fine-tuning, on the generalisation of signer independent models, and show the effects of different input representations, namely variations in image data and pose estimation. We go on to investigate the sensitivity of current pose estimation models in order to establish their limitations and areas in need of improvement. The results show that accurate pose estimation outperforms raw RGB image data, even when relying on pre-trained image models. Following on from this, we investigate image texture as a potential contributing factor to the gap in performance between signer-dependent and signer-independent models using counterfactual testing images and discuss potential ramifications for low-resource sign languages.

Keywords: Sign language recognition, Transfer learning, Irish Sign Language, Low-resource languages

1. Introduction

Modern deep learning techniques rely heavily on large scale datasets. However this becomes a significantly limiting factor when such large datasets are unavailable or difficult to obtain, as is the case with many low-resource sign languages. This limitation is not unique to sign language recognition, with several techniques being proposed to perform image classification within this resource-constrained setting (Larochelle et al., 2008; Sharif Razavian et al., 2014). Sign language recognition adds an additional nuance to this challenge as models not only need to generalise to different variations of hand signs but also to new signers. Training models on a low number of signers causes them to learn the characteristics of particular individuals leading to significant levels of bias in the models and limited applicability in real-world settings (Kim et al., 2016).

In this work, we first quantify the disparity in performance between signer independent and signer-dependent models for Irish Sign Language (ISL) letter hand shape recognition. We show the effects of different input representations on the performance of signer-independent models trained on low-resource data and the tendency of raw image data to lead to significant bias, even when transfer learning is used. The experiments show that pose estimation alone may lead to increased performance in this scenario. To study the efficacy of pose estimation models, the effects of colour on existing pose estimation models are shown. Finally, we experiment with different levels of fine-tuning to assess whether this provides a regularisation effect.

The remainder of this paper is structured as follows. Section 2 describes current works studying the area of low resource datasets and signer-independent models along with the preprocessing techniques used; Section 3 describes our approach to evaluating transfer learning and input representations for low-resource sign language recognition; Section 4 describes the details of the dataset used in our experiments, models and evaluation techniques. We present and discuss the results of these experiments in Section 5. Finally, we conclude with a summary of our findings and a discussion on potential future work in Section 6.

2. Related Work

One of the over-arching issues associated with sign language recognition research is a distinct lack of large-scale, diverse datasets. In particular, less prevalent languages such as ISL and Italian sign language (LIS) whose users number approximately just 40,000-60,000 (Leeson et al., 2015; Branchini and Mantovan, 2020) experience this to a greater degree.

Due to the low-resource nature of these types of datasets, it is imperative that we consider the potential influences this has on real-world recognition scenarios. While differences in camera quality, lighting, and scenery are all valid and important considerations, it is also important that our methods properly account for diversity of signer. We must therefore also be considerate of gender, skin-tone, fluency, age, disability, etc (Bragg et al., 2019).

The lack of signer variety that comes with low-resource datasets is a recurring challenge in the literature. Specifically, there are many sign languages where data is extremely limited, both in availability and size. For example, (Nakjai and Katanyukul, 2019; Fagiani et al., 2015; Oliveira et al., 2017a; Oliveira et al., 2017c) experiment on datasets with fewer than 12 signers. This inevitably leads to bias in the models trained on these datasets. For example, the dataset used in our experiments consist of just 6 signers (3 male, 3 female), all of whom are of similar skin-tone, dressed in dark long sleeves, and are recorded in extremely similar studio conditions. It is therefore clear that we need to address both preprocessing and training in a different way compared with scenarios where signers and data are in abundance.

In terms of preprocessing, several works have utilised raw images as input or a combination of images and auxillary features. Both Openpose (Cao et al., 1812) pose estimation and RGB values were used by (De Coster et al., 2021), optical flow and RGB values were combined by (Shi et al., 2018), data augmentation on raw images was performed by (Pigou et al., 2016) including rotation, stretching and shifting, while (Oliveira et al., 2017c) experiment with raw images alone. Other works take a more domain specific approach, using several image processing and feature selection techniques. (Nakjai and Katanyukul, 2019) perform thresholding and calculate the maximum contour area of each image before classification, (Fagiani et al., 2015) obtain the centroid coordinates of the hands with respect to the face, (Oyedotun and Khashman, 2017) convert images to binary and apply noise filtering while (Oliveira et al., 2017a; Oliveira et al., 2017c) also experiment with PCA and image blurring. (Fowley and Ventresque, 2021) create synthetic data for ISL fingerspelling recognition, achieving high performance in a signer independent setting. Though the authors are approaching a similar problem to that we aim to tackle, we instead focus on a less language specific-approach that does not require synthetic dataset design. Signer independent models are also addressed by (Kim et al., 2016) using neural network adaptation, however this assumes that a small number of examples from the test signer is available which we assume will be unavailable in our work.

While other works have studied signer independent models (Fowley and Ventresque, 2021; Kim et al., 2016), we do so explicitly in a low resource context. We experiment with the most effective preprocessing techniques in the literature and determine their contribution to classification performance in this context. Specifically, we examine the generalisability of different input representations in isolation, determine the most useful method of fine-tuning for pre-trained models, and discuss the impact of these experimental design choices on the overall classification performance.

3. Adapting to Low Resource Sign Languages

For languages where availability of data is limited, i.e. *low-resource languages*, training deep learning algorithms can be challenging due to their dependence on large-scale datasets (LeCun et al., 2015). Furthermore, as with other tasks that utilise bio-metric data, performance of subject-independent models tends to be distinctly lower than subject-dependent models (Kim et al., 2016; Lockhart and Weiss, 2014). This negative effect on performance tends to be amplified for low resource datasets as the number of subjects contained within them will naturally be lower.

3.1. Transfer Learning

An obvious choice for learning with limited image data is transfer learning (Sharif Razavian et al., 2014) due to the wide availability of pre-trained image models. However, the degree of fine-tuning needed to exploit the features learned from pre-trained models for sign language recognition is less obvious. In this paper we investigate the effect of fine-tuning an entire network on this domain-specific data versus fine-tuning only the final classifier. We assess whether it is necessary to adjust the parameters in the earlier layers of the network in order to adapt to this task or whether the potential regularising effects of simply training the final layers are more beneficial. We also assess this specifically in the signer-independent scenario compared to the signer-dependent scenario to determine whether signer-independent models benefit more from this regularising effect.

3.2. Input Representation

Though transfer learning alone vastly improves the ability of a network to learn image features with a small amount of data, there remains a question as to whether these are, in fact, the features the network *should* be learning in order to generalise to the largest number of signers possible. We seek to directly compare two of the most common input representations for sign-language recognition: raw image data with minimal pre-processing and pose estimation keypoints. Below is a discussion on the motivation for this comparison for low-resource sign language data.

3.2.1. Raw Image Data

The use of raw image data in deep learning models has become ubiquitous in computer vision. Raw color values, for instance, are vital in order to identify varying objects and textures. However, for low resource computer vision, there is a question as to whether color features are desirable to learn directly from the data relating to the task at hand. The role of incorrect white-balance, for instance, has been found to cause errors in deep learning models due to bias in datasets towards white-balanced data (Afifi and Brown, 2019). When we keep in mind that low-resource datasets have a low number of signers, the potential for the particular characteristics of signers such as skin tone, dress colour etc. to bias datasets is undeniable. We will show the sensitivity of sign language recognition models to colour by determining the disparity in performance between greyscale and RGB images.

3.2.2. Pose Estimation

Given the potential dependence of low resource computer vision models on less than optimal features, we seek to determine whether extracted pose estimation could potentially outperform raw images (even with pre-trained models) and generalise better to signers not in the training data. Though many state-of-the-art pose estimation tools also use raw images as training data, they are typically trained on far more data than could ever be collected in a low-resource scenario. We hypothesise that using a highly accurate pose estimation model's output as sign language recognition model's input will allow for better generalisation, as the sign language recognition model is forced to learn only from the features that matter the most, i.e. the coordinates of body parts and their relationship to each other, with minimal dependence on the personal characteristics of the signer.

4. Experimental Setup

4.1. Dataset

The following section describes the dataset used for experiments. We describe the different dataset configurations we created to assess the affect of certain attributes on the overall performance and generalisation.

4.1.1. ISL Hand-shape Dataset

The dataset of Irish Sign Language Hand-shapes (ISL-HS) was originally curated by (Oliveira et al., 2017b) and is publicly available for download[1].

The dataset consists of 468 RGB24 videos of 3 male and 3 female signers performing the 26 ISL alphabet hand-shapes. Each hand-shape was recorded three times at 30 frames per second (fps) and resolution of 640 x 480 pixels. The curators of this dataset have also extracted the frames from these videos, converted them to greyscale and removed background features using a pixel-value threshold. The resulting frames include just the single hand and forearm used to perform the hand-shape. These hand-shapes can be further distinguished into two subcategories:

1. **Static hand-shapes**: All English letters with the exception of 'J', 'X' and 'Z' which include no dynamic movement in their action. These signs were performed using an arcing motion (vertical to horizontal) to better simulate real-world gestural permutations. There are on average 2291 grey-scale frames per hand-shape.
2. **Dynamic hand-shapes**: English letters 'J', 'X' and 'Z' which were performed only using the motion of the gesture itself thus resulting in relatively fewer frames on average (1809 frames per hand-shape) with 'X' having the least of all (1443).

4.1.2. Data Configurations

In order to ascertain the disparity in performance of signer-dependent versus signer-independent models, we create the following two dataset configurations.

[1]https://github.com/marlondcu/ISL

1. **Signer-dependent dataset**: Three trials of each letter are signed by each person in the dataset. The first trial is used for training, the second for validation and third for testing. This ensures that data from all signers present is available for training, validation and testing, while ensuring the frames used in each set are different. We also assess the effect of image colour composition on performance with the following variations.
   (a) The greyscale frames provided by (Oliveira et al., 2017b), see Figure 1a.
   (b) The RGB frames we extracted from the videos provided by (Oliveira et al., 2017b), see Figure 1b. We noted that this process lead to 143 fewer frames than the greyscale data provided in the public dataset. This is seemingly due to a small number of the original videos being very slightly longer than those provided in the public data.
2. **Signer-independent dataset**: To keep the signers in each set separate, data from *Person 1* and *2* is used for training, *Person 3* and *4* is used for validation and *Person 5* and *6* is used for testing. This also ensures that a similar number of examples are present in each set of this dataset as the signer-dependent dataset. Next we perform pose estimation on the signer-independent dataset to create a third data configuration. This is to assess the extent to which pose estimation can close the gap in performance between signer-dependent and signer-independent models. We use MediaPipe Hands (Zhang et al., 2020). Where the detection confidence surpasses a minimum threshold, we plot the pose estimation co-ordinates in 2D, modifying the default pose estimation plots to prevent landmarks from becoming visually overcrowded, see Figure 1c. Where the pose estimation confidence does not meet this minimum criteria, the raw frame is simply used. The minimum detection confidence set for our experiments was 0.5. We stress that though it is certainly possible to use the pose estimation co-ordinates directly as input features, this transformation into a 2D "image" allows a direct comparison of the same model architectures irrespective of the input and to hold all other algorithmic features and hyper-parameters constant. The following data configurations are used:
   (a) Greyscale frames provided by (Oliveira et al., 2017b)
   (b) RBG frames of from the videos provided by (Oliveira et al., 2017b). In the same way as the signer-dependent dataset, this lead to fewer RGB frames for each video than those provided in the grey-scale dataset.
   (c) Pose estimation images for greyscale frames.

(a) Greyscale. (b) RGB. (c) Pose estimation.

Figure 1: The letter U performed by *Person 2* in Greyscale, RGB and the corresponding pose estimation.

(d) Pose estimation images for RGB frames.

4.2. Models

For all experiments the same deep architecture and hyperparameters are used. This was done in order to ensure that all but the desired aspects of the data or model being tested were kept constant.

Table 1: Hyperparameters used across all VGG models.

Hyperparameter	Value
Normalisation	Standard for VGG16 [a]
Image resizing	(120, 160)
Optimiser	Adam
Initial learning rate	0.0001
Batch size	64
Number of epochs	50

[a] https://pytorch.org/vision/stable/models.html.

4.2.1. VGG network

For this network, we used an ImageNet pre-trained VGG network (Simonyan and Zisserman, 2014)[2]. An additional layer with 4000 unit, with ReLU (Nair and Hinton, 2010) activation and Dropout (Srivastava et al., 2014) of 0.5 was added along with and a classification layer with 26 outputs.

4.2.2. Fine-tuning

Fine-tuning was performed in two ways for each model:

1. The added layers of the network alone were fine-tuned on the ISL training set.
2. The entire network, including pre-trained layers, were fine-tuned.

This process was performed to determine whether a regularisation effect could be achieved by excluding the pre-trained layers from the fine-tuning process.

[2] https://pytorch.org/hub/pytorch_vision_vgg/

5. Results

This section first details the results of signer independent compared to signer dependent models in subsection 5.1. We then move on to compare raw images to a pose estimation representation in subsection 5.2. Additionally, we provide a discussion on our results and further analysis in subsection 5.3.

5.1. Signer-Independent Models

We can see in Table 2 that there is a sizable disparity between signer-independent and signer-dependent models, trained on greyscale images, even for a relatively homogeneous dataset. It is reasonable to expect that there would be an even larger gap in performance between these models for signers with significantly different characteristics to those in this dataset, highlighting the challenge with datasets of this size. One may expect that this drop in performance is an indicator of over-fitting however when we plot the validation accuracy over all 50 epochs in Figure 2, we can see that these models never perform anywhere near as well as their signer-dependent counterparts. This, once again, highlights the tendency of these models to learn characteristics of the training images not useful to generalisation. With respect to fine-tuning, interestingly, signer-independent models gain slightly more benefit from fine-tuning all layers in the network more than the signer-dependent models.

This disparity in performance is not unique to sign-language models with similar behaviour to be seen in fields like activity recognition (Lockhart and Weiss, 2014) and electroencephalography classification (Zhang et al., 2019). The performance of the signer-independent models shown here closely mirror that achieved by other authors (Fagiani et al., 2015; Shi et al., 2018) - diverting from the higher performance results achieved in the signer-dependent work of (Nakjai and Katanyukul, 2019; Oyedotun and Khashman, 2017; Oliveira et al., 2017a; Oliveira et al., 2017c).

All this indicates that models trained on raw images have a tendency to utilise signer-specific features when classifying hand shapes. Of course, a larger number of signers would likely help remedy this behaviour, though for low-resource languages such as ISL, this data tends not to be available. Therefore we con-

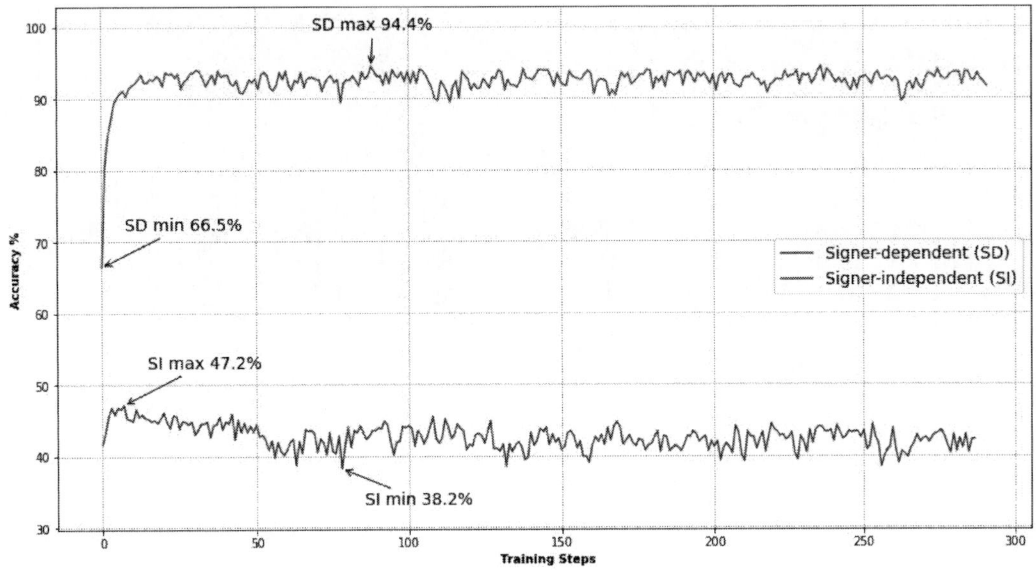

Figure 2: Validation accuracy for the signer-dependent and signer-independent models trained on greyscale images with only layers added to the pre-trained VGG network fine-tuned. Minimum and maximum values are labeled.

clude that signer-independent models using raw RGB images have limited generalisability for these low resource scenarios, even when pre-trained image classification models are used. This motivates a more generalisable input representation.

Table 2: Signer-dependent versus signer independent models on greyscale data. *Added layers* refers to models where only the layers added to the end of a pre-trained network were fine-tuned. *All layers* refers to models where all layers of a pre-trained model were fine-tuned.

Type	Fine-tuning	F1-Score
Signer-Dependent	Added layers	0.885
	All layers	0.882
Signer-Independent	Added layers	0.433
	All layers	0.463

5.2. Raw Images vs. Pose Estimation

Table 3: Pre-trained VGG network's performance on signer-independent data.

Fine-tuning	Input	F1-score
Added layers	Greyscale (∼48% MP frames)	0.486
	RGB	0.369
	RGB (∼99% MP frames)	**0.545**
All layers	Greyscale (∼48% MP frames)	0.468
	RGB	0.399
	RGB (∼99% MP frames)	0.542

For our main results in 3, we first look at the effect of converting greyscale images to MediaPipe landmarks, with roughly 48% of these images being successfully converted. We can see that these pose-estimation features increased the performance for greyscale images, especially when pre-trained weights are kept fixed, with this variation achieving a 4.8% increase over the best performing signer-independent model in Table 2. We also evaluated models trained on the corresponding RGB frames. Neither models trained on raw RGB images exceed the performance of the best model trained on greyscale images. Again, we can see in Figure 3 that validation accuracy for raw RGB data remains in this region of performance for the entire training period. This, at first, seems surprising given that pre-trained models are trained on colour images. However, we hypothesise that this is caused by features that are signer-specific, but irrelevant to the characteristics of a given sign, being more successfully learned by these models, leading to poor generalisation. This is despite the fact that regularisation is used in the form of Dropout in the second to last layer added to the VGG network. This behaviour is actually exacerbated when pre-trained weights are not fine-tuned. We can see that fine-tuning all layers leads to slightly increased performance for raw RGB images. In fact, we can see that both raw greyscale and RGB images show that a similar increase in performance can be gained from fine-tuning all layers of the network. Interestingly, we do not see such an increase when including pose images generated from MediaPipe.

Finally, we look at the effect of converting RBG images to MediaPipe pose estimation landmarks, with over 99% of images successfully converted. There is over

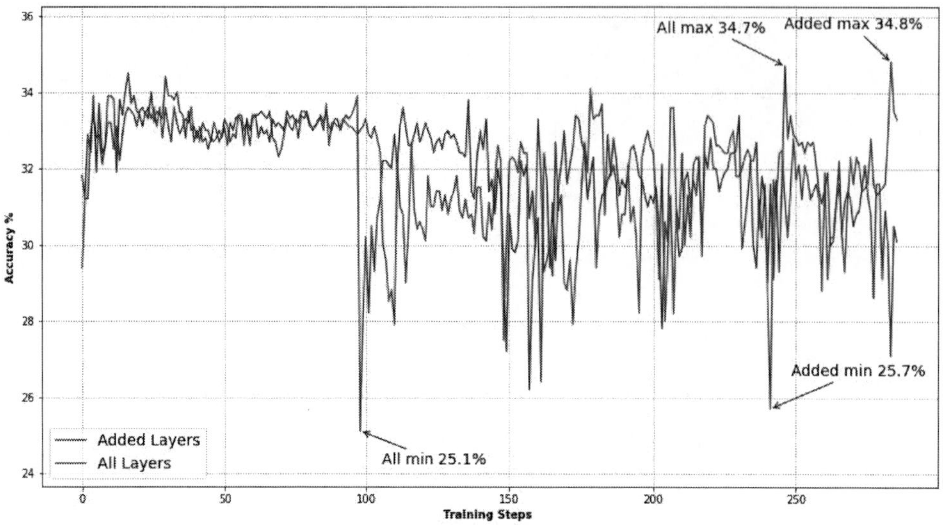

Figure 3: Validation accuracy for raw RGB frames with fine-tuning on added layers and for raw RGB frames with fine-tuning on all layers.

an 11% improvement compared to the next best models (greyscale images converted to MediaPipe, added layers fine-tuned), a pronounced boost in performance. It is fascinating that models trained on raw RGB images, in fact, come last in terms of performance. This provides evidence that pose estimation with minimal use of RGB images (less than 1% due to low pose estimation confidence) provides greater generalisation to unseen signers than utilising RGB images for a low resource dataset. We also observe greater performance when excluding pre-trained layers from fine-tuning.

5.3. Feature Analysis

We observed that some features had a significant effect on the overall performance of both pose estimation and sign recognition. We discuss some of our further analysis and observations below.

5.3.1. Pose Estimation

The effect of removing colour from images on pose estimation performance, even when using a popular pose estimation model trained on a large amount of data, illustrates the sensitivity of such models to colour in images. Table 4 compares the number of successfully converted greyscale images compared to RGB images. Figures 4a and 4b further break down this comparison by letter and signer ID respectively.

Table 4: Results of the Mediapipe conversion on both greyscale and RGB frames

Frame Type	# Frames Available	# Frames Converted	No. Frames Non-Converted	% Frames Converted
Grey-scale	58,114	27,840	30,274	47.9
RGB	57,971	57,850	121	99.7

On the face of it, this may not appear to be a problem, due to the fact that modern images are unlikely to be in greyscale. However, the reliance on colour indicates that performance could also be greatly affected by lighting conditions and scenes not present in the training data. This type of behaviour has been observed in other computer vision tasks (Afifi and Brown, 2019). This should be taken into consideration if sign language recognition systems rely on such models and might motivate other types of feature pre-processing before pose estimation such as optical flow.

5.3.2. Signer-specific Characteristics

The large gap between signer-dependent and signer-independent models in the case of raw RGB images is challenging as it can be difficult to determine which of the characteristics specific to each signer is being learned when trained on low-resource data. Models pre-trained on ImageNet have indeed been found to be biased towards image texture over shapes of objects within images (Geirhos et al., 2018), which in this case translates to the texture of the clothes being worn by the signer and their skin texture. To evaluate whether this could be a large contributing factor, we create counterfactual examples of the signer-independent RGB test set described in 4.1.2 by applying a Gaussian blur to images to smooth the image texture. We do, in fact, see a decrease in performance for the model which was trained on raw RGB images which suggests that this is a contributing factor. This feature alone, however, is clearly just a single aspect that influences this gap in performance and further evaluations are needed to ascertain other contributing factors.

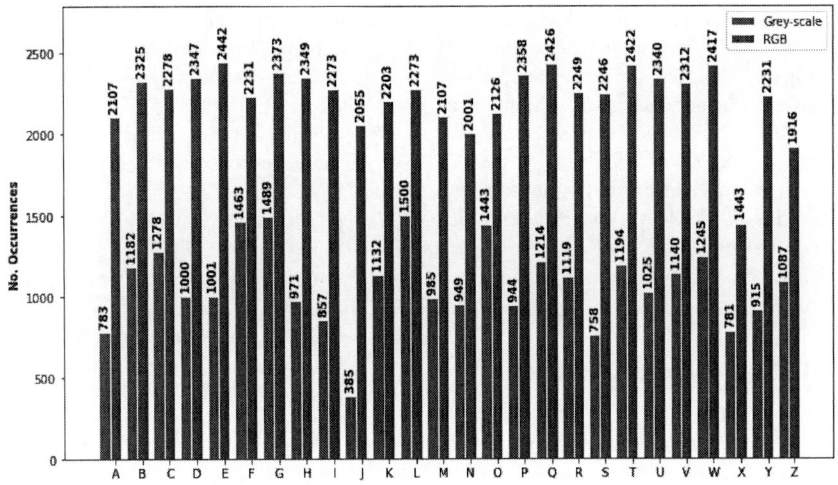

(a) Hand-shapes.

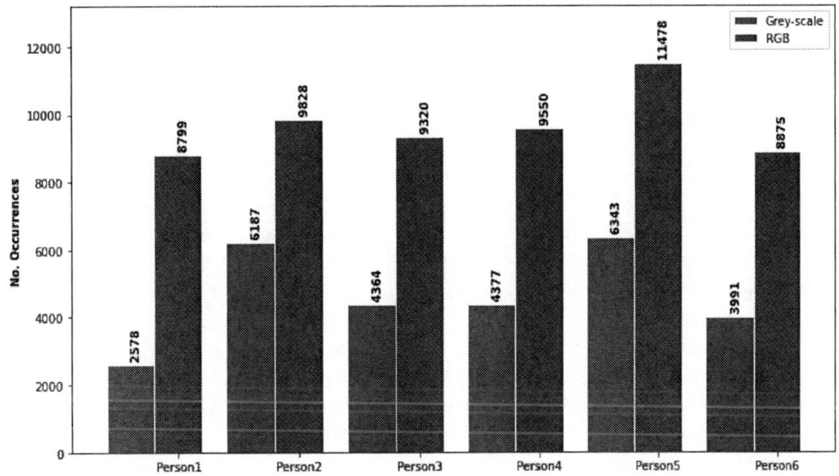

(b) Signers.

Figure 4: The number of frames converted to pose estimation for both hand-shapes and signers between the grey-scale and RGB images.

Table 5: VGG model with a Gaussian blur applied to test set

Fine-tuning	Input	F1-score
Added layers	RGB	0.359
All layers	RGB	0.384

6. Conclusion

In this work we have illustrated the large performance disparity between signer-independent and signer-dependent models in Irish Sign Language. We show that using accurate pose estimation as input when training on low-resource sign language datasets increases recognition performance. We have investigated the improvements needed for pose estimation models to become more effective and have used counterfactual examples to show the effect of texture on models using raw RGB data. It should be noted that these images account for just a small subset of ISL manual hand shapes. We also recognise that the resolution of the images used in these experiments and their distinct lack of background noise is often an overly optimistic representation of real-world finger spelling. However, this work is merely the beginning of a line of research that will perform more extensive analysis on the effects of input representation, the ways that this representation can be made more robust and the role of the network architecture in improving signer-independent generalisation.

7. Acknowledgements

We would like to warmly thank our colleague Thomas Laurent for his valuable feedback and comprehensive proofreading assistance on several drafts of this manuscript. This work was supported, in part, by SignON, a project funded by the European Union's Horizon 2020 Research and Innovation programme under grant No. 101017255; and by Science Foundation Ireland grant 13/RC/2094 P2 to Lero - the Science Foundation Ireland Research Centre for Software (www.lero.ie); F. Fowley is funded by the Science Foundation Ireland Centre for Research Training in Digitally-Enhanced Reality (D-REAL) under Grant No. 18/CRT/6224.

8. Bibliographical References

Afifi, M. and Brown, M. S. (2019). What else can fool deep learning? addressing color constancy errors on deep neural network performance. In *ICCV*, pages 243–252.

Bragg, D., Koller, O., Bellard, M., Berke, L., Boudreault, P., Braffort, A., Caselli, N., Huenerfauth, M., Kacorri, H., Verhoef, T., et al. (2019). Sign language recognition, generation, and translation: An interdisciplinary perspective. In *ASSETS*, pages 16–31.

Branchini, C. and Mantovan, L. (2020). *A Grammar of Italian Sign Language (LIS)*. 12.

Cao, Z., Hidalgo, G., Simon, T., Wei, S.-E., and Sheikh, Y. (1812). Openpose: Realtime multi-person 2d pose estimation using part affinity fields. arxiv 2018. *arXiv preprint arXiv:1812.08008*.

De Coster, M., Van Herreweghe, M., and Dambre, J. (2021). Isolated sign recognition from rgb video using pose flow and self-attention. In *CVPR*, pages 3441–3450.

Fagiani, M., Principi, E., Squartini, S., and Piazza, F. (2015). Signer independent isolated italian sign recognition based on hidden markov models. *Pattern Analysis and Applications*, 18(2):385–402.

Fowley, F. and Ventresque, A. (2021). Sign language fingerspelling recognition using synthetic data. In *AICS*, pages 84–95.

Geirhos, R., Rubisch, P., Michaelis, C., Bethge, M., Wichmann, F. A., and Brendel, W. (2018). Imagenet-trained cnns are biased towards texture; increasing shape bias improves accuracy and robustness. *arXiv preprint arXiv:1811.12231*.

Kim, T., Wang, W., Tang, H., and Livescu, K. (2016). Signer-independent fingerspelling recognition with deep neural network adaptation. In *ICASSP*, pages 6160–6164. IEEE.

Larochelle, H., Erhan, D., and Bengio, Y. (2008). Zero-data learning of new tasks. In *AAAI*, volume 1, page 3.

LeCun, Y., Bengio, Y., and Hinton, G. (2015). Deep learning. *Nature*, 521(7553):436–444.

Leeson, L., Saeed, J. I., and Grehan, C. (2015). 18 irish sign language (isl). *Sign Languages of the World: A Comparative Handbook*, page 449.

Lockhart, J. W. and Weiss, G. M. (2014). Limitations with activity recognition methodology & data sets. In *Pervasive and Ubiquitous Computing*, pages 747–756.

Nair, V. and Hinton, G. E. (2010). Rectified linear units improve restricted boltzmann machines. In *ICML*.

Nakjai, P. and Katanyukul, T. (2019). Hand sign recognition for thai finger spelling: An application of convolution neural network. *Journal of Signal Processing Systems*, 91(2):131–146.

Oliveira, M., Chatbri, H., Ferstl, Y., Farouk, M., Little, S., O'Connor, N. E., and Sutherland, A. (2017a). A dataset for irish sign language recognition. In *IMVIP*.

Oliveira, M., Chatbri, H., Ferstl, Y., Farouk, M., Little, S., O'Connor, N. E., and Sutherland, A. (2017b). A dataset for irish sign language recognition. In *IMVIP*.

Oliveira, M., Chatbri, H., Little, S., Ferstl, Y., O'Connor, N. E., and Sutherland, A. (2017c). Irish sign language recognition using principal component analysis and convolutional neural networks. In *DICTA*, pages 1–8. IEEE.

Oyedotun, O. K. and Khashman, A. (2017). Deep learning in vision-based static hand gesture recognition. *Neural Computing and Applications*, 28(12):3941–3951.

Pigou, L., Van Herreweghe, M., and Dambre, J. (2016). Sign classification in sign language corpora with deep neural networks. In *LREC*, pages 175–178.

Sharif Razavian, A., Azizpour, H., Sullivan, J., and Carlsson, S. (2014). Cnn features off-the-shelf: an astounding baseline for recognition. In *CVPR*, pages 806–813.

Shi, B., Del Rio, A. M., Keane, J., Michaux, J., Brentari, D., Shakhnarovich, G., and Livescu, K. (2018). American sign language fingerspelling recognition in the wild. In *SLT*, pages 145–152.

Simonyan, K. and Zisserman, A. (2014). Very deep convolutional networks for large-scale image recognition. *arXiv preprint arXiv:1409.1556*.

Srivastava, N., Hinton, G., Krizhevsky, A., Sutskever, I., and Salakhutdinov, R. (2014). Dropout: a simple way to prevent neural networks from overfitting. *The journal of machine learning research*, 15(1):1929–1958.

Zhang, D., Yao, L., Chen, K., and Monaghan, J. (2019). A convolutional recurrent attention model for subject-independent eeg signal analysis. *IEEE Signal Processing Letters*, 26(5):715–719.

Zhang, F., Bazarevsky, V., Vakunov, A., Tkachenka, A., Sung, G., Chang, C.-L., and Grundmann, M. (2020). Mediapipe hands: On-device real-time hand tracking. *arXiv preprint arXiv:2006.10214*.

Proceedings of the 7th International Workshop on Sign Language Translation and Avatar Technology (SLTAT 7), pages 53–58
Language Resources and Evaluation Conference (LREC 2022), Marseille, 20-25 June 2022

Improved Facial Realism through an Enhanced Representation of Anatomical Behavior in Sign Language Avatars

Ronan Johnson
DePaul University
Chicago, USA
sjohn165@depaul.edu

Abstract

Facial movements and expressions are critical features of signed languages, yet are some of the most challenging to reproduce on signing avatars. Due to the relative lack of research efforts in this area, the facial capabilities of such avatars have yet to receive the approval of those in the Deaf community. This paper revisits the representations of the human face in signed avatars, specifically those based on parameterized muscle simulation such as FACS and the MPEG-4 file definition. An improved framework based on rotational pivots and pre-defined movements is capable of reproducing realistic, natural gestures and mouthings on sign language avatars. The new approach is more harmonious with the underlying construction of signed avatars, generates improved results, and allows for a more intuitive workflow for the artists and animators who interact with the system.

Keywords: signing avatars, sign language representation, computer animation

1. Introduction

The translation of spoken language to signed language is not only a translation of meaning, but also modality. It is therefore the place of the signing avatar to act as the intermediary between verbal and visual communication. In spoken language, most of the linguistic and syntactic information is conveyed by voice through the mouth while the hands provide secondary gesture and nuance. Signed languages are the opposite, with most of the lexical information occurring on the hands, allowing the face to supply grammatical and prosodic information. While research efforts have made progress on generating the primary hand and arm movements of signed languages, the processes on the face have not been examined so thoroughly, although the Deaf community has expressed their concerns on this matter (Verlinden, et al., 2001; Kipp, et al., 2011; Ebling, et al., 2015; Huenerfauth, et al., 2011).

Due to the complexity of the task, a perfect recreation of a real human is both unnecessary in practice and logistically untenable. Therefore, a major challenge in developing a representation of a human avatar is simplification. Any framework for a signed avatar must be complex enough to achieve the desired results while being simple enough to be workable by artists and procedural algorithms.

2. Previous Work

One of the primary descriptions of human facial movement is the Facial Action Coding System (FACS) (Ekman and Friesen, 1978). The basis for this system is a set of combined facial muscle movements first described by (Hjorstjo, 1970) and coded as a set of action units, each defining a specific motion on the face. These action units can be combined to classify all possible movements of the human face based on the underlying musculature. FACS has continued to be an on-going resource to industry professionals and academics studying the motion of the human face (Seymour, 2019).

FACS has been widely influential in the parameterization of human facial movements. One such example is the standardized facial representation in the MPEG-4 file description (Pandzic and Forshheimer, 2003). This attempted to define a minimal set of parameters necessary to recreate the facial actions observed by descriptive systems such as FACS. These parameters are conceptualized as a set of markers across key portions of the face. Each marker acts as a feature point for either an artist or procedural computer algorithm to control the shape and position the facial features. Figure 1 shows the control points defined for the mouth.

This implementation has been the foundation for previous developments in signed avatar technology such as the work of EMBR Virtual Human Animation System (Huenerfauth and Kacorri, 2015), the VSign sign synthesis web tool (Papadogiorgaki et.al., 2004), and the Paula avatar of DePaul University's American Sign Language Avatar Project (Wolfe, et al., 2018), the latter of which will be used by way of example. In Paula's case, the original underlying framework defines the landmarks as a set of joints that are skinned to the mesh, allowing the avatar's geometry to follow the movements of the joint.

Machine learning implementations for generating expressive facial animation, such as the Tacotron2 developed by Apple, yield promising results (Hussen Abdelaziz et.al., 2021). However, their major drawback is the sheer amount of data needed to adequately train an algorithm, especially a neural network. Tacotron2 used a dataset consisting of 10 hours of data captured from real human performance to train their convolutional neural network (CNN). Another research group based in the United Kingdom implemented a similar system using a temporal generative adversarial net (GAN) which used over 26 hours of video for its training data (Vougioiukas et.al., 2019). Even projects that have achieved success with far less training data such as the one developed by (Laine et.al., 2017) still require every desired facial movement be present in the training data. These restrictions make such models expensive to develop. They also require entirely separate data to properly model movements and gestures in other languages, limiting their generalizability.

Motion-tracking based frameworks such as the ARTUS project (Bailly et.al., 2006) present an alternative that is more extendible and can be used in broader real-time applications such television broadcasts. Their use of marker-less tracking also allows their system to function on a variety of video clips in order to generate clearer lip movements for Deaf and hearing-impaired viewers to follow, as opposed to traditional subtitles. This methodology has proven to be effective in generating realistic facial movements, but is reliant on the underlying video. Further research would be beneficial to evaluate its performance in generating original movements in the absence of human video.

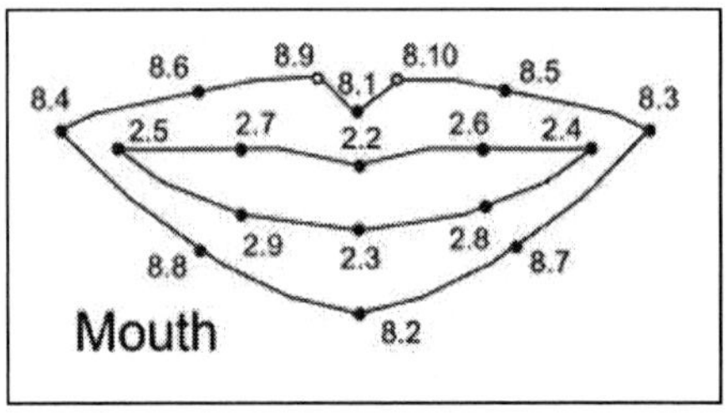

Figure 1: The mouth landmarks from MPEG-4 (Ekman and Friesen, 1978).

3. Revisiting Avatar Facial Representations

While they must appear similar in their final renderings, humans and avatars have little in common in terms of underlying structure. Humans are made up of layers of skin, fat, muscle, and bone. Mobility is achieved via the contraction of various muscles that pull on the underlying bones and ligaments. In contrast, signing avatars are defined primarily by geometric positioning and color information. Any movement is caused by some sequence of matrix operations on the avatar's positional data. These two highly contrasting modalities must nevertheless facilitate the same results: realistic and believable phonemes, visemes, and gestures.

The previous implementation of these facial processes on the Paula avatar utilized a FACS-based approach using the MPEG-4 facial marker definition. Although FACS is good at describing the process of observed actions on real human faces, an avatar framework instead needs to mathematically manipulate geometry to produce a final effect. The MPEG-4 representation attempts to define a complex series of muscle contractions with 28 points of positional control in two dimensions. Not only is there no strong structural connection between these modalities, but insistence on anatomical accuracy can distract from the ultimate goal of rendering expressive movement that garners the approval of the Deaf community. Ultimately, the underlying structure is only as useful as its ability to generate results. An improved model will be more congruent with the medium of avatar technology while allowing for greater artistic freedom and expediency.

Probably the biggest shortcoming of the MPEG-4 modality is its reliance on positional movement while ignoring rotation. For example, when the muscles around the sides of the mouth are activated, they pull the corners of the lips out towards the sides of the face. However, instead of simply shifting all the muscle and fat farther to the side, the lips are pulled around the curvature of the teeth in an arc. This kind of curved movement path is so fundamental to animation and recreating naturalistic motion, it is one of the twelve foundational principles of animation as defined by the original Disney animators (Johnston and Thomas, 1995).

This lack of rotation also creates an inability to reproduce several of Ekman's action units, in particular, the Lip Funneler (AU 22) and the Lip Suck (AU 28) as seen in Figure 2. These two actions are particularly challenging to recreate with positional movement because of the way the lips curl over the teeth and push away from the face towards the camera. These limitations have led to undesirable results on the avatar.

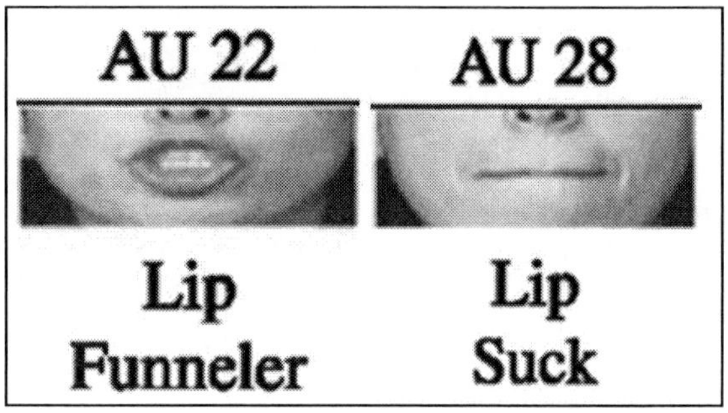

Figure 2: Two action units from FACS (Ekman and Friesen, 1978) that are difficult to recreate using only positional facial markers.

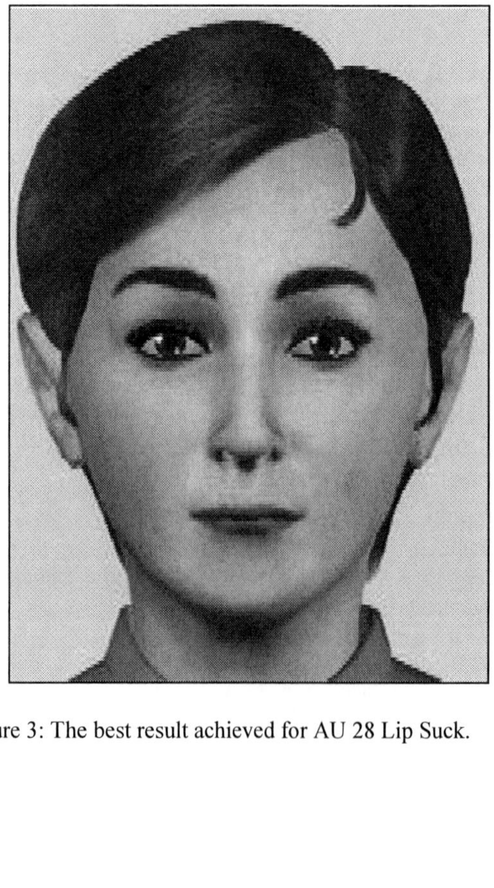

Figure 3: The best result achieved for AU 28 Lip Suck.

4. An Improved Framework

4.1 Geometric Marker Placement

In light of these considerations, the new representation is based not on positional translation, but rather the rotation of 44 individual mouth landmarks about a series of local pivot points. These landmarks lie along the surface of the geometry, centered on significant underlying geometry, and following the curvature of the lips. The original MPEG-4 landmarks are based on a general model of the movement of human facial anatomy, following the underlying muscles that pull on the lips. However, in a geometric representation, the landmarks should follow the underlying geometry that they will be transforming. This allows the model to work with the structural form of the avatar rather than retro-fitting a technique developed for an entirely separate modality. While this does technically increase the absolute number of control points from 28 to 44, through the use of rotational movement, the final structure allows maximum control to the artist with far fewer controls.

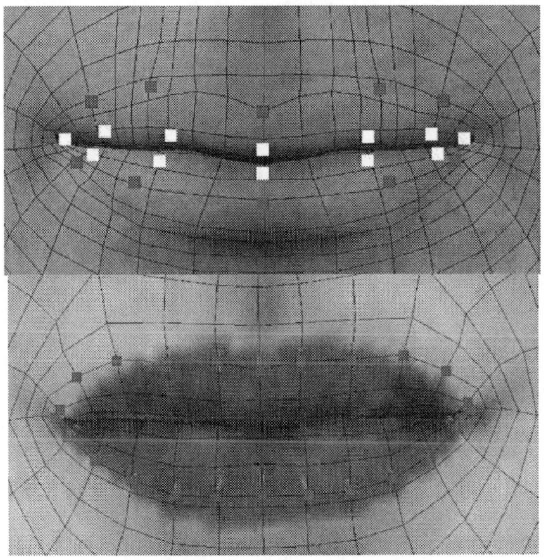

Figure 4: The original set of 28 control points (top); Red markers are the outer lip controls, white markers are the inner lip controls. Compare to the new set of control points and their geometric positioning (bottom).

It should be noted that there are a number of approaches to determining optimal marker placement. The work of (Le et.al., 2013) attempts to find a minimal layout that is effective for motion capture retargeting based on their effectiveness at recreating a given series of deformations in motion. Additionally, (Reverdy et.al., 2015) and (Will et.al., 2018) find compelling results on their motion tracker placement by using clustering methods to identify areas of the mesh with the strongest deformations while performing a series of expressions. This research does find marker placements that appear to perform more efficiently than the empirical placements such as the ones presented here. However, the primary goal of this new approach on the Paula avatar is to reduce the complexity of the work required of skilled artists, not necessarily the underlying computation.

Of particular concern is the number of control points surrounding the lips. The proposed optimization methods take the entire face into account when evaluating performance, which may mask underlying issues with localized performance in certain deformations. With the use of parameterized script controls as described in section 4.2, there can be greater flexibility in the absolute number of markers without placing undue strain on the artists' workflow. This yields the additional advantage of allowing the more complex control to be exposed to the artist if necessitated by a specific situation.

4.2 Major controls

Instead of the artist directly manipulating all 44 control points, the new system defines twelve major lip movements based on industry best practices (Osipa, 2010):

1. Lip spread
2. Jaw drop
3. Upper lip roll
4. Lower lip roll
5. Left lip corner
6. Right lip corner
7. Show upper teeth
8. Show lower teeth
9. Left upper snarl
10. Right upper snarl
11. Left lower snarl
12. Right lower snarl

The artist control structure for this system is presented as a set of sliders, each one dictating the intensity of each of these twelve movements. Here, 'intensity' refers to how extreme the movement appears on the face and is defined by a set of positional and rotational values for each relevant marker. These values are obtained by artist-generated extreme poses, intended to represent the most intense form of the movement an animator is likely to need. The slider values are normalized to lie between 0 and 100. This abstracts the complexities of generating the final shape to a single number, easily understood and manipulated by artists. When used in conjunction with one another, it is possible to recreate a wider range of action units than Paula's previous MPEG-4 framework with only a dozen single values for the artist to manage.

Each slider is connected to its relevant landmarks on the face with a script. These short pieces of code contain the needed positions and rotations of the landmarks to generate the most extreme form of the movement. They are also responsible for managing the intensity of the pose by interpolating between the neutral and the extreme. The slider value dictates the proportion by which this interpolation should occur. For example, when a user moves the jaw drop slider to open the mouth and sets the value to 50, the markers will move from their neutral values to 50% of their most extreme positions.

Further implementation details concerning the technologic connection between the landmarks and the sliders is presented in (McDonald, et al., 2022).

This interface gives artists complex control over the geometry with a minimal number of controls to manage. Furthermore, not all controls must be used to produce every individual mouth movement, reducing the complexity of the animators' work. Extended controls can be revealed to the user as needed should smaller corrections be needed. Other potential uses for this slider interface could include connecting the slider values to motion tracking markers, allowing for the retargeting of motion capture data.

4.3 Marker Pivot Placement

A rotation is defined by movement about some axis and centered around a pivot point. These define the local deformations of the geometry by the facial landmarks to portray the desired shape. For the lip landmarks, pivot points are derived from the sweep of the arc that the final movement must follow. For example, in the case of lip spread, the control points need to follow a curved path to simulate the pull of the lips across the teeth in a real human. Figure 5 shows the derivation of such a path with a simple circle following the curvature of the teeth as a guide. The circumference of the circle should extend past the teeth just enough to account for the mass of the lips sitting on top. The center of this circle is the pivot point for each lip landmark during any movement that spreads the lips wide. The arrow shows the connection between the circle center and the position of the landmark.

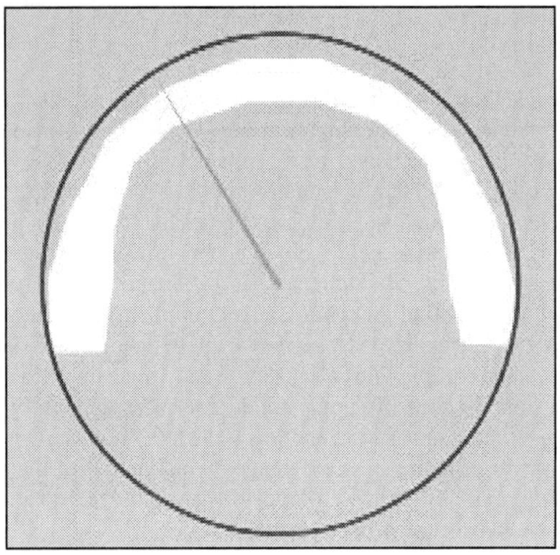

Figure 5: The guide circle for determining the appropriate pivot point of the lip spread control markers.

This same principle can be applied on an orthogonal plane to achieve the rotation necessary for AU 22 and AU 28. The difference in these movements is the location of the pivot. Instead of sweeping across the teeth, the lips in AU 28 need to curl under the teeth. Additionally, each landmark needs its own custom pivot point based on its exact location on the lips. This is because in order to avoid collisions with the teeth, the amount of rotation will be variable depending on the thickness of the lip at that location. This inward rotation must also account for the naturally curved orientation of the landmarks as the lips follow the curvature of the teeth, even when in a neutral pose. The same guiding curve of the previous example can determine the precise locations of these pivots as well. Instead of following the curvature of the teeth, this guide curve follows the thickness of the lips along the orientation of the geometry defining that section.

Human artists determined the exact position and orientation of these curves based on the orientation of the underlying geometry, specifically the edge loops that define the shape of the lips. While these positions have yet to be determined analytically, the initial results of the new approach were promising enough to continue with development. Future improvements may include optimization of these orientations, especially for application in the general case of any humanoid avatar.

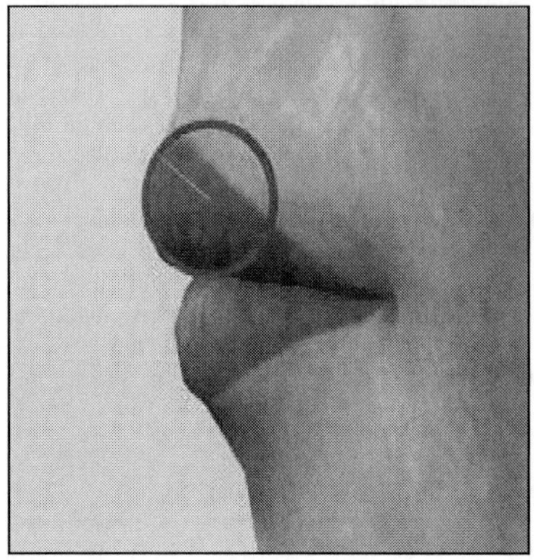

Figure 6: The guide circle for determining the appropriate pivots for the lip roll control markers.

By utilizing this rotational movement rather than relying exclusively on positional information, the markers naturally follow the curvatures of the face, yielding more realistic results. Additionally, rotational movement allows for the complex lip behaviors that were difficult to replicate with the previous MPEG-4 landmarks.

5. Results

The new system of empirically-placed facial markers driven by pre-set animation scripting is capable of reproducing all poses the original MPEG-4 framework could manage, while surpassing it in both control and flexibility. While each marker maintains only a small area of influence during a deformation, the combination of all markers working together gives more complex results with a far simpler interface for the artists. The results on the avatar are much improved in range of motion and expressivity.

One of the most compelling aspects of this design is its extendibility. The framework can accommodate any number of additions by simply defining another set of pivot points for each landmark. Figures 7 and 8 demonstrate the capabilities of the new parameterized framework. Artists are able to recreate subtle, intricate nuance in the shape of the mouth with relatively few controls. Further extensions may include generalized parameterization of the placement of the markers and their pivots for application to other avatars.

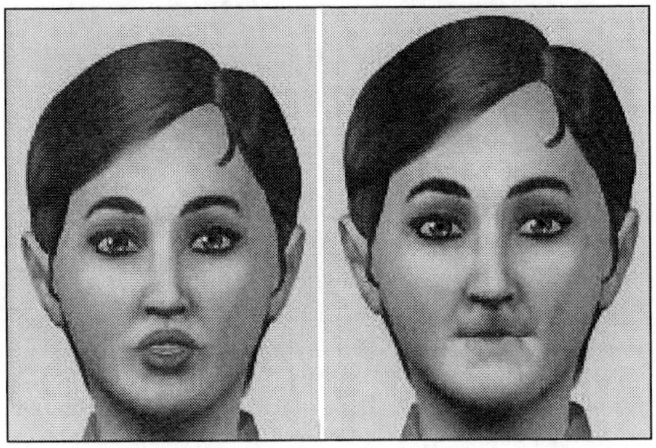

Figure 7: AU 22 (left) and AU 28 (right) created by an artist using the new framework. AU 28 can be generated by adjusting only two sliders.

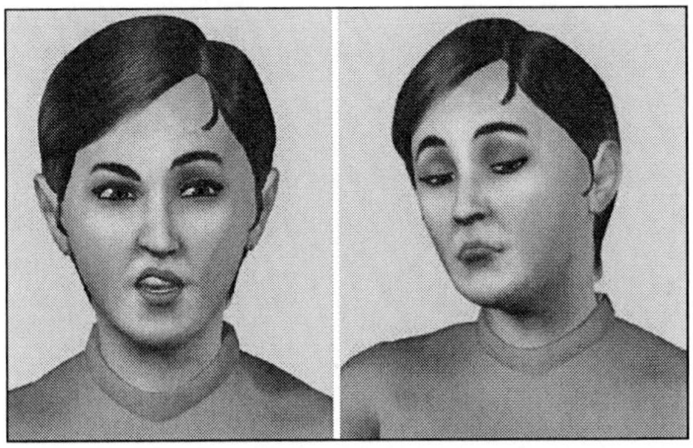

Figure 8: Example expressions created on Paula using the new framework. The system is capable of generating a wide range of expressions and mouth postures.

6. Future Work

Due to the extendibility of the system, future work will include additional support for many signed languages including German Sign Language (DGS) and French Sign Language (LSF). Some expressive features of these languages require additional capabilities beyond those of both the new framework and the MPEG-4 description. For instance, there are several DGS mouth gestures that require interaction between the tongue and cheek. This complex deformation has yet to be recreated satisfactorily on a signing avatar.

Previous research on clustering-based facial marker placement may be of use in extending the expressivity of the Paula avatar. One area in need of improvement is the extent to which the cheeks and surrounding areas react to wide movements on the lips. While there are landmarks in areas such as the upper cheeks that are scripted to react to certain artist input, informal subjective assessment of the results indicates that additional naturalism might be possible without increasing the workload on the artists. These studies could inform the optimal locations of additional markers to allow more flexibility in these secondary movements.

Furthermore, a perceptual user study will be conducted to better assess the subjective quality of the final results compared to previous attempts on the Paula avatar.

7. Acknowledgements

Many thanks to Nicole Barnekow for her fantastic work creating facial expressions with the new framework.

8. Bibliographic References

Bailly, G., Attina, V., Baras, C., Bas, P., Baudry, S., Beautemps, D., ... & Nguyen, P. (2006). ARTUS: synthesis and audiovisual watermarking of the movements of a virtual agent interpreting subtitling using cued speech for deaf televiewers. *Modelling, measurement and control C, 67(2, supplement: handicap),* 177-187.

Ebling, S., Wolfe, R., Schnepp, J., Baowidan, S., McDonald, J., Moncrief, R., . . . Tissi, K. (2015). Synthesizing the finger alphabet of Swiss German Sign Language and evaluating the comprehensibility of the resulting animations. *Proceedings of SLTAT 2015: 6th Workshop on Speech and Language Processing for Assistive Technologies,* 10-16.

Ekman, P., & Friesen, W. V. (1978). Facial action coding system. *Environmental Psychology & Nonverbal Behavior.*

Hjortsjö, C. H. (1969). *Man's face and mimic language.* Studentlitteratur.

Huenerfauth, M., Lu, P., & Rosenberg, A. (2011). Evaluating importance of facial expression in American Sign Language and pidgin signed English animations. *The proceedings of the 13th international ACM SIGACCESS conference on Computers and accessibility* (pp. 99-106).

Huenerfauth, M., & Kacorri, H. (2015). Augmenting EMBR virtual human animation system with MPEG-4 controls for producting ASL facial expressions. *International symposium on sign language translation and avatar technoloty* (Vol. 3, p. 94).

Hussen Abdelaziz, A., Kumar, A. P., Seivwright, C., Fanelli, G., Binder, J., Stylianou, Y., & Kajareker, S. (2021). Audiovisual Speech Synthesis using Tacotron2. *In Proceedings of the 2021 International Conference on Multimodal Interaction* (pp. 503-511).

Kipp, M., Heloir, A., & Matthes, S. (2011). Assessing the deaf user perspective on sign language avatars. *The proceedings of the 13th international ACM SIGACCESS conference on Computers and accessibility. ACM,* (pp. 107-114).

Laine, S., Karras, T., Aila, T., Herva, A., Saito, S., Yu, R., & Lehtinen, J. (2017). Production-level facial performance capture using deep convolutional neural networks. *In Proceedings of the ACM SIGGRAPH/Eurographics symposium on computer animation* (pp. 1-10).

Le, B. H., Zhu, M., & Deng, Z. (2013). Marker optimization for facial motion acquisition and deformation. *IEEE transactions on visualization and computer graphics, 19(11),* 1859-1871.

McDonald, J., Wolfe, R., Johnson, R. (2022). A novel approach to managing lower face complexity in signing avatars (submitted). *Seventh Sign Language Translation and Avatar Technology Workshop, Language resources and Evaluation Conference.* Marseilles: ELRA

Osipa, J. (2010). *Stop staring: facial modeling and animation done right.* John Wiley & Sons.

Pandzic, I. S., & Forchheimer, R. (Eds.). (2003). *MPEG4 facial animation: the standard, implementation and applications.* John Wiley & Sons.

Papadogiorgaki, M., Grammalidis, N., Sarris, N., & Strintzis, M. G. (2004, May). Synthesis of virtual reality animations from SWML using MPEG-4 body animation parameters. In *Workshop on the Representation and Processing of Sign Languages, 4th International Conference on Language Resources and Evaluation LREC 2004.*

Reverdy, C., Gibet, S., & Larboulette, C. (2015). Optimal marker set for motion capture of dynamical facial expressions. *In Proceedings of the 8th ACM SIGGRAPH Conference on Motion in Games* (pp. 31-36).

Seymour, M. (2019). FACS at 40: facial action coding system panel. In *ACM SIGGRAPH 2019 Panels* (pp. 1-2).

Thomas, F., Johnston, O., & Thomas, F. (1995). *The illusion of life: Disney animation* (p. 28). New York: Hyperion.

Verlinden, M., Tijsseling, C., & Frowein, H. (2001). A Signing Avatar on the WWW. *International Gesture Workshop,* (pp. 169-172).

Vougioukas, K., Petridis, S., & Pantic, M. (2019). End-to-End Speech-Driven Realistic Facial Animation with Temporal GANs. *CVPR Workshops* (pp. 37-40).

Will, A. D., De Martino, J. M., & Bezerra, J. (2018). An Optimized Marker Layout for 3D Facial Motion Capture. *In STAG* (pp. 107-113).

Wolfe, R., Hanke, T., Langer, G., Jahn, E., worsek, S., Bleicken, J., …, Johnson, R. (2018). Exploring Localication for Muothings in Sign Language Avatars. *Language Resources and Evaluation Converence* (pp. 207-212). Miyazaki, Japan: European Language Resurces Association (ELRA).

Proceedings of the 7th International Workshop on Sign Language Translation and Avatar Technology (SLTAT 7), pages 59–66
Language Resources and Evaluation Conference (LREC 2022), Marseille, 20-25 June 2022

KoSign Sign Language Translation Project: Introducing The NIASL2021 Dataset

Mathew Huerta-Enochian[1] Du Hui Lee[1] Hye Jin Myung[2]
Kang Suk Byun[2] Jun Woo Lee[2]
[1]EQ4ALL
11, Nonhyeon-ro 76-gil, Gangnam-gu, Seoul. Republic of Korea.
{mathew, scottlee}@eq4all.co.kr
[2]Kangnam University
40, Gangnam-ro, Giheung-gu, Yongin-si, Gyeonggi-do. Republic of Korea.
{acq57rep, byunkang-suk, knudeaf}@kangnam.ac.kr

Abstract

We introduce a new sign language production (SLP) and sign language translation (SLT) dataset, NIASL2021, consisting of 201,026 Korean-KSL data pairs. KSL translations of Korean source texts are represented in three formats: video recordings, keypoint position data, and time-aligned gloss annotations for each hand (using a 7,989 sign vocabulary) and for eight different non-manual signals (NMS). We evaluated our sign language elicitation methodology and found that text-based prompting had a negative effect on translation quality in terms of naturalness and comprehension. We recommend distilling text into a visual medium before translating into sign language or adding a prompt-blind review step to text-based translation methodologies.

1. Introduction

In this paper, we introduce a new Korean and Korean Sign Language (KSL) translation dataset, NIASL2021, containing 201,026 paired Korean-KSL samples from the emergency alert message and weather broadcast domains. NIASL2021 was created to support KoSign, a sign language translation (SLT) and sign language production (SLP) development project, and can thus be used for SLT and SLP and serve as a reference for avatar development. We also present a critical evaluation of the translation methodology used in NIASL2021 to inform future collection methodologies. Our contributions are:

- Introduction of the complete NIASL2021 dataset
- Quantitative evaluation of the translation methodology used in NIASL2021, which revealed that text-free prompting produced better translations than text-based prompting.

In section 2 we briefly review relevant research and development projects before introducing the new translation dataset in section 3. We then present a quantitative evaluation of our translation methodology in section 4 and present our conclusions in section 5.

2. Background

The primary language for many Deaf and hard of hearing (DHH) individuals is their region's sign language. While hearing people can easily access a wide variety of news sources, DHH signers are usually limited to a handful of deaf news services or must consume media through text. Though using an interpreting service is reasonable for large events and critical news broadcasts, it is usually impractical to do so for daily news, weather reports or non-critical alert messages. We suggest that an automatic sign language translation engine targeting this domain would be highly impactful to DHH signers as a supplement to existing interpreting services, underscoring the need for new emergency-situation translation datasets.

2.1. Translation Data Collection

Translation datasets are multilingual datasets with a semantic alignment between each language. A common trend in collection methodologies for monolingual datasets is to prompt for expressions in the informants native language or in a neutral medium (like images) to reduce the influence of a foreign language as is mentioned in (Filhol and Hadjadj, 2018), (Nishio et al., 2010), and (Hong et al., 2009). However, for translation datasets, a non-native language prompt is usually used to create translations. Even when employing professional translators, an increase in so-called translationese is unavoidable. See (Koppel and Ordan, 2011) for a discussion. If the training data is intended to be non-directional, a common method to reduce translationese imbalance is to collect an equal proportion of source data from each language as in (Bojar et al., 2018), where 50% of language A is translated into language B and 50% of language B is translated into language A for every language pair A and B in the dataset. Source language texts are usually collected from existing material.

Since sign languages are extremely low-resource, existing sign language source material for a given translation topic will be insufficient. Therefore, the above 50-50 solution must be abandoned or data must be manually generated from structured, semi-structured, or unstructured interviews for sign language datasets. Unstructured interviews will yield inconsistent content while structured interviews that allow fine control over content will be subject to unwanted language influence and translationese. We are not aware of any accepted solution to this problem, and most projects assume that using professional interpreters will minimize the severity of translationese.

The two most common benchmark translation datasets for sign languages are RWTH-PHOENIX-Weather 2014T from (Camgoz et al., 2018) and How2Sign (Duarte et al., 2020). RWTH-PHOENIX-Weather 2014T contains German and German Sign Language (DGS) translation pairs from weather broadcasts while How2Sign contains English and American Sign Language (ASL) translation pairs from a variety of domains. Both feature text, sign video translations, and single-channel gloss annotations. Recently, (Camgöz et al., 2021) introduced several news and weather broadcast sign language datasets with an order of magnitude more data than in RWTH-PHOENIX-Weather 2014T.

Sign language datasets use the terms sign, type, and gloss to encode and explain a signed passage. We refer to (Johnston and Schembri, 1999)'s definition of a sign: signs are "a relatively stable, identifiable visual-gestural act with an associated meaning which is reproduced with consistency by native signers and for which, consequently, particular agreed values can be given for hand shape, orientation, location, and movement." Types are a fixed naming system for signs, and each type is distinct in appearance or in meaning. We refer to (Konrad et al., 2020) for further discussion of types. Finally, glosses are the text representations or annotations of a sign.

2.2. Sign Language Production

Though there is some overlap in the usage of "sign language translation" (SLT) and "sign language production" (SLP), literature is becoming clearer in using SLT to refer to translating sign into text or speech (a natural extension of sign language recognition) and SLP to refer to translating text or speech into sign language. However, SLP also covers topics of avatar generation and how to digitally express signing.

2.3. The KoSign Project

KoSign is an ongoing SLT and SLP engine development project that started in 2021 and is funded by the Korean Ministry of Trade, Industry, and Energy.[1] The project is a collaboration between five domestic member organizations: EQ4ALL, KETI, KAIST, TestWorks, and the Korean Association of the Deaf. To support continued development, we secured additional funding for a large-scale Korean-KSL translation data collection project (see section 3) and are continuing to acquire funding for other projects in support of KoSign. The scope of this project is two-fold:

- Research machine-learning-based SLT and SLP (including relevant avatar technologies)
- Develop a usable, bi-directional Korean-KSL translation engine

We are leading the project and conducting SLP research and development. We utilize transformer-like models to predict type tokens and sign timing data, decoding into a multi-channel signing space. We are conducting human evaluations for our models and will release our results in the future.

A brief overview of our avatar player was provided in (Kim et al., 2022). We divide our avatar into five channels: left hand, right hand, body, lower face, and upper face. We then use inverse kinematics (IK) and animation composition to model each channel and combine them into one animation. This method is a simple way to expand a limited number of animations into a large set of complex animations.

2.4. Other Sign Language Production Projects

There are a number of ongoing projects of similar size and scope to KoSign. (EASIER, Accessed 2022 04 04) and (SignON, Accessed 2022 04 04) are two projects funded by the EU's Horizon 2020 research program. Both projects aim to create models for automatic translation between sign languages and spoken/written languages. Both projects target multiple European sign and spoken languages. (AVASAG, Accessed 2022 04 04) (Avatar-basierter Sprachassistent zur automatisierten Gebärdenübersetzung) on the other hand is a research project focusing on developing a real-time controlled avatar for translating German texts into sign language.

3. NIASL2021

We[2] introduce NIASL2021,[3] a new Korean-KSL translation dataset, collected over the domains of Korean government emergency alert messages and weather broadcasts. Collection was a multi-organization effort and native signers were intimately involved in the process.

NIASL2021 contains 201,026 unique data samples (segmented at the Korean sentence and multi-sentence level) and can be used to train both SLT and SLP (gloss-, pose-, or video-generating) models. KSL translations use 7,989 unique types, and all samples feature a single signer only. Data samples are organized into one of forty-three categories: weather and forty-two emergency alert categories. There are many similar categories, and since multiple disaster events often co-occur, there is significant overlap between categories.

[1] 산업통상자원부 in Korean.

[2] In this section, we use "we" to refer to our work and the passive voice for work conducted by other parties.

[3] The project was funded by the Korean National Information Society Agency (NIA). The dataset will be released in late 2022, accessible through https://aihub.or.kr/; we will host an in-depth user guide at https://eq4all-data.github.io from the fourth quarter of 2022.

For example, the landslide and flooding categories have overlap with heavy rain and typhoon categories.

Each sample in the dataset has five components: metadata about the sample, Korean text, a KSL video translation of the text, gloss annotations, and automatically-extracted keypoint estimations. For simplicity, we bundle the metadata, Korean text, gloss annotations, and keypoint data together in a JSON file so that each sample can be expressed with only a video file and a human-readable data file.

Since there is an abundance of emergency alert and weather broadcasts available in Korean and none originally in KSL, KSL videos in every sample are translated from the associated Korean text. As discussed in 2.1, this may introduce undesired translationese in the KSL samples, but we took as many steps as possible to reduce this risk.

Note that a subset of NIASL2021 was used in (Kim et al., 2022).

3.1. Korean Text Data

Korean text was initially scraped from government alert and news websites to create a raw Korean text dataset. This dataset had extreme class imbalance. Categories related to recent issues like Covid-19 had many samples, but other categories like terrorism had few or none. Additional samples were manually created based on government text outlines for categories with too few samples.

This raw text dataset was split into two subsets, one subset set aside for the final dataset and one subset used to train a series of GPT2-like natural language generation models for offline-augmentation as in (Kumar et al., 2020). Using these models, each category was oversampled (except for weather broadcasts and the infectious diseases alert categories, which already had a sufficient number of samples). Generated sequences were then reviewed based on grammar and similarity with training samples to ensure that synthetic data was in distribution. Synthetic samples were then combined with the unused text subset to create the final set of Korean text. Note that sample metadata indicates if it is a synthetic or original sample.

3.2. KSL Video and Annotation Data

Based on feedback from KSL experts, we allowed multiple translations to be made for each Korean source text. For each source, KSL experts determined how many sign language translations should be prepared, ranging from one to three translations. Researchers should be aware of this detail when using the dataset as over one-fourth of the data is made up of one-to-many translations. If needed, researchers can reduce the dataset to a 148,984 sample subset of one-to-one translations.

3.2.1. Translation and Video Capture

After translation duplicity was determined for a source text, we would assign the text to a translator and an evaluator three days before a scheduled translation filming date. We instructed translators and evaluators to research each sample and prepare for translation and evaluation, respectivley, during this three-day period. On the day of filming, evaluators would review the prepared translations. Translations that required little or no correction could be filmed, and translations judged as insufficient were corrected right away or returned to the translator for improvement. Based on initial discussion with KSL experts, we felt that this method should be effective for producing high-quality translations.

Translations were filmed either in a studio with two or five cameras or were crowd-sourced and filmed with phone cameras or web cams. Of the 201,026 samples in the dataset, 127,624 (63.49%) samples were created in-studio and 73,402 (36.51%) were crowd-sourced. The multi-camera setups captured one frontal view of the signer and one or four 45° angled view(s) of the signer (45° views were offset from above, down, left, and right for the five-camera setup and left for the two-camera setup).

All translators and evaluators were native signers and had previous experience translating Korean into KSL. Official translation videos may feature the translator or may be filmed with a different signer who re-signed the prepared translation exactly. Translator, evaluator, and signer IDs were all collected in sample metadata.

Though all signers and evaluators were native signers, we received feedback from participants that the crowd-sourced videos may be of a lower quality than in-studio translations. This is to be expected from crowd sourcing but also indicates the need for more strict review of crowd-sourced translations in the future.

3.2.2. Annotation

Filmed translations were annotated by hand with 90-95% of samples annotated by deaf participants and the remaining 5-10% by hearing signers. Additionally, our type system was created and managed by deaf participants.

A single-channel gloss list would not sufficiently preserve the meaning of the KSL translations in this domain. For example, one common translation pattern was a disaster event like a fire that would be expressed with one hand while the other hand explained what to do about the event (take a detour, go the opposite way, etc.). After consulting with KSL experts, we decided to annotate the dominant hand[4] and non-dominant hand separately, as well as eight types of non-manual signals (NMS): puffed cheeks (denoted Ci), head shake (Hs), eye brow furrow (EBf), head nod (Hno), mouthings (Mmo), rounded lips (Mo1), tongue out (Tbt), and smile (Mctr). We refer to these ten different annotation types as tiers. All annotations are time aligned to the corresponding translation video.

Following the convention from (Kita et al., 1997), hand signs can be segmented into four movements: prepara-

[4]All recorded signers self reported as right-handed.

tion, stroke, hold, and retraction. The movement most associated with a sign is the stroke. Preparation and retraction are more akin to inter-sign movements and hold is an optional movement where the articulator is held in the sign or gesture's final position. We instructed annotators to align annotations with the start of the stroke and the end of the hold.

Each annotation in the sign tiers was from one of four categories: type, dynamic number (signs combining number hand shapes with gestures to express certain quantities, such as dates, times, durations, and ages), fingerspelling (FS), and number. We annotated FS and numbers separately since a series of digits and a multi-digit number need to be expressed differently (for example, 555 can be either "five five five" or "five hundred and fifty five"), and annotating groups of FS numbers together significantly eased the annotation burden given the frequent phone numbers, addresses, and quantity expressions in the dataset.

Though existing annotation tools like ELAN (Wittenburg et al., 2006) are well-developed, we designed our own webtool to have more control over the annotation interface and for better integration into our online data pipeline. This allowed us to create a separate annotation insertion menu for each of the annotation categories, streamlining the user interface.

In addition to the manual gloss annotations, pose data was automatically extracted from each KSL video using OpenPose. For videos filmed from more than one angle (the in-studio five-camera and two-camera videos), OpenPose-generated 2D keypoints from two separate camera angles were used to calculate 3D keypoints for each frame using MATLAB. Since crowd-sourced videos only have a single view, they contain 2D keypoint data.

3.3. Challenges

3.3.1. Signing Dates

In KSL, the day of the month cannot be signed without also signing the month. For example, "the 11th" cannot be signed by itself in KSL, but "the 11th of January" can be signed. However, it is common to express only the day of the month in Korean, especially in emergency alert messages and weather broadcasts since these sources are not intended to be relevant outside of a small temporal window. To create realistic training data, we included samples with this pattern and instructed translators to denote the month using the zero value hand shape when translating. We also added a flag in sample metadata so researchers can choose to remove these data points or find some other work around.

3.3.2. Translating Unclear Context

One of the biggest hurdles was translating low-context and unclear phrases into KSL. There were two root causes for this ambiguity: differing context requirements between Korean and KSL and poor Korean source text segmentation.

The first problem refers to when something in Korean can be expressed with ambiguity, but any translation to KSL (as with most sign languages) is highly context-dependent.

Since recording long sequences increases the need for multiple takes and increases signer fatigue, source text was intentionally segmented into short sequences. Additionally, most of the synthetic text data (see section 3.1) was generated at the sentence level. This led to the second problem mentioned above. Many such cases were removed, but we allowed some to be translated since it was not always clear what samples reflected real-world data (because of the first problem above) and what samples were vague due to processing error.

For future projects, we recommend segmenting at a higher level or assigning consecutive samples to the same translator.

3.3.3. Annotating Productive Signs

Following (Johnston and Schembri, 1999), we differentiate between two classes of signs in NIASL2021: established and productive signs. Established signs are simply signs collectively known to users of a sign language. Productive signs are created through a novel combination of sign building-blocks (known as phonomorphemes) or the selective modification of one or more established signs or phonomorphemes. These are new or modified signs spontaneously expressed based on the signing context.

We annotated productive signs by labeling them with the most similar type (referred to as its "parent type") and adding up to three special symbols and an optional string identifier. We added a "#" character to the end of every productive sign annotation, and optionally added a short explanatory string after the "#" character. If the sign terminated prematurely, we added a "@" character after the "#" and optional string. Finally, when the hand shape varied from the hand shape of the parent type, we added a "&" character to the beginning of the annotation.

For example, if the signer indicates that a car turns left using a productive sign derived from the parent type "car1", then we might annotate the type as "car1#turnleft". If the hand is shaped a little tighter to indicate that the car is small, it will be annotated as "&car1#turnleft". Finally, if the signer indicates that the car starts to turn left but stops the sign abruptly (perhaps to indicate that left turns are not allowed), the annotation would be "car1#turnleft@". Note that actual types are in Korean.

4. Translation Methodology Evaluation

Anecdotally, we noticed that some of the KSL translations were unclear without checking the Korean source. Based on qualitative review, we tentatively identified two reasons for low quality signing: unclear Korean source passages (see section 3.3) and spoken language influence on translations (see section 2.1). We can mitigate source ambiguity by aligning longer segments, but

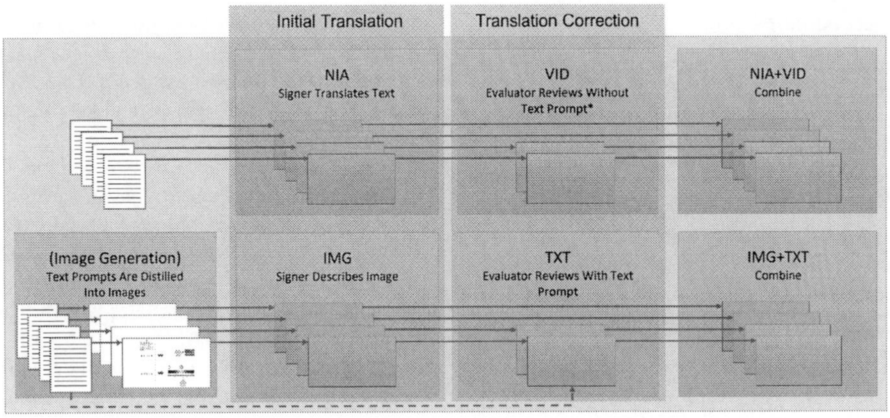

Figure 1: Overview of evaluation video generation. Best viewed in color.
*Source text is made available after initial review.

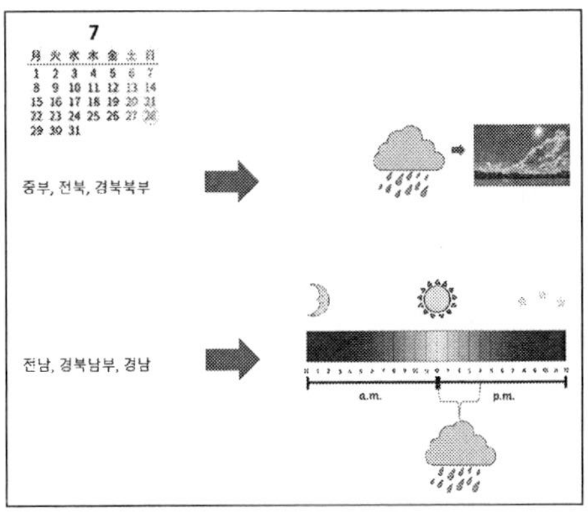

Figure 2: Example of an image prompt created from part of a weather report. Only location names and morning/evening abbreviations are expressed as text.

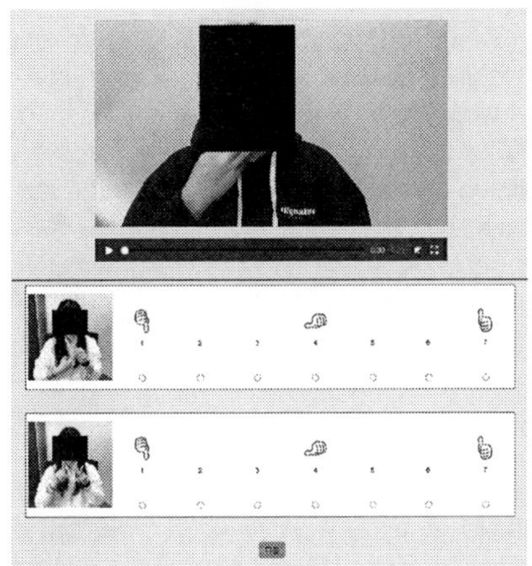

Figure 3: An example from our evaluation web tool.

avoiding spoken language influence will require a new translation methodology.

To evaluate translation quality and to explore the influence of spoken language in prompted sign language translation, we designed two new translation methodologies: NIA+VID and IMG+TXT. Both are two step methodologies with an initial translation (what we call NIA and IMG video translations, respectively) and a translation correction (VID and TXT corrected translations, respectively). Thus, NIA+VID and IMG+TXT videos refer to corrected videos and any initial translations that are not corrected.

NIA+VID uses the NIASL2021 translation methodology as the initial translation (for convenience, we use translations from the dataset) and an initially prompt-blind evaluation step. For IMG+TXT, prompts are first converted into image representations. Signers then describe the image as the initial translation. The signer is then shown the original prompt and given the option to update their initial translations. See figure 1 for a visual overview of the two methodologies.

We further define signing quality as the aggregate of signing naturalness and comprehensibility, evaluated on a likert scale, and make the following hypotheses:

H_1: TXT < IMG Text-aware correction decreases the signing quality.

H_2: NIA < VID Text-unaware correction increases the signing quality.

H_3: NIA < IMG Image-prompted translations are of a higher quality than text-prompted translations.

H_4: NIA+VID < IMG+TXT Image-prompted translations are of a higher quality than text-prompted translations, even with corrections.

Finally, it is important that we validate the adequacy of all sign videos with respect to the source texts as there are likely trade offs in adequacy, naturalness, and comprehensibility.

4.1. Methodology

We sampled fifty source sentences from NIASL2021 and worked with four native signers to generate video translations for each sample following the two procedures outlined above. The four signers do professional work related to sign language.

To measure the effects of prompting, it was important that no signer translated the same source text for both NIA+VID and IMG+TXT, so we used a round-robin assignment method.

In total, signers created 148 videos: 50 NIA videos, 9 VID videos, 50 IMG videos, and 29 TXT videos. We then had two native signers review the videos to find cases where video quality or lack of signer preparation may interfere with evaluations. These videos were re-signed exactly (including hand signs and NMS) according to the original video but with a more stable camera and with the signer having practiced before filming.

We then arranged for nine native signers to evaluate the videos. Three of the evaluators work professionally in sign language translation and annotation with us, one is involved in sign language research, and five work in fields unrelated to sign language. Similar with the translation procedure assignment above, it was crucial that evaluators not review multiple videos corresponding to the same source sentence since this could affect comprehensibility. We used the latin-square method to balance evaluator assignments and guarantee that each video was reviewed at least two times.

We required evaluators to watch an introductory video of a native signer explaining the goal of the research, the importance of honest feedback, and how to interpret the likert items. We also worked with our sign language team to design an online evaluation tool for deaf users. To encourage evaluations without influence from written or spoken language, we removed as much text from the evaluation interface as possible. We replaced the standard likert text prompts with video prompts that play when activated by the mouse cursor. Using text was reported as too confusing and hard to look at, and using continuous video prompts was reported as being too distracting. The likert scale was also based on significant user feedback. Rather than text labels, we used three symbols to augment number labels: a thumbs down over 1, a horizontal thumb over 4, and a thumbs up over 7. The naturalness and comprehensibility prompts translate as "the signing in this video is natural" and "the signing in this video is understandable", respectively. The scale values range from 1 for strongly disagree to 7 for strongly agree. The evaluation interface can be seen in figure 3.

After videos were evaluated, we became aware of a possible quality difference between crowd-sourced translations and in-house translations (see section 3.2.1). To avoid introducing bias into our analysis, we removed samples that used crowd-sourced translations from NIA and VID. This removed a total of nine videos and twenty-seven evaluations from our analysis.

We also arranged for two professional interpreters to evaluate all 148 videos in terms of adequacy with the source texts (i.e., source-based direct assessment). This evaluation used two two-point likert items and one four-point likert item for each video. The first prompt translates to English as "Compared to the Korean, the KSL translation has added content" with a true/false response. The second prompt translates similarly as "Compared to the Korean, the KSL translation has missing content" with identical response values. Finally, the third prompt translates as "The main points of the Korean and the KSL translation are..." with a response of 1 for the same, 2 for slightly different but acceptable, 3 for different and unacceptable, and 4 for very different and unacceptable.

4.2. Results

We collected a total of 304 likert scale evaluations for naturalness and comprehensibility. Raw likert results are summarized in table 1.

We calculated Cronbach's alpha for the two likert items to be 0.889. According to (Nunnally, 1994)'s interpretation for applied research, this is a sufficient level of reliability between the two indicators, and we combined the scores into one aggregate quality score. For hypothesis testing, we applied ordinal logistic modeling with mixed effects to measure the effect of video type on signing quality. For tests between IMG and TXT and between NIA and VID, we limit IMG and NIA to videos matching TXT and VID, respectively. We also present quality z-scores normalized over evaluators in table 2 to build intuition.

Treating video type as a fixed effect and evaluator and source sentence as random effects produced the best fitting model for all four tests. We used Holm-Bonferroni correction for multiple hypothesis testing to recalculate p value thresholds. Models were implemented using the "ordinal" R package, and we used likelihood ratio tests to calculate p values as per (Christensen, 2019).

For H_1, we restricted analysis to IMG (encoded as 0) and TXT (encoded as 1) videos. For H_2, we restricted analysis to NIA (encoded as 0) and VID (encoded as 1) videos. For H_3, we restricted analysis to NIA (encoded as 0) and IMG (encoded as 1) videos. For H_4, we used the combined video sets NIA+VID (encoded as 0) and IMG+TXT (encoded as 1). See table 3 for results.

Regarding adequacy scores, IMG+TXT videos scored higher than NIA+VID on average, but no statistically significant differences could be found, and the estimated effect size (based on Cliff's Delta) is below the minimal small threshold according to both (Vargha and Delaney, 2000) and (Romano et al., 2006).

4.3. Discussion

The mode of scores for all translation videos is six or seven for both likert items. By subdividing our scale into disagreement (responses 1, 2, or 3), neutral (response 4), and agreement (responses 5, 6, and 7), we found that, for naturalness, NIA videos had a 66.33%

Video	Total	1	2	3	4	5	6	7	5+6+7
NIA	101	5.94%	2.97%	6.93%	17.82%	18.81%	**26.73%**	20.79%	66.33%
VID	12	8.33%	0.00%	0.00%	8.33%	25.00%	**33.33%**	25.00%	83.33%
IMG	127	0.00%	3.15%	6.30%	12.60%	19.69%	25.98%	**32.28%**	77.95%
TXT	64	4.69%	1.56%	9.38%	15.63%	18.75%	**29.69%**	20.31%	68.75%
NIA+VID	101	6.93%	1.98%	2.97%	17.82%	20.79%	**26.73%**	22.77%	73.29%
IMG+TXT	133	2.26%	3.01%	9.02%	10.53%	20.30%	**27.82%**	27.07%	75.19%
NIA	101	1.98%	6.93%	5.94%	13.86%	22.77%	23.76%	**24.75%**	71.28
VID	12	0.00%	0.00%	0.00%	16.66%	25.00%	**33.33%**	25.00%	83.33
IMG	127	0.79%	0.00%	8.66%	11.81%	15.75%	23.62%	**39.37%**	78.74
TXT	64	1.56%	6.25%	10.94%	7.81%	12.50%	**32.81%**	28.13%	73.44
NIA+VID	101	1.98%	5.94%	4.95%	12.87%	23.76%	23.76%	**26.73%**	74.25
IMG+TXT	133	1.50%	3.01%	9.02%	10.53%	14.29%	27.82%	**33.08%**	75.19

Table 1: *Top*: Naturalness likert results. *Bottom*: Comprehension likert results. VID and TXT are included for reference, but NIA+VID and IMG+TXT are more informative for comparison. Mode response values are in bold.

Type	Total	mean	std
NIA	101	-0.3051	1.1148
IMG	127	**0.2432**	0.8292
NIA (matched)	12	-0.5439	1.5002
VID (matched)	12	**0.2450**	0.8091
IMG (matched)	64	**0.1923**	0.7584
TXT (matched)	64	-0.0471	1.0399
NIA+VID	101	-0.2114	1.0430
IMG+TXT	133	**0.1257**	0.9746

Table 2: Signing quality z scores (calculated over evaluator). For comparison, scores are grouped by translation step, and high scores are presented in **bold**.

rate of agreement while VID and IMG (both created from text-free prompts) had an agreement rate of over 75%. Furthermore, NIA agreement for naturalness increased to over 73% after text-free correction was introduced (NIA+VID). On the other hand, IMG agreement dropped slightly to 75.19% when the text-aware correction was introduced (IMG+TXT). While agreement for comprehensibility scores follows the same trend, it did not vary as drastically.

Based on the above and on user-normalized z-scores for the aggregate signing quality score, all of our hypotheses seem to be supported. However, statistical tests revealed that we can reject the null hypotheses only for H_3 and H_4 and not for H_1 or H_2.

Given that there was no loss in adequacy, it is clear that text-free prompting produced better translations then text-based prompting (H_3: NIA $<$ IMG), and the IMG+TXT procedure produced better translations than those from the NIA+VID procedure (H_4: NIA+VID $<$ IMG+TXT). Both produced better translations on average than NIA translations.

5. Conclusion

We introduced NIASL2021, providing an overview of the dataset, the collection methodology, and challenges. We then provided an evaluation of the translation methodology used for NIASL2021. We found that text-free prompting produced better translations than text-based prompting. We recommend the following for future data collection projects:

1. Prompting from visual media. Text-to-image distillation can be used for small projects or when a standardized rubric can be developed.

2. (If text-based prompts are used) introducing an evaluation step where the evaluator does not have access to the source text.

6. Acknowledgements

This work was supported by the Bio Industry Core Technology Development Project funded by the Korean Ministry of Trade, Industry, and Energy (MOTIE, Korea) [Grant Number: 20014406], supported by the Data Construction Business for AI funded by the National Information Society Agency (NIA, Korea) [Grant Number: 69], and supported by the Citizen-Customized Life Safety Technology Development Program funded by the Ministry of the Interior and Safety (MOIS, Korea) [Grant Number: 2021-MOIS61-003].

7. Bibliographical References

AVASAG. (Accessed: 2022-04-04). Avatar-basierter sprachassistent zur automatisierten gebärdenübersetzung. *https://www.avasag.de/* by AVASAG 2022.

Bojar, O., Federmann, C., Fishel, M., Graham, Y., Haddow, B., Koehn, P., and Monz, C. (2018). Findings of the 2018 conference on machine translation (WMT18). In *Proceedings of the Third Conference on Machine Translation: Shared Task Papers*, pages

H_i	Coeff	p-value	Threshold	Cliff's Delta*	Reject NH†
H_1	-0.400	$= 0.259$	0.05	0.1474 (small)	No
H_2	1.528	$= 0.0854$	0.025	0.4000 (medium)	No
H_3	0.986	$= 0.0001$	0.0125	0.1885 (small)	Yes
H_4	0.6445	$= 0.0105$	0.0167	0.0830 ($<$ small)	Yes

Table 3: Regression results.

*Interpretation based on (Romano et al., 2006). †If the null hypothesis is rejected, we conclude that H_i is correct.

272–303, Belgium, Brussels, October. Association for Computational Linguistics.

Camgoz, N. C., Hadfield, S., Koller, O., Ney, H., and Bowden, R. (2018). Neural sign language translation. In *Proceedings of the IEEE Conference on Computer Vision and Pattern Recognition (CVPR)*, June.

Camgöz, N. C., Saunders, B., Rochette, G., Giovanelli, M., Inches, G., Nachtrab-Ribback, R., and Bowden, R. (2021). Content4all open research sign language translation datasets. In *2021 16th IEEE International Conference on Automatic Face and Gesture Recognition (FG 2021)*, pages 1–5. IEEE.

Christensen, R. H. B. (2019). A tutorial on fitting cumulative link mixed models with clmm2 from the ordinal package. *Tutorial for the R Package ordinal https://cran.r-project.org/web/packages/ordinal*, 1.

Duarte, A. C., Palaskar, S., Ghadiyaram, D., DeHaan, K., Metze, F., Torres, J., and Giró-i-Nieto, X. (2020). How2sign: A large-scale multimodal dataset for continuous american sign language. *CoRR*, abs/2008.08143.

EASIER. (Accessed: 2022-04-04). Intelligent automatic sign language translation. *https://www.project-easier.eu/* by EASIER PROJECT 2021-2023.

Filhol, M. and Hadjadj, M. N. (2018). Elicitation protocol and material for a corpus of long prepared monologues in sign language. In *Proceedings of the Eleventh International Conference on Language Resources and Evaluation (LREC 2018)*, Miyazaki, Japan, May. European Language Resources Association (ELRA).

Hong, S.-E., Hanke, T., König, S., Konrad, R., Langer, G., and Rathmann, C. (2009). Elicitation materials and their use in sign language linguistics. In *Poster presented at the Workshop "Sign Language Corpora: Linguistic Issues" in London*.

Johnston, T. and Schembri, A. C. (1999). On defining lexeme in a signed language. *Sign language & linguistics*, 2(2):115–185.

Kim, J.-H., Hwang, E. J., Cho, S., Lee, D. H., and Park, J. C. (2022). Sign language production with avatar layering: A critical use case over rare words. In *Language Resources and Evaluation Conference*.

Kita, S., Gijn, I. v., and Hulst, H. v. d. (1997). Movement phases in signs and co-speech gestures, and their transcription by human coders. In *International Gesture Workshop*, pages 23–35. Springer.

Konrad, R., Hanke, T., Langer, G., König, S., König, L., Nishio, R., and Regen, A. (2020). Öffentliches DGS-Korpus: Annotationskonventionen / Public DGS Corpus: Annotation conventions. Project Note AP03-2018-01, DGS-Korpus project, IDGS, Universität Hamburg, Hamburg, Germany.

Koppel, M. and Ordan, N. (2011). Translationese and its dialects. In *Proceedings of the 49th Annual Meeting of the Association for Computational Linguistics: Human Language Technologies - Volume 1*, HLT '11, page 1318–1326, USA. Association for Computational Linguistics.

Kumar, V., Choudhary, A., and Cho, E. (2020). Data augmentation using pre-trained transformer models. *arXiv preprint arXiv:2003.02245*.

Nishio, R., Hong, S.-E., König, S., Konrad, R., Langer, G., Hanke, T., and Rathmann, C. (2010). Elicitation methods in the dgs (german sign language) corpus project. In *sign-lang@ LREC 2010*, pages 178–185. European Language Resources Association (ELRA).

Nunnally, J. C. (1994). *Psychometric theory 3E*. Tata McGraw-hill education.

Romano, J., Kromrey, J. D., Coraggio, J., Skowronek, J., and Devine, L. (2006). Exploring methods for evaluating group differences on the nsse and other surveys: Are the t-test and cohen'sd indices the most appropriate choices. In *annual meeting of the Southern Association for Institutional Research*, pages 1–51. Citeseer.

SignON. (Accessed: 2022-04-04). Sign language translation mobile application and open communications framework. *https://signon-project.eu/* by SignON PROJECT 2021-2023.

Vargha, A. and Delaney, H. D. (2000). A critique and improvement of the cl common language effect size statistics of mcgraw and wong. *Journal of Educational and Behavioral Statistics*, 25(2):101–132.

Wittenburg, P., Brugman, H., Russel, A., Klassmann, A., and Sloetjes, H. (2006). ELAN: a professional framework for multimodality research. In Nicoletta Calzolari, et al., editors, *5th International Conference on Language Resources and Evaluation (LREC 2006)*, pages 1556–1559, Genoa, Italy, May. European Language Resources Association (ELRA).

Proceedings of the 7th International Workshop on Sign Language Translation and Avatar Technology (SLTAT 7), pages 67–72
Language Resources and Evaluation Conference (LREC 2022), Marseille, 20-25 June 2022

A Novel Approach to Managing Lower Face Complexity in Signing Avatars

John C. McDonald, Rosalee Wolfe, Ronan Johnson
DePaul University
Chicago, USA
jmcdonald@cs.depaul.edu, {rwolfe,sjohn165}@depaul.edu

Abstract

An avatar that produces legible, easy-to-understand signing is one of the essential components to an effective automatic signed/spoken translation system. Facial nonmanual signals are essential to natural signing, but unfortunately signing avatars still do not produce acceptable facial expressions, particularly on the lower face. This paper reports on an innovative method to create more realistic lip postures. The approach manages the complexity of creating lip postures, thus making fewer demands on the artists making them. The method will be integral to our efforts to develop libraries containing lip postures to support the generation of facial expressions for several sign languages.

Keywords: signing avatars, sign language representation, computer animation

1. Introduction

To improve deaf accessibility, multiple efforts have explored automatic translation from spoken to signed language. However, since signed languages have no widely accepted written form, any output from machine translation will necessarily require a display on a computer-generated human form. One of the most promising methods is a signing avatar, and while efforts to utilize avatars have been ongoing since the late 90's, the acceptability of signing avatars in the Deaf community has been lukewarm at best (Austrian Association of Applied Linguistics, 2019).

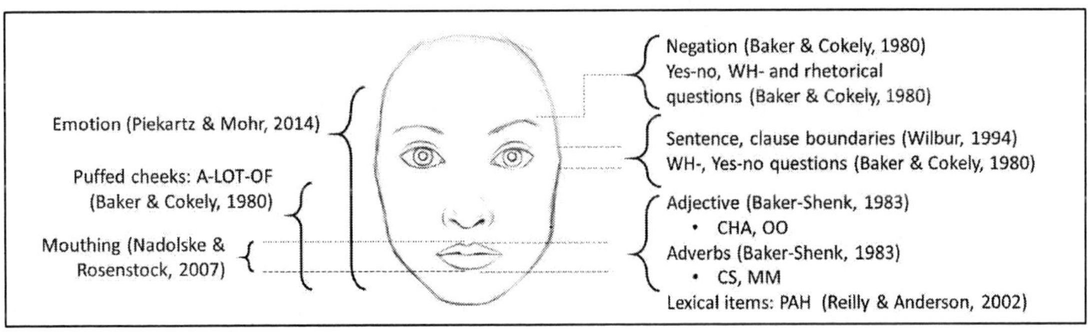

Figure 1: No linguistic or extralinguistic process has an exclusive franchise on a facial feature.

One of the primary criticisms from the Deaf community has been the lack of adequate motion on the face, including the lack of adequate mouthing (Verlinden, Tijsseling, & Frowein, 2001), (Kipp, Nguyen, Heloir, & Matthes, 2011), (Ebling, et al., 2015). This paper revisits the existing technologies for mouthing on human avatars and proposes a novel approach that is tuned to the unique requirements of sign language, allowing for greater expressivity, and imposing fewer demands on the artists creating signed discourse.

2. Background

The technology of applying mouthing to a signing avatar draws on the traditional lip sync process used in character animation (Parent, King, Fujimura, & Osamu, 2002). The process involves four steps:

1. Generate phonemes corresponding to a spoken word.
2. Map each phoneme to a viseme, which is the phoneme's visual appearance.
3. Retrieve facial poses (or settings) corresponding to each viseme from a library.
4. Apply facial poses to the avatar as animation keys.

A prerequisite to this process is the creation of a library of visemes. Creating a realistic set of facial postures to portray visemes is a difficult and time-consuming task that does not always yield satisfactory results (Brumm, Johnson, Hanke, Grigat, & Wolfe, 2019). This paper describes an innovative approach to viseme creation that manages the complexity of the process in an animator-friendly way. The approach is sufficiently general that it also supports the creation of postures for mouth gestures as well as for visemes.

There are two main approaches to creating visemes: using morph targets[1] and using muscle simulation. Morph targets have the advantage of simplicity (Alexa, 2002). To create a library of visemes, artists manually sculpt each viseme from

[1] Another term commonly used in the animation industry is "blend shapes".

a copy of the original model and can utilize their favorite sculpting tools. From a software development standpoint, morphing is straightforward to implement. However, the same simple implementation can create unanticipated effects. All changes in position in morphing follow a linear path, which is not compatible with human facial anatomy. Additionally, there is a deeper concern because in sign language, no one linguistic or extralinguistic process has an exclusive franchise over a facial feature and multiple processes can co-occur. With a morph implementation, multiple morphs will directly affect the same regions of the face simultaneously, but in an additive manner. The resulting effects are not natural-looking. Finally, from an implementation standpoint, morph representations require extensive in-memory storage. This is not necessarily a problem in desktop environments, but it can become a consideration on mobile devices.

3. Previous Work

Previous signing avatars have used both the morph-based (Jennings, Elliott, & Kennaway, 2010), (Kipp, Heloir, & Nguyen, 2011) and the muscle-based (Wolfe, et al., 2018) approaches, but feedback from deaf communities indicated that the mouth postures were not satisfactory. These avatars relied on the MPEG-4 H-Anim standard for manipulating the mouth (Ostermann, 2002). In the standard, there are 28 landmarks available to control lip postures. This was sufficient for early interactive agents to demonstrate the approach, but a rig capable of accurately portraying lip postures required more landmarks. Johnson (2018). developed a rig with 44 landmarks instead of 28. This facilitated smoother lip postures and made it possible to portray a wider variety of mouth postures than with the original H-Anim landmarks.

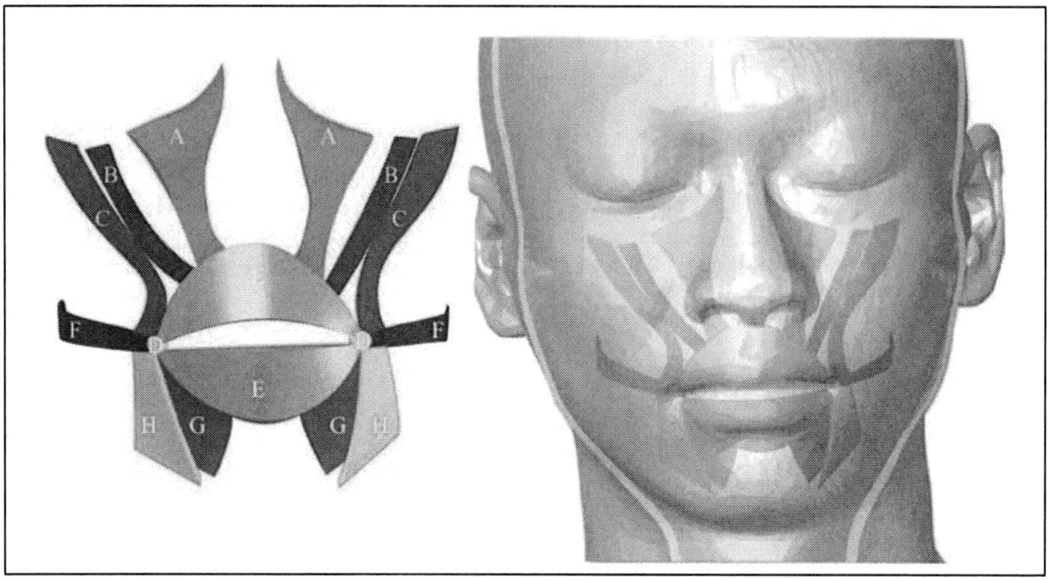

Figure 2: Selected muscles affecting lip shape, including levator labii superioris (A), zygomaticus minor (B), zygomaticus major (C), orbicularis oris (E), risorius (F), depressor labii inferioris (G) and depressor anguli oris (H) (Chen, et al., 2012).

The alternative to morph-based systems are muscle-based systems. Park and Waters (2008) examined facial structure beneath the skin and developed a parametric representation to simulate muscles. A muscle-based approach has the advantage of producing more natural results, as the underlying representation more closely mimics the muscle behavior in a human face. A distinct disadvantage of this approach is the increased burden placed on an artist using the system. A case in point is simulating the orbicularis oris to control lip shape.

The orbicularis oris is a complex multi-layered set of muscles that attach to the upper and lower lip. Researchers point out that, although anatomically it is a single muscle, from a functional viewpoint it actually consists of several components that either act independently or in concert with other facial muscles (Jain & Rathee, 2021). Figure 2 displays a simplified schematic of 10 of the 20 muscles attached to the orbicularis oris.

4. An Improved Approach

With the new capabilities for precision and a wider range of expressive possibilities came problems with usability. From an animator's perspective, the new rig was a step backwards. Instead of working with 28 landmarks to manipulate the face, the animator was confronted with the prospect of 44 landmarks to manipulate. In this state, the new workflow made it more difficult, not less difficult, to create believable mouth poses.

To counter this problem, Johnson began by organizing the facial muscles into groups, based on the perceived effect each group has on the face. He characterized the effect of various muscle groups on the lips, with the goal of making the lip posing process more manageable. Not surprisingly, the orbicularis oris is a member of each group. The other muscles in a group create localized changes to the geometry of the orbicularis oris. For a discussion of building the muscle representation, please see (Johnson, 2022).

The muscle groups are attached to controls in the user interface in DePaul's Expression Builder (Schnepp, Wolfe, McDonald, & Toro, 2013). Each control is simply a slider, and there is one slider for each muscle group. The first six groups listed in Table 1 appear in the Lips panel, as seen in Figure 3. (The second six groups appear in the Teeth panel of the interface.) Per Table 1 all the sliders involve the orbicularis oris. Most of the sliders also manipulate connecting muscles that in turn affect the orbicular oris. In all, an artist has access to twelve sliders to manipulate the lips. This compares quite favorably to the 28 H-Anim landmarks and certainly a better approach than requiring the manipulation of a set of 44 landmarks. Artists can use this system to create not only visemes suitable for mouthing, but also postures for mouth gestures.

	Effect	Cooperating muscle group	Layer
1	Lip Spread	left/right risorius, left/right buccinator, obicularis oris	1
2	Jaw Drop	left/right depressor labii inferioris, mentalis, orbicularis oris	2
3	Upper Lip Roll	obicularis oris	4
4	Lower Lip Roll	left/right mentalis, left/right depressor labii inferioris, obicularis oris	4
5	Left Lip Corner	left Zygomaticus major, left Depressor anguli oris, obicularis oris	3
6	Right Lip Corner	right Zygomaticus major, right Depressor anguli oris, obicularis oris	3
7	Show Upper Teeth	left/right zygomaticus minor, left/right levator labii superioris alaeque nasi, obicularis oris	5
8	Show Lower Teeth	left/right depressor labii inferioris, left/right mentalis, obicularis oris	5
9	Left Upper Snarl	left levator anguli oris, left levator labii superioris alaeque nasi, obicularis oris	6
10	Right Upper Snarl	right levator anguli oris, right levator labii superioris alaeque nasi, obicularis oris	6
11	Left Lower Snarl	left depressor labii inferioris, left depressor anguli oris, obicularis oris	6
12	Right Lower Snarl	right depressor labii inferioris, right depressor anguli oris, obicularis oris	6

Table 1: Muscle groups and their effect on the lips.

5. Implementing the approach

The last part of this approach involves developing the infrastructure required to manage the behavior of the 44 landmarks in response to the manipulation of the sliders. Consider a single slider "Lip Spread" from the interface. It controls the effects of the buccinator muscles, which compress the orbicularis oris and the risorius muscles which spread it. Moving the Lip Spread slider to the left activates the buccinator which puckers the lips. Moving the Lip Spread slider to the right activates the risorius which widens the mouth.

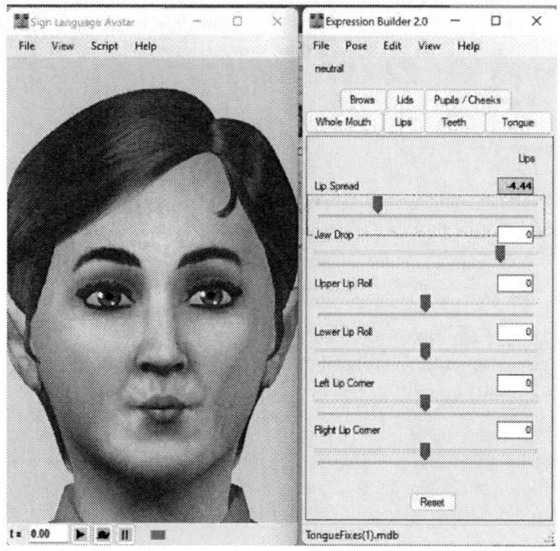

A negative Lip Spread compresses the lips.

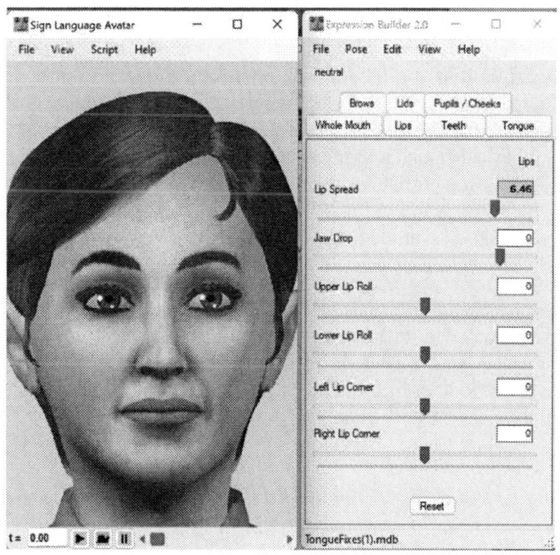

A positive Lip Spread widens the lips.

Figure 3: Artists use sliders in the interface to create facial postures

5.1 Basic algorithm

Now consider a single landmark of the 44 landmarks on the mouth. The landmark has three positions of interest – one when the lips are fully pursed, one when the lips are fully spread and one when the lips are in the neutral position.

These three points define a path. Instead of following a straight line from one extreme to neutral to the other extreme, as in a morphing approach, the transition path follows an arc which approximates the local contour of the head. This creates a natural-looking transition, with no awkward or unnatural intermediate positions.

A script within the landmark connects[2] the landmark's position to the user interface slider "Lip Spread". The slider value controls the landmark's position along its path. Each of the 44 landmarks has a customized script connected to the "Lip Spread" slider that controls its path movement. When an animator adjusts the slider, the landmarks all move in concert, see Figure 3. The same scalar from the slider controls the rotations for all the landmarks.

Thus, the slider value is the parameter for all of the landmark scripts. This requires creating a strict consistency in the slider values in the user interface. For each parameter, a value of zero corresponds to the neutral position on the landmark. For symmetric sliders, the range is always -10 to 10. For asymmetric sliders, the range is always 0 to 10. (The jaw drop slider is slightly different for historic reasons, but its neutral position is at zero.)

Adhering to this consistency results in shorter scripts, and quicker code development. Further, resetting the entire face to neutral is simply a matter of setting all of the values of the user interface sliders to zero.

We used the scripting capability of a commercial animation package to prototype the approach. Figure 4 gives the pseudocode script for a landmark controlled by the Lip Spread slider. The initial statement designates the user interface slider as the connecting parameter; the second line ensures that the incoming parameter absolute value is no more than 1. The if statement distinguishes between the spread (positive) and pucker (negative) cases. The slerp (spherical linear interpolation) function calculates the angle of rotation for the landmark. Note that a single slerp operation between qmaxPucker and qmaxSpread cannot in general be assumed here because the half-way point between the two rotations may not be identity.

Some landmarks, particularly those on or near the center line, will be influenced by multiple muscles, and each muscle will have a different behavior. Scripts can accommodate this situation and blend the influences to derive a smoothly changing transition.

```
dependsOn LipSpreadSlider
t = LipSpreadSlider / 10
if t >= 0 then
 slerp identity qmaxSpread  t
else
 slerp identity qmaxPucker -t
```

Figure 4: Pseudocode to control landmark position from user interface.

[2] Commercial animation packages refer to these as "wires".

5.2 Organizing multiple influences

As is demonstrated in Figure 4, the scripts for controlling a single cooperating muscle group are straightforward. However, on the human face, the orbicularis oris has multiple influences from many sets of cooperating muscles. Attempting to incorporate all influences into the landmark scripts would become unmanageable.

To accommodate the many influences while keeping script complexity under control resulted in a layered organization. Instead of having a single set of 44 landmarks, there are six sets of landmarks, one each for spread, jaw drop, lip roll, (mouth) corners, show teeth and snarl. Table 1 lists their layer assignments, with smaller layer numbers being more global (proximal) in the hierarchy. Each layer has its own set of scripts, and the complete lip posture is a result of multiplying the transform matrices of the corresponding landmarks in each layer.

5.3 From prototype to production

Our avatar modeling, rigging, and texturing occur in several commercially available animation packages (3ds Max, Maya, Substance Painter), and a custom exporter package converts these into a format compatible with our real-time avatar display. Likewise, the scripts connecting the user interface to the landmarks originated in a commercial package and needed to be exported to the real-time system. This presented a knotty problem, because the complexity of the scripts would require the addition of a parser to export them.

As an alternative, we added a specially formatted comment line at the beginning of each script. A colon-delimited line specifies

- Number of muscles influencing the movement
- Names of slider controlling the movement
- Whether the range of the slider control is symmetric or asymmetric
- Extreme maximum value of the landmark rotation (positive values of slider)
- Extreme minimum value of the landmark rotation (negative values of slider)
- Normative factors to convert incoming parameters from sliders to range from -1 to 1 or 0 to 1, depending on whether the parameter range is symmetric or asymmetric
- Weights corresponding to the influence of each muscle

For the pseudocode in Figure 4, the pseudo comment line would be

```
--:1:LipSpreadSlider:symmetric:qmaxSpread:
qmaxPucker:10:-10:100:100
```

Please note that the strictures of the paper format required a line break. Thus, the exporter only had to consider the first (comment) line of a script when exporting it. Given the adherence to a consistent writing style for the scripts, we were able to express the intent of the scripts in the form of a comment line. The exporter required only a few additional lines of code to process the scripts, and a single, generalized shader in the real-time avatar display accommodated all the scripted behavior.

6. Controlling motion

Posture is, of course, only part of the equation when dealing with avatars, since much of what distinguishes natural vs. robotic signing is carried in the motion between the animation keys. Thus, intuitive control of the interpolation between animation keys is critical, and the new facial bone structure and control set has several distinct advantages over both the MPEG-4 H-Anim localized control and the original Paula rig:

- A more compact control count (56 as opposed to 800) affords more space in the database for velocity/acceleration control,
- Each of the controls is a single scalar rather than a 3D position or set of Euler Angle rotations, so a single animation control can affect all of position/rotation information encoded in each script. Interpolating a scalar is more straightforward than interpolating a position and certainly more straightforward than interpolating a rotation,
- Each control affects multiple bones in a coordinated and intuitive manner, e.g., lip spread, rather than controlling highly localized position on the skin. This allows a single animation control to affect multiple bones with a more coordinated and predictable result for the animator.

To compliment the Expression Builder, the Paula system provides an interface (Figure 5) offering the following animation parameters for each facial muscle control group. They are based on a Tension-Bias-Continuity interpolator (Bartels, Beatty, & Barsky, 1995), but with the parameters renamed to give a more intuitive set of controls for the animator:

- Speed: maps to the Tension parameter and controls the rate of change of the control values through the key
- Bounce: maps to the Continuity parameter and controls the degree to which the speed changes abruptly or more smoothly at a key
- Overshoot: controls the degree and direction of overshoot through a key which is an inherent feature of most interpolators and can be beneficial for creating abrupt "snap" effects
- Ease In/Out: Controls the classical Disney style animation features of ease at a key
- Compound controls: These are special controls that coordinate settings of the other controls for specific effects

These controls afford the animator with more direct ways to create the explosive motion out of a B or a P, or to create softer entries more subtle motions into a pose.

7. Conclusion and future work

We have retooled all the controls in the Expression Builder to this scripted approach. It gives artists more flexibility in creating not only lip postures, but convincing poses involving the entire face.

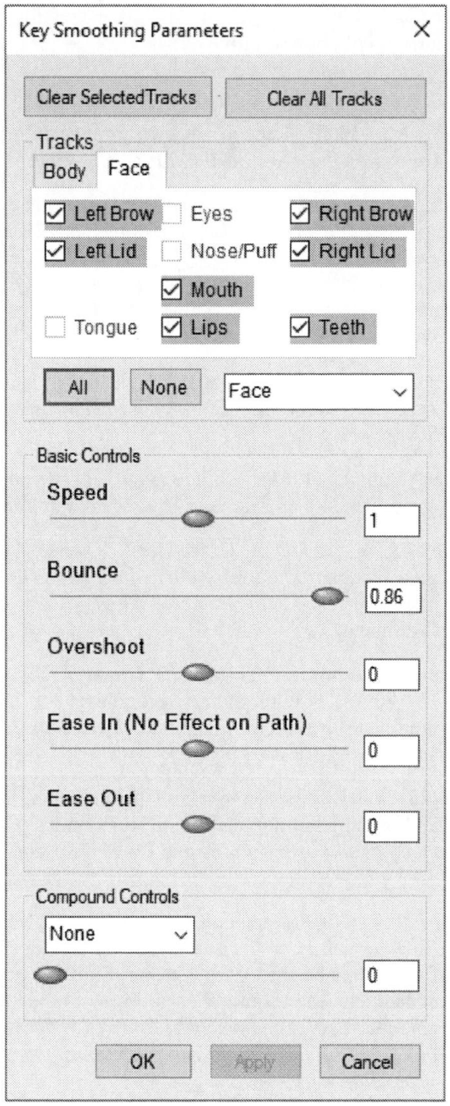

Figure 5: Animation controls.

The approach has also lightened data storage demands. The previous version of the Expression Builder required over 800 values to record a single facial pose. Now the Expression Builder only stores the 56 slider values from the user interface, but the slimmed-down value set allows for more precision and flexibility in creating lip postures and eye apertures. Additionally, the more compact representation has made it possible to control the local speed of the motion of a slider at each key using Tension-Continuity-Bias controls that makes it easy to control overshoot, bounce, and many other dynamical properties. Future plans are to create additional viseme sets to support mouthing in multiple signed languages, including LSF, GSL, DGS and DSGS, and then to test the resulting animations with the Deaf community.

8. Acknowledgements

Many thanks to Ben Sturr, Anthony Bonzani, Nicole Barnekow, Syd Klinghoffer, and Andrew Alexander, the incredible team of modelers and animators of The American Sign Language Avatar Project at DePaul University for their dedication, enthusiasm, and good humor in creating fabulous animations with buggy software.

9. Bibliographic References

Alexa, M. (2002). Recent advances in mesh morphing. *Computer Graphics Forum, 21*(2), 173-198.

Austrian Association of Applied Linguistics. (2019, August). *Position Paper on Automated Translations and Signing Avatars.* Récupéré sur verbal; Verband für Angewandte Linguistik Österreich: https://www.verbal.at/stellungnahmen/Position_Paper-Avatars_verbal_2019.pdf

Baker, C., & Cokely, D. (1980). American sign language. *A Teacher's Resource Text on Grammar and Culture. Silver Spring, MD: TJ Publ.*

Baker-Shenk, C. (1983). A microanalysis of the nonmanual components of questions in American Sign Language.

Bartels, R. H., Beatty, J. C., & Barsky, B. A. (1995). *An introduction to splines for use in computer graphics and geometric modeling.* Los Altos, CA: Morgan Kaufmann.

Brumm, M., Johnson, R., Hanke, T., Grigat, R.-R., & Wolfe, R. (2019). Use of avatar technology for automatic mouth gesture recognition. *SignNonmanuals 2.*

Chen, S., Lou, H., Guo, L., Rong, Q., Liu, Y., & Xu, T.-M. (2012). 3-D finite element modelling of facial soft tissue and preliminary application in orthodontics. *Computer methods in biomechanics and biomedical engineering, 15*(3), 255-261.

Ebling, S., Wolfe, R., Schnepp, J., Baowidan, S., McDonald, J., Moncrief, R., . . . Tissi, K. (2015). Synthesizing the finger alphabet of Swiss German Sign Language and evaluating the comprehensibility of the resulting animations. *Proceedings of SLPAT 2015: 6th Workshop on Speech and Language Processing for Assistive Technologies*, 10-16.

Jain, P., & Rathee, M. (2021). *Anatomy, Head and Neck, Orbicularis Oris Muscle.* Treasure Island, Florida: StatPearls Publishing.

Jennings, V., Elliott, R., & Kennaway, R. (2010). Requirements for a signing avatar. *Workshop on Copora and Sign Language Technologies (CSLT), LREC*, (pp. 133-136). Malta.

Johnson, R. (2022). Improved facial realism through an enhanced representation of anatomical behavior in signing avatars (submitted). *Seventh Sign Language Translation and Avatar Technology Workshop, Language resources and Evaluation Conference.* Marseilles: ELRA.

Johnson, R., Brumm, M., & Wolfe, R. (2018). An Improved Avatar for Automatic Mouth Gesture Recognition. *Language Resources and Evaluation Conference* (pp. 107-108). Myazaki, Japan: European Language Resources (ELRA).

Kipp, M., Heloir, A., & Nguyen, Q. (2011). Sign language avatars: Animation and comprehensibility. *International Workshop on Intelligent Virtual Agents*, (pp. 113–126).

Kipp, M., Nguyen, Q., Heloir, A., & Matthes, S. (2011). Assessing the deaf user perspective on sign language avatars. *The proceedings of the 13th international ACM SIGACCESS conference on Computers and accessibility. ACM*, (pp. 107-114).

Nadolske, M. A., & Rosenstock, R. (2007). Occurrence of mouthings in American Sign Language: A preliminary study. *Visible variation: Comparative studies on sign language structure*, 35–61.

Ostermann, J. (2002). Face Animation in MPEG-4. *MPEG-4 Facial Animation: The Standard, Implementation And Applications*, 17-55.

Parent, R., King, S., Fujimura, & Osamu. (2002). Issues with lip sync animation: can you read my lips? *Computer Animation 2002 (CA 2002)* (pp. 3-10). Geneva, Switzerland: IEEE.

Parke, F. I., & Waters, K. (2008). *Computer facial animation.* Boca Raton, Florida: CRC Press.

Piekartz, H. v., & Mohr, G. (2014). Reduction of head and face pain by challenging lateralization and basic emotions: a proposal for future assessment and rehabilitation strategies. *Journal of Manual & Manipulative Therapy, 22*, 24–35.

Reilly, I., & Anderson, D. (2002). FACES: The aquisition of non-manual morphology in ASL. *Directions in sign language acquisition , 2*, 159--182.

Schnepp, J., Wolfe, R., McDonald, J., & Toro, J. (2013). Generating Co-occurring Facial Nonmanual Signals in Synthesized American Sign Language. *Eighth International Conference on Computer Graphics Theory and Applications GRAPP/IVAPP*, (pp. 407-416). Barcelona.

Verlinden, M., Tijsseling, C., & Frowein, H. (2001). A Signing Avatar on the WWW. *International Gesture Workshop*, (pp. 169–172).

Wilbur, R. (1994). Eyeblinks & ASL phrase structure. *Sign Language Studies, 84*, 221–240.

Wolfe, R., Hanke, T., Langer, G., Jahn, E., Worsek, S., Bleicken, J., . . . Johnson, R. (2018). Exploring Localization for Mouthings in Sign Language Avatars. *Language Resources and Evaluation Conference* (pp. 207-212). Myazaki, Japan: European Language Resources Association (ELRA).

Proceedings of the 7th International Workshop on Sign Language Translation and Avatar Technology (SLTAT 7), pages 73–78
Language Resources and Evaluation Conference (LREC 2022), Marseille, 20-25 June 2022

A Software Toolkit for Pre-processing Sign Language Video Streams

Fabrizio Nunnari
German Research Center for Artificial Intelligence (DFKI)
Saarland Informatics Campus D3.2
fabrizio.nunnari@dfki.de

Abstract

We present the requirements, design guidelines, and the software architecture of an open-source toolkit dedicated to the pre-processing of sign language video material. The toolkit is a collection of functions and command-line tools designed to be integrated with build automation systems. Every pre-processing tool is dedicated to standard pre-processing operations (e.g., trimming, cropping, resizing) or feature extraction (e.g., identification of areas of interest, landmark detection) and can be used also as a standalone Python module. The UML diagrams of its architecture are presented together with a few working examples of its usage. The software is freely available with an open-source license on a public repository.

Keywords: sign language, video pre-processing, open source toolkit, software engineering

1. Introduction and Related Work

In these years, there is a consistent amount of public-funded research on sign language recognition and translation. In particular, two EU-funded projects, SignOn[1] (Shterionov et al., 2021) and EASIER[2], attempt to provide bi-directional translation from and to spoken and sign languages of different European languages.

In addition to its contribution to the EASIER project, the German Research Center for Artificial Intelligence (DFKI) works on the nationally funded AVASAG[3] (Nunnari et al., 2021a) and SocialWear[4] (Nunnari et al., 2021b) projects. All of those projects share the use of the latest generation of artificial intelligence techniques, based on neural networks, for video analysis. In all cases, video material needs to be analysed and pre-processed before being fed to convolutional neural networks (CNN) architectures.

In machine learning, data pre-processing is a common task that ensures some form of data normalization and possibly some pre-computation of features that facilitates the training of the neural architectures.

In the realm of sign language, such video pre-processing might include identifying body parts (hands, face, lips, eyes) and cropping the portion of video frames containing a higher resolution of such items. Other pre-processing steps might include the identification of landmarks (i.e., transiting from pixel-based features to 2D/3D vector information).

However, despite being recognized as a necessary step, pre-processing is performed again and again among different projects using highly customized scripts that are hardly reusable across projects or datasets. This is due to many factors. One of them is the storage format of the video material, which is for example available as images sequence in the PHOENIX corpus (Forster et al., 2012) and as compressed videos in the Hamburg DGS corpus (Hanke et al., 2020). Other typical differences relate to different ways of organizing and naming the video sources.

For those reasons, the DFKI started a software project with the goal of collecting in a single open-source repository all of the algorithms broadly needed to perform pre-processing of sign language videos, to maximize reusability across projects, but leaving out the specific details that are hindering its portability.

The project is called Sign Language Video processing Tools[5] and it is available as a public open-source repository on the popular GitHub platform. The software package is essentially a collection of command-line tools, usable also as Python modules, developed by aggregating several popular open-source libraries and tools such as ffmpeg[6], MediaPipe (Lugaresi et al., 2019), OpenCV (Bradski and Kaehler, 2000), MTCNN (Xiang and Zhu, 2017). Figure 1 shows some examples of the toolkit in action.

The added values of this toolkit, compared to directly using directly its underlying libraries, are described in detail in section 2. Section 3 lists the tools implemented so far. Finally, section 4 summarizes the paper and describes future work.

2. Framework Goals and Design

The framework has been designed to fulfill the three following requirements:

1. Usable both as command line tools as well as Python functions;

[1] `https://signon-project.eu`
[2] `https://www.project-easier.eu`
[3] `https://avasag.de`
[4] `https://affective.dfki.de/socialwear-bmbf-2020-2024/`

[5] Sign Language Video Processing Tools code repository: `https://github.com/DFKI-SignLanguage/VideoProcessingTools`
[6] `https://ffmpeg.org`

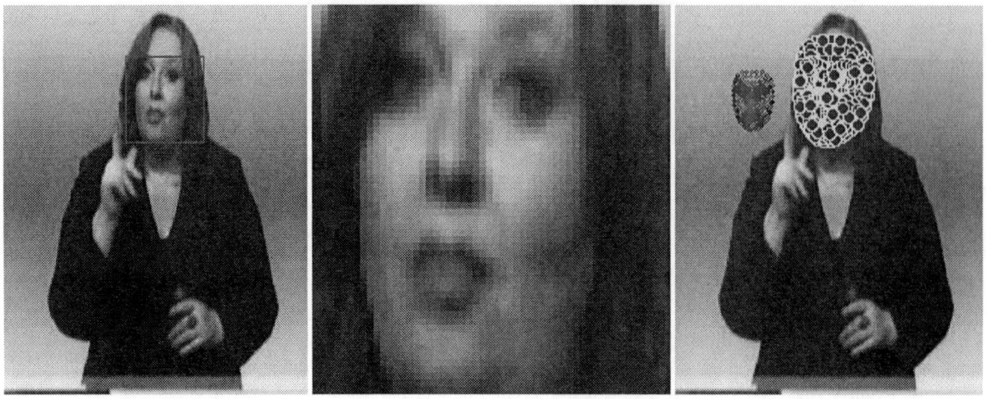

Figure 1: Examples of the toolkit applied to a test video of the PHOENIX corpus. From left to right: face bounds detection, cropping, detection, and normalization of facial landmarks. For the latter, the blue dots are the landmarks detected by MediaPipe, while the red dots are the landmarks after normalization of the head orientation.

2. Support video streams both as encoded videos and as image sequences;
3. The parameters of the command-line tools are designed to be concatenated with build automation tools.

In the following, we describe how those requirements have been addressed.

As for **Requirement 1**, all of the video processing tools are organized as stand-alone Python modules. Figure 2 shows a UML diagram of the top-level `slvideotools` package, which contains a sub-package for each of the available tools. Packages and sub-packages are implemented as Python sub-modules. Every sub-module acts as *wrapper* for a specific functionality. Each wrapping sub-module contains a top-level code acting as the `main` execution point, parsing the command line arguments, and invoking the corresponding video processing function; the latter has the same name as the containing sub-module.
For example, the `crop_video` tool is implemented in the `slvideotools.crop_video` sub-package and can be invoked as CLI command:

```
python -m slvideotools.crop_video\
    --inframes myface.mp4\
    --inbounds face_bounds.json\
    --outframes cropped_frames/
```

At the same time, the function `crop_video(...)` is available within pure Python code and can be imported and reused:

```
from slvideotools.crop_video import crop_video
from slvideotools.datagen import\
    create_frame_producer, create_frame_consumer

with create_frame_producer(
        dir_or_video="myface.mp4") as prod,\
     create_frame_consumer(
        dir_or_video="cropped_frames") as cons:

    with open("face_bounds.json", "r") as bounds_fp:
        bounds = json.load(bounds_fp)

    crop_video(frames_producer=prod,
        bounds_tuple=bounds,
        frames_consumer=cons)
```

The next paragraph describes what are frame producers and consumers.

Requirement 2 Sign language video material is often stored as a video stream. However, in some cases, to more easily feed single frames to a convolutional classifier, or to avoid video compression artifacts, videos are stored as a sequence of single images, usually collected inside a folder. To seamlessly support frame sequencing from both videos and image folders, the class structure depicted in Figure 3 was adopted. The production and the consumption of frames are managed through two abstract classes: `FrameProducer` and `FrameConsumer`. Their subclasses are responsible for implementing a method to read frames from a video or a directory, and to store frames in a video or directory. To further facilitate code flexibility, two factory methods (Gamma et al., 1994) create the correct Producer/Consumer subclass by checking if the source or the destination is a video file or a directory. Finally, the Producer/Consumer top classes support the *context management* interface[7], allowing for for automatic resource disposal through the `with ... as ...` statement.
As a result, the typical recipe to process frames from/to video containers or directories is illustrated in the following code snippet.

```
from slvideotools.datagen import\
    create_frame_producer, create_frame_consumer

with create_frame_producer(
        dir_or_video="my/frames/") as prod,\
     create_frame_consumer(
        dir_or_video="my_final_video.mp4") as cons:
```

[7] `https://docs.python.org/3/reference/datamodel.html#context-managers`

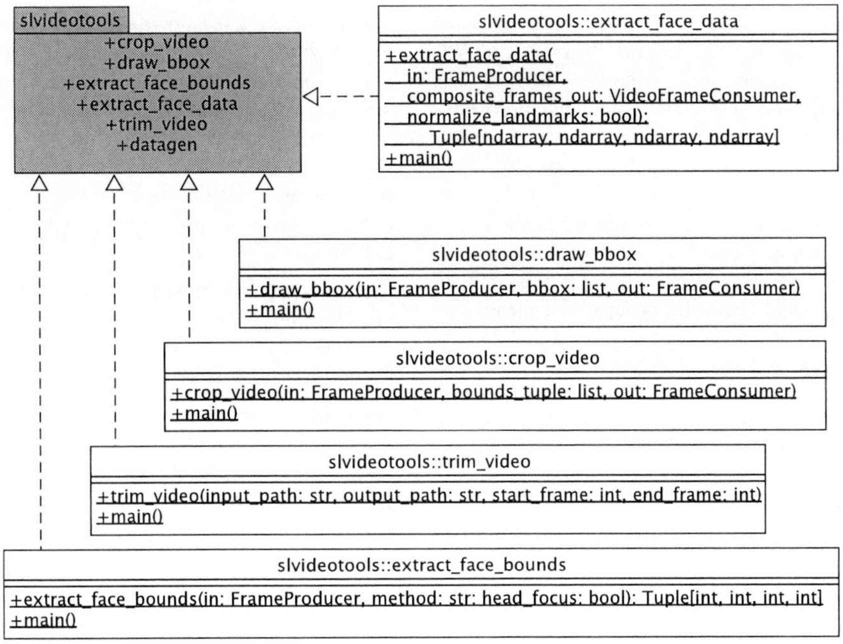

Figure 2: The UML diagram of the data video processing tools package.

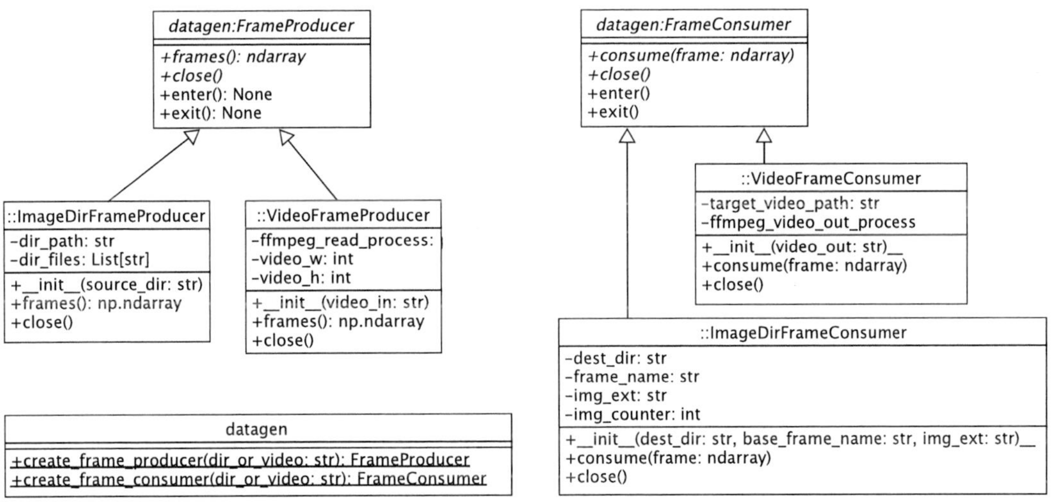

Figure 3: The UML diagram of the data generation subpackage.

```
for in_frame in prod.frames():
    # Process your frame
    # out_frame = ...

    # Feed the frame to output video
    cons.consume(frame=out_frame)
```

Finally, for **Requirement 3**, the command line tools must be usable from wrapping build automation systems like the popular GNU Make[8] or equivalent more advanced systems like Luigi[9].

Video datasets can grow consistently, and running video preprocessing over many video samples can be time and resource-consuming. Hence, when preparing a new dataset, it is important to avoid the repetition of a video processing step (e.g., feature extraction) when not required, e.g., when only a few new samples are added or a few samples are updated (e.g., re-takes).

To fulfill this requirement two simple guidelines were

[8] https://www.gnu.org/software/make/

[9] https://github.com/spotify/luigi

followed. First, the command line interfaces have been designed to take explicit filenames as input and output, avoiding any automatic generation of filenames or any custom convention about naming. For example, automatic filename composition, like appending a timestamp to a base file naming, is avoided. Automatic filename generation can be handy to run several tests while avoiding overriding previous results, but hinders reproducibility and increases the complexity in the maintenance of data folders (also, potentially leading to uncontrolled space occupation). Hence, file names must be unambiguously provided and naming conventions are left to project-specific needs. Second, every script is designed to manage single files (or single folders containing video frames). Iteration over files or directories, which normally requires dealing with peculiar naming conventions, is left to external automation tools.

For example, the following `Makefile` scans a directory for videos with extension `.mp4` and for each video generates a corresponding `.bounds` JSON file with information on the bounding box containing the face of the speaker in the video.

```
# Directory containing the .mp4 files
DIR=videos
# Lists all of the MP4 videos
invideofiles := $(wildcard $(DIR)/*.mp4)
# Compose the names of output .bound files.
boundfiles := $(subst .mp4,.bounds,$(invideofiles))

all: $(boundfiles)
	@echo "Extracted␣face␣bounds."

$(boundfiles): $(DIR)/%.bounds: $(DIR)/%.mp4
	@echo "Finding␣bounds␣for␣video␣$<␣..."
	python -m slvideotools.extract_face_bounds \
	    --invideo $< \
	    --outbounds $@
	@echo "Saved␣to␣$@."
```

Every time the `make` command is invoked, each `.bounds` file will be created or updated if the corresponding source video is renewed.

The use of automated dependency checking systems is of extreme advantage when dealing with evolving datasets where single animation clips might be added or updated as the dataset is populated. Using dependency systems ensures that only the minimal set of video processing operations is performed to keep the dataset in a consistent state.

3. Implemented Tools

At the moment of writing, the following command-line tools and functions are fully implemented.

extract_face_bounds This tool analyzes a video clip and identifies frame-by-frame a bounding rectangle containing the face of a speaker. The bounding box (upper-left x and y corner, width, height) of the full video is then computed so that the face is always visible during the whole video. For sign language analysis this approach helps in dealing with frames where the hands cover the face. In those situations, face detection tools fail. By gracefully skipping frames without a visible face, the global bounds containing the face for the whole video can still be inferred from the other video frames, where the face is detected. Two detection methods are currently supported: using the MediaPipe library (Lugaresi et al., 2019), which is faster, or the MTCNN (Zhang et al., 2016), which is more robust for faces at variable distances from the camera. The bounding information is saved into a simple JSON array file.

draw_bbox This tool takes as input a video and bounding box information and produces a new video with the bounding information as an overlay. This is useful for debugging the face detection procedure.

crop_video takes as input a video and bounding box files and outputs a cropped video. This is useful for cropping the face, hands, lips, or any other information which requires zooming on a body part for normalizing image size, increasing resolution, removing noisy information, and thus improving further analysis.

extract_face_data is a complex tool able to extract four kind of information. First, it uses Mediapipe to extract the set of 468 landmarks describing the movement of the face of a subject. Second, it outputs the position of the tip of the nose, which can be used as reference to identify the position of the face in a video frame. Third, it infers the rotation of the head; this is done with vector operations involving the landmarks at the border of the forehead, which are not involved by facial muscle activation (Figure 4 shows the process). Fourth, it calculates a scaling factor, estimating the distance of the face from the camera, useful to normalize the face size before using it in further facial expression recognition algorithms, such as the classification of facial expressions (Savchenko, 2021).

trim_video is useful to trim out initial and ending frames of a video, for example to insulate stroke and hold phases of a motion while removing the preparation and release phases. This script is the only one not using the Producer/Consumer mechanism, but takes as parameters the input and output video file paths, and relies of the `ffmpeg` core functionality to trim a video while avoiding uncompressing and recompressing the stream (which might hinder video quality).

Command	Elapsed	frames/sec
extract_face_bounds (MTCNN)	44s	5,5
extract_face_bounds (MediaPipe)	<1s	>242
draw_bbox	6s	40,33
crop_video	2s	121
extract_face_data	9s	28,89
trim_video	< 1s	> 242

Table 1: Results of the speed test measuring the execution time on a 242-frame sample video.

To measure performances, we monitored the time needed for the execution of all the implemented com-

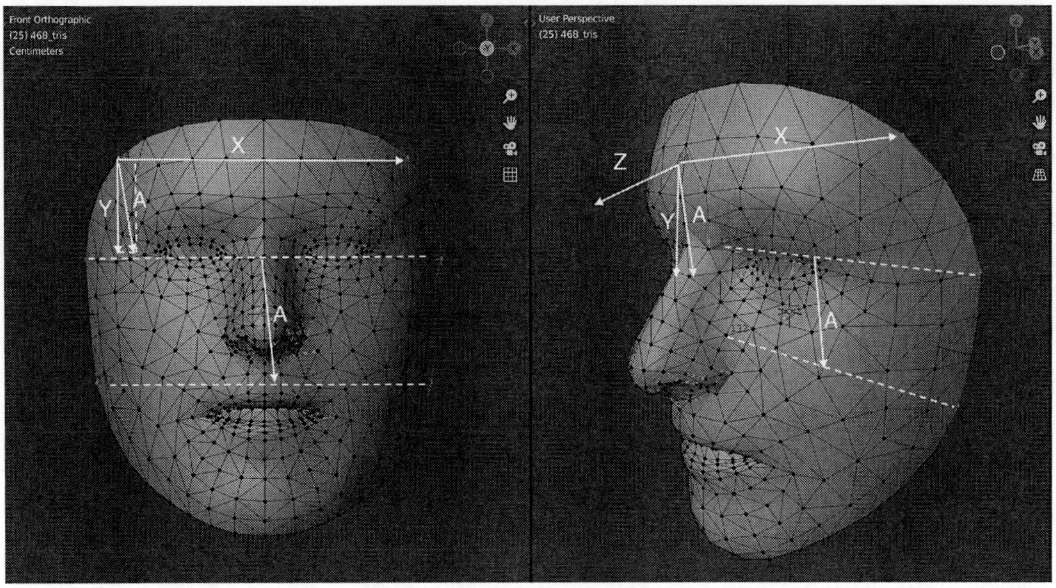

Figure 4: Computing the head rotation from the Mediapipe 3D facial landmarks. To calculate the rotation of the head, we need to define a new orthogonal system with axes X, Y, and Z, which must be already approximately aligned with the absolute reference axes x,y,z when the subject is looking straight forward. The new system must be computed using landmarks that do not move with the facial muscles. The new X axis is computed by considering two landmarks on the forehead. A new A axis is computed considering the midpoints of two horizontal segments joining the sides of the face. Because of noisy information and approximations, A is rarely perfectly orthogonal to X; hence, the new Y is computed from A by subtracting its projection on X. Finally, the new Z is the cross-product between X and Y. The new XYZ reference system is then compared with the global xyz axes to produce a 3x3 rigid rotation matrix.

mands on a sample sign language video. The sample video is the longest found in the PHOENIX 2014-T corpus: 242 frames, resolution 210 X 260 pixels. The reference hardware is a MacBookPro (model 2019) with Intel i9 CPU. Table 1 reports the results. It can be noticed that the slowest process is the extraction of the face bounds with MTCNN, while the same process executed with MediaPipe lasts less than one second. It is worth specifying that the test machine doesn't support GPU acceleration, meaning that MTCNN might perform significantly better on other hardware.

4. Conclusions

We presented the requirements and architecture design of an open-source software toolkit dedicated to the pre-processing of sign language videos. The goal of such a toolkit is to centralize, into a single repository, pieces of code that are often copied and scattered around many projects requiring pre-processing for developing sign language recognition systems. The software architecture of the toolkit has been designed with extensibility in mind.

The toolkit offers already the scripts needed to process face information and will be extended to integrate ad-hoc analysis of other body parts (head, upper body, hands) and features (eye blinks, eye gaze, etc.). Other tools will be likely dedicated to color normalization.

We are updating this toolkit with the code that we developing for three different projects dedicated to sign language analysis and translation. Our goal is to help the research community in speeding up video material pre-processing, without re-implementing it from scratch, and involve other researchers in sharing other pre-processing techniques in a common open repository.

Acknowledgements

The author would like to thank Yasser Hamidullah for his contribution to some parts of the code, and Cristina España-Bonet and Eleftherios Avramidis for their collaboration on the several sign language projects and for the review of this manuscript.

This work has been partially funded by BMBF (German Federal Ministry of Education and Research) within project AVASAG (Avatar-basierter Sprachassistent zur automatisierten Gebärdenübersetzung, grant number: 16SV8491) and project SOCIALWEAR (Socially Interactive Smart Fashion, DFKI Kst 22132), and by the EU Horizon 2020 programme within the EASIER project (Grant agreement ID: 101016982).

5. Bibliographical References

Bradski, G. and Kaehler, A. (2000). Opencv. *Dr. Dobb's journal of software tools*, 3:2.

Forster, J., Schmidt, C., Hoyoux, T., Koller, O., Zelle, U., Piater, J., and Ney, H. (2012). RWTH-PHOENIX-Weather: A Large Vocabulary Sign Language Recognition and Translation Corpus. In *Language Resources and Evaluation*, pages 3785–3789, Istanbul, Turkey, May.

Gamma, E., Helm, R., Johnson, R., and Vlissides, J. (1994). *Design patterns: elements of reusable object-oriented software*. Addison-Wesley.

Hanke, T., Schulder, M., Konrad, R., and Jahn, E. (2020). Extending the public DGS corpus in size and depth. In *Proceedings of the LREC2020 9th Workshop on the Representation and Processing of Sign Languages: Sign Language Resources in the Service of the Language Community, Technological Challenges and Application Perspectives*, pages 75–82.

Lugaresi, C., Tang, J., Nash, H., McClanahan, C., Uboweja, E., Hays, M., Zhang, F., Chang, C.-L., Yong, M. G., Lee, J., Chang, W.-T., Hua, W., Georg, M., and Grundmann, M. (2019). MediaPipe: A Framework for Building Perception Pipelines. *arXiv:1906.08172 [cs]*, June. arXiv: 1906.08172.

Nunnari, F., Bauerdiek, J., Bernhard, L., España-Bonet, C., Jäger, C., Unger, A., Waldow, K., Wecker, S., André, E., Busemann, S., Dold, C., Fuhrmann, A., Gebhard, P., Hamidullah, Y., Hauck, M., Kossel, Y., Misiak, M., Wallach, D., and Stricker, A. (2021a). AVASAG: A German Sign Language Translation System for Public Services. In *1st International Workshop on Automatic Translation for Signed and Spoken Languages (AT4SSL)*. Association for Machine Translation in the Americas, August.

Nunnari, F., España-Bonet, C., and Avramidis, E. (2021b). A Data Augmentation Approach for Sign-Language-To-Text Translation In-The-Wild. In Dagmar Gromann, et al., editors, *3rd Conference on Language, Data and Knowledge (LDK 2021)*, volume 93 of *Open Access Series in Informatics (OASIcs)*, pages 36:1–36:8, Dagstuhl, Germany. Schloss Dagstuhl – Leibniz-Zentrum für Informatik. ISSN: 2190-6807.

Savchenko, A. V. (2021). Facial expression and attributes recognition based on multi-task learning of lightweight neural networks. In *2021 IEEE 19th International Symposium on Intelligent Systems and Informatics (SISY)*, pages 119–124. IEEE.

Shterionov, D., Vandeghinste, V., Saggion, H., Blat, J., Coster, M. D., Dambre, J., Heuvel, H. V. d., Murtagh, I., Leeson, L., and Schuurman, I. (2021). The SignON project: a Sign Language Translation Framework. In *Proceedings of the 31st Meeting of Computational Linguistics in The Netherlands (CLIN 31)*, July. event-place: Ghent.

Xiang, J. and Zhu, G. (2017). Joint face detection and facial expression recognition with mtcnn. In *2017 4th international conference on information science and control engineering (ICISCE)*, pages 424–427. IEEE.

Zhang, K., Zhang, Z., Li, Z., and Qiao, Y. (2016). Joint Face Detection and Alignment Using Multitask Cascaded Convolutional Networks. *IEEE Signal Processing Letters*, 23(10):1499–1503, October.

Proceedings of the 7th International Workshop on Sign Language Translation and Avatar Technology (SLTAT 7), pages 79–84
Language Resources and Evaluation Conference (LREC 2022), Marseille, 20-25 June 2022

Greek Sign Language Recognition for the SL-ReDu Learning Platform

Katerina Papadimitriou [1], Gerasimos Potamianos [1], Galini Sapountzaki [2], Theodor Goulas [3], Eleni Efthimiou [3], Stavroula-Evita Fotinea [3], Petros Maragos [4]

[1] Department of Electrical & Computer Engineering, University of Thessaly, Volos, Greece
[2] Department of Special Education, University of Thessaly, Volos, Greece
[3] Institute for Language & Speech Processing, Athena Research & Innovation Center, Athens, Greece
[4] School of Electrical & Computer Engineering, National Technical University of Athens, Greece

aipapadimitriou@uth.gr, gpotam@ieee.org, gsapountz@sed.uth.gr,
{tgoulas, eleni_e, evita}@athenarc.gr, maragos@cs.ntua.gr

Abstract

There has been increasing interest lately in developing education tools for sign language (SL) learning that enable self-assessment and objective evaluation of learners' SL productions, assisting both students and their instructors. Crucially, such tools require the automatic recognition of SL videos, while operating in a signer-independent fashion and under realistic recording conditions. Here, we present an early version of a Greek Sign Language (GSL) recognizer that satisfies the above requirements, and integrate it within the SL-ReDu learning platform that constitutes a first in GSL with recognition functionality. We develop the recognition module incorporating state-of-the-art deep-learning based visual detection, feature extraction, and classification, designing it to accommodate a medium-size vocabulary of isolated signs and continuously fingerspelled letter sequences. We train the module on a specifically recorded GSL corpus of multiple signers by a web-cam in non-studio conditions, and conduct both multi-signer and signer-independent recognition experiments, reporting high accuracies. Finally, we let student users evaluate the learning platform during GSL production exercises, reporting very satisfactory objective and subjective assessments based on recognition performance and collected questionnaires, respectively.

Keywords: Greek Sign Language recognition, MediaPipe, MobileNet, ResNet, CNN, BiLSTM, sign language learning, user evaluation

1. Introduction

Sign languages (SLs) involve a complex non-vocal means of communication in the 3D visible space around the signer, with both manual and non-manual articulation carrying linguistic content of a set of glosses (Armstrong et al., 2002). Such complexity renders SL education a difficult and time-consuming process (Kemp, 1998) for both learners and their instructors, thus motivating recently the development of automatic SL assessment and tutoring tools (Aran et al., 2009; Zafrulla et al., 2011; Ebling et al., 2018; Joy et al., 2019; Mohammdi and Elbourhamy, 2021). A critical functionality in such applications is the ability to assess the validity of the learners' SL productions, necessitating automatic SL recognition (SLR) of the produced videos in a signer-independent fashion and under realistic, non-ideal recording conditions. Not surprisingly, this constitutes a challenging problem, due to the aforementioned complexity of SL production, coupled with the intricacies of robust video processing (detection, tracking, representation) and inherent inter-signer production variability.

Motivated by the above, in conjunction with the lack of learning tools in the under-resourced Greek Sign Language (GSL), we have recently initiated the "SL-ReDu" project (Potamianos et al., 2020). This aims to considerably advance the current state-of-the-art in automatic recognition of GSL from videos, while focusing on the use-case of standardized GSL teaching as a second language. For this purpose, in previous work we have already developed a suitable platform that allows "passive"-type GSL learning exercises (e.g., multiple-choice questions) and populated it with appropriate learning material (Sapountzaki et al., 2021; Efthimiou et al., 2021). However, we have not yet enabled "active", production-type assessment, which requires an appropriate SLR module.

In this paper, we proceed to enable such functionality, presenting our initial GSL recognition module that we integrate to the SL-ReDu platform. In particular, we focus on two recognition problems: (i) that of isolated GSL signs within a medium-size vocabulary, developing separate models for numerals and non-numerals, and (ii) that of continuous sequences of fingerspelled letters of the Greek alphabet. Note that the latter task plays a critical role in SLs, as it is regularly used for words that lack unique signs, such as names, technical phrases, and foreign words, among others (Armstrong et al., 2002).

We develop the corresponding SLR module incorporating state-of-the-art deep-learning techniques. Specifically, we utilize the MediaPipe library for detecting the signer and relevant landmarks from RGB video (Lugaresi et al., 2019), thus avoiding the use of special sensing equipment, such as hand gloves (Mehdi and Khan, 2002) or depth cameras (Ren et al., 2011). Fur-

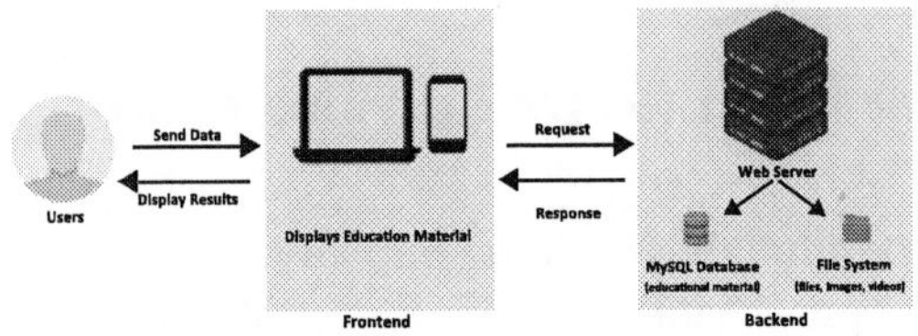

Figure 1: Illustration of the SL-ReDu prototype system web-based architecture.

ther, we employ convolutional neural networks (CNNs) for visual feature learning, namely a 3D CNN (Tran et al., 2018) and MobileNet (Howard et al., 2017). Finally, in the case of fingerspelling, for sequence learning we use a bidirectional long short-term memory (BiLSTM) encoder (Schuster and Paliwal, 1997) and connectionist temporal classification (CTC) based decoding (Graves et al., 2006).

We train and evaluate the recognition module on a suitable GSL corpus, collected as part of this work. The data contain multiple signers, recorded using a typical web-cam in non-studio conditions. We report both multi-signer and signer-independent recognition experiments on this corpus. Moreover, we evaluate the SL-ReDu platform and its recognition functionality with a small number of student users that conduct GSL production exercises, reporting both objective and subjective evaluation results.

The rest of the paper is structured as follows: Section 2 overviews the SL-ReDu platform; Section 3 describes the developed SLR module; Section 4 presents the SLR corpus and its evaluation; Section 5 discusses the user evaluation; and Section 6 concludes the paper.

2. The SL-ReDu Platform

The SL-ReDu platform attempts to handle the drawbacks of conventional practice and testing strategies in learning GSL as a second language by enabling self-monitoring of learning and objective learner evaluation. For the system's design all aspects of GSL linguistics are being considered, i.e. GSL semantics, as well as morpho-syntactic effects in both GSL recognition and GSL production. In particular, teaching techniques and content are integrated into the system design, including various SL practice assignments that cover GSL phenomena from sign formation to complicated syntactic and semantic utterance production. Ordinary multiple-choice questions that utilize images, videos, and text to elicit a response from the user, as well as user feedback by means of video recordings of GSL production, are examples of exercise types. With the integration of SLR technology, SL-ReDu enables the user to actively sign and be assessed for the capacity to appropriately generate signs.

The SL-ReDu prototype system is a web-based application that runs on a web server managing the end-user's interaction. Self-monitoring and objective assessment system modalities entail a variety of components, namely the system database, the front-end and back-end user interfaces, as well as image and video files. Further, the system involves a content management system (back-end) that is exploited by the instructor to create learners' assessment tests and track performance over time. Figure 1 depicts the adopted architecture.

To build the dynamic web platform, the PHP programming language in conjunction with HTML5, CSS3, and JavaScript is used. A MySQL open-source database is employed for the construction of the web application, including the storage of the content, as well as the results of the platform users. An Apache Web Server hosts the web application.

SLR represents a separate module of the system that runs as standalone on the learner's device (typically a higher-end laptop with an available camera). The technical details of the communication between the web server and the SLR engine are available in a Technical Report (Potamianos et al., 2021).

3. The GSL Recognition Module

We next detail the SLR module for the two GSL recognition tasks considered, namely that of isolated signs and continuous fingerspelling. The module also contains a pre-processing stage.

3.1. Pre-processing

This stage is employed to detect the signer, extract the region-of-interest (RoI), and provide feedback in case signer positioning is incorrect.

Specifically, the recorded video frames are fed to the MediaPipe holistic tool (Lugaresi et al., 2019). This is a multi-stage pipeline that integrates separate models for pose, face, and hand components, extracting 543 whole-body landmarks from RGB data (33 pose, 468 face, and 21 hand landmarks per hand). Lack of detected landmarks of the two hands, face, and upper torso is assumed to imply incorrect user positioning with respect to the camera field of view. In such case, the signer is prompted by the system to reposition.

If user positioning is correct, the detected landmarks are utilized to extract the RoI for subsequent appearance feature generation. In the case of isolated signs, where multiple articulators may participate in signing, the entire upper body is cropped producing the RoI (see also Figure 2(a)). This is then normalized to the subsequent CNN input layer size (i.e., 256×256 pixels of ResNet2+1D). In the case of fingerspelling though, where typically one hand constitutes the sole articulator, the RoI consists of the signing hand only (see also Figure 2(b)), which is determined based on the motion of the landmarks (3D skeletal keypoints) of each hand in the video. The RoI is then normalized to the input layer size of the MobileNet CNN (i.e., 224×224 pixels). Note that we use the estimated landmarks exclusively for RoI extraction, thus minimizing the impact of occasional MediaPipe failures (Moryossef et al., 2021).

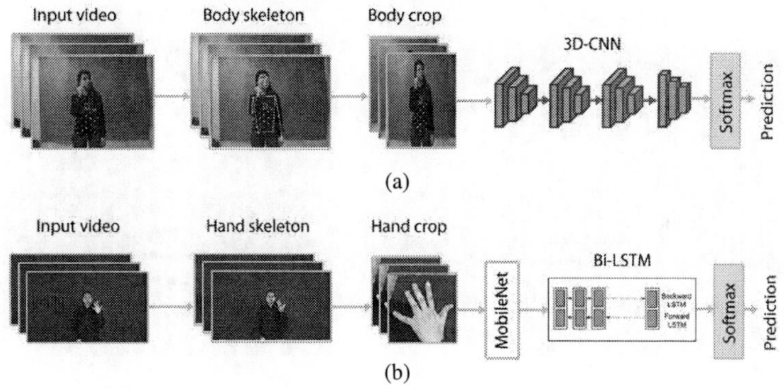

Figure 2: Schematics of GSL recognition modules for (a) isolated signs and (b) continuous fingerspelling.

3.2. Isolated Sign Recognition

A 3D CNN is employed for isolated sign recognition (see also Figure 2(a)). Specifically, the 18-layer ResNet2+1D model is used (Tran et al., 2018) that separates spatial and temporal convolutions of 3D CNNs. Note that two recognition subtasks are considered employing separate models, one for numeral signs with a vocabulary size of 18, and a second for non-numeral ones with a vocabulary size of 36.

Note that in all cases the CNN is pretrained on the Kinetics dataset (Carreira et al., 2018). Model training (finetuning) then proceeds via the Adam optimizer (Kingma and Ba, 2014) with initial learning rate set to 0.0001 and weight decay 0.0001. For sign prediction, the cross-entropy loss is used with label smoothing (Szegedy et al., 2016). The mini-batch size is fixed to 16.

3.3. Continuous Fingerspelling Recognition

A CNN-BiLSTM combination is employed for recognizing continuously fingerspelled sequences of the 24 Greek alphabet letters. In the adopted approach (see also Figure 2(b)), the CNN serves as visual feature learner of each video frame and the BiLSTM learns their temporal relations. Specifically, the CNN uses the MobileNet architecture (Howard et al., 2017), pretrained on the ImageNet corpus (Deng et al., 2009). Feature maps are generated by taking the output of the last fully-connected layer, yielding 1024-dimensional (dim) features. These are then fed to a linear projection layer for size reduction, resulting in 512-dim features. Subsequently, a two-layer BiLSTM encoder is employed with 512-dim hidden states (Schuster and Paliwal, 1997) followed by CTC decoding (Graves et al., 2006) for letter sequence prediction.

The model's linear projection layer is jointly trained with the BiLSTM. Training is conducted using the Adam optimizer with initial learning rate equal to 0.001, decayed by a factor of 0.1 if the validation score remains consistent for 9 steps. In addition, a dropout rate of 0.1 is used, and the mini-batch size is fixed to 16. Finally, during inference, beam search decoding is adopted with beam width 3. Note also that no letter language model is employed.

4. GSL Data and Experiments

To support the development of the GSL recognizer, we have collected a suitable database. We describe it next, followed by the adopted experimental framework and our GSL recognition experiments on it.

4.1. The GSL Database

Signing data by multiple volunteer informants (both native and non-native in GSL) have been collected to allow isolated GSL recognition of numerals (18-sign vocabulary), isolated SLR of non-numerals (36-sign GSL vocabulary), and continuous recognition of fingerspelled sequences of the 24 Greek alphabet letters.[1]

The data have been recorded indoors, under realistic, non-studio conditions with varying background and lighting, using a Logitech C615 web-camera at a frame rate of 30 Hz, YUV411 video format, and 640×480-pixel resolution.

In the case of numeral signs, data from 20 signers have been collected. Each signer articulated the 18 numerals 5 consecutive times, resulting in a total of 1,800 database videos.

In the case of non-numeral signs, data from 17 signers have been collected. Each informant articulated the 36 signs five times. In addition, these data have been supplemented with videos from the publicly available ITI GSL corpus (Adaloglou et al., 2022), resulting to 7 more informants signing the same 36 signs five times. Note that the latter have been recorded using an Intel RealSense D435 RGB-D camera under studio-quality conditions, but here only the RGB stream is utilized. Thus, the combined data contain 24 (17 + 7) signers and a total of 4,320 videos.

Finally, in the case of fingerspelling, data from 12 signers have been recorded. Each informant signed once the 24 Greek alphabet letters in isolation, as well as 50 fingerspelled words (unique to each signer) composed

[1]All informants have signed consent forms, and the data will become publicly available in the future, as part of a larger data release of SL-ReDu project resources.

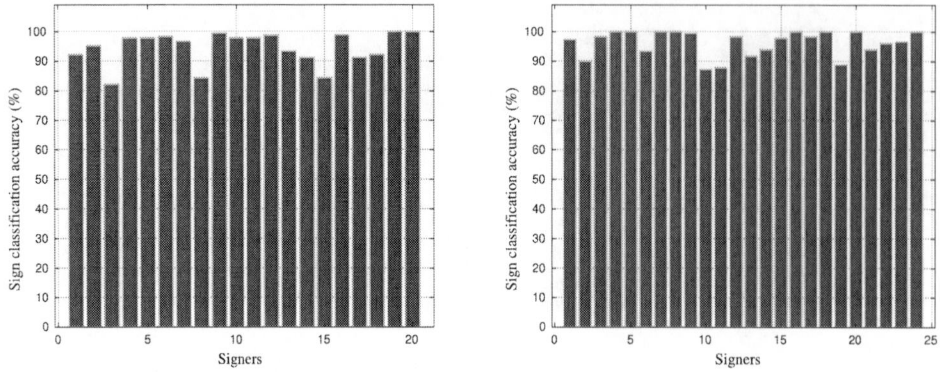

(a) (b)

Figure 3: SI isolated GSL recognition accuracy (%) per signer for (a) numerals and (b) non-numeral signs.

of 4-5 letters. In addition, 7 informants performed 16 words (common to all) composed of 3-7 letters, and 3 signers expressed an extra 71 words of 4-5 letters. This process resulted in a total of 1,071 videos. Note that each informant has signed each letter at least 4 times.

4.2. Experimental Framework

We are interested primarily in signer-independent (SI) SLR, since learner users of the SL-ReDu platform are typically "unseen" during GSL model training. For comparison purposes, we also report multi-signer (MS) recognition results, where data from all signers are used for both training and test sets (with the sets remaining disjoint), being an easier learning scenario.

In the MS case, we use ten-fold cross-validation. In each fold, we allocate 80% of all videos to training (numerals: 1,440; non-numerals: 3,456; fingerspelling: 857), 10% to validation (numerals: 180; non-numerals: 432; fingerspelling: 107), and the remaining 10% to testing (same number of videos as in validation).

In the SI scenario, we employ 20-fold cross-validation in the numerals case, 24 folds for non-numerals, and 12 ones for fingerspelling. In all cases, each fold contains one test signer, while the model is trained on all others.

In addition to these paradigms, GSL models are also trained to be used by the SL-ReDu platform in its user-evaluation, as reported in Section 5. For this purpose, we allocate 90% of the available videos to training (numerals: 1,620; non-numerals: 3,888; fingerspelling: 964) and the remaining 10% to validation (numerals: 180; non-numerals: 432; fingerspelling: 107).

4.3. Recognition Results

In Table 1, we report the recognition performance of the isolated GSL and continuous fingerspelling tasks on the datasets of Section 4.1, under both MS and SI training/testing paradigms of Section 4.2. Results are reported in word accuracy (WAcc), %, and in the case of fingerspelling in letter accuracy (LAcc), %, as well. In all cases, performance degrades in the SI case, compared to the MS scenario, which is not surprising. Nevertheless, WAcc remains satisfactory in both isolated SLR tasks (in the 95% WAcc range for SI), showing the potential of utilizing the module in learning platforms like SL-ReDu. Note also that performance varies among signers, as shown in Figure 3 for the isolated tasks in the SI case, remaining nevertheless well above 80% WAcc, even for the worse performing ones.

Concerning continuous fingerspelling, it is natural that performance suffers at the WAcc level, since letter recognition errors (including insertions and deletions) accumulate at the word level, especially for longer letter sequences. This effect is exacerbated due the lack of a language model in the recognizer, as well as the significantly smaller amount of collected data and number of signers compared to the isolated tasks. As expected, LAcc results are higher, but clearly further improvement is needed.

5. User Evaluation of SL-ReDu Platform

We have also conducted a user evaluation of the SL-ReDu platform, producing both objective results (focusing on GSL recognition performance), as well as a subjective assessment based on user responses to a questionnaire.

5.1. Volunteer Users

Two groups of students (with the Department of Special Education at University of Thessaly) and two professional volunteers participated in the preliminary SL-

GSL recog. task	Metric	MS	SI	Eval.
iso. numerals	WAcc	97.78	94.48	98.61
iso. non-numerals	WAcc	99.44	96.20	97.22
cont. fingerspelling	WAcc	75.22	65.30	90.28
	LAcc	86.12	77.66	91.03

Table 1: GSL recognition performance for the various tasks considered here under MS and SI training/testing on the GSL corpus of Section 4.1. Also shown, at the right-most column, is the recognition performance during user evaluation of the SL-ReDu platform (Section 5.2). Results are reported in word accuracy (WAcc, %) or letter accuracy (LAcc, %).

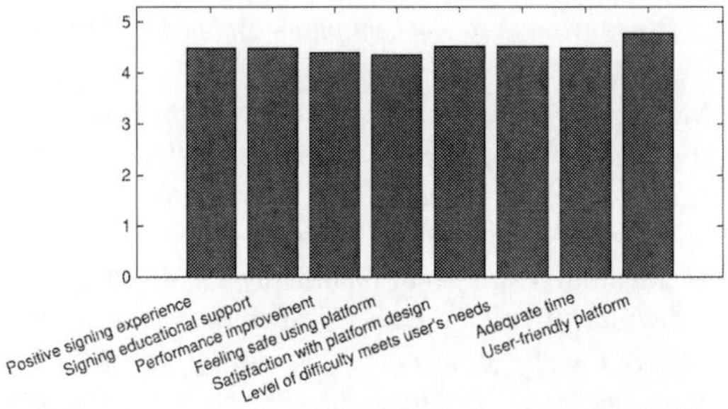

Figure 4: Mean values (on the 1-5 Likert scale) of the platform subjective user assessment along eight aspects.

ReDu evaluation. The first group (10 students) involved true beginners, i.e. university students who had had some contact with GSL for less than five months, the second group (11 students) was made up of students who had recently achieved the target A0-A1 level and had more than five months of experience, and the third group (2 experts) consisted of GSL experts who served as teachers to the student volunteer groups. The demographic characteristics of the student users were consistent with the demographics of the overall student population at the particular department, with ages between 19 and 22 years old and females outnumbering males.

5.2. Objective Evaluation of GSL Recognizer

This evaluation was carried out via "active"-type exercises that require SL production by the learner, captured by a camera and fed to the SL recognition module to provide learner binary feedback. For the isolated GSL recognition of numerals, we incorporated 3 assignments to the platform, each consisting of six GSL production questions of a numeral. For non-numerals we included 6 corresponding six-question production assignments. Finally, for continuous fingerspelling we used 6 six-question assignments that include letters as well as words that do not appear in the training set.

As already mentioned, the system also provides feedback to the user for correct positioning with respect to the camera. Note that participants are allowed to try twice each exercise in case of incorrect positioning feedback. Additionally, "active"-type exams designed by the instructor are automatically graded by the system, while limiting user interaction within prespecified time constraints.

For "active" GSL production and recognition evaluation, a subset of volunteers participated, namely 12 users, including 7 A0 level students, 4 A1 level students, and 1 expert, each performing 3 six-question assignments (one per task, totaling 18 questions).

The objective evaluation results in terms of WAcc (as well as LAcc for fingerspelling) are reported at the right-most column of Table 1. We observe that the results achieved are better than SI recognition performance of the isolated tasks on the collected GSL corpus of Section 4.1. This fact is probably due to the very careful signing and possible over-articulation by the volunteers. The difference is even larger in fingerspelling, due to the additional fact that the corresponding questions involved production of shorter words than those of the GSL corpus.

5.3. Subjective Assessment of the Platform

After signing the relevant consent forms and completing both self-monitoring and GSL production sessions of the SL-ReDu platform, participants were handed an anonymous subjective experience questionnaire that measures eight aspects concerning ease of use, usefulness, design, and user trust on the one-to-five Likert scale. The analysis of the filled subjective experience questionnaires provided valuable input, both in the form of numerical trends and via textual comments. In half (four out of eight) questions of the subjective evaluation the majority of the users provided the highest assessment ("very much"). More specifically, most of the users were completely satisfied with platform design, considered it to be a user-fiendly platform, felt that the level of difficulty meets their needs, and that signing educationally supports them (see also Figure 4 for the mean scores returned).

6. Conclusion

In this paper, we present a GSL recognizer capable of recognizing a medium-size vocabulary of isolated signs and continuously fingerspelled letter sequences, that is integrated in the SL-ReDu learning platform. The recognition module incorporates state-of-the-art deep-learning based visual detection, feature extraction, and classification, and is capable of operating in a signer-independent fashion in non-ideal visual environments. The designed module performs very well, as evidenced by recognition experiments on a suitable dataset collected for this purpose. Further, it yields very satisfactory objective and subjective user evaluation assessment of the SL-ReDu platform.

7. Acknowledgments

This research work was supported by the Hellenic Foundation for Research and Innovation (H.F.R.I.) under the "1st Call for H.F.R.I. Research Projects to support Faculty Members & Researchers and the procurement of high-cost research equipment grant" (Project "SL-ReDu", Project Number 2456).

8. Bibliographical References

Adaloglou, N., Chatzis, T., Papastratis, I., Stergioulas, A., Papadopoulos, G., Zacharopoulou, V., Xydopoulos, G. J., Atzakas, K., Papazachariou, D., and Daras, P. (2022). A comprehensive study on sign language recognition methods. *IEEE Transactions on Multimedia*, 24:1750–1762.

Aran, O., Ari, I., Akarun, L., Sankur, B., Benoit, A., Caplier, A., Campr, P., Carrillo, A. H., and Fanard, F.-X. (2009). SignTutor: An interactive system for sign language tutoring. *IEEE MultiMedia*, 16(1):81–93.

Armstrong, D. F., Karchmer, M. A., and VanCleve, J. V. (2002). *The Study of Signed Languages: Essays in Honor of William C. Stokoe*. Gallaudet University Press, Washington, DC.

Carreira, J., Noland, E., Banki-Horvath, A., Hillier, C., and Zisserman, A. (2018). A short note about Kinetics-600. *CoRR*, arXiv:1808.01340.

Deng, J., Dong, W., Socher, R., Li, L.-J., Li, K., and Fei-Fei, L. (2009). ImageNet: A large-scale hierarchical image database. In *Proc. IEEE Conference on Computer Vision and Pattern Recognition (CVPR)*, pages 248–255.

Ebling, S., Camgöz, N. C., Braem, P. B., Tissi, K., Sidler-Miserez, S., Stoll, S., Hadfield, S., Haug, T., Bowden, R., Tornay, S., Razavi, M., and Magimai-Doss, M. (2018). SMILE Swiss German Sign Language Dataset. In *Proc. Int. Conference on Language Resources and Evaluation (LREC)*, pages 4221–4229.

Efthimiou, E., Fotinea, S.-E., Flouda, C., Goulas, T., Ametoglou, G., Sapountzaki, G., Papadimitriou, K., and Potamianos, G. (2021). The SL-ReDu environment for self-monitoring and objective learner assessment in Greek Sign Language. In *Proc. Conference on Universal Access in Human-Computer Interaction. Access to Media, Learning and Assistive Environments (HCII)*, volume LNCS-12769, pages 72–81.

Graves, A., Fernández, S., Gomez, F., and Schmidhuber, J. (2006). Connectionist temporal classification: Labelling unsegmented sequence data with recurrent neural networks. In *Proc. Int. Conference on Machine Learning (ICML)*, pages 369–376.

Howard, A. G., Zhu, M., Chen, B., Kalenichenko, D., Wang, W., Weyand, T., Andreetto, M., and Adam, H. (2017). MobileNets: Efficient convolutional neural networks for mobile vision applications. *CoRR*, arXiv:1704.04861.

Joy, J., Balakrishnan, K., and Sreeraj, M. (2019). SignQuiz: A quiz based tool for learning fingerspelled signs in Indian Sign Language using ASLR. *IEEE Access*, 7:28363–28371.

Kemp, M. (1998). Why is learning American Sign Language a challenge? *American Annals of the Deaf*, 143(3):255–259.

Kingma, D. P. and Ba, J. (2014). Adam: A method for stochastic optimization. *CoRR*, arXiv:1412.6980.

Lugaresi, C., Tang, J., Nash, H., McClanahan, C., Uboweja, E., Hays, M., Zhang, F., Chang, C.-L., Yong, M., Lee, J., Chang, W.-T., Hua, W., Georg, M., and Grundmann, M. (2019). MediaPipe: A framework for perceiving and processing reality. In *Proc. Workshop on Computer Vision for AR/VR at IEEE CVPR*.

Mehdi, S. A. and Khan, Y. N. (2002). Sign language recognition using sensor gloves. In *Proc. Int. Conference on Neural Information Processing (ICONIP)*, pages 2204–2206.

Mohammdi, H. M. and Elbourhamy, D. M. (2021). An intelligent system to help deaf students learn Arabic Sign Language. *Interactive Learning Environments*.

Moryossef, A., Tsochantaridis, I., Dinn, J., Camgöz, N. C., Bowden, R., Jiang, T., Rios, A., Müller, M., and Ebling, S. (2021). Evaluating the immediate applicability of pose estimation for sign language recognition. In *Proc. IEEE/CVF Conference on Computer Vision and Pattern Recognition Workshops (CVPRW)*, pages 3429–3435.

Potamianos, G., Papadimitriou, K., Efthimiou, E., Fotinea, S. E., Sapountzaki, G., and Maragos, P. (2020). SL-ReDu: Greek sign language recognition for educational applications. Project description and early results. In *Proc. PErvasive Technologies Related to Assistive Environments Conference (PETRA)*.

Potamianos, G., Papadimitriou, K., Efthimiou, E., Fotinea, S.-E., Goulas, T., Flouda, C., and Ametoglou, G. (2021). SL-ReDu Deliverable D5.2: Technical specifications and system architecture definition. Technical report. [Online:] https://sl-redu.ece.uth.gr/deliverable/Deliverable_D5.2.pdf.

Ren, Z., Yuan, J., and Zhang, Z. (2011). Robust hand gesture recognition based on finger-earth mover's distance with a commodity depth camera. In *Proc. ACM Int. Conference on Multimedia (MM)*, pages 1093–1096.

Sapountzaki, G., Efthimiou, E., Fotinea, S. E., Papadimitriou, K., and Potamianos, G. (2021). Educational material organization in a platform for Greek Sign Language self monitoring and assessment. In *Proc. Int. Conference on Education and New Learning Technologies (EDULEARN)*, pages 3322–3331.

Schuster, M. and Paliwal, K. K. (1997). Bidirectional recurrent neural networks. *IEEE Transactions on Signal Processing*, 45(11):2673–2681.

Szegedy, C., Vanhoucke, V., Ioffe, S., Shlens, J., and Wojna, Z. (2016). Rethinking the Inception architecture for computer vision. In *Proc. IEEE Conference on Computer Vision and Pattern Recognition (CVPR)*, pages 2818–2826.

Tran, D., Wang, H., Torresani, L., Ray, J., LeCun, Y., and Paluri, M. (2018). A closer look at spatiotemporal convolutions for action recognition. In *Proc. IEEE/CVF Conference on Computer Vision and Pattern Recognition (CVPR)*, pages 6450–6459.

Zafrulla, Z., Brashear, H., Presti, P., Hamilton, H., and Starner, T. (2011). CopyCat: An American Sign Language game for deaf children. In *Proc. IEEE Int. Conference on Automatic Face and Gesture Recognition (FG)*.

Proceedings of the 7th International Workshop on Sign Language Translation and Avatar Technology (SLTAT 7), pages 85–90
Language Resources and Evaluation Conference (LREC 2022), Marseille, 20-25 June 2022

Signing Avatars in a New Dimension: Challenges and Opportunities in Virtual Reality

Lorna C. Quandt, Jason Lamberton, Carly Leannah, Athena Willis, & Melissa Malzkuhn
Gallaudet University
800 Florida Ave NE Washington, DC 20002
{lorna.quandt, jason.lamberton, carly.leannah, athena.willis, melissa.malzkuhn}@gallaudet.edu

Abstract

With improved and more easily accessible technology, immersive virtual reality (VR) head-mounted devices have become more ubiquitous. As signing avatar technology improves, virtual reality presents a new and relatively unexplored application for signing avatars. This paper discusses two primary ways that signed language can be represented in immersive virtual spaces: 1) Third-person, in which the VR user sees a character who communicates in signed language; and 2) First-person, in which the VR user produces signed content themselves, tracked by the head-mounted device and visible to the user herself (and/or to other users) in the virtual environment. We will discuss the unique affordances granted by virtual reality and how signing avatars might bring accessibility and new opportunities to virtual spaces. We will then discuss the limitations of signed content in virtual reality concerning virtual signers shown from both third- and first-person perspectives.

Keywords: signing avatars, virtual reality, motion capture

1. Introduction

Immersive virtual reality (VR) continues to become more popular, with almost 10 million VR devices shipped in 2021 alone (Alsop, 2022). Along with this proliferation of new technology comes the possibility of new ways of communicating, socializing, or learning in virtual spaces. Likewise, interest in technology-supported sign language instruction is growing. Unlike spoken language, which can be taught and evaluated using smartphones or computers, the three-dimensional nature of signed languages and facial expression's impact on meaning has created a severe barrier to technology-based sign language instruction. In-person classes are expensive and difficult to access in many areas. The other available options include books, videos, or smartphone apps that cannot fully demonstrate the highly spatial nature of signed language or provide real-time feedback. Emerging technologies like mixed and virtual reality allow the development of three-dimensional interactions in immersive environments. By taking advantage of the three-dimensional (3D) nature of immersive VR, it may be possible to create immersive learning experiences to engage learners' bodies and minds more effectively and enhance learning. In this paper, we will discuss the possibility of signing avatars in a VR environment, considering both the opportunities afforded by the current technology and the limitations.

Our work focuses on American Sign Language (ASL), but these considerations may also apply to other signed languages. We direct our attention primarily toward using VR for supporting sign language learning (Quandt et al., 2020). However, sign language in VR is also relevant for entertainment, gaming, and socialization in virtual spaces.

While developers are designing many different types of learning experiences in VR, the applications of VR for learning signed languages are particularly encouraging. A fundamental theory in learning science, called embodied learning, posits that greater involvement of conceptually-aligned movement and action during learning can lead to better understanding and higher recall (Kontra et al., 2012; Kontra et al., 2015; Lindgren & Johnson-Glenberg, 2013; Weisberg & Newcombe, 2017). The immersive and spatially rich nature of VR allows for the possibility of embodied learning. Learning signed languages in VR may represent a step toward the potential far-reaching application of embodied learning through signed languages.

Many new ASL learners use online two-dimensional videos to learn introductory signs, but these pre-recorded videos have no interactive features and may not engage all learners (Shao et al., 2020). By contrast, immersive VR creates a powerful experience wherein people feel as if they are physically present in a 3D virtual space (Bailenson, 2018; Lindgren & Johnson-Glenberg, 2013). This immersive, spatially rich environment is particularly well-suited to the highly spatial nature of ASL, in which space is used as a core feature of the language. In one study, interaction with a signing avatar in augmented reality (e.g., the avatar is overlaid upon the real-world view) led to improved ASL learning outcomes compared to learning by video or book (Shao et al., 2020). Throughout our work on signing avatars, a critical guiding goal has been to ensure that the movements of the animated signing are as natural (i.e., human-like) as possible. It is crucial to ensure that animated sign language accurately delivers the nuances and inflections of the original linguistic content, rather than relying on automated animations which do not include smooth transitions or natural movements (Quandt et al., 2022). Even a slight error in the synchronization of the animation can affect the interpretation of a signed production. Motion capture enables the highest quality animation (Joerg, Hodgins, & O'Sullivan, 2010), although it does come at a high processing cost.

Our group has established the feasibility of an immersive VR ASL learning environment populated with high-quality signing avatars. In this work, we created a prototype for teaching ASL in immersive VR (Quandt et al., 2020), in which both a virtual Teacher avatar and the VR user are present in the virtual environment (Fig. 1). This scenario

Figure 1: Two types of signing present in an immersive virtual reality environment.

encapsulates the two types of signing which may present in the virtual space: 1) Third-person Perspective, wherein one or more signing avatars are present in front of the VR user in space; and 2) First-person perspective, wherein the VR user's own hands can be seen in the virtual space and can potentially be animated with real-time signing based on hand-tracking the user's actual signing (Fig. 1). These two signers in virtual space bring about different challenges and opportunities, which we will discuss in this paper.

2. The State of Signing Avatars in VR

Signing avatars are not commonly seen in virtual spaces yet, but as VR becomes more affordable, and research development continues in this area, we are becoming more familiar with what is possible regarding signing in VR. The newest publicly available models of VR head-mounted devices have better-performing hardware and software, which makes the representation of ASL in VR more feasible. For example, newer VR headsets are wireless, which allows for better head and body mobility. They also include better video resolution and built-in cameras to aid in hand-tracking. Recent software updates have further improved the hand tracking capabilities of some devices (Henry, 2022). We expect this trajectory to continue as VR becomes more mainstream. Particularly relevant to signing in virtual spaces, the Oculus Quest 2 contains built-in hand-tracking cameras. Currently, some publicly available software (e.g., Waltz of the Wizard; Hand Physics Lab) use hand-tracking to control user interfaces or as an integral part of the gameplay, while many programs still rely on controller-based commands. We use the built-in hand tracking of the head-mounted Oculus Quest 2 device in our current work, but other options may be commercially available, and developers regularly release new hardware with updated capabilities. Some external hardware could enhance hand-tracking capabilities (e.g., Kinect, depth sensors), however, users much prefer a fully wireless experience, especially if they are moving their hands around to learn and produce signs (Quandt et al., 2020). Keeping the equipment manageable and avoiding physically burdensome add-ons is an intentional design choice.

Socialization and community-building are growing activities within VR, allowing users to connect with others in a natural, immersive environment (Li, Vinayagamoorthy, Williamson, Shama, & Cesar, 2021). Virtual avatars have already been hacked to communicate in sign languages for casual conversation and social interaction. VRChat is a community accessible to any VR user wherein people can virtually navigate a built environment, inhabiting a character that they customize. Users can chat and form online communities with other users. An emergent sign-language using community has emerged in VRChat, including drop-in sign language chats and informal sign language lessons in several different signed languages (Davis, 2019). Since not all users have devices that can track hand movements, VRChat users cannot sign naturally with their hands. Instead, they use controllers to produce signs. Some controllers give the user the ability to make certain handshapes, with the thumb and the index and middle fingers, and the ability to open and close your fist. Within those limitations, a user can sign in a modified way, involving a limited number of moveable fingers and opening and closing their fists. The hands can move freely in the space around the user, allowing for sign location to be represented reasonably well. This emerging signing community in VRChat demonstrates interest in the casual use of signed languages for socialization and learning in VR and highlights the adaptations that communities come up with to work around technological limitations.

One significant limitation of signed communication in VR is the difficulty animating natural facial expressions, especially for real-time communication as in VRChat described above. In ASL, and all signed languages, facial expressions, including the mouth, eye, cheek, and eyebrow movements, are intricate and nuanced, adding and changing the meaning and structure of signs produced by the hands. To successfully capture facial expressions in VR, the capture technology must pick up on the slightest differences and changes in the face that accompany the hand movements of ASL. The two distinct types of signers in VR each present different opportunities and challenges, which we will discuss below.

3. Third-person perspective signing

3.1 Opportunities

Third-person perspective signing—in which the user views a signing avatar in front of them (Fig. 1) is the more straightforward representation of sign language in VR. This scenario is similar to animating a signing avatar outside of VR. Developers create the avatar using development pipelines the same way they do for non-VR use. The 3D avatar file is then placed in the VR environment. The 3D nature of the virtual environment means that a user can see the avatar's movements with rich spatial detail. For instance, in VR, a signing avatar can be seen from all angles in ways that accurately represent signing movements in space.

3.2 Challenges

With the third-person signing avatar, the primary challenge is creating avatars that are not too resource-heavy, since typical animations are made up of too many polygons and become a burden on the VR platform. Polygon count is a critical consideration when developing and populating virtual environments. Essentially, the more polygons, the more computing power is needed. There is a tradeoff between quality and the ability of the VR platform to handle the torrent of data efficiently. To ensure real-time interactivity, we ensure that the system maintains stability by keeping the avatar's animation within reasonable limits for polygon count.

Figure 2. The built-in hand-tracking cameras on a VR device (located at the blue dots) can capture movements in certain locations well, as shown in the green areas. However, areas on the user's head and body are not easily captured by the cameras, as shown in red. This schematic is generic and not specific to any specific device.

In the past, our team used motion capture markers on the face. However, the markers only captured a subset of facial movements, overlooking other possible facial expressions, and could not track eye movements. The Faceware system (Faceware Tech, Austin, TX, USA) has proved to be effective in capturing a broader range of a signer's facial expressions and eye movements, resulting in an avatar that portrays ASL facial expressions accurately. Our project requires the use of a customized Faceware helmet camera which allows for natural movements of the hands near the signer's face (Quandt et al., 2020). One remaining issue is that whenever the hands cover the signer's face during recording, there are gaps in the facial data, which must be hand-animated in later in the development pipeline.

4. First-person perspective signing

4.1 Opportunities

When hand-tracking in enabled on a VR device, the user can see his or her own hands moving in the virtual world. Seeing one's own hands moving in VR provides a strong sense of embodiment—especially if the virtual hands correctly represent the users' real-life movements. If and when hand-tracking technology develops sufficiently to accurately track signed language handshapes and movements, users will be able to sign while wearing VR devices and will be able to see their signs in the virtual space. The user's signing will also be visible to other online users, as in the example of VRChat in Section 2. Popular VR devices have recently improved their hand-tracking capabilities (Henry, 2022), deploying updates remotely to all users. These updates have mitigated some of the major limitations of hand-tracking, but some issues still remain (see Section 4.2).

In our ongoing research (Quandt et al., 2020), we have evaluated which ASL signs are best captured by existing hand-tracking technology. Most of our team members are deaf, which affords us the unique opportunity to self-evaluate the representation of signs in VR. For example, we evaluated a list of potential signs and decided whether different signs would work well with the Oculus Quest 2 and

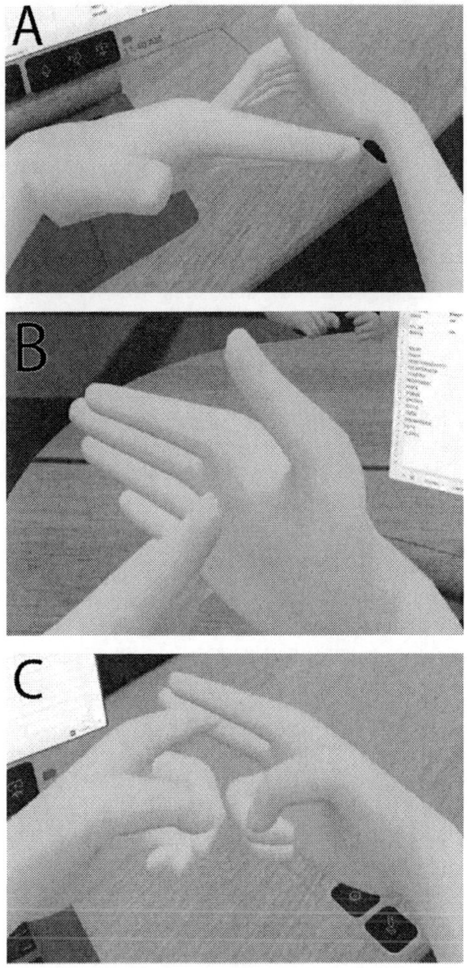

Figure 3. ASL signs as captured by Oculus Quest 2 (v38). A) the sign BREAD is represented well, with no occlusion or disfigurements. B) the sign WOOD resulting in unnatural overlap of the hands. C) the sign EGGS resulting in overlap and inaccurate handshape.

modified the signs as needed. Because there are often different signs for the same word, we track what variations of a sign are most compatible with the device's current hand tracking capabilities. With a Deaf-centric team, the ability to make quick informed decisions to make the whole system work well is an advantage.

4.2 Challenges

Animating hands in real-time as a camera tracks a signer's hands is a significant challenge. Our team has identified several specific issues remaining before real-time ASL can be well represented in VR. All currently available VR headsets protrude several inches away from the bridge of the nose and eyes. Headsets with built-in hand-tracking capabilities have cameras embedded that look outward, and each camera has a cone of view that expands as the distance from the camera increases (Fig. 2). Close to the cameras, there are significant blind spots. Additionally, as the user moves their head to look around in space, the field of view which the cameras can see changes. Thus, the space in which the device can sense signs is inherently limited and changes depending on where the user is looking. Signs located outside the space in front of the signer are poorly captured by the cameras. This limited field of view causes technological limitations in recognizing three key visuospatial parameters of ASL: 1) handshapes, 2) physical location, and 3) facial expressions. These parameters are necessary to convey communication accurately and effectively in ASL and other signed languages (Friedman, 1976).

A crucial parameter of ASL is the physical location in which signed words are produced. In ASL, location in signing space is inherent to each sign's meaning. However, the many signs which are located near the body present a challenge for representation in VR. For example, the common sign for PARENT uses the "5" hand shape with all five fingers extended, touching the lower cheek, then touching the upper cheek. Because this sign includes touching the face near where the device rests, the normal production of the sign is prohibited, and the cameras cannot capture the sign.

Another challenge is the representation of ASL handshapes in VR headsets. While some current VR devices allow for improved hand-tracking, the technology still has limitations with recognizing certain handshapes, especially handshapes that require fingers crossing one another. For instance, the ASL handshape R involves the middle finger crossing over the index finger and is often not well tracked by current devices. Occlusions can also happen with two-handed signs if the hands or fingers cross one another, as with the word EGG (Fig. 3). In ASL, EGG is signed as the index and middle finger on both hands together, each hand forming the "H" handshape and tapping once, then moving downwards slightly away from each other. These shapes and movement tend to produce a great deal of occlusion when tracked by VR headset cameras.

To address the challenges related to sign location and occlusion, our current work focuses on signs that the hardware cameras can most accurately capture. When hands or fingers are placed on top of each other, it is difficult for the built-in cameras to see the hidden hand or fingers. The software interpolates the missing information, and often the resulting visualization is distorted (Fig. 3). Signs that avoid those handshapes and movement patterns are better represented in current VR devices.

Lastly, current hardware cannot capture a user's facial expressions. While it appears that developers are testing various approaches to capturing users' facial and eye movements while wearing a VR device (Wen et al., 2022), no options are commercially available at the time of writing. Naturally, given the importance of facial expression to signed languages, this still constitutes a major challenge for the progress of ASL in VR.

5. Conclusion

There is much room for improvement and undoubtedly, developers are racing to produce sophisticated hardware with better hand tracking, resolution, and capture for signing in virtual spaces. However, VR devices continue to be an obstacle given that in natural signed communication, many signs touch the face and body. We expect that advances in artificial intelligence will help solve some of the computer-vision related problems in this area. Signing in VR remains novel but brings much potential for learning, teaching, and interacting in virtual environments. Our research group is pursuing signing in VR in both the first- and third-person perspectives, and while the representation of signed languages improve in those two dimensions, we continue to identify remaining problems. Fluency and clarity of signing are essential and cannot be compromised without harming communication. Without the accurate representation of sign language, researchers risk compromising the representation of deaf people in virtual spaces.

6. Acknowledgements

The authors acknowledge the support of National Science Foundation grants #2118742, 2012924, and 2123626 to LQ and MM. We also thank Sarah Miller, Yiqiao Wang. Jianye Wang, Myles de Bastion, and Heather Smith for their contributions to this work.

7. Bibliographical References

Alsop, T. (2022). AR/VR headset shipments worldwide 2019-2023. Statista. https://www.statista.com/statistics/653390/worldwide-virtual-and-augmented-reality-headset-shipments/

Bailenson, J. (2018). *Experience on demand: What virtual reality is, how it works, and what it can do*. WW Norton & Company.

Davis, R. N. (2019). *Deaf VRChat players are inventing their own sign language*. https://www.gamerevolution.com/news/617632-deaf-vrchat-players-asl-sign-language-index-vr

Friedman, L. A. (1976). *Phonology of a soundless language: phonological structure of the American sign language*. University of California, Berkeley.

Henry, J. (2022). *Meta rolls out hand tracking update on Oculus Quest 2*. Tech Times. https://www.Techtimes.com/articles/274566/20220421/meta-rolls-out-hand-tracking-update-oculus-quest-2-here.htm

Jörg, S., Hodgins, J., & O'Sullivan, C. (2010, July). The perception of finger motions. In *Proceedings of the 7th Symposium on Applied Perception in Graphics and Visualization*, pp. 129-133.

Kontra, C., Lyons, D. J., Fischer, S. M., & Beilock, S. L. (2015). Physical experience enhances science learning. *Psychological Science*, 26(6), 737-749.

Kontra, C., Goldin-Meadow, S., & Beilock, S. L. (2012). Embodied learning across the life span. *Topics in Cognitive Science*, 4(4), pp. 731-739.

Li, J., Vinayagamoorthy, V., Williamson, J., Shama, D. & Cesar, P. (2021). Social VR: A New Medium for Remote Communication and Collaboration. In *CHI EA '21: Extended Abstracts of the 2021 CHI Conference on Human Factors in Computing Systems*, 81, pp. 1-6.

Lindgren, R., & Johnson-Glenberg, M. (2013). Emboldened by embodiment: Six precepts for research on embodied learning and mixed reality. *Educational Researcher*, 42(8), pp. 445-452.

Quandt, L. C., Lamberton, J., Willis, A. S., Wang, J., Weeks, K., Kubicek, E., & Malzkuhn, M. (2020). Teaching ASL signs using signing avatars and immersive learning in virtual reality. *The 22nd International ACM SIGACCESS Conference on Computers and Accessibility (ASSETS '20)*, 98, 1-4.

Quandt, L. C., Willis, A. W., Schwenk, M., Weeks, K., &

Ferster, R. (2022). Attitudes toward signing human avatars vary depending on hearing status, age of signed language acquisition, and avatar type. *Frontiers in Psychology*, 13.

Shao, Q., Sniffen, A., Blanchett, J., Hillis, M. E., Shi, X., Haris, T. K., Liu, J., Lamberton, J., Malzkuhn, M., Quandt, L. C., Mahoney, J., Kraemer, D. J. M., Zhou, X., & Balkcom, D. (2020). Teaching American Sign Language in mixed reality. In *Proceedings of the ACM on Interactive, Mobile, Wearable and Ubiquitous Technologies (IMWUT)*, 4, 152.

Weisberg, S. M., & Newcombe, N. S. (2017). Embodied cognition and STEM learning: Overview of a topical collection in CR: PI. *Cognitive Research: Principles and Implications*, 2(1), pp. 1-6.

Wen, L., Zhou, J., Huang, W., & Chen, F. (2022). A Survey of Facial Capture for Virtual Reality, in *IEEE Access*, vol. 10, pp. 6042-6052.

Proceedings of the 7th International Workshop on Sign Language Translation and Avatar Technology (SLTAT 7), pages 91–94
Language Resources and Evaluation Conference (LREC 2022), Marseille, 20-25 June 2022

Mouthing Recognition with OpenPose in Sign Language

María Del Carmen Sáenz
Computing & Digital Media, DePaul University
Chicago, IL. USA
msaenz@depaul.edu

Abstract

Many avatars focus on the hands and how they express sign language. However, sign language also uses mouth and face gestures to modify verbs, adjectives, or adverbs; these are known as non-manual components of the sign. To have a translation system that the Deaf community will accept, we need to include these non-manual signs. Just as machine learning is being used on generating hand signs, the work we are focusing on will be doing the same, but with mouthing and mouth gestures. We will be using data from The National Center for Sign Language and Gesture Resources. The data from the center are videos of native signers focusing on different areas of signer movement, gesturing, and mouthing, and are annotated specifically for mouthing studies. With this data, we will run a pre-trained Neural Network application called OpenPose. After running through OpenPose, further analysis of the data is conducted using a Random Forest Classifier. This research looks at how well an algorithm can be trained to spot certain mouthing points and output the mouth annotations with a high degree of accuracy. With this, the appropriate mouthing for animated signs can be easily applied to avatar technologies.

Keywords: Avatar technology, American Sign Language, OpenPose, Nonmanual signs, Mouthing, Mouth gestures

1. Introduction

Many Deaf people have American Sign Language (ASL) as their native language; their native tongue is usually secondary. Most people have limited reading and writing skills in said spoken language, leading to disadvantages in everyday situations such as health, education, and work. Communication barriers can occur especially in emergencies or government spaces. For example, if an emergency announcement is made on a train, there will be a delay in communication for a Deaf individual. An automatic translation system, such as an avatar, can provide rudimentary communication, in ASL on a public address system. These non-invasive technologies have been explored for the last 20 years to present sign languages. Many prototypes have been explored to accelerate Deaf-accessible systems, such as weather reports, airport security personnel, and government offices (Wolfe et. al, 2021).

Studies using a signing avatar combined with automatic translation systems, have focused on the hands more so than any other part of the avatar. Even though, it is well known that non-manual components of a sign, such as mouthing and mouth gestures, are used to discern signs that are closely related semantically as they may share the same movements or handshapes (Koller et. al, 2015). Mouthing itself is from spoken language in which you partially or fully mouth a word (Bickford and Fraychineaud, 2006). While mouth gestures come from the Deaf community, with no clear origin, such as mouthing "CHA" after signing the word "big" (Bickford and Fraychineaud, 2006). Just like in spoken language, the mood is conveyed with facial expressions and how words are said (mouthed). Having no facial expressions or mouthing/mouth gestures in sign language, according to Baldassarri et al., "is like speaking in a monotonic voice: more boring, less expressive and, in some cases, ambiguous" (2009).

Through the years as technology has advanced, so has avatar technology. However, there are still many inquiries regarding how to display information linguistically and pragmatically on the avatar's face (Wolfe et. al, 2021). Currently, work done with the face and mouth with present-day technologies available have long rendering times and can be incompatible with interactive graphic applications (Wolfe et. al, 2021).

Just like the work being done on algorithms for animating hand signs, this research aims to train how to spot mouthing points with exactitude to automate and apply it in avatar technologies for appropriate mouthing/mouth gestures for animated signs.

2. Related Work

The earliest research about mouthing, was in 1968 by Fisher (Koller et. al, 2015) distinguishing between a viseme and phonemes. Phonemes are the smallest units that compromise spoken language. While a viseme is made up of several speech sounds (phonemes). A viseme is "a set of phonemes which have an identical appearance on the lips" as they are the visual twin of phonemes (Bear and Harvey, 2017). As more research was being done in understanding how to visualize mouth movement to create speech, the audio-visual speech recognition field was born. This, in turn, led to the studying of the correlation of facial expression recognition with mouth shape creation via algorithms.

Usually mouthing and mouth gestures regarding sign language detection are overlooked (Koller et. al, 2015), but interest has been developing in this field (Antonakos et. al, 2015). Automatic Sign Language Recognition (ASLR) systems have been looking into the shape and motion of the mouth to determine critical cues versus ones done carelessly. For example, in ASL the tongue going through the front teeth is something done carelessly, therefore not a cue (Antonakos et. al, 2015). However, a critical cue is when one can recognize the state of the mouth. Such as open, closed, or very closed mouth during facial recognition (Koller et. al, 2015). Other related work has looked at using sequential pattern trees (Koller et. al, 2015) for general facial tracking or weak supervision models for facial features (Koller et. al, 2015). Overall, many models and analyses have been done on the face and head movements, which have partially included mouthing and/or mouth gestures.

On the other side, we must consider the progress in Computer Generated Imagery (CGI) and how it has advanced facial and mouthing in various spaces.

One of the first computer-animated faces called *Tony* from 1985, took 3 years to create a 7.5-minute film. Although it won many prizes for its innovation, this character today suffers from the phenomenon called *uncanny valley (*Wolfe et. al, 2021*)*; which gives the viewer a feeling of uneasiness or repulsion of seeing the humanoid figure. To avoid this, many animations use cartoon or alien humanoids, because since they are less human-like, they are more accepting of their emotions and expressions (Wolfe et. al, 2021). The best effects for facial and mouthing imagery in more complex visuals, still take hours to render a frame even though we have faster computers. There is also the painstaking task of doing some work manually, especially for frame transitions (Wolfe et. al, 2021).

With many advancements done in computational imagery and graphics, as well as in modeling, it takes time to fully capture the facial expressions. As well as creating reliable and most of all, believable mouthing, and mouth gestures. Just as many efforts are put into automating hand signs for signed languages, one must put in work on non-manual signs to have an avatar-based translation system be accepted in the Deaf community. The work proposed in this paper is attempting to bridge the gap in its usage of modeling and analyzing visual data to attempt to output mouthing points that can be used in automation for avatar usage.

3. Data Analysis

Motion capture is one way of data collecting to analyze sign languages. Much of this data is, again, primarily focused on the hands and how they move. Another way of studying sign languages is by using images or videos of native signers that are already available. OpenPose is a pre-trained Neural Network that analyzes video and images for a "real-time multi-person system to jointly detect human body, hand, facial, and foot keypoints." (Cao et. al, 2021). With 135 keypoints overall and 70 face keypoints, we will be analyzing videos of native signers which are publicly available.

3.1 Video Dataset

The dataset that is used was specifically captured to study ASL, which demonstrates the necessary parts of Sign Language accurately. The National Center for Sign Language and Gesture Resources (B.U., 1999), has a significant corpus of ASL videos of native signers. It contains multiple synchronized video files showing views from different angles and close-ups of the face. The corpus is a collection of 2,617 videos in MP4 format that has been compressed from 60 frames per second to 30 frames per second.

Figure 1: Example frames of video dataset

To coincide with each video, DePaul University has created an ELAN (also known as EUDICO annotation format) formatted file that groups different areas of the signer's mouthing and mouth gestures. The ELAN formatted file offered many mouthing annotations, but we focused on 9 annotations with a minimum of 35 examples as a requirement.

The 9 annotations we focused on were:

- Open and corners down
- Intense
- Raised upper lip
- Lips spread and corners down
- Lips pursed: mm
- Open (as in mouth open)
- Onset (mouth movement start)
- Offset (mouth movement end)

3.2 OpenPose Dataset

Although OpenPose has 70 face keypoint estimations that we can use on the video dataset, we will be focusing on points 48, 54, and 60-67 which pertain to the mouth.

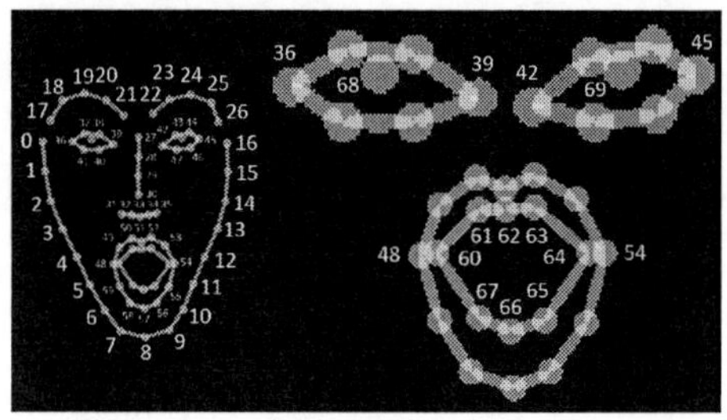

Figure 2: Facial keypoints in OpenPose

When we run the dataset through OpenPose the output visually shows the facial keypoints being mapped to the video.

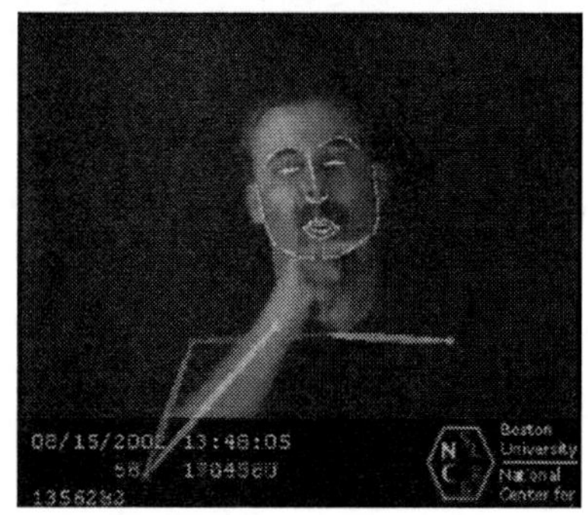

Figure 3: OpenPose keypoints on Video Dataset

4. Modeling

OpenPose is a powerful tool that was used to build highly confident mappings of the mouth. It works such that it uses two parallel divisions of convolutional network layers (Cao et. al, 2021); the first predicting 18 confidence maps, while the other predicts 38-part affinity fields. The confidence maps denote the specific part of the human pose skeleton, and the affinity fields denote the level of association between the parts (Cao et. al, 2021). In the last stages of the OpenPose algorithm, it cleans up its predictions made by the branches, weaker links are pruned via the PAF values, and the keypoints are then estimated and allocated on the video itself. Before OpenPose, some libraries were using different models such as Alpha-Pose and Mask R-CNN.

Comparing the runtime analysis of all 3, OpenPoses' runtime is constant, while Alpha-Pose and Mask R-CNN grow linearly with more people in the video. Although we are only focusing on one person in our video datasets, future work with multiple signers would be easier to evaluate using this software, especially with its constant runtime analysis.

After running OpenPose on 2,617 videos, we join the video JSON output with its respective ELAN annotation file by converting both into data frames and joining them via timestamp keyframe. This allowed us to analyze what annotations we wanted to focus on and at the same time have more than 35 videos available with said annotations. We were left with about 1,800 videos and used a matplotlib animator to manually look over the keyframes for occlusion and obstruction of the face by the hands. The filtering of the videos was only for extreme distortions and others were left to train the model effectively in the next phase.

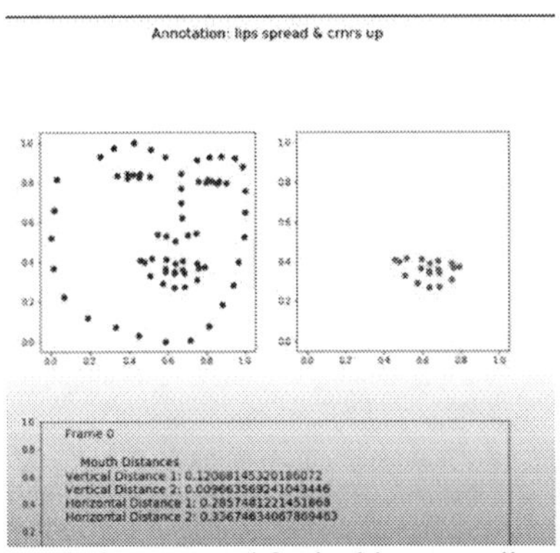

Figure 3: Animator used for looking over distortions

Combing through the data were left with 2,217 videos that had one or many of the annotations that we were interested in further analyzing using other modeling techniques. The next modeling technique we used, was a Random Forest Classifier (RFC) Model, an ensemble method, that has been utilized before to study Sign Languages (Su et. al, 2016). Going through the output of the OpenPose datasets, there was one sample size that had most of the data. To take advantage of this classifier, we used an oversampling method, called SMOTE (Synthetic Minority Oversampling Technique) (Chawla et. al, 2002), to improve the random oversampling. For comparison's sake, we ran the RFC without resampling and with resampling. A Grid Search was used to find the best hyperparameters for both the resampled and the non-resampled data, coming up with the same hyperparameters.

5. Results

Overall, the dataset showed a higher accuracy with the resampled data as opposed to the non-resampled data in the test balanced accuracy of the model and the validation accuracy of the annotations on the facial points themselves.

Dataset	**Validation Accuracy**	**Test Balance Accuracy**
With Resampling	0.96 (+/- 0.01)	0.6664373289281572
Without Resampling	0.43 (+- 0/03)	0.4392537365588655

Table 1: General Results of RFC

The classification reports also show that the recall is higher when there is more data to analyze for each facial keypoint and their respective annotation.

=== Classification Report ===

	precision	recall	f1-score	support
OFFSET	1.00	0.32	0.48	38
ONSET	0.60	0.11	0.19	27
intense	0.87	0.70	0.78	98
lips pursed:mm	0.86	0.85	0.85	91
lips spread	0.87	0.79	0.83	153
lips spread & crnrs down	0.80	0.96	0.87	532
open	0.90	0.88	0.89	174
open & corners down	0.85	0.76	0.80	111
raised upper lip	0.94	0.82	0.88	111
accuracy			0.84	1335
macro avg	0.85	0.69	0.73	1335
weighted avg	0.85	0.84	0.83	1335

Figure 4: RFC without resampling of the dataset

=== Classification Report ===

	precision	recall	f1-score	support
OFFSET	0.68	0.68	0.68	38
ONSET	0.47	0.52	0.49	27
intense	0.80	0.94	0.86	98
lips pursed:mm	0.92	0.92	0.92	91
lips spread	0.80	0.86	0.83	153
lips spread & crnrs down	0.90	0.86	0.88	532
open	0.92	0.94	0.93	174
open & corners down	0.85	0.86	0.85	111
raised upper lip	0.93	0.85	0.89	111
accuracy			0.87	1335
macro avg	0.81	0.82	0.82	1335
weighted avg	0.87	0.87	0.87	1335

Figure 5: RFC with resampling of the dataset

6. Conclusion

A CNN with an RFC can prove to give a high accuracy in knowing which annotation is which on the facial keypoints. However, to have more balance in the tree, we need more data to work with from credible resources. Many institutions are sharing their corpus with other universities and agencies. Then we can add known annotations, like ELAN to the corpora that can assist in researching further the automation of mouthing and mouth gestures. Although the dataset used was small, we can see that a model can be trained to be effective in figuring out what mouth gestures are being used on specific facial points. For avatar translation systems, automation of the correct hand and mouthing/mouth gestures will be highly beneficial in getting us towards a system that will be acceptable to the Deaf community. As well as bridging the gap between the Hearing and Deaf communities.

7. Bibliographical References

Baldassarri, Sandra & Cerezo, Eva & Royo-Santas, Francisco. (2009). Automatic Translation System to Spanish Sign Language with a Virtual Interpreter. 5726. 196-199. 10.1007/978-3-642-03655-2_23.

Bear, Helen L. and Richard Harvey. "Phoneme-to-viseme mappings: the good, the bad, and the ugly." ArXiv abs/1805.02934 (2017): n. pag.

Bickford, J. and Fraychineaud, K. (2006). Mouth Morphemes in ASL: A closer look Theoretical Issues in Sign Language Research 9, 32–47.

Boston University. "Corpus of American Sign Language (ASL) Video Data from Native Signers". National Center for Sign Language and Gesture Resources at B.U., Dec. 1999, https://www.bu.edu/asllrp/cslgr/.

Chawla, N. et al. "SMOTE: Synthetic Minority Over-sampling Technique." J. Artif. Intell. Res. 16 (2002): 321-357.

E. Antonakos, A. Roussos and S. Zafeiriou, "A survey on mouth modeling and analysis for Sign Language recognition," 2015 11th IEEE International Conference and Workshops on Automatic Face and Gesture Recognition (FG), 2015, pp. 1-7, doi: 10.1109/FG.2015.7163162.

Koller, Oscar & Ney, Hermann & Bowden, Richard. (2015). Deep Learning of Mouth Shapes for Sign Language. 10.1109/ICCVW.2015.69.

San-Segundo, Rubén & Montero, Juan & Cordoba, Ricardo & Sama, V. & Fernández-Martínez, Fernando & D'Haro, Luis & López-Ludeña, Verónica & Sánchez, D. & García, A.. (2012). Design, development, and field evaluation of a Spanish into sign language translation system. Pattern Analysis and Applications. 15. 10.1007/s10044-011-0243-9.

Su, Ruiliang & Xiang, Chen & Cao, Shuai & Zhang, Xu. (2016). Random Forest-Based Recognition of Isolated Sign Language Subwords Using Data from Accelerometers and Surface Electromyographic Sensors. Sensors. 16. 100. 10.3390/s16010100.

Wolfe, R., Hanke, T., Langer, G., Jahn, E., Worseck, S., Bleicken, J., McDonald, J. & Johnson, S. Exploring Localization for Mouthings in Sign Language Avatars. Proceedings of the International Conference on Language Resources and Evaluation (LREC) 2018

Wolfe, R., McDonald, J., Johnson, R., Moncrief, R., Alexander, A., Sturr, B., Klinghofer, S., Conneelly, F. Saenz, M. & Choudhry, S. State of the Art and Future Challenges of the Portrayal of Facial Nonmanual Signals by Signing Avatar. International Conference on Human- Computer Interaction pp. 639-655. Springer, Cham. 2021

Z. Cao, G. Hidalgo, T. Simon, S. -E. Wei and Y. Sheikh, "OpenPose: Realtime Multi-Person 2D Pose Estimation Using Part Affinity Fields," in IEEE Transactions on Pattern Analysis and Machine Intelligence, vol. 43, no. 1, pp. 172-186, 1 Jan. 2021, doi: 10.1109/TPAMI.2019.2929257.

Proceedings of the 7th International Workshop on Sign Language Translation and Avatar Technology (SLTAT 7), pages 95–102
Language Resources and Evaluation Conference (LREC 2022), Marseille, 20-25 June 2022

Skeletal Graph Self-Attention: Embedding a Skeleton Inductive Bias into Sign Language Production

Ben Saunders, Necati Cihan Camgoz, Richard Bowden
University of Surrey
{b.saunders, n.camgoz, r.bowden}@surrey.ac.uk

Abstract

Recent approaches to Sign Language Production (SLP) have adopted spoken language Neural Machine Translation (NMT) architectures, applied without sign-specific modifications. In addition, these works represent sign language as a sequence of skeleton pose vectors, projected to an abstract representation with no inherent skeletal structure.

In this paper, we represent sign language sequences as a skeletal graph structure, with joints as nodes and both spatial and temporal connections as edges. To operate on this graphical structure, we propose Skeletal Graph Self-Attention ($SGSA$), a novel graphical attention layer that embeds a skeleton inductive bias into the SLP model. Retaining the skeletal feature representation throughout, we directly apply a spatio-temporal adjacency matrix into the self-attention formulation. This provides structure and context to each skeletal joint that is not possible when using a non-graphical abstract representation, enabling fluid and expressive sign language production. We evaluate our Skeletal Graph Self-Attention architecture on the challenging RWTH-PHOENIX-Weather-2014**T** (PHOENIX14**T**) dataset, achieving state-of-the-art back translation performance with an 8% and 7% improvement over competing methods for the dev and test sets.

Keywords: Sign Language Production (SLP), Graph Neural Network (GNN), Computational Sign Language

1. Introduction

Sign languages are rich visual languages, the native languages of the Deaf communities. Comprised of both manual (hands) and non-manual (face and body) features, sign languages can be visualised as spatio-temporal motion of the hands and body (Sutton-Spence and Woll, 1999). When signing, the local context of motions is particularly important, such as the connections between fingers in a sign, or the lip patterns when mouthing (Pfau et al., 2010). Although commonly represented via a graphical avatar, more recent deep learning approaches to Sign Language Production (SLP) have represented sign as a continuous sequence of skeleton poses (Saunders et al., 2021a; Stoll et al., 2018; Zelinka and Kanis, 2020).

Due to the recent success of Neural Machine Translation (NMT), computational sign language research often naively applies spoken language architectures without sign-specific modifications. However, the domains of sign and spoken language are drastically different (Stokoe, 1980), with the continuous nature and inherent spatial structure of sign requiring sign-dependent architectures. Saunders *et al* (Saunders et al., 2020c) introduced *Progressive Transformers*, an SLP architecture specific to a continuous skeletal representation. However, this still projects the skeletal input to an abstract feature representation, losing the skeletal inductive bias inherent to the body, where each joint upholds its own spatial representation. Even if spatio-temporal skeletal relationships can be maintained in an latent representation, a trained model may not correctly learn this complex structure.

Graphical structures can be used to represent pairwise relationships between objects in an ordered space. GNNs are neural models used to capture graphical relationships, and predominantly operate on a high-level graphical structure (Bruna et al., 2014), with each node containing an abstract feature representation and relationships occurring at the meta level. Conversely, skeleton pose sequences can be defined as spatio-temporal graphical representations, with both intra-frame spatial adjacency between limbs and inter-frame temporal adjacency between frames. In this work, we employ attention mechanisms as global graphical structures, with each node attending to all others. Even though there have been attempts to combine graphical representations and attention (Yun et al., 2019; Dwivedi and Bresson, 2020; Veličković et al., 2017), there has been no work on graphical self-attention specific to a spatio-temporal skeletal structure.

In this paper, we represent sign language sequences as spatio-temporal skeletal graphs, the first SLP model to operate with a graphical structure. As seen in the centre of Figure 1, we encode skeletal joints as nodes, $\mathcal{J}$ (blue dots), and natural limb connections as edges, $\mathcal{E}$, with both spatial (blue lines) and temporal (green lines) relationships. Operating on a graphical structure explicitly upholds the skeletal representation throughout, learning deeper and more informative features than using an abstract representation.

Additionally, we propose Skeletal Graph Self-Attention ($SGSA$), a novel spatio-temporal graphical attention layer that embeds a hierarchical body inductive bias into the self-attention mechanism. We directly mask the self-attention by applying a sparse adjacency matrix to the weights of the value computation, ensuring a spatial information propagation. To the best of our knowledge, ours is the first work to embed a graphical

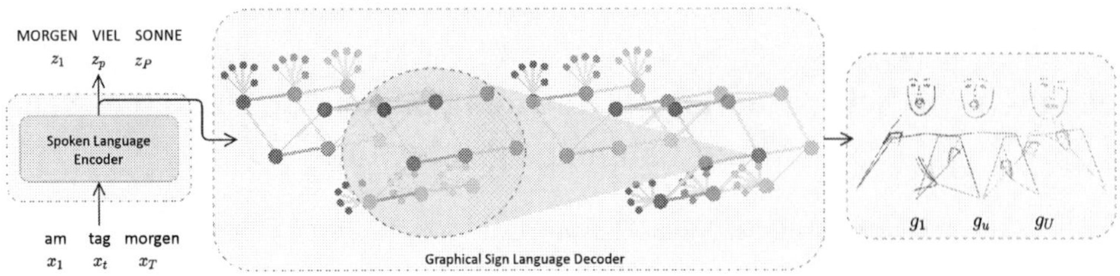

Figure 1: An overview of our proposed SLP network, showing an initial translation from a spoken language sentence using a text encoder, with gloss supervision. A subsequent skeletal graphical structure is formed, with multiple proposed Skeletal Graph Self-Attention layers applied to embed a skeleton inductive bias and produce expressive sign language sequences.

structure directly into the self-attention mechanism. In addition, we expand our model to the spatio-temporal domain by modelling the temporal adjacency only on $\mathcal{N}$ neighbouring frames.

Our full SLP model can be seen in Figure 1, initially translating from spoken language using a spoken language encoder with gloss supervision. The intermediary graphical structure is then processed by a graphical sign language decoder containing our proposed $SGSA$ layers, with a final output of sign language sequences. We evaluate on the challenging RWTH-PHOENIX-Weather-2014**T** (PHOENIX14**T**) dataset, performing spatial and temporal ablation studies of the proposed $SGSA$ architecture. Furthermore, we achieve state-of-the-art back translation results for the text to pose task, with an 8% and 7% performance increase over competing methods for the development and test sets respectively.

The contributions of this paper can be summarised as:

- The first SLP system to model sign language as a spatio-temporal graphical structure, applying both spatial and temporal adjacency.
- A novel Skeletal Graph Self-Attention ($SGSA$) layer, that embeds a skeleton inductive bias into the model.
- State-of-the-art Text-to-Pose SLP results on the PHOENIX14**T** dataset.

2. Related Work

Sign Language Production The past 30 years has seen extensive research into computational sign language (Wilson and Anspach, 1993). Early work focused on isolated Sign Language Recognition (SLR) (Grobel and Assan, 1997), with a subsequent move to continuous SLR (Camgoz et al., 2017). The task of Sign Language Translation (SLT) was introduced by Camgoz *et al* (Camgoz et al., 2018) and has since become a prominent research area (Yin, 2020; Camgoz et al., 2020a). Sign Language Production (SLP), the automatic translation from spoken language sentences to sign language sequences, was initially tackled using avatar-based technologies (Elliott et al., 2008). The rule-based Statistical Machine Translation (SMT) achieved partial success (Kouremenos et al., 2018), albeit with costly, labour-intensive pre-processing.

Recently, there have been many deep learning approaches to SLP proposed (Zelinka and Kanis, 2020; Stoll et al., 2018; Saunders et al., 2020b), with Saunders *et al* achieving state-of-the-art results with gloss supervision (Saunders et al., 2021b). These works predominantly represent sign languages as sequences of skeletal frames, with each frame encoded as a vector of joint coordinates (Saunders et al., 2021a) that disregards any spatio-temporal structure available within a skeletal representation. In addition, these models apply standard spoken language architectures (Vaswani et al., 2017), disregarding the structural format of the skeletal data. Conversely, in this work we propose a novel spatio-temporal graphical attention layer that injects an inductive skeletal bias into SLP.

Graph Neural Networks A graph is a data structure consisting of nodes, $\mathcal{J}$, and edges, $\mathcal{E}$, where $\mathcal{E}$ defines the relationships between $\mathcal{J}$. Graph Neural Networks (GNNs) (Bruna et al., 2014) apply neural layers on these graphical structures to learn representations (Zhou et al., 2020), classify nodes (Yan et al., 2018; Yao et al., 2019) or generate new data (Li et al., 2018). A skeleton pose representation can be structured as a graph, with joints as $\mathcal{J}$ and natural limb connections as $\mathcal{E}$ (Straka et al., 2011; Shi et al., 2019). GNNs have been proposed for operating on such dynamic skeletal graphs, in the context of action recognition (Yan et al., 2018; Shi et al., 2019) and human pose estimation (Straka et al., 2011). Attention networks can be formalised as a fully connected GNN, where the adjacency between each word, $\mathcal{E}$, is a weighting learnt using self-attention. Expanding this, Graph Attention Networks (GATs) (Veličković et al., 2017) define explicit weighted adjacency between nodes, achieving state-of-the-art results across multiple domains (Kosaraju et al., 2019). Recently, there have been multiple graphical transformer architectures proposed (Yun et al., 2019; Dwivedi and Bresson, 2020), which have been extended to the spatio-temporal domain for applications such as multiple object tracking (Chu et al., 2021) and pedestrian tracking (Yu et al., 2020).

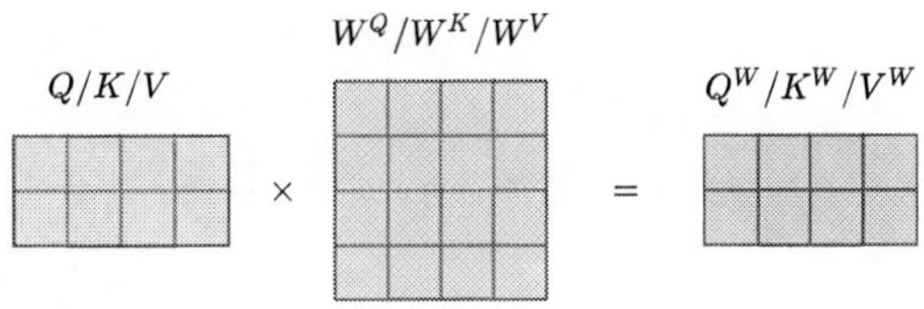

Figure 2: Weighted calculation of Queries, Q, Keys, K and Values, V, for global self-attention.

However, there has been no work on graphical attention mechanisms where the features of each time step holds a relevant graphical structure. We build a spatio-temporal graphical architecture that operates on a skeletal representation per frame, explicitly injecting a skeletal inductive bias into the model. There have been some applications of GNNs in computational sign language in the context of SLR (de Amorim et al., 2019; Flasiński and Myśliński, 2010). We extend these works to the SLP domain with our proposed Skeletal Graph Self-Attention architecture.

Local Attention Attention mechanisms have demonstrated strong Natural Language Processing (NLP) performance (Bahdanau et al., 2015), particularly with the introduction of transformers (Vaswani et al., 2017). Although proposed with global context (Bahdanau et al., 2015), more recent works have selectively restricted attention to a local context (Yang et al., 2018) or the top-k tokens(Zhao et al., 2019), often due to computational issues or to enable long-range dependencies. In this paper, we propose using local attention to represent temporal adjacency within our graphical skeletal structure.

3. Background

In this section, we provide a brief background on self-attention. Attention mechanisms were initially proposed to overcome the information bottleneck found in encoder-decoder architectures (Bahdanau et al., 2015). Transformers (Vaswani et al., 2017) apply multiple scaled self-attention layers in both encoder and decoder modules, where the input is a set of queries, $Q \in \mathbb{R}^{d_k}$, and keys, $K \in \mathbb{R}^{d_k}$, and values, $V \in \mathbb{R}^{d_v}$. Self-attention aims to learn a context value for each time-step as a weighted sum of all values, where the weight is determined by the relationship of the query with each corresponding key. An associated weight vector, $W^{Q/K/V}$, is first applied to each input, as shown in Figure 2, as:

$$Q^W = Q \cdot W^Q, \quad K^W = K \cdot W^K, \quad V^W = V \cdot W^V \tag{1}$$

where $W^Q \in \mathbb{R}^{d_{model} \times d_k}$, $W^K \in \mathbb{R}^{d_{model} \times d_k}$ and $W^V \in \mathbb{R}^{d_{model} \times d_v}$ are weights related to each input variable and d_{model} is the dimensionality of the self-attention layer. Formally, scaled self-attention (SA) outputs a weighted vector combination of values, V^W, by the relevant queries, Q^W, keys, K^W, and dimensionality, d_k, as:

$$\text{SA}(Q, K, V) = \text{softmax}(\frac{Q^W (K^W)^T}{\sqrt{d_k}})V^W \tag{2}$$

Multi-Headed Attention (MHA) applies h parallel attention mechanisms to the same input queries, keys and values, each with different learnt parameters. In the initial architecture (Vaswani et al., 2017), the dimensionality of each head is proportionally smaller than the full model, $d_h = d_{model}/h$. The output of each head is then concatenated and projected forward, as:

$$\text{MHA}(Q, K, V) = [head_1, ..., head_h] \cdot W^O, \quad \text{where } head_i = \text{SA}(Q^W, K^W, V^W) \tag{3}$$

where $W^O \in \mathbb{R}^{d_{model} \times d_{model}}$. In this paper, we introduce Skeletal Graph Self-Attention layers that inject a skeletal inductive bias into the self-attention mechanism.

4. Methodology

The ultimate goal of SLP is to automatically translate from a source spoken language sentence, $\mathcal{X} = (x_1, ..., x_T)$ with $\mathcal{T}$ words, to a target sign language sequence, $\mathcal{G} = (g_1, ..., g_U)$ of $\mathcal{U}$ time steps. Additionally, an intermediary gloss[1] sequence representation can be used, $\mathcal{Z} = (z_1, ..., z_P)$ with P glosses. Current approaches (Saunders et al., 2021a; Stoll et al., 2018; Zelinka and Kanis, 2020) predominantly represent sign language as a sequence of skeletal frames, with each frame containing a vector of body joint coordinates. In addition, they project this skeletal structure to an abstract representation before being processed by the model (Saunders et al., 2020c). However, this approach removes all spatial information contained within the skeletal data, restricting the model to only learning the internal relationships within a latent representation.

Contrary to previous work, in this paper we represent sign language sequences as spatio-temporal skeletal graphs, $\mathcal{G}$, as in the centre of Figure 1. As per graph theory (Bollobás, 2013), $\mathcal{G}$ can be formulated as a function of nodes, $\mathcal{J}$ and edges, $\mathcal{E}$. We define $\mathcal{J}$ as the skeleton pose sequence of temporal length $\mathcal{U}$ and spatial width $\mathcal{S}$, with each node representing a single skeletal joint coordinate from a single frame (blue dots in Fig. 1). $\mathcal{S}$ is therefore the dimensionality of the skeleton representation of each frame. $\mathcal{E}$ can be represented as a spatial adjacency matrix, $\mathcal{A}$, defined as the natural limb connections between skeleton joints both of its own frame (blue lines) and of neighbouring frames (green lines).

[1]Glosses are a written representation of sign, defined as minimal lexical items.

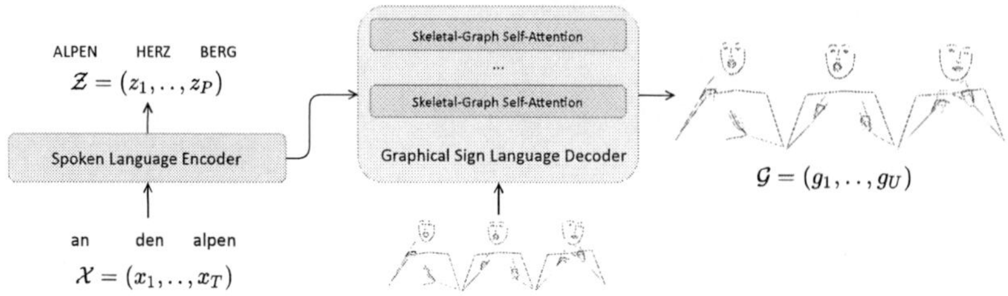

Figure 3: Overview of the proposed model architecture, detailing the Spoken Language Encoder (Sec. 4.1) and the Graphical Sign Language Decoder (Sec. 4.2). We propose novel Skeletal Graph Self-Attention layers to operate on the sign language skeletal graphs, $\mathcal{G}$.

As outlined in Sec. 3, classical self-attention operates with global context over all time-steps. However, a skeletal inductive bias can be embedded into a model by restricting attention to only the natural limb connections within the skeleton. To embed a skeleton inductive bias into self-attention, we propose a novel Skeletal Graph Self-Attention ($SGSA$) layer that operates with sparse attention. Modeled within a transformer decoder, $SGSA$ retains the original skeletal structure throughout multiple deep layers, ensuring the processing of spatio-temporal information contained in skeletal pose sequences. In-built adjacency matrices of both intra- and inter-frame relationships provide structure and context directly to each skeletal joint that is not possible when using a non-graphical abstract representation.

In this section, we outline the full SLP model, containing a spoken language encoder and a graphical sign language decoder, with an overview shown in Figure 3.

4.1. Spoken Language Encoder

As shown on the left of Figure 3, we first translate from a spoken language sentence, $\mathcal{X}$, of dimension $\mathcal{E} \times \mathcal{T}$, where $\mathcal{E}$ is the encoder embedding size, to a sign language representation, $\mathcal{R} = (r_1, ..., r_U)$ (Fig. 1 Left). We build a classical transformer encoder (Vaswani et al., 2017) that applies self-attention using the global context of a spoken language sequence. $\mathcal{R}$ is represented with a spatio-temporal structure, containing identical temporal length, $\mathcal{U}$, and spatial shape, $\mathcal{S}$, as the final skeletal graph, $\mathcal{G}$. This structure enables a graphical processing by the proposed sign language decoder. Additionally, as proposed in (Saunders et al., 2021b), we employ a gloss supervision to the intermediate sign language representation. This prompts the model to learn a meaningful latent sign representation for the ultimate goal of sign language production.

4.2. Graphical Sign Language Decoder

Given the intermediary sign language representation, $\mathcal{R} \in$, we build an auto-regressive transformer decoder containing our novel Skeletal Graph Self-Attention (SGSA) layers (Figure 3 middle). This produces a graphical sign language sequence, $\hat{\mathcal{G}}$, of spatial shape, $\mathcal{S}$, and temporal length, $\mathcal{U}$.

Spatial Adjacency We define a spatial adjacency matrix, $\mathcal{A} \in \mathbb{R}^{\mathcal{S} \times \mathcal{S}}$, expressed as a sparse attention map, as seen in Figure 4. $\mathcal{A}$ contains a spatial skeleton adjacency structure, modelled as the natural skeletal limb connections within a frame (blue lines in Fig. 1). $\mathcal{A}$ can be formalised as:

$$\mathcal{A}_{i,j} = \begin{cases} 1, & \textit{if} \, \text{Con}(i,j) \\ 0, & \textit{otherwise} \end{cases} \tag{4}$$

where $\text{Con}(i,j) = True$ if joints i and j are connected. For example, the skeletal elbow joint is connected to the skeletal wrist joint. We use an undirected graph representation, defining $\mathcal{E}$ as bidirectional edges.

Temporal Adjacency We expand the spatial adjacency matrix to the spatio-temporal domain by modelling the inter-frame edges of the skeletal graph structure (green lines in Fig. 1). The updated spatial-temporal adjacency matrix can be formalised as $\mathcal{A} \in \mathbb{R}^{\mathcal{S} \times \mathcal{S} \times \mathcal{U}}$. We set $\mathcal{N}$ as the temporal distance that defines 'adjacent', where edges are established as both same joint connections and natural limb connections between the $\mathcal{N}$ adjacent frames. In the standard attention shown in Sec. 3, each time-step can globally attend to all others, which can be modelled as $\mathcal{N} = \infty$. We formalise our spatio-temporal adjacency matrix, as:

$$\mathcal{A}_{i,j,t} = \begin{cases} 1, & \textit{if} \, \text{Con}(i,j) \, \textit{and} \, t \leq \mathcal{N} \\ 0, & \textit{otherwise} \end{cases} \tag{5}$$

where t is the temporal distance from the reference frame, $t = u - u_{\text{ref}}$.

Self-loops and Normalisation To account for information loops back to the same joint (Bollobás, 2013), we add self-loops to $\mathcal{A}$ using the identity matrix, $\mathcal{I} \in \mathbb{R}^{\mathcal{S} \times \mathcal{S}}$. In practice, due to our multi-dimensional skeletal representation, we add self-loops from each coordinate of the joint both to itself and all other coordinates of the same joint, which we define as $\mathcal{I}^* \in \mathbb{R}^{\mathcal{S} \times \mathcal{S}}$. Furthermore, to prevent numerical instabilities and exploding gradients (Bollobás, 2013), we normalise the adjacency matrix by inversely applying the degree matrix, $\mathcal{D} \in \mathbb{R}^{\mathcal{S}}$. $\mathcal{D}$ is defined as the numbers of edges a node is connected to. Normalisation is formulated as:

$$\mathcal{A}^* = \mathcal{D}^{-1}(\mathcal{A} + \mathcal{I}^*) \tag{6}$$

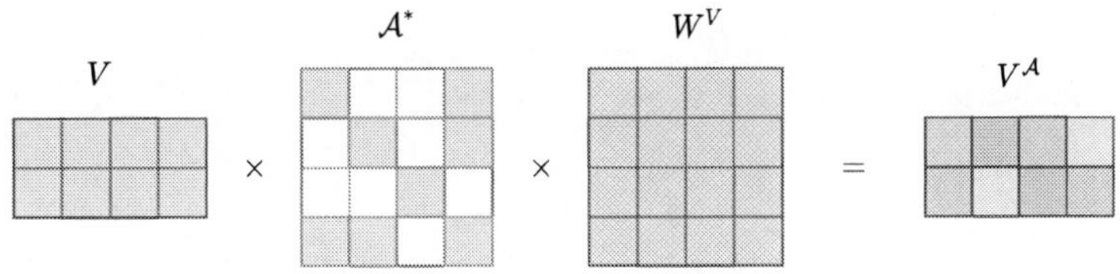

Figure 4: Skeletal Graph Self-Attention: Weighted calculation of Values, V, masked with a spatio-temporal adjacency matrix $\mathcal{A}^*$ to embed a skeleton inductive bias.

where $\mathcal{A}^*$ is the normalised adjacency matrix.

Skeletal Graph Self-Attention We apply $\mathcal{A}^*$ as a sparsely weighted mask over the weighted value calculation, $V^W = V \cdot W^V$, (Eq. 1), ensuring that values used in the weighted context for each node are only impacted by the adjacent nodes of the previous layer:

$$V^{\mathcal{A}} = V \cdot \mathcal{A}^* \cdot W^V \tag{7}$$

where Figure 4 shows a visual representation of the sparse adjacent matrix $\mathcal{A}^*$ containing spatio-temporal connections, applied as a mask to the weighted calculation. With a value matrix containing a skeletal structure, $V \in \mathbb{R}^{\mathcal{S}}$, $\mathcal{A}^*$ restricts the information propagation of self-attention layers only through the spatial and temporal skeletal edges, $\mathcal{E}$, and thus embeds a skeleton inductive bias into the attention mechanism.

We formally define a Skeletal Graph Self-Attention ($SGSA$) layer by plugging both the weighted variable computation of Eq. 1 and the adjacent weighted computation of Eq. 7 into the self-attention Eq. 2, as:

$$SGSA(Q, K, V, A) = \text{softmax}(\frac{Q \cdot W^Q (K \cdot W^K)^T}{\sqrt{d_k}}) V \cdot \mathcal{A}^* \cdot W^V \tag{8}$$

where $d_{model} = \mathcal{S}$. This explicitly retains the spatial skeletal shape, $\mathcal{S}$, throughout the sign language decoder, enabling a spatial structure to be extracted.

To extend this to a multi-headed transformer decoder, we replace self-attention in Eq. 3 with our proposed $SGSA$ layers. To retain the spatial skeletal representation within each head, the dimensionality of each head is kept as the full model dimension, $d_h = d_{model} = \mathcal{S}$, with the final projection layer enlarged to $h \times \mathcal{S}$.

We build our auto-regressive decoder with $\mathcal{L}$ multi-headed $SGSA$ sub-layers, interleaved with fully-connected layers and a final feed-forward layer, each with a consistent spatial dimension of $\mathcal{S}$. A residual connection and subsequent layer norm is employed around each of the sub-layers, to aid training. As shown on the right of Figure 3, the final output of our sign language decoder module is a graphical skeletal sequence, $\hat{\mathcal{G}}$, that contains $\mathcal{U}$ frames of skeleton pose, each with a spatial shape of $\mathcal{S}$.

We train our sign language decoder using the Mean Squared Error (MSE) loss between the predicted sequence, $\hat{\mathcal{G}}$, and the ground truth sequence, $\mathcal{G}^*$. This is formalised as $\mathcal{L}_{\mathcal{MSE}} = \frac{1}{U} \sum_{i=1}^{u} \hat{g}_{1:U} - {g^*}_{1:U})^2$, where $\hat{g}$ and g^* represent the frames of the produced and ground truth sign language sequences, respectively. We train our full SLP model end-to-end with a weighted combination of the encoder gloss supervision (Saunders et al., 2021b) and decoder skeleton pose losses.

4.3. Sign Language Output

Generating a sign language video from the produced graphical skeletal sequence, $\hat{\mathcal{G}}$, is then a trivial task, animating each frame in temporal order. Frame animation is done by connecting the nodes, $\mathcal{J}$, using the natural limb connections defined by $\mathcal{E}$, as seen in Fig. 1.

5. Experiments

Dataset We evaluate our approach on the PHOENIX14T dataset introduced by Camgoz et al. (Camgoz et al., 2018), containing parallel sequences of 8257 German sentences, sign gloss translations and sign language videos. Other available sign datasets are either simple sentence repetition tasks of non-natural signing not appropriate for translation (Zhang et al., 2016; Efthimiou and Fotinea, 2007), or contain larger domains of discourse that currently prove difficult for the SLP field (Camgoz et al., 2021). We extract 3D skeletal joint positions from the sign language videos to represent our spatio-temporal graphical skeletal structure. Manual and non-manual features of each video are first extracted in 2D using OpenPose (Cao et al., 2017), with the manuals lifted to 3D using the skeletal model estimation model proposed in (Zelinka and Kanis, 2020). We normalise the skeleton pose and set the spatial skeleton shape, $\mathcal{S}$, as 291, with 290 joint coordinates and 1 counter decoding value (as in (Saunders et al., 2020c)). Adjacency information, $\mathcal{A}$, is defined as the natural limb connections of 3D body, hand and face joints, as in (Zelinka and Kanis, 2020), where each coordinate of a joint is adjacent to both the coordinates of its own joint and all connected joints. We define the counter value as global adjacency, with connections to all joints.

Implementation Details We setup our SLP model with a spoken language encoder of 2 layers, 4 heads and an embedding size, $\mathcal{E}$, of 256, and a graphical sign language decoder of 5 layers, 4 heads and an embedding size of $\mathcal{S}$. Our best performing model contains 9M trainable parameters. As proposed by Saunders *et*

Skeletal Graph	DEV SET					TEST SET				
Layers, $\mathcal{L}$:	BLEU-4	BLEU-3	BLEU-2	BLEU-1	ROUGE	BLEU-4	BLEU-3	BLEU-2	BLEU-1	ROUGE
0 (4 SA)	14.25	17.73	23.47	34.79	37.65	13.64	17.03	23.09	35.03	36.59
1	14.37	17.67	23.13	33.95	36.98	13.63	17.08	23.17	35.39	37.05
2	14.50	18.14	24.10	35.96	38.09	13.85	17.23	23.14	34.93	37.33
3	14.53	18.02	24.00	35.71	37.62	13.72	17.23	23.10	34.45	36.99
4	14.68	18.30	**24.31**	**36.16**	38.51	14.05	17.59	23.73	35.63	37.47
5	**14.72**	**18.39**	24.29	35.79	**38.72**	**14.27**	**17.79**	**23.79**	**35.72**	**37.79**

Table 1: Impact of Skeletal Graph Self-Attention layers, $\mathcal{L}$, on model performance.

al (Saunders et al., 2020c), we apply Gaussian noise augmentation with a noise rate of 5. We train all parts of our network with Xavier initialisation, Adam optimization with default parameters and a learning rate of 10^{-3}. Our code is based on Kreutzer et al.'s NMT toolkit, JoeyNMT, and implemented using PyTorch.

Evaluation We use the back translation metric (Saunders et al., 2020c) for evaluation, which employs a pre-trained SLT model (Camgoz et al., 2020b) to translate the produced sign pose sequences back to spoken language. We compute BLEU and ROUGE scores against the original input, with BLEU n-grams from 1 to 4 provided. The SLP evaluation protocols on the PHOENIX14**T** dataset have been set by (Saunders et al., 2020c). We share results on the *Text to Pose (T2P)* task which constitutes the production of sign language sequences directly from spoken language sentences, the ultimate goal of an SLP system. We omit Gloss to Pose evaluation to focus on the more important spoken language translation task.

Skeletal Graph Self-Attention Layers We start our experiments on the proposed Skeletal Graph Self-Attention layers, evaluating the effect of stacking multiple $SGSA$ layers, $\mathcal{L}$, each with a multi-head size, h, of 4. We first ablate the effect of using no $SGSA$ layers, and replacing them with 4 standard self-attention layers, as described in Section 3. We then build our graphical sign language decoder with 1 to 5 $SGSA$ layers, with each model retaining a constant spoken language encoder size and a global temporal adjacency.

Table 1 shows that using standard self-attention layers achieves the worst performance of 14.25 BLEU-4, showing the benefit of our proposed $SGSA$ layers. Increasing the number of $SGSA$ layers, as expected, increases model performance to a peak of 14.72 BLEU-4. A larger number of layers enables a deeper representation of the skeletal graph and thus provides a stronger skeleton inductive bias to the model. In lieu of this, for the rest of our experiments we build our sign language decoder with five $SGSA$ layers.

Temporal Adjacency In our next experiments, we examine the impact of the temporal adjacency distance, $\mathcal{N}$, (Sec. 4.2). We set $\mathcal{N}$ by analysing the trained temporal attention matrix of the best performing decoder evaluated above. We notice that the attention predominantly falls on the last 3 frames, as the model learns to attend to the local temporal context of skeletal motion. Manually restricting the temporal attention provides this information as an inductive bias into the model, rather than relying on this being learnt.

Table 2 shows results of our temporal adjacency evaluation, ranging from an infinite adjacency (no constraint) to $\mathcal{N} \in [1, 5]$. A temporal adjacency distance of one achieves the best BLEU-4 performance. Note: Although we report BLEU of n-grams 1-4 for completeness, we use BLEU-4 as our final evaluation metric to enable a clear result. Although counter-intuitive to the global self-attention utilised by a transformer decoder, we believe this is modelling the Markov property, where future frames only depend on the current state. Due to the intermediary gloss supervision (Saunders et al., 2021b), the defined sign language representation, $\mathcal{R}$, should contain all frame-level information relevant to a sign language translation. The sign language decoder then has the sole task of accurately animating each skeletal frame. Therefore, a single temporal adjacency in the graphical decoder makes sense, as no new information is required to be learnt from temporally distant frames.

Baseline Comparisons We compare the performance of the proposed Skeletal Graph Self-Attention architecture against 4 baseline SLP models: 1) Progressive transformers (Saunders et al., 2020c), which applied the classical transformer architecture to sign language production. 2) Adversarial training (Saunders et al., 2020a), which utilised an adversarial discriminator to prompt more expressive productions, 3) Mixture Density Networks (MDNs) (Saunders et al., 2021a), which modelled the variation found in sign language using multiple distributions to parameterise the entire prediction subspace, and 4) Mixture of Motion Primitives

Temporal	DEV SET					TEST SET				
Adjacency, $\mathcal{N}$:	BLEU-4	BLEU-3	BLEU-2	BLEU-1	ROUGE	BLEU-4	BLEU-3	BLEU-2	BLEU-1	ROUGE
∞	14.72	18.39	24.29	35.79	38.72	14.27	17.79	23.79	35.72	37.79
1	**15.15**	18.67	24.47	35.88	38.44	**14.33**	17.77	23.72	35.26	37.96
2	15.09	18.51	24.43	36.17	38.04	14.07	17.62	23.91	**36.28**	37.82
3	15.08	**18.84**	24.89	36.66	38.95	14.32	**17.95**	**24.04**	36.10	**38.38**
5	14.90	18.81	**25.30**	**37.31**	**39.55**	14.21	17.79	23.98	35.88	38.44

Table 2: Impact of Temporal Adjacency, $\mathcal{N}$, on $SGSA$ model performance

	DEV SET					TEST SET				
Approach:	BLEU-4	BLEU-3	BLEU-2	BLEU-1	ROUGE	BLEU-4	BLEU-3	BLEU-2	BLEU-1	ROUGE
Progressive Transformers	11.82	14.80	19.97	31.41	33.18	10.51	13.54	19.04	31.36	32.46
Adversarial Training	12.65	15.61	20.58	31.84	33.68	10.81	13.72	18.99	30.93	32.74
Mixture Density Networks	11.54	14.48	19.63	30.94	33.40	11.68	14.55	19.70	31.56	33.19
Mixture of Motion Primitives	14.03	17.50	23.49	35.23	37.76	13.30	16.86	23.27	**35.89**	36.77
Skeletal Graph Self-Attention	**15.15**	**18.67**	**24.47**	**35.88**	**38.44**	**14.33**	**17.77**	**23.72**	35.26	**37.96**

Table 3: Baseline comparisons on the PHOENIX14**T** dataset for the *Text to Pose* task.

(MOMP) (Saunders et al., 2021b), which split the SLP task into two distinct jointly-trained sub-tasks and learnt a set of motion primitives for animation.

Table 3 presents *Text to Pose* results, showing that $SGSA$ achieves 15.15/14.33 BLEU-4 for the development and test sets respectively, an 8/7% improvement over the state-of-the-art. These results highlight the significant success of our proposed $SGSA$ layers. We have shown that representing sign pose skeletons in a graphical skeletal structure and embedding a skeletal inductive bias into the self-attention mechanism enables a fluid and expressive sign language production.

6. Conclusion

In this paper, we proposed a skeletal graph structure for SLP, with joints as nodes and both spatial and temporal connections as edges. We proposed a novel graphical attention layer, Skeletal Graph Self-Attention, to operate on the graphical skeletal structure. Retaining the skeletal feature representation throughout, we directly applied a spatio-temporal adjacency matrix into the self-attention formulation, embedding a skeleton inductive bias for expressive sign language production. We evaluated $SGSA$ on the challenging PHOENIX14**T** dataset, achieving state-of-the-art back translation performance with an 8% and 7% improvement over competing methods for the dev and test set. For future work, we aim to apply $SGSA$ layers to the wider computational sign language tasks of SLR and SLT.

7. Acknowledgements

This work received funding from the SNSF Sinergia project 'SMILE' (CRSII2 160811), the European Union's Horizon2020 research and innovation programme under grant agreement no. 762021 'Content4All' and the EPSRC project 'ExTOL' (EP/R03298X/1). This work reflects only the authors view and the Commission is not responsible for any use that may be made of the information it contains.

8. Bibliographical References

Bahdanau, D., Cho, K., and Bengio, Y. (2015). Neural Machine Translation by Jointly Learning to Align and Translate. *Proceedings of the International Conference on Learning Representations (ICLR)*.

Bollobás, B. (2013). *Modern graph theory*. Springer Science & Business Media.

Bruna, J., Zaremba, W., Szlam, A., and LeCun, Y. (2014). Spectral Networks and Locally Connected Networks on Graphs. In *Proceedings of the International Conference on Learning Representations (ICLR)*.

Camgoz, N. C., Hadfield, S., Koller, O., and Bowden, R. (2017). SubUNets: End-to-end Hand Shape and Continuous Sign Language Recognition. In *Proceedings of the IEEE International Conference on Computer Vision (ICCV)*.

Camgoz, N. C., Hadfield, S., Koller, O., Ney, H., and Bowden, R. (2018). Neural Sign Language Translation. In *Proceedings of the IEEE Conference on Computer Vision and Pattern Recognition (CVPR)*.

Camgoz, N. C., Koller, O., Hadfield, S., and Bowden, R. (2020a). Multi-channel Transformers for Multi-articulatory Sign Language Translation. In *Assistive Computer Vision and Robotics Workshop (ACVR)*.

Camgoz, N. C., Koller, O., Hadfield, S., and Bowden, R. (2020b). Sign Language Transformers: Joint End-to-end Sign Language Recognition and Translation. In *Proceedings of the IEEE Conference on Computer Vision and Pattern Recognition (CVPR)*.

Cao, Z., Hidalgo, G., Simon, T., Wei, S.-E., and Sheikh, Y. (2017). OpenPose: Realtime Multi-Person 2D Pose Estimation using Part Affinity Fields. In *Proceedings of the IEEE Conference on Computer Vision and Pattern Recognition (CVPR)*.

Chu, P., Wang, J., You, Q., Ling, H., and Liu, Z. (2021). TransMOT: Spatial-Temporal Graph Transformer for Multiple Object Tracking. *arXiv preprint arXiv:2104.00194*.

de Amorim, C. C., Macêdo, D., and Zanchettin, C. (2019). Spatial-Temporal Graph Convolutional Networks for Sign Language Recognition. In *International Conference on Artificial Neural Networks*.

Dwivedi, V. P. and Bresson, X. (2020). A Generalization of Transformer Networks to Graphs. *arXiv preprint arXiv:2012.09699*.

Elliott, R., Glauert, J. R., Kennaway, J., Marshall, I., and Safar, E. (2008). Linguistic Modelling and Language-Processing Technologies for Avatar-based Sign Language Presentation. *Universal Access in the Information Society*.

Flasiński, M. and Myśliński, S. (2010). On The Use of Graph Parsing for Recognition of Isolated Hand Postures of Polish Sign Language. *Pattern Recognition*.

Grobel, K. and Assan, M. (1997). Isolated Sign Language Recognition using Hidden Markov Models. In *IEEE International Conference on Systems, Man, and Cybernetics*.

Kosaraju, V., Sadeghian, A., Martín-Martín, R., Reid, I.,

Rezatofighi, S. H., and Savarese, S. (2019). Social-BiGAT: Multimodal Trajectory Forecasting using Bicycle-GAN and Graph Attention Networks. In *Advances in Neural Information Processing Systems (NIPS)*.

Kouremenos, D., Ntalianis, K. S., Siolas, G., and Stafylopatis, A. (2018). Statistical Machine Translation for Greek to Greek Sign Language Using Parallel Corpora Produced via Rule-Based Machine Translation. In *IEEE 31st International Conference on Tools with Artificial Intelligence (ICTAI)*.

Li, Y., Vinyals, O., Dyer, C., Pascanu, R., and Battaglia, P. (2018). Learning Deep Generative Models of Graphs. *arXiv preprint arXiv:1803.03324*.

Pfau, R., Quer, J., et al. (2010). *Nonmanuals: Their Grammatical and Prosodic Roles*. Cambridge University Press.

Saunders, B., Camgoz, N. C., and Bowden, R. (2020a). Adversarial Training for Multi-Channel Sign Language Production. In *Proceedings of the British Machine Vision Conference (BMVC)*.

Saunders, B., Camgoz, N. C., and Bowden, R. (2020b). Everybody Sign Now: Translating Spoken Language to Photo Realistic Sign Language Video. *arXiv preprint arXiv:2011.09846*.

Saunders, B., Camgoz, N. C., and Bowden, R. (2020c). Progressive Transformers for End-to-End Sign Language Production. In *Proceedings of the European Conference on Computer Vision (ECCV)*.

Saunders, B., Camgoz, N. C., and Bowden, R. (2021a). Continuous 3D Multi-Channel Sign Language Production via Progressive Transformers and Mixture Density Networks. In *International Journal of Computer Vision (IJCV)*.

Saunders, B., Camgoz, N. C., and Bowden, R. (2021b). Mixed SIGNals: Sign Language Production via a Mixture of Motion Primitives. In *Proceedings of the International Conference on Computer Vision (ICCV)*.

Shi, L., Zhang, Y., Cheng, J., and Lu, H. (2019). Skeleton-based Action Recognition with Directed Graph Neural Networks. In *Proceedings of the IEEE Conference on Computer Vision and Pattern Recognition (CVPR)*.

Stokoe, W. C. (1980). Sign Language Structure. *Annual Review of Anthropology*.

Stoll, S., Camgoz, N. C., Hadfield, S., and Bowden, R. (2018). Sign Language Production using Neural Machine Translation and Generative Adversarial Networks. In *Proceedings of the British Machine Vision Conference (BMVC)*.

Straka, M., Hauswiesner, S., Rüther, M., and Bischof, H. (2011). Skeletal Graph Based Human Pose Estimation in Real-Time. In *Proceedings of the British Machine Vision Conference (BMVC)*.

Sutton-Spence, R. and Woll, B. (1999). *The Linguistics of British Sign Language: An Introduction*. Cambridge University Press.

Vaswani, A., Shazeer, N., Parmar, N., Uszkoreit, J., Jones, L., Gomez, A. N., Kaiser, Ł., and Polosukhin, I. (2017). Attention Is All You Need. In *Advances in Neural Information Processing Systems (NIPS)*.

Veličković, P., Cucurull, G., Casanova, A., Romero, A., Lio, P., and Bengio, Y. (2017). Graph Attention Networks. In *Proceedings of the International Conference on Learning Representations (ICLR)*.

Wilson, B. J. and Anspach, G. (1993). Neural Networks for Sign Language Translation. In *Applications of Artificial Neural Networks IV*. International Society for Optics and Photonics.

Yan, S., Xiong, Y., and Lin, D. (2018). Spatial Temporal Graph Convolutional Networks for Skeleton-Based Action Recognition. In *Proceedings of the AAAI Conference on Artificial Intelligence*.

Yang, B., Tu, Z., Wong, D. F., Meng, F., Chao, L. S., and Zhang, T. (2018). Modeling Localness for Self-Attention Networks. In *Proceedings of the 2018 Conference on Empirical Methods in Natural Language Processing (EMNLP)*.

Yao, L., Mao, C., and Luo, Y. (2019). Graph Convolutional Networks for Text Classification. In *Proceedings of the AAAI Conference on Artificial Intelligence*.

Yin, K. (2020). Sign Language Translation with Transformers. *arXiv preprint arXiv:2004.00588*.

Yu, C., Ma, X., Ren, J., Zhao, H., and Yi, S. (2020). Spatio-Temporal Graph Transformer Networks for Pedestrian Trajectory Prediction. In *Proceedings of the European Conference on Computer Vision (ECCV)*.

Yun, S., Jeong, M., Kim, R., Kang, J., and Kim, H. J. (2019). Graph Transformer Networks. In *Advances in Neural Information Processing Systems (NIPS)*.

Zelinka, J. and Kanis, J. (2020). Neural Sign Language Synthesis: Words Are Our Glosses. In *The IEEE Winter Conference on Applications of Computer Vision (WACV)*.

Zhao, G., Lin, J., Zhang, Z., Ren, X., Su, Q., and Sun, X. (2019). Explicit Sparse Transformer: Concentrated Attention Through Explicit Selection. *arXiv preprint arXiv:1912.11637*.

Zhou, J., Cui, G., Hu, S., Zhang, Z., Yang, C., Liu, Z., Wang, L., Li, C., and Sun, M. (2020). Graph Neural Networks: A Review of Methods and Applications.

9. Language Resource References

Camgoz, Necati Cihan and Saunders, Ben and Rochette, Guillaume and Giovanelli, Marco and Inches, Giacomo and Nachtrab-Ribback, Robin and Bowden, Richard. (2021). *Content4All Open Research Sign Language Translation Datasets*.

Efthimiou, Eleni and Fotinea, Stavroula-Evita. (2007). *GSLC: Creation and Annotation of a Greek Sign Language Corpus for HCI*.

Zhang, Jihai and Zhou, Wengang and Xie, Chao and Pu, Junfu and Li, Houqiang. (2016). *Chinese Sign Language Recognition with Adaptive HMM*.

Proceedings of the 7th International Workshop on Sign Language Translation and Avatar Technology (SLTAT 7), pages 103–108
Language Resources and Evaluation Conference (LREC 2022), Marseille, 20-25 June 2022

Multi-Track Bottom-Up Synthesis from Non-Flattened AZee Scores

Paritosh Sharma , Michael Filhol
Laboratoire Interdisciplinaire des Sciences du Numérique (LISN), CNRS, Université Paris–Saclay, Orsay, France
paritosh.sharma@lisn.upsaclay.fr, michael.filhol@cnrs.fr

Abstract

We present an algorithm to improve the pre-existing bottom-up animation system for AZee descriptions to synthesize sign language utterances. Our algorithm allows us to synthesize AZee descriptions by preserving the dynamics of underlying blocks. This bottom-up approach aims to deliver procedurally generated animations capable of generating any sign language utterance if an equivalent AZee description exists. The proposed algorithm is built upon the modules of an open-source animation toolkit and takes advantage of the integrated inverse kinematics solver and a non-linear editor.

Keywords: AZee, sign language, avatar

1. Introduction

Sign language synthesis is a technique for converting a sign language utterance description into an avatar animation. Such avatars are commonly referred to as signing avatars. Automating this process can provide a flexible way to generate sign language content while preserving the signer's anonymity. This also provides means to customize the sign language content more conveniently than fixed video recordings of signers.

Various systems for sign language synthesis have been developed over the years. Most of them relied on descriptions that modeled sign language utterances as sequences of glosses. This approach has several limitations ranging from synchronisation to contextual variations of signs. Hence, various utterance representations have been developed over these years to address one or more of these problems. EMBRScript (Kipp et al., 2011) added timing information to these sequences of glosses. The P/C model (Huenerfauth, 2006) solves the problem of synchronisation and concurrency of signs by allowing for partitions in utterance descriptions. The ATLAS project (Lombardo et al., 2010; Bertoldi et al., 2010) addresses the issue of sign variations using modifiers. Finally, the HLSML model (López-Colino and Pasamontes, 2011; López-Colino and Pasamontes, 2012) addresses the issue of timing information and sign variations.

Unlike those mentioned above, the AZee model (Filhol et al., 2014) allows us to write parameterised signed forms for semantic functions. A sign language utterance is encoded in the form of a hierarchy of applied production rules instead of a sequence. Given a description, it produces a timeline specifying all parts of the utterance to render with the avatar, thereby addressing the issues of non-manual features synchronisation, sign concurrency, and timing. Furthermore, AZee's timeline specifications also carry interpolation information and are essential for synthesising the utterance.

These features of AZee are essential for our work since modern animation systems use a multi-track timeline and allow for non-linear editing of animation blocks. This paper aims at synthesising AZee input with such type of software, namely Blender in our case.

We first present two prior approaches complementing each other that worked on animating from AZee, and explain a fundamental limitation found in one of them. We then propose a novel algorithm to animate AZee descriptions that allow for better synthesis. Lastly, we present our implementation in Blender and snapshots of output results we were able to generate.

2. State of the Art

To animate AZee, Filhol et al. (2017) follow a fundamental guiding principle, according to which the coarser the basic animation blocks, the more natural the final animation. To apply this principle, we should try to work from coarse AZee blocks as much as possible and fall back on synthesising from lower levels of AZee specification only if necessary. If this top-down search in the hierarchy of the AZee expression is not attempted, or indeed if it reaches the bottom of the hierarchy, the animation needs to be built from the bottom-up, i.e., work from the minimal articulatory constraints provided by AZee in its block specifications. In this section, we first review the Paula system, the only one attempting a top-down search for synthesis from an AZee description. Then we look into a Blender implementation, the only one proposed for a bottom-up synthesis of AZee.

2.1. Top-Down Approach

The Paula sign synthesis system provides a multi-track animation system close to how AZee describes sign language utterances. The system uses multiple animation techniques, capitalising on their strengths. Currently, it principally relies on pre-animated clips made by artists whose work is made simpler by using procedural techniques such as spine-assisted computation (Mcdonald et al., 2015); hence they do not have to be an expert in keyframe animation or armatures. These clips, representing coarse animation blocks, are essential in encapsulating the natural motions (McDonald et al., 2016) which are vital to improving sign language generation. Furthermore, the system has been extended to enable natural proform synthesis (Filhol and Mcdonald, 2018). Various extensions have been made for better facial model synthesis (Wolfe et al., 2021). Overall, this gives a more natural animation since it encapsulates movements that would be natural to a human signer. All of this is done on a multi-track animation timeline.

Using coarse blocks improves natural synthesis. However, it relies on a large set of shortcut clips, and does not address solving minimal constraints in the case none exists for a given segment.

2.2. Bottom-Up Synthesis: Building from Minimal Constraints

In contrast, a bottom-up approach proposes working from small articulation constraints and then combining and evaluating them to generate an animated utterance on a timeline. Thus, while it generates motion that looks more robotic, it can generate any sign language utterance description, and therefore give complete coverage of the AZee language description. This method of synthesis from AZee was most recently attempted by (Nunnari et al., 2018).

To understand it better, let's consider the AZee expression *nicht-sondern(arbre, armoire)* from their work, which means "not a tree but a wardrobe." Evaluating this expression with the AZee interpreter yields a set of time-bounded intervals arranged on a timeline. These intervals can be represented as blocks on a horizontal axis such as those shown in Figure 1. This arrangement is called an AZee score. Each of these intervals contains articulatory constraints such as, *placements* (e.g. place fingertip at forehead), *orientations* (e.g. orient forearm along upward vector), *transpaths* (e.g. fingertip must transition on a circular path) and *holds* (e.g. hold block UNIT0 for a duration).

In such a score, we notice that these constraints can apply simultaneously Figure 2. For example, PALMS DOWN, which refers to the orientation of palms downwards, while HANDS CONTACT, which refers to the contact of palms. Since both these blocks affect common bones of a bone chain, animating them separately is a problem.

To avoid this problem, Nunnari et al. chose to *flatten* the AZee score to create a linear sequence of keyframes comprising of,

- the constraints corresponding to the boundaries of the original blocks (example k_1, k_2 in Figure 1)
- additional keyframes to control interpolations as specified by transpaths (example k_{12}, k_{13}, ... k_{18} in Figure 1)

Each of the former kinds contains all of the articulatory constraints applied at that time, collecting from any block starting, ending, or crossing over that keyframe. A keyframe of the latter kind contains the same, plus the additional place constraints generated by the transpaths.

When flattening, all the underlying constraints within the blocks are projected on a single timeline. For example, in Figure 1, the constraints in PALMS DOWN and HANDS CONTACT are combined to make one single set of constraints for the keyframe k_9.

This *flattened* score is then used to animate the posture. This is done by resolving the sets of constraints associated with each keyframe in chronological order on the timeline. The constraints are then eventually resolved into the rotation of bone joints. Thus, a posture with n bones can be represented as the following:

$$X(i) = \{bone\_rot_1(i), bone\_rot_2(i), ..., bone\_rot_n(i)\}$$

where X is the state of the posture for the i-th frame.

A problem with this approach is that, even though the system fixes the issue of concurrent constraints depending on each other, it loses the information brought by the parallelism of the blocks while flattening. This means that the only information we have for interpolation are the constraints present on k_1, k_2, ..., and so on. Moreover, every interpolation between each pair of successive keyframes will be distributed on all the bones, including those that should not be affected. Thus, we lose the dynamics of the present blocks, and there is no information on how the system should interpolate amongst these flattened constraints. Also, even if the concurrent blocks comprised of constraints not affecting the same bone chains, there was never a need to flatten in the first place.

In the following section, we propose to fix this using an algorithm that does not flatten by presenting a multi-track bottom-up synthesis of an AZee description.

3. Algorithm for Multi-Track Synthesis

We aim to build a multi-track system without flattening the AZee score. Our work focuses on synthesising the *non-flattened* AZee score in Figure 1. Since the score is constructed based on linguistic descriptions which can be non-linear, we need to impose a certain set of rules while constructing the multi-track timeline, which were previously resolved by flattening the score. Similar to the previous work, we focus on placements and orientation constraints. However, since we are not *flattening*, the *transpath* and *hold* constraints will not be resolved, and we have to deal with them separately.

3.1. Resolving Conflicting Cases

We chose to resolve the conflicting cases by applying the following rules.

3.1.1. Rule 1: Timely Evaluation

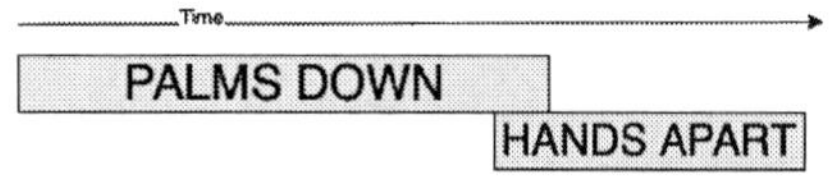

Figure 3: Timely evaluation

Problem: Time overlapping blocks containing constraints that act on the same bone chain but do not start at the same time. For example, in Figure 3, HANDS APART shouldn't be evaluated before PALMS DOWN.

Response: In this scenario(Figure 3), the evaluation of HANDS APART has to account for the fact that the palms are already facing downwards since both blocks act on the same kinematic chain. Thus, to fix this, time overlapping blocks acting on the same bone chains have to be evaluated chronologically.

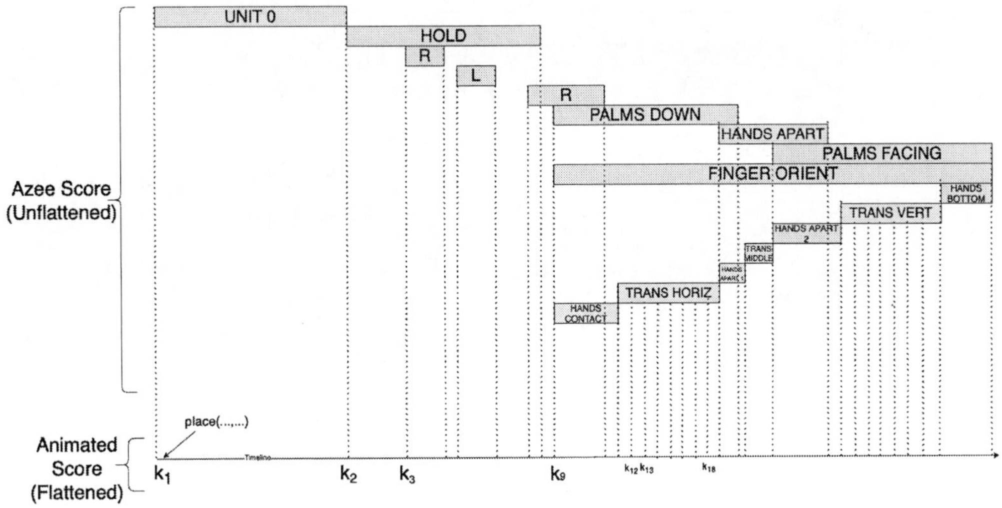

Figure 1: Arrangement of blocks in an AZee score(top) and the equivalent flattened score(bottom)

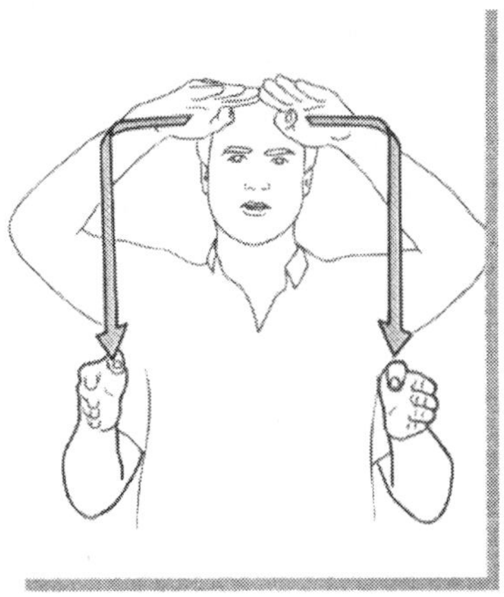

Figure 2: HANDS CONTACT and PALMS DOWN in :armoire (Moody, 1997)

3.1.2. Rule 2: Constraint Precedence

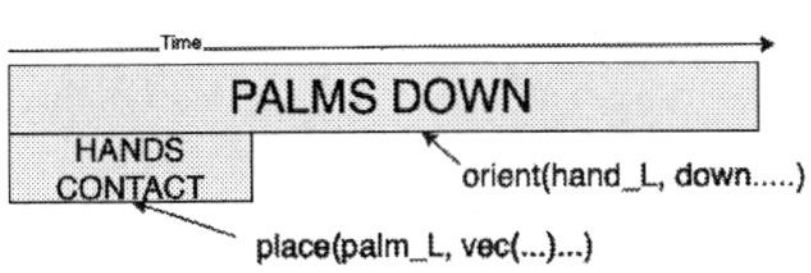

Figure 4: Constraint Precedence

Problem: Time overlapping blocks containing constraints that act on the same bone chain but start at the exact same time. For example, in Figure 4, HANDS CONTACT contains placements while PALMS DOWN contains orientations.

Response: In this scenario(Figure 4), the evaluation of PALMS DOWN has to account for the fact that the hands are already in contact. Thus, to fix this, precedence has to be given to the block containing placement constraints over those with orientation constraints.

3.1.3. Rule 3: Second Pass for Transpaths

Problem: A block contains a transpath constraint.

Response: The transpaths represent transitioning of the posture along some path for an effector of the body. It depends on the evaluation of surrounding blocks and all subsequent interpolations. The solution is, therefore, to evaluate blocks containing transpaths in a Second Pass(Figure 5) after all other blocks have been animated.

3.1.4. Rule 4: Second Pass for Holds

Problem: A block contains a hold constraint.

Response: A block containing the hold constraint specifies that constraints of some other block have to be held for a duration. It, therefore, depends on the animation of that reference block. Hence, blocks containing holds have to be evaluated in a Second Pass (Figure 5) as well.

3.2. Non-Conflicting Cases

Any case not mentioned above will be clear of conflicts and can be evaluated independently. These include:

- all blocks not overlapping each other on the timeline;
- overlapping blocks that act on different bone chains;
- other constraints such as morph and look act independently from the others.

4. Implementation and Experimental Results

The above system has been implemented as an add-on in Blender(v3.1). The interface (Figure 6) shows the Blender interface configured for AZee synthesis. Its main components include:

AZee editor (a) An editor to evaluate AZee expressions. It also includes settings for armature configuration, toggling constraints, and managing body sites.

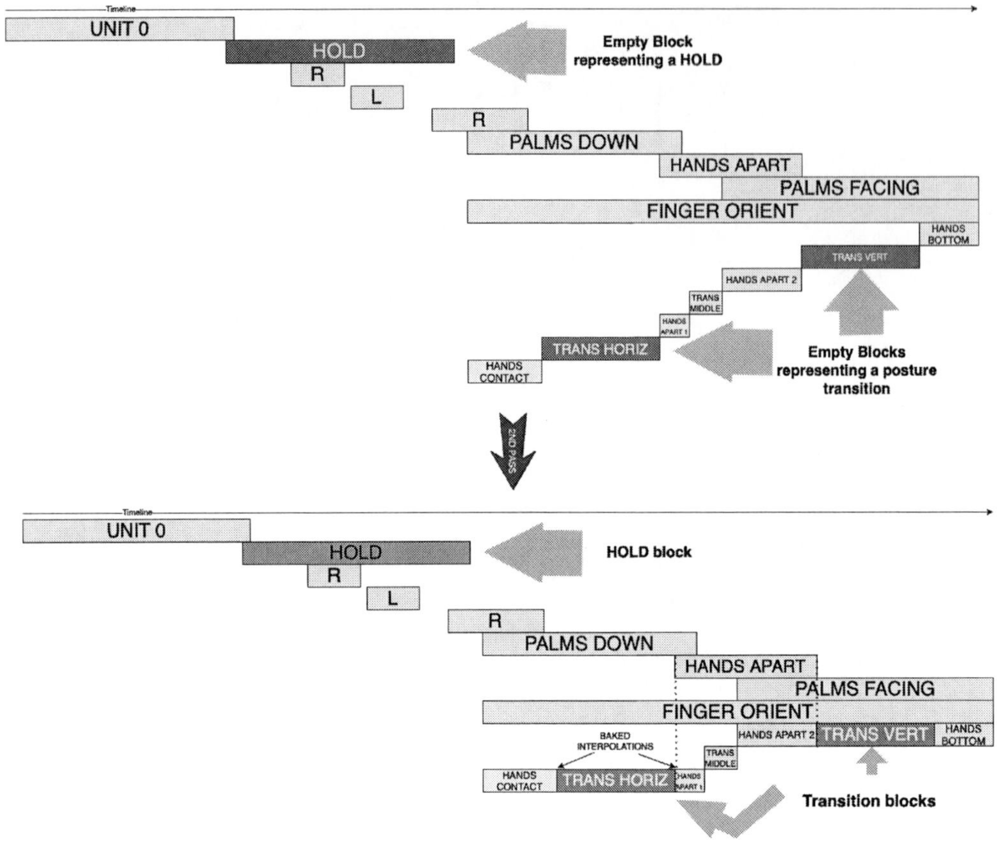

Figure 5: Second Pass to resolve transpaths and holds for *:nicht-sondern(:arbre, :armoire)*

Viewport (b) Shows the 3D scene with the avatar

Non-linear Editor (c) To place all the baked AZee blocks after evaluation.

Properties (d) Modify inverse kinematics (IK) settings, access pose library, and animation layers.

To implement IK solving, we chose to use the iTaSc IK solver (Smits et al., 2008). The reason for that choice is its popularity and that it is already integrated into Blender.
Our implementation is still under development, but the current state of progress already allows to visualise timelines and extract renders, as shown in Figure 7. Here, we present various synthesised AZee descriptions such as *:bien*, *:armoire*, *:arbre*, *:bonjour*.
The current implementation produces satisfactory utterances of simple descriptions but needs more testing and debugging for complex utterances. These occur mainly when there joint orientations get close to the rotation limits. This can be observed in *:armoire* in Figure 7 where the hand rotation limits are reached to satisfy the orientations and placements. But we see that the linguistic constraints on the forearm, hand, and finger orientations, for example, are well satisfied.
As a result of not flattening the score, we preserve the dynamics of individual blocks. This can be seen in *armoire_comparison.mp4* available at `https://doi.org/10.5281/zenodo.6563373` where (A) shows an *:armoire* synthesised using a flattened score while (B) shows the one synthesised using our approach. For (A) we observe that the interpolations are distributed on all bones while for (B) they distribute only over the relevant bones of the blocks shown in the Non-linear Editor.

5. Conclusion and Future Prospects

In this work, we proposed an algorithm that allows for developing the first multi-track animation system for AZee bottom-up synthesis. This proposed algorithm is a step forward in sign language synthesis, allowing for individual AZee blocks to be synthesised independently and ensuring that the dynamics of these blocks are preserved by not flattening. We also integrate our algorithm as an add-on in the open-source Blender software.
Eventually, we want to integrate our work with a top-down technique to have a complete hybrid approach to animate AZee descriptions. The implementation should allow shortcuts using pre-animated clips, MoCap data, or processes that animate these blocks. This would create a system leveraging the advantages of both techniques, as proposed in the AZee–Paula effort.
The current system doesn't resolve AZee morph constraints. More research is needed to handle the bottom-up synthesis of morph constraints and integrate it with our current work. Furthermore, the AZee constraint dependencies

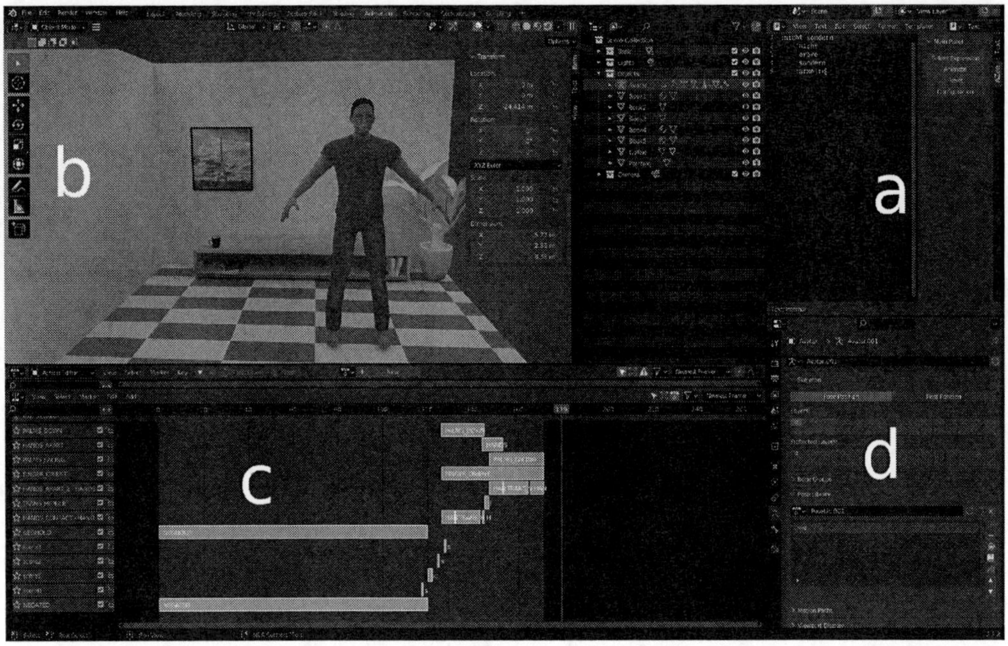

Figure 6: Main Blender interface. (a) AZee editor. (b) 3D Viewport. (c) Non-linear Editor. (d) Properties panel.

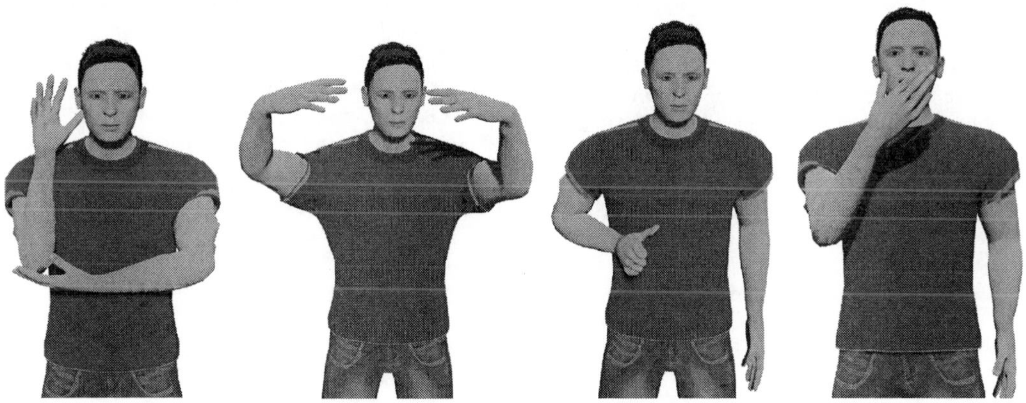

(a) *:arbre* (b) *:armoire* (c) *:bien* (d) *:bonjour*

Figure 7: Results

can eventually be mapped as a dependency graph (Zhang et al., 2021; Watt et al., 2012) which can be solved using a multi-pass system.
Lastly, this work can be extended to make the bottom-up synthesis less robotic using ambient noise analysis and style transfer techniques (Holden et al., 2017).

6. Acknowledgement

This work has been funded by the Bpifrance investment "Structuring Projects for Competitiveness" (PSPC), as part of the Serveur Gestuel project (IVès et 4Dviews Companies, LISN — University Paris-Saclay, and Gipsa-Lab — Grenoble Alpes University).

7. Bibliographical References

Bertoldi, N., Tiotto, G., Prinetto, P., Piccolo, E., Nunnari, F., Lombardo, V., Mazzei, A., Damiano, R., Lesmo, L., and Del Principe, A. (2010). On the creation and the annotation of a large-scale Italian-LIS parallel corpus. In Philippe Dreuw, et al., editors, *Proceedings of the LREC2010 4th Workshop on the Representation and Processing of Sign Languages: Corpora and Sign Language Technologies*, pages 19–22, Valletta, Malta, May. European Language Resources Association (ELRA).

Community, B. O., (2018). *Blender - a 3D modelling and rendering package*. Blender Foundation, Stichting Blender Foundation, Amsterdam.

Filhol, M. and Mcdonald, J. (2018). Extending the azee-paula shortcuts to enable natural proform synthesis. In *Workshop on the Representation and Processing of Sign Languages*.

Filhol, M., Hadjadj, M., and Choisier, A. (2014). Non-manual features: the right to indifference. In *International Conference on Language Resources and Evaluation*.

Filhol, M., Mcdonald, J., and Wolfe, R. (2017). Synthesizing sign language by connecting linguistically structured descriptions to a multi-track animation system. pages 27–40, 05.

Holden, D., Habibie, I., Kusajima, I., and Komura, T. (2017). Fast neural style transfer for motion data. *IEEE computer graphics and applications*, 37(4):42–49.

Huenerfauth, M. (2006). *Generating American Sign Language classifier predicates for English-to-ASL machine translation*. Ph.D. thesis, Citeseer.

Kipp, M., Héloir, A., and Nguyen, Q. (2011). Sign language avatars: Animation and comprehensibility. pages 113–126, 09.

Lombardo, V., Nunnari, F., and Damiano, R. (2010). A virtual interpreter for the italian sign language. volume 6356, pages 201–207, 09.

López-Colino, F. J. and Pasamontes, J. C. (2011). The synthesis of lse classifiers: From representation to evaluation. *J. Univers. Comput. Sci.*, 17:399–425.

López-Colino, F. J. and Pasamontes, J. C. (2012). Spanish sign language synthesis system. *J. Vis. Lang. Comput.*, 23:121–136.

Mcdonald, J., Wolfe, R., Hochgesang, J., Jamrozik, D., Stumbo, M., Berke, L., Bialek, M., and Thomas, F. (2015). An automated technique for real-time production of lifelike animations of american sign language. *Universal Access in the Information Society*, 15, 05.

McDonald, J. C., Wolfe, R., Wilbur, R., Moncrief, R., Malaia, E., Fujimoto, S., Baowidan, S., and Stec, J. (2016). A new tool to facilitate prosodic analysis of motion capture data and a datadriven technique for the improvement of avatar motion. In *sign-lang@ LREC 2016*, pages 153–158. European Language Resources Association (ELRA).

Moody, B. (1997). *La langue des signes, dictionnaire bilingue élémentaire*.

Nunnari, F., Filhol, M., and Heloir, A. (2018). Animating azee descriptions using off-the-shelf ik solvers. In *Workshop on the Representation and Processing of Sign Languages*.

Smits, R., De Laet, T., Claes, K., Bruyninckx, H., and De Schutter, J. (2008). itasc: a tool for multi-sensor integration in robot manipulation. In *2008 IEEE International Conference on Multisensor Fusion and Integration for Intelligent Systems*, pages 426–433.

Watt, M., Cutler, L. D., Powell, A., Duncan, B., Hutchinson, M., and Ochs, K. (2012). Libee: A multithreaded dependency graph for character animation. In *Proceedings of the Digital Production Symposium*, DigiPro '12, page 59–66, New York, NY, USA. Association for Computing Machinery.

Wolfe, R., McDonald, J., Johnson, R., Moncrief, R., Alexander, A., Sturr, B., Klinghoffer, S., Conneely, F., Saenz, M., and Choudhry, S. (2021). State of the art and future challenges of the portrayal of facial nonmanual signals by signing avatar. In *International Conference on Human-Computer Interaction*, pages 639–655. Springer.

Zhang, J.-Q., Xu, X., Shen, Z.-M., Huang, Z.-H., Zhao, Y., Cao, Y.-P., Wan, P., and Wang, M. (2021). Write-an-animation: High-level text-based animation editing with character-scene interaction. In *Computer Graphics Forum*, volume 40, pages 217–228. Wiley Online Library.

Proceedings of the 7th International Workshop on Sign Language Translation and Avatar Technology (SLTAT 7), pages 109–116
Language Resources and Evaluation Conference (LREC 2022), Marseille, 20-25 June 2022

First Steps Towards a Signing Avatar for Railway Travel Announcements in the Netherlands

Britt van Gemert, Richard Cokart, Lyke Esselink, Maartje de Meulder, Nienke Sijm, Floris Roelofsen
Universiteit van Amsterdam, Radboud Universiteit, Hogeschool Utrecht,
Nederlands Gebarencentrum, Nederlandse Spoorwegen
britt-van-gemert@live.nl, r.cokart@gebarencentrum.nl, l.d.esselink@uva.nl,
maartje.demeulder@hu.nl, nienke.sijm@hu.nl, f.roelofsen@uva.nl

Abstract

This paper presents first steps towards a sign language avatar for communicating railway travel announcements in Dutch Sign Language. Taking an interdisciplinary approach, it demonstrates effective ways to employ co-design and focus group methods in the context of developing sign language technology, and presents several concrete findings and results obtained through co-design and focus group sessions which have not only led to improvements of our own prototype but may also inform the development of signing avatars for other languages and in other application domains.

Keywords: text-to-sign translation, signing avatars, co-design, Dutch Sign Language, railway travel information

1. Introduction

This paper presents initial results of a project which aims to develop a sign language avatar for communicating railway travel announcements in Dutch Sign Language (Nederlandse Gebarentaal, NGT), in collaboration with the Dutch national railway company (NS).

For developing responsible and ethical signed language technologies that are adopted by deaf end users, interdisciplinary collaboration between specialists in Deaf Studies, Sign Linguistics, Computer Science, Artificial Intelligence, Human Computer Interaction, Language Policy, and Sign Language Interpreting Studies is essential (Bragg and others, 2019; Bragg and others, 2021; Yin et al., 2021). Such collaboration increases the quality of the developed technologies, ensures that they incorporate deaf communities' demands and values, and guarantees that there is consideration for design and appropriate user interfaces (De Meulder, 2021).

The present project is an example of such interdisciplinary collaboration. Our team consists of three deaf researchers with a background in Applied Sign Linguistics (Cokart, de Meulder) and Deaf Studies (de Meulder, Sijm) and three hearing researchers with a background in AI and Linguistics (Esselink, van Gemert, Roelofsen). Esselink and van Gemert have elementary proficiency in NGT, Roelofsen intermediate. Cokart and Sijm use NGT as their primary sign language and use it in different domains, De Meulder uses NGT primarily in professional contexts. Cokart, De Meulder and Sijm all have knowledge of various other sign languages and are involved in various deaf networks and communities.

The paper makes two contributions. The first is methodological: it exemplifies how co-design and focus group methods can be used effectively in the context of developing sign language technology, and offers some recommendations as to how these methods may be adapted to this specific purpose. The second is technological: it discusses several concrete findings and results obtained through co-design and focus group sessions which have not only led to improvements of our own prototype but may also inform the development of signing avatars for other languages and in other application domains.

2. Brief Background on Sign Languages

Evidently, we cannot provide a comprehensive overview here of the (socio)linguistic properties of sign languages in general (Baker et al., 2016), nor of NGT in particular (Klomp, 2021). We will, however, highlight some important features which any text-to-sign translation system needs to take into account.

First of all, sign languages have naturally evolved in deaf communities around the world (Kusters and Lucas, 2022). This means that, contrary to a rather common misconception, there is not a single, universal sign language used by all deaf people worldwide, but many different sign languages used on different scales by different deaf and hearing signers (Hou and de Vos, 2022).

Second, although sign languages exist in language ecologies in close contact with spoken languages, there is generally no direct correspondence between the sign language used in a given country and the spoken language used in that same country. For instance, while English is the mainstream spoken language both in the US and in the UK, American Sign Language (ASL) and British Sign Language (BSL) differ considerably from each other, as well as from spoken English. Such differences do not only pertain to the lexicon, but also to grammatical features such as word order. This means in particular that, to translate a sentence from English to ASL or BSL it does not suffice to translate every word in the sentence into the corresponding sign in ASL/BSL and then put these signs together in the same order as the words in the English sentence.

Third, making travel information available in the form of written text does not necessarily make it equally comprehensible for all deaf passengers. Depending on the complexity and time-sensitiveness of the message, textual information may be difficult to process, which may lead to misinterpretation. At the same time, the time-sensitive character of travel information entails specific demands concerning the comprehensibility of avatars.

Fourth, signs are generally not just articulated with the hands, but often also involve facial expressions and/or movements of the head, mouth, shoulders, or upper body. These are referred to as the *non-manual* components of a sign. A text-to-sign translation system has to take both manual and non-manual components of signs into account. These movement qualities (fluid movement) seem to be a crucial aspect for the rating of avatars by deaf end users (e.g. Quandt et al. (2021)).

Fifth, related to the previous point, non-manual elements are not only part of the *lexical* make-up of many signs, but are also often used to convey certain *grammatical* information (comparable to intonation in spoken languages). For instance, raised eyebrows may indicate that a given sentence is a question rather than a statement, and a head shake often expresses negation. Such non-manual grammatical markers are typically 'supra-segmental', meaning that they do not co-occur with a single lexical sign but rather span across a sequence of signs in a sentence. Sign language linguists use so-called *glosses* to represent sign language utterances. For instance, the gloss in (1) represents the NGT translation of the question *Have you already eaten?*.

(1) $\overline{\text{YOU EAT ALREADY}}^{\text{brow raise}}$

Lexical signs are written in small-caps. They always involve a manual component and often non-manual components as well. The upper tier shows non-manual grammatical markers, and the horizontal line indicates the duration of these non-manual markers. In this case, 'brow raise' is used to indicate that the utterance is a question. A text-to-sign translation system should thus be able to integrate non-manual elements that convey grammatical information with manual and non-manual elements that belong to the lexical specification of the signs in a given sentence (Wolfe et al., 2011). This means that a system which translates sentences word by word, even if it re-orders the corresponding signs in accordance with the word order rules of the target sign language, will not be fully satisfactory. More flexibility is needed: word by word translation can be a first step, but the corresponding signs as specified in the lexicon, must generally be adapted when forming part of a sentence to incorporate non-manual markers carrying grammatical information.

Sixth, in the context of machine learning, just like some smaller spoken languages, (most) sign languages belong to the category of 'low-resourced languages', which refers to a lack of available training data and the fragmentation of efforts in resource development (Sayers et al., 2021). For sign languages there is the additional issue of a different language modality, which makes data collection and machine training much more challenging than for most spoken languages.

3. Related Work

We cannot provide a comprehensive overview of all work related to the present project. We restrict ourselves to highlighting some relevant work on (i) signing avatars for NGT, (ii) signing avatars in the railway domain, (iii) co-design and focus group methodologies, and (iv) user feedback on existing avatars.

Signing avatars for NGT Previous research on sign language technology for NGT is rather limited. Prins and Janssen (2014) developed a first prototype signing avatar for NGT to translate an episode of a Dutch TV program for children. Roelofsen et al. (2021) developed an avatar to address concerns in the Dutch deaf community during the COVID pandemic about the difficulty of communicating with healthcare professionals in case sign language interpreters would not be permitted into the hospital (Smeijers and Roelofsen, 2021). This avatar supports basic one-way communication from healthcare professionals to patients, e.g. to inform a patient about the results of their COVID test.

Signing avatars in the railway domain There has been discussion in the literature and the user communities about possible application domains of signing avatars. In general, announcements in public transportation are seen as a 'safe' application domain (Krausneker and Schügerl, 2021; WFD and WASLI, 2018) because their grammar is highly constrained and predictable, and the information that is shared is impersonal. This is different for application domains where the stakes are higher and miscommunication can potentially lead to life-threatening situations.

Prototype avatars for railway travel announcements have been developed for several sign languages, including Italian Sign Language (Battaglino et al., 2015), Swiss German Sign Language (Ebling and Glauert, 2016), and Sign Language of French-speaking Belgium David and Bouillon (2018).

The basic aim of Battaglino et al. (2015) was similar to ours, but the approach quite different. Their project involved a technical development phase and a quantitative assessment of the translation accuracy of the system. Our approach instead involves co-design and focus group methods so as to improve the system through various iterations. The findings we report are qualitative in nature rather than quantitative.

Closer to our project is the work of Ebling and Glauert (2016) and David and Bouillon (2018). These projects involved an initial development phase, a focus group session to collect suggestions for improvements, and a second development phase to implement these suggestions. These projects were similar to ours in that they used a qualitative method for evaluation, and involved multiple (in their case two) development iterations. One difference is that our project did not only include a focus group session, but also several co-design sessions, interleaved with multiple development iterations. Moreover, there is a difference in focus group methodology. These previous projects presented focus group members with a number of sentences signed by an avatar and elicited general feedback on the basis of these sentences. We instead discussed eight specific topics with our focus group members which had arisen during the co-design sessions. In each case we presented three different avatar animations for comparison, in order to make the discussion more targeted and to elicit more specific recommendations.

Co-design and focus group methodologies Co-design of sign language technologies with deaf end users improves the quality of the developed technologies, ensures appropriateness for the intended purpose, and stimulates acceptance. Conversely, lack of co-design may not only lead to sub-optimal technologies but also ones that could negatively impact deaf communities (Bragg and others, 2021).

Community-based co-design has been performed for several sign languages, including South African sign language (Blake et al., 2014). For example, for the design of a Deaf culture website, combining iterative co-design and focus group methods yielded insights in the native point of view and actionable insights on culturally rooted conventions for user experience (Pylvänen et al., 2013). Moreover, it can uncover hidden cultural norms, values, beliefs and attitudes (Chininthorn, 2021). Focus groups are used to elicit perceptions and opinions in early development stages. Young and Hunt (2011) emphasise the importance of avoiding visual distractions in focus group sessions: no busy walls or clothing, and a setting that ensures a good view for all participants.

User feedback User feedback has been collected for several existing signing avatars. We will highlight only some of the most recent studies, which involves state-of-the-art avatars. Krausneker and Schügerl (2021) compared perceptions of avatars vs. human interpreters through focus groups. Deaf participants criticized avatars for "lacking facial expressions, imprecise co-ordination of manual and non-manual components of a sign, missing phrase melody, jerky, hard, mechanical, wooden, robotic, somnolent, unnatural, incomplete signs and missing transitions between signs." They also mentioned "lack of mobility of upper body, shoulders, cheeks, unclear mouthing, comic face, artificial figure." Younger participants were often more familiar with the uncanny valley effect. Older participants sometimes felt that it was inappropriate that they were informed by a playful cartoon character, because they felt it exacerbated the infantilisation of sign languages — and by extension, deaf people (see also Wolfe et al. (2021)). Participants further reported that "maximal cognitive attention" was needed to understand the avatar.

Quandt et al. (2021) found that deaf respondents rated an avatar based on motion capture significantly more positively than an avatar based on (scripted) keyframe animation, but still not as positively as a human signer. Participants who had learned ASL later in life were more open to signing avatars in general, but also gave more negative ratings to the avatar based on keyframe animation. Participants who learned ASL earlier in life were more sensitive to movement quality issues in the keyframe animation avatar.

4. Design Process

4.1. Phase 1: Initial Design

First, we obtained a list of railway announcement templates from NS (e.g. 'The intercity train to destination X departs at time Y from platform Z'). The Dutch Sign Language Centre (Nederlands Gebarencentrum, NGc) provided NGT translations of these templates (for randomly picked X's, Y's, and Z's).

We created an initial basic system based on these translations. The signing avatar mimicked the video translations as closely as possible, and had the ability to sign several variations of the announcement templates (with different X's, Y's, and Z's). We made use of the JASigning avatar engine for implementation of the avatar (e.g. Ebling and Glauert (2016)). This engine takes phonetic representations of signs as input (specified in the Sign Gesture Markup Language, SiGML for short) and yields an avatar animation as output. This approach allowed us to efficiently create a large number of variations of the given set of templates, without expensive equipment (e.g. motion capture).

In addition, we developed an online user interface to facilitate further development of the basic initial system in subsequent phases of the project.

A general strategy for inclusive collaboration methods was defined through a brainstorm session involving two deaf and two hearing researchers. We opted for a *combination* of multiple co-design sessions and a focus group. The former allows for iterative development with a relatively small, highly engaged and fully dedicated team. The latter ensures input from a larger and more diverse group of potential end users. We envisioned that a combination of the two methods would work particularly well because the co-design sessions could result in specific topics to be discussed in the focus group. Indeed, we feel that this has made the focus group particularly fruitful (see below).

4.2. Phase 2: Iterative Co-design

4.2.1. Method

We held three co-design sessions (2x2 hours on campus with two deaf researchers, two hearing, and two interpreters; 1x1 hour online with one deaf researcher, two hearing, and one interpreter). These sessions focused on improving various aspects of the avatar's signing (e.g., manual movements, facial expressions, mouthing, grammar, transitions between signs) as well as non-linguistic aspects of the animations (e.g., camera angle, speed). Following each session, all suggestions made by the deaf researchers were implemented by the developers, often in several variations, so that they could be reconsidered and possibly further refined during the next session. In some cases, suggested improvements were implemented on the fly and evaluated immediately.

4.2.2. Results

The co-design sessions led to major adjustments of the avatar, pertaining to both linguistic and non-linguistic aspects. Below we discuss a selection of these adjustments.

Greeting All NS announcements start with a greeting, BESTE REIZIGERS *(DEAR PASSENGERS)*. This is not a natural greeting in NGT. At first, we removed the greeting entirely. However, it also functions as a way of getting people's attention and provides a 'time buffer', so that passengers don't miss the first part of the actual announcement. As an alternative, we opted for the greeting HALLO (HELLO), which is commonly used in NGT, both in formal and in informal settings. The avatar initially signed HALLO with a 5-handshape, with all selected fingers stretched. This looked unnatural. We adapted the sign, opting for a handshape that lies between the 5-handshape and the B1-handshape. A subtle difference, but the resulting sign looks substantially more natural.

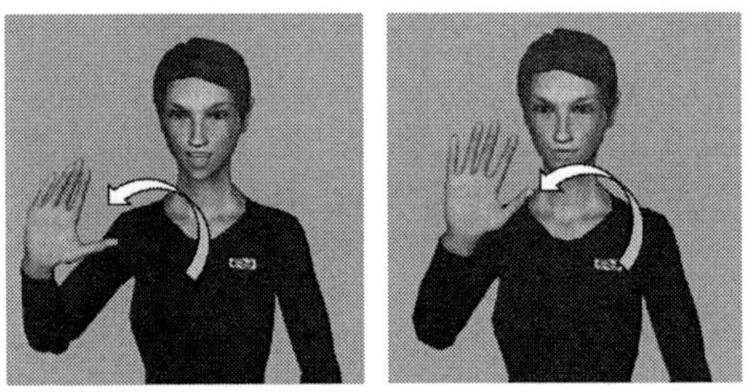

(a) HALLO - Version 1 (b) HALLO - Version 2

Fig. 1: HALLO - Multiple versions

Mouthings The JAsigning avatar engine offers limited possibilities to produce natural-looking mouthings. The engine requires a specification of the mouthing in SAMPA notation. But SAMPA is a notation system for *phonemes*, and there is no one-to-one mapping between phonemes and mouth movements. For instance, the 's' in 'sun' and the 's' in 'silver' involve different mouth shapes. This makes it difficult to generate correct mouthings for NGT in JAsigning, and in several cases we did not succeed in doing so. For instance, the mouthing for VIJFENVIJFTIG *(fiftyfive)* was initially coded in SAMPA as 'vE_ifv@nvE_iftIx'. After multiple adjustments we ended up with 'vE_ifE_iftI'. While this improved the animation, the last part 'tig' is still unsatisfactory.

Formal vs informal registers The distinction between formal and informal registers proved to be highly relevant for the perception of the avatar. Clear signing is not sufficient; the avatar's signing style and choice of vocabulary also need to fit the particular context of use. For instance, the sign WEGGAAN (*LEAVE*) which is frequently used in casual interactions (e.g., in 'the train already left') was deemed too informal for official announcements and was replaced by the more formal sign VERTREKKEN (*DEPART*).

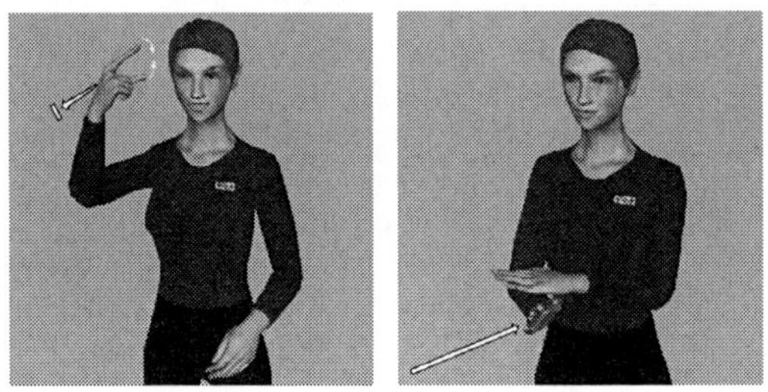

(a) WEGGAAN (b) VERTREKKEN

Fig. 2: WEGGAAN and VERTREKKEN

Intensity Preferences regarding the intensity of body movements and facial expressions varied. On the one hand, for station names such as ENSCHEDE and UTRECHT CENTRAAL, the manual movements and facial expressions of the avatar were considered too exaggerated, even aggressive, and had to be 'toned down'. On the other hand, for certain other signs (e.g. BIJNA *(ALMOST)*) they were considered too subtle and had to be intensified.

Transitions In phrases of the form NAAR X *(TO X)*, where X is the name of some destination, the transition between the two signs was sometimes unnatural. For instance, as can be seen in Figure 3(a), the path movement of the sign NAAR ends by default in the upper right corner of the signing space (from the perspective of the signer), but if the initial position of the subsequent sign, e.g. ALMELO in Figure 3(c), is in the upper left corner of the signing space, there is an unnatural prolonged transition between the two signs. This issue was also observed for other destinations, such as MAASTRICHT and AMSTERDAM. This was resolved by manually adapting the sign NAAR whenever needed. Ideally, however, future iterations of the system would be able to automatically adjust the direction of signs like NAAR, depending on the next sign.

Eye gaze In several phrases, the avatar's eye gaze was too static. For instance, when a destination is signed (e.g., Amsterdam), it is natural for the eyes to be directed at the location of the sign in the signing space and to follow the path movement of the sign.

(a) NAAR (b) Transition (c) First pose of ALMELO

Fig. 3: Transition between NAAR and ALMELO

Camera angle Initially, the camera angle was front-view, the default in JAsigning. This, however, resulted in poor visibility for some signs, e.g., VIJFTIEN *(FIFTEEN)*. By changing the camera angle 13° to the left, and adjusting the head position and eye gaze of the avatar in such a way that she still faced the addressee by default, visibility was significantly improved.

Sentence structure Due to grammatical differences between NGT and Dutch, the signed sentence structure sometimes had to be adjusted. For example, in NGT, certainties should be positioned at the start of the sentence and uncertainties at the end (e.g. 'over een nog onbekende tijd' *(in a yet unknown time)* should be positioned at the end). The structure of sentences containing a final destination and several intermediate destinations was adapted as well: the preference was to mention the final destination before the intermediate destinations. In both cases, the preferred structure in NGT differs from the structure of the original NS announcements in Dutch.

Lists In phrases like *the train to Almelo, Hengelo and Enschede*, the avatar initially used a 'count hand' to list the three destinations, a grammatical construction that is commonly used in NGT for conjunctions and lists. In the present context, however, this gave the wrong impression that the announcement concerned multiple trains. Therefore, all count hand signs were removed.

Indexing There was much discussion about the appropriate use of INDEX signs. For instance, the video translations that served as our point of reference rendered the phrase *The intercity to...* as INDEX INTERCITY NAAR, where the function of the INDEX sign was to place the intercity in the signing space for future anaphoric reference. While grammatically correct, this usage of the INDEX sign seemed superfluous if the announcement did not involve any anaphoric reference to the intercity (which was the case in most announcements). A similar issue arose for phrases like *from platform two*, which were translated as VAN INDEX SPOOR TWEE. No consensus on this issue was established during the co-design process. Moreover, it was suggested that some INDEX signs, if present at all, should be shorter (less prominent) than others. We decided to create several variants for a number of sentences, with index signs present or absent in several positions, and with shorter or longer movements, to be further discussed in the focus group session.

Visual elements If an announcement is a repetition of a previously made announcements, its spoken version always starts with *Herhaling* (*Repetition*). In the signed version, however, starting with the sign HERHALING would not be effective for passengers who miss the beginning of the announcement. We therefore removed the sign and instead added a red bar under the animation displaying the text *Herhaling* to indicate the repetition.

Appearance The avatar's fingers were perceived as being unnaturally long. This affected the appearance of some hand shapes, e.g. in SPOOR *(PLATFORM)*. When properly signed, SPOOR involves a baby-C handshape with extended fingers. Due to the the long fingers of the avatar, this baby-C handshape had an unnatural curved shape.
The deaf researchers in the team also commented on the general appearance of the avatar. It was perceived as somewhat grumpy, not friendly. We added a smile right at the beginning of each announcement, before and during the greeting HALLO. This was an improvement, but a more friendly-looking avatar should be developed/adopted in future work (the JAsigning engine is limited in this regard – it includes some avatars other than the one we used, but not ones that are more suitable for our present purposes). Users should preferably also be able to adapt the clothing of the avatar, and to choose a male, female or androgyn-looking avatar.

Semantic refinement In some cases, a Dutch phrase cannot be univocally translated to NGT without making more specific what its intended semantic interpretation is. For instance, the proper translation of *De trein naar... rijdt niet* (*The train to... is cancelled*) depends on whether it's just a single train that is cancelled or the problem is structural. In the first case, the phrase RIJDEN NIET *(DEPART NOT)* is used, where NIET is signed with a 1-handshape moving from a central position in the signing space towards the upper right corner accompanied by a headshake, while in the second case the sign ANNULEREN *(CANCEL)* is more appropriate (drawing a cross in the signing space).

Times and numbers In phrases like INTERCITY NAAR AMSTERDAM TIJD TIEN TWINTIG (*INTERCITY TO AMSTERDAM TIME TEN TWENTY*), it is clear that the numeral phrase TIEN TWINTIG refers to the departure time. The sign TIJD was felt to be redundant and was therefore removed. Instead the preposition VAN *(OF)* was inserted, corresponding to the preposition that is used in Dutch, e.g., *De trein* *van 10:20* (*'The train of 10:20'*). No consensus was reached on whether to include a sign for the ':' symbol in times like 10:20, and if so, which sign. We created several variations to be discussed further during the focus group session.

Topics for focus group As already alluded to in several places above, we identified a number of specific topics during the co-design sessions that required further discussion in a larger and more diverse group of deaf people (e.g. indexing, time punctuation). For this purpose, multiple variations were created to facilitate comparison and stimulate targeted discussion.

4.3. Phase 3: Focus Group

4.3.1. Method

A 3-hour focus group session with six participants was held. Participants were selected by the deaf team members from their personal and professional network. They represented different regions, age groups and school backgrounds (see Table 1). In advance, participants received a link to an online demo of the avatar. Specific topics for discussion were not sent in advance.

	Age	Home, work and school region
D1	31-40	Noord-Holland, Utrecht, Groningen
D2	41-50	Noord-Holland, Utrecht, Noord-Brabant
D3	18-30	Utrecht, Gelderland, Groningen
D4	51-60	Utrecht, Groningen
D5	18-30	Noord-Holland, Groningen
D6	41-50	Flevoland, Amsterdam

Table 1: Focus Group Participants

The session was held at the University of Amsterdam in a room with a big screen. One team member acted as host and moderator (hearing, intermediate signer), one team member controlled the screen and took detailed minutes (hearing, minimal knowledge of NGT, developer), and two team members took part in the discussion (both deaf). One NGT-English interpreter was present. Having a signing moderator who is familiar with the research terms and project itself is an advantage over solely communicating through the interpreter (less engaging, time lag between communication types) (Orfanidou et al., 2014; Harris et al., 2009).

The discussion concentrated on eight topics determined by the team in advance, including time punctuation, subtitles, animation speed, mouthing, indexing, pauses and choice of vocabulary. In each case, three variants of a sign or a phrase were presented for comparison and participants discussed their perspectives and opinions. At the end of the focus group, participants were asked how and where they would like to see the avatar put to use.

4.3.2. Results

We provide an overview of our main findings.

Subtitles We asked participants whether subtitles might be helpful, and if so, which format would be preferred (per sign vs per sentence). Participants indicated that subtitles could indeed be useful, and had a clear preference for subtitles for entire sentences rather than for individual signs. If the text in the subtitles is used as an information source, displaying the entire sentence at once makes it easier to obtain complete information at once.

Animation speed The JASigning avatar engine offers speed adjustments ranging from 0.00 to +3.00. Participants of the focus group considered an animation speed of +0.40 optimal for comprehension. Lower speed was perceived as too slow. For most participants, a higher speed (e.g. +0.60) was comprehensible as well, but required more cognitive effort.

Indexing We asked participants for their preference concerning the use of INDEX signs (see Section 4.2). They indicated a preference for the use of INDEX sign even if they were strictly speaking redundant, but also indicated that INDEX signs should by default be subtle and not too prominent, often involving just a change of handshape and/or a subtle movement of the wrist, otherwise keeping the body and arms roughly in the same position as where the previous sign ended. For instance, the preferred translation of *The intercity to Almelo departs from platform five* was: INDEX1 (subtle) INTERCITY NAAR ALMELO INDEX1 (subtle) VERTREKKEN SPOOR 5 INDEX2 (subtle).

Time punctuation No consensus was reached for time punctuation, i.e., the sign for the ':' in times like '15:31'. In fact, among our six participants, three different signs were used, and preferences seemed to depend on age group.

Personal pronouns In some sentences the avatar used a first person pronoun IK/WIJ *(I/WE)*. The original Dutch announcements of NS involve *impersonal* pronouns instead, but these do not have a direct translation in NGT. However, our focus group participants indicated that the use of first person pronouns was not suitable, as this suggested that the avatar herself was the source of the information, rather than NS.

Pauses In general, animations without any pauses between signs were preferred, or with very short pauses based on the syntactic structure of the sentence (i.e., somewhat longer pauses between conjoined sentences and shorter ones between noun phrases).

User interface Participants made some specific user interface suggestions. They indicated that it would be useful for the avatar to be displayed on screens at train stations and in trains, as well as in the mobile NS app. Drawing passengers' attention before an announcement starts is essential – otherwise, passengers might miss part of the announcement. At train stations and in trains, flickering lights on the ground could serve this purpose. In the mobile app, a vibrate alert would be a natural choice, and passengers should be enabled to replay the announcement if they want to. It would be good if deaf users of the mobile app could choose to receive automatic alerts for announcements related to their personal itinerary.

5. Discussion and Conclusion

The combined expertise from various disciplines in the co-design process and the input from a diverse focus group led to significant improvements of our prototype (manual movements, facial expressions, mouthing, grammar, transitions between signs, camera angle, speed), many of which may well be transferable to other languages and application domains.
It is evident, however, that the development of a fully satisfactory signing avatar for railway announcements in NGT requires much further work. Below we highlight some specific limitations of the methodological choices we made and the results obtained so far, as well as some natural avenues for further research.

5.1. Initial design

Reference material As an initial point of reference for our avatar translations, we obtained video recordings of the Dutch Sign Language Centre. However, sign languages are 3D, and videos 2D. In several cases, the video translations, filmed with a front-view camera angle, were not quite sufficient as reference material, since signs could not be viewed from multiple directions. Additional video's with different camera angles could possibly resolve this issue.

Avatar engine The JAsigning avatar engine which we used to generate avatar animations currently has a number of limitations. In particular, important features of the overall appearance of the avatar cannot be adjusted (e.g. excessively long fingers, somewhat unfriendly look) and control over mouth movements and facial expressions is too restricted. Such limitations form a real bottleneck for the development of a truly satisfactory signing avatar. Overcoming them would require substantial further development of the engine, or alternatively, adopting an altogether different approach to generating animations based on motion capture. We aim to explore both routes in future work.

5.2. Co-design

Iterative nature The iterative nature of our co-design process resulted in a thorough analysis of several aspects and considerable changes in the design of the avatar. Nevertheless, many other aspects had to be left for future iterations (e.g. eye gaze direction, facial expressions, topic-marking).

Live vs online sessions Three co-design sessions took place, of which two live and one online. We feel that the live sessions were much more effective, because they ensured a good view of the participants' signing, including their facial expressions and body language. Moreover, they provided the possibility to point out some details on a big screen, write on a chalkboard and point at the screen or at the board while signing the same time. The duration of the live sessions (2 hours) was quite demanding. In the future, more and shorter sessions would be preferable.

Interpreters During the sessions, interpreter(s) were present and some of the communication happened indirectly. Signers sometimes had to wait for interpreters to catch up, become familiar with research terms, or repeat signs so that the person taking notes could see the intended movements. Working with the same interpreters during all sessions is beneficial for familiarity with the relevant terms. However, it should always be kept in mind that if there is no shared language among all researchers and therefore some of the communication has to be mediated by an interpreter, there is always a higher chance of miscommunication. *Iterative* co-designs overcomes this issue to some extent: possible misunderstandings are often identified when suggestions are implemented and re-evaluated.

5.3. Focus Group

Recording vs minutes Detailed minutes were taken during the focus group. However, these minutes only provide a textual transcription, mediated by an interpreter, of what was actually signed during the session. This loss of information could be overcome by capturing the discussion on video, with multiple cameras to ensure a good view of all participants. This would also prevent overlooking information when multiple participants are signing at the same time – in many such cases, interpreter-mediated transcriptions will only capture what one of the participants signed. We should note that in order to make such video data searchable and usable for analysis it would have to be annotated in quite some detail, which would be a labor intensive process. But the information retained in this way could be very beneficial.

Developer presence The presence of the developers during our focus group may well have affected the discussion, as participants may have felt less comfortable criticizing the system. On the other hand, not having developers present during a focus group sessions would result in less direct input and would take away the possibility of directly implementing and evaluating certain suggestions.

Generalising results Our focus group was quite diverse in terms of age group and region. However, for further development it is necessary to organise more focus groups with more diversity in terms of age group, region, educational level, and reading level, among other things. For example, seniors and people from the southern part of the Netherlands were not represented in our focus group. Moreover, use of the avatar in a real-life setting is under-researched. This may affect our current results, especially given the time-sensitiveness of the context in which the avatar needs to provide information.

6. Acknowledgements

We are grateful to the participants of our focus group, and to Martijn van Beek, Babette van Blijenburgh, Stijn van den Brand, Bastien David, Marjon Fonville, John Glauert, Richard Kennaway, and Martha Larson for their help with various aspects of the project. We gratefully acknowledge financial support from NS and the Netherlands Organization for Scientific Research (NWO).

7. Bibliographical References

Baker, A., van den Bogaerde, B., Pfau, R., and Schermer, T. (2016). *The linguistics of sign languages: An introduction*. John Benjamins.

Battaglino, C., Geraci, C., Lombardo, V., and Mazzei, A. (2015). Prototyping and preliminary evaluation of a sign language translation system in the railway domain. In Margherita Antona et al., editors, *Universal Access in Human-Computer Interaction*, pages 339–350.

Blake, E., Tucker, W., and Glaser, M. (2014). Towards communication and information access for deaf people. *South African Computer Journal*, 54:10–19.

Bragg, D. et al. (2019). Sign language recognition, generation, and translation: An interdisciplinary perspective. In *The 21st international ACM SIGACCESS conference on computers and accessibility*, pages 16–31.

Bragg, D. et al. (2021). The fate landscape of sign language ai datasets: An interdisciplinary perspective. *ACM Transactions on Accessible Computing (TACCESS)*, 14(2):1–45.

Chininthorn, P. (2021). Community-based co-design for accessible health information for deaf people in a context with societal complexity.

David, B. V. C. and Bouillon, P. (2018). Prototype of Automatic Translation to the Sign Language of French-speaking Belgium. *Modelling, Measurement and Control C*, 79(4):162–167.

De Meulder, M. (2021). Is "good enough" good enough? Ethical and responsible development of sign language technologies. In *Proc. of the 1st Int. Workshop on Automatic Translation for Signed and Spoken Languages (AT4SSL)*, pages 12–22.

Ebling, S. and Glauert, J. (2016). Building a Swiss German Sign Language avatar with JASigning and evaluating it among the Deaf community. *Universal Access in the Information Society*, 15(4):577–587.

Harris, R., Holmes, H. M., and Mertens, D. M. (2009). Research ethics in sign language communities. *Sign Language Studies*, 9(2):104–131.

Hou, L. and de Vos, C. (2022). Classifications and typologies: Labeling sign languages and signing communities. *Journal of Sociolinguistics*, 26(1):118–125.

Klomp, U. (2021). *A descriptive grammar of Sign Language of the Netherlands*. Ph.D. thesis, University of Amsterdam.

Krausneker, V. and Schügerl, S. (2021). Best practices protocol on the use of sign language avatars.

Kusters, A. and Lucas, C. (2022). Emergence and evolutions: Introducing sign language sociolinguistics. *Journal of Sociolinguistics*, 26(1):84–98.

Orfanidou, E., Woll, B., and Morgan, G. (2014). *Research methods in sign language studies: A practical guide*. John Wiley & Sons.

Prins, M. and Janssen, J. B. (2014). Automated sign language. TNO technical report.

Pylvänen, S., Raike, A., Rainò, P., et al. (2013). Co-design for accessibility in academia for deaf students. *Co-Create 2013*.

Quandt, L. C., Willis, A., Schwenk, M., Weeks, K., and Ferster, R. (2021). Attitudes toward signing human avatars vary depending on hearing status, age of signed language exposure, and avatar type. Manuscript archived at PsyArXiv, June 25, doi:10.31234/osf.io/g2wuc.

Roelofsen, F., Esselink, L., Mende-Gillings, S., and Smeijers, A. (2021). Sign language translation in a healthcare setting. In *Proceedings of the Translation and Interpreting Technology Online Conference*, pages 110–124.

Sayers, D., Sousa-Silva, R., Höhn, S., et al. (2021). The dawn of the human-machine era: A forecast of new and emerging language technologies. *Report for EU COST Action CA19102 'Language in the Human-Machine Era'*.

Smeijers, A. S. and Roelofsen, F. (2021). Communicatiebehoeften en ervaringen van dove patiënten in Nederland tijdens de COVID-19 pandemie (communication needs and experiences of deaf patients in the netherlands during the covid-19 pandemic). Dutch report available through `https://zorgbeter.info/`, with per-section summaries in NGT.

WFD and WASLI. (2018). World Federation of the Deaf and World Association of Sign Language Interpreters Statement on Use of Signing Avatars. `https://wfdeaf.org/news/wfd-wasli-issue-statement-signing-avatars/`.

Wolfe, R., Cook, P., McDonald, J. C., and Schnepp, J. (2011). Linguistics as structure in computer animation: Toward a more effective synthesis of brow motion in American Sign Language. *Sign Language & Linguistics*, 14(1):179–199.

Wolfe, R., Mcdonald, J., Efthimiou, E., Fotinea, E., Picron, F., Van Landuyt, D., Sioen, T., Braffort, A., Filhol, M., Ebling, S., et al. (2021). The myth of signing avatars. In *1st International Workshop on Automatic Translation for Signed and Spoken Languages*.

Yin, K., Moryossef, A., Hochgesang, J., Goldberg, Y., and Alikhani, M. (2021). Including signed languages in natural language processing. *arXiv preprint arXiv:2105.05222*.

Young, A. and Hunt, R. (2011). Research with d/deaf people. *Methods Reviews*, 9.

Proceedings of the 7th International Workshop on Sign Language Translation and Avatar Technology (SLTAT 7), pages 117–124
Language Resources and Evaluation Conference (LREC 2022), Marseille, 20-25 June 2022

Changing the Representation: Examining Language Representation for Neural Sign Language Production

Harry Walsh, Ben Saunders, Richard Bowden

University of Surrey
{harry.walsh, b.saunders, r.bowden}@surrey.ac.uk

Abstract

Neural Sign Language Production (SLP) aims to automatically translate from spoken language sentences to sign language videos. Historically the SLP task has been broken into two steps; Firstly, translating from a spoken language sentence to a gloss sequence and secondly, producing a sign language video given a sequence of glosses. In this paper we apply Natural Language Processing techniques to the first step of the SLP pipeline. We use language models such as BERT and Word2Vec to create better sentence level embeddings, and apply several tokenization techniques, demonstrating how these improve performance on the low resource translation task of Text to Gloss. We introduce Text to HamNoSys (T2H) translation, and show the advantages of using a phonetic representation for sign language translation rather than a sign level gloss representation. Furthermore, we use HamNoSys to extract the hand shape of a sign and use this as additional supervision during training, further increasing the performance on T2H. Assembling best practise, we achieve a BLEU-4 score of 26.99 on the MineDGS dataset and 25.09 on PHOENIX14T, two new state-of-the-art baselines.

Keywords: Sign Language Translation (SLT), Natural Language Processing (NLP), Sign Language, Phonetic Representation

1. Introduction

Sign languages are the dominant form of communication for Deaf communities, with 430 million users worldwide (WHO, 2021). Sign languages are complex multichannel languages with their own grammatical structure and vocabulary (Stokoe, 1980). For many people, sign language is their primary language, and written forms of spoken language are their secondary languages.

Sign Language Production (SLP) aims to bridge the gap between hearing and Deaf communities, by translating from spoken language sentences to sign language sequences. This problem has historically been broken into two steps; 1) translation from spoken language to gloss[1] and 2) subsequent production of sign language sequences from a sequence of glosses, commonly using a graphical avatar (Elliott et al., 2008; Efthimiou et al., 2010; Efthimiou et al., 2009) or more recently, a photo-realistic signer (Saunders et al., 2021a; Saunders et al., 2021b). In this paper, we improve the SLP pipeline by focusing on the Text to Gloss (T2G) translation task of step 1.

Modern deep learning is heavily dependent upon data. However, the creation of sign language datasets is both time consuming and costly, restricting their size to orders of magnitude smaller than their spoken language counterparts. State-of-the-art datasets such as RWTH-PHOENIX-Weather-2014**T** (PHOENIX14**T**), and the newer MineDGS (mDGS), contain only 8,257 and 63,912 examples respectively (Koller et al., 2015; Hanke et al., 2020), compared to over 15 million examples for common spoken language datasets (Vrandečić and Krötzsch, 2014). Hence, sign languages can be considered as low resource languages.

In this work, we take inspiration from NLP techniques to boost translation performance. We explore how language can be modeled using different tokenizers, more specifically Byte Pair Encoding (BPE), Word-Piece, word and character level tokenizers. We show that finding the correct tokenizer for the task helps simplify the translation problem.

Furthermore, to help tackle our low resource language task, we explore using pre-trained language models such as BERT (Devlin et al., 2018) and Word2Vec (Mikolov et al., 2013b) to create improved sentence level embeddings. We also fuse contextual information from the embedding to increase the amount of information available to the network. We show that using models trained on large corpuses of data improves translation performance.

Previously the first step of the SLP pipeline used T2G translation. We explore using a phonetic representation based on the Hamburg Notation System (HamNoSys) which we define as Text to HamNoSys (T2H). HamNoSys encodes signs using a set of symbols and can be viewed as a phonetic representation of sign language (Hanke, 2004). There are three main components when representing a sign in HamNoSys; a) its initial configuration b) it's hand shape and c) it's action. An example of HamNoSys can be seen in Fig. 1 along with its gloss and text counterparts.

We evaluate our SLP models on both the mDGS and PHOENIX14**T** datasets, showing state-of-the-art performance on T2G (mDGS & PHX) and T2H (mDGS)

[1] Gloss is the written word associated with a sign

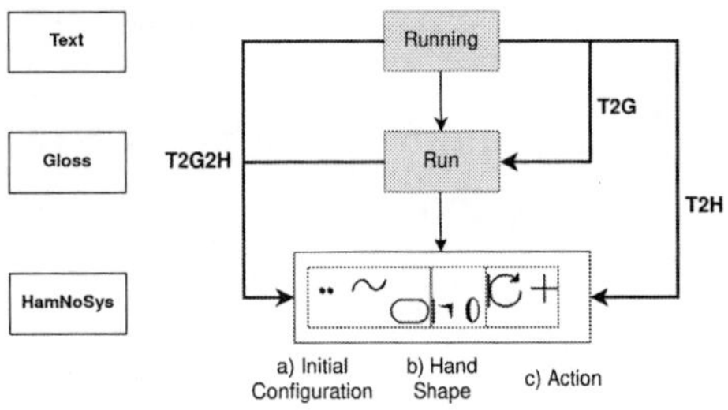

Figure 1: A graph to show the word "running" which would be 'glossed' as RUN and the associated sequence of HamNoSys, Top: Text, Middle: Gloss, Bottom: HamNoSys. HamNoSys is split into: a) it's initial configuration b) it's hand shape 3) it's action

tasks. We achieve a BLEU-4 score of 26.99 on mDGS, a significant increase compared to the state-of-the-art score of 3.17 (Saunders et al., 2022).

The rest of this paper is structured as follows; In section 2 we review the related work in the field. Section 3 presents our methodology. Section 4 shows quantitative and qualitative results. Finally, we draw conclusions in section 5 and suggest future work.

2. Related Work

Sign Language Recognition & Translation: Computational sign language research has been studied for over 30 years (Tamura and Kawasaki, 1988). Research started with isolated Sign Language Recognition (SLR) where individual signs were classified using CNNs (Lecun et al., 1998). Recently, the field has moved to the more challenging problem of Continuous Sign Language Recognition (CSLR), where a continuous sign language video needs to be segmented and then classified (Koller et al., 2015). Most modern approaches to SLR and CSLR rely on deep learning, but such approaches are data hungry and therefore are limited by the size of publicly available datasets.

The distinction between CSLR and Sign Language Translation (SLT) was stressed by Camgoz et al. (2018). SLT aims to translate a continuous sequence of signs to spoken language sentences (Sign to Text (S2T)) or vice versa (Text to Sign (T2S)), a challenging problem due to the changes in grammar and sequence ordering.

Sign Language Production (SLP): focusses on T2S, the production of a continuous sign language sequence given a spoken language input sentence. Current state-of-the-art approaches to SLP use transformer based architectures with attention (Stoll et al., 2018; Saunders et al., 2020). In this paper, we tackle the SLP task of neural sign language translation, defined as T2G or T2H translation.

HamNoSys has been used before for statistical SLP, with some success (Kaur and Kumar, 2014; Kaur and Kumar, 2016). However, the produced motion becomes robotic and is not practical for real world applications. Note that these approaches first convert the HamNoSys to SiGML, an XML format of HamNoSys (Kaur and Kumar, 2016).

Neural Machine Translation (NMT): NMT aims to generate a target sequence given a source sequence using neural networks (Bahdanau et al., 2014) and is commonly used for spoken language translations. Initial approaches used recurrence to map a hidden state to an output sequence (Kalchbrenner and Blunsom, 2013), with limited performance. Encoder-decoder structures were later introduced, that map an input sequence to an embedding space (Wu et al., 2016). To address the bottleneck problem, attention was introduced to measure the affinity between sections of the input and embedding space and allow the model to focus on specific context (Bahdanau et al., 2014). This was improved further with the introduction of the transformer (Vaswani et al., 2017) that used Multi-Headed Attention (MHA) to allow multiple projections of the learned attention. More recently, model sizes have grown with architectures introduced such as GPT-2 (Radford et al., 2019) and BERT (Devlin et al., 2018).

Different encoding/decoding schemes have been explored. BPE was first introduced in Sennrich et al. (2015), to create a set of tokens given a set vocabulary size. This is achieved by merging the most commonly occurring sequential characters. WordPiece, a similar tokenizer to BPE, was first introduced in Schuster and Nakajima (2012) and is commonly used when training language models such as BERT, DistilBERT and Electra. Finally, word and character level tokenizers break up a sentence based on white space and unique symbols respectively.

Natural Language Processing: NLP has many applications, for example Text Simplification, Text Classification, and Speech Recognition. Recently, deep learning approaches have outperformed older statistical methods (Vaswani et al., 2017). A successful NLP model must understand the structure and context of language, learned via supervised or unsupervised methods. Pretrained language models have been used to boost performance in other NLP tasks (Clinchant et al., 2019; Zhu et al., 2020), such as BERT (Devlin et al., 2018) achieving state-of-the-art performance. Zhu et al., 2020 tried to fuse the embedding of BERT into a traditional transformer architecture using attention, increasing the translation performance by approximately 2 BLEU score.

Other methods have used Word2Vec to model language, this has been applied to many NLP tasks (Mikolov et al., 2013b). Word2Vec is designed to give meaning to a numerical representation of words. The central idea being that words with similar meaning should have a small euclidean distance between the vector representation.

In this paper, we take inspiration from these techniques to boost performance of the low resource task of T2G and T2H sign language production.

3. Methodology

The task of neural sign language production aims to map a source sequence of spoken language sentences, $x = (x_1, x_2, ..., x_W)$ with W words, to a sequence of glosses, $y = (y_1, y_2, ..., y_G)$ with G glosses (Text to Gloss (T2G)), or a sequence of HamNoSys, $z = (z_1, z_2, ..., z_H)$ with H symbols (Text to HamNoSys (T2H)). T2G and T2H tasks thus learn the conditional probabilities $p(y|x)$ and $p(z|x)$ respectively. Sign language translation is not a one to one mapping as several words can be mapped to a single gloss $(W > G)$, $(W > H)$. This increases the complexity of the problem as the model must learn to attend to multiple words in the input sequence.

Fig. 2 shows the general architecture of our model used to translate from spoken language to gloss/HamNoSys. For means of comparison, our baseline model is an encoder-decoder transformer with MHA. The input and output sequence are tokenized using a word level tokenizer and the embedding for a given sequence is created using a single linear layer. We later build on this base model using different tokenizers, embedding and supervision techniques. We train our model using a cross-entropy loss between the predicted target sequence, $\hat{x}$ and the ground truth sequence, x^*, defined as L_T.

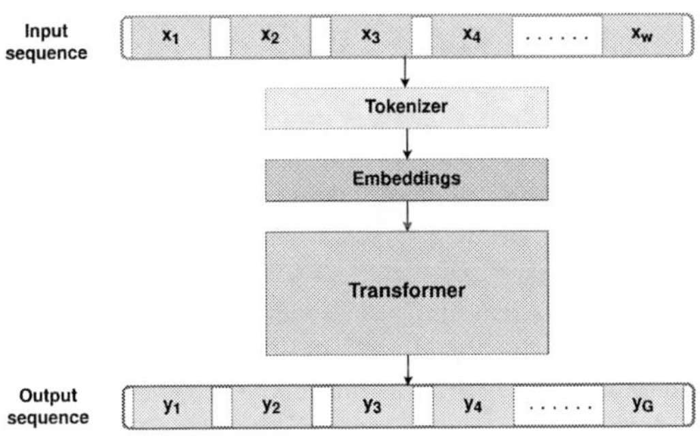

Figure 2: An overview of the different configuration of our architecture for SLT

In this section, we follow the structure of Fig. 2 from top to bottom. We start by describing the different tokenizers used to split the source text and produce tokens (Sec. 3.1). Next, we explain the different embedding techniques used to create a vector from the input tokens (Sec. 3.2). Finally, we talk about the advantages of using extra supervision and explain how this is implemented in conjunction with the translation loss.

3.1. Tokenizers

Several tokenizer schemes can be used on both the input and output such as BPE, Word, character and WordPiece. BPE (Sennrich et al., 2015), character and WordPiece (Schuster and Nakajima, 2012) all change the vocabulary size of the model by breaking sentences into sub-units. This reduces the number of singletons and reduces lexical inflections in the input and output sequences (Wolf et al., 2019).

Word A word level tokenizer segments the input sentence based on white space. Therefore, a normal sentence is split into whole words.

Character A character level tokenizer segments the text based on the individual symbols, reducing the vocabulary to simply the alphabet plus punctuation.

BPE BPE creates a base vocabulary containing all the unique symbols in the data, from which it learns a number of merge rules based on the most commonly occurring sequential symbols. An example of the BPE algorithm being applied to HamNoSys is shown in Fig. 3, with the coloured boxes indicating what merges are made at each step. Merging continues until a specific vocabulary size is reached. This helps reduce word inflections e.g. the words low, lowest and lower can be segmented to low, est and er. Over the whole corpus the suffix's (est and er) can be reused, collapsing the vocabulary in this example from 3 to 1.

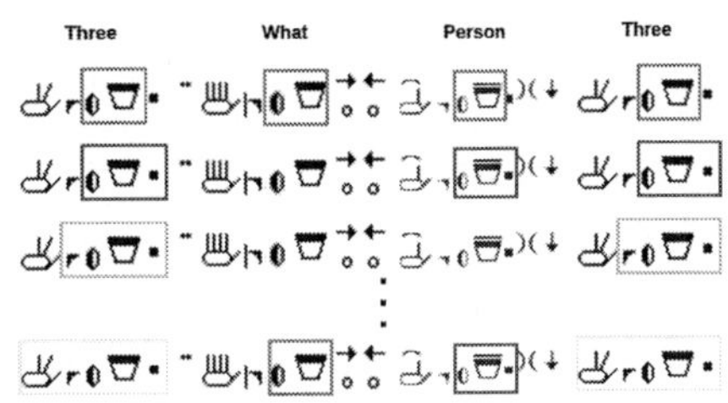

Figure 3: An example of how BPE can be applied to HamNoSys.

WordPiece We only apply a WordPiece tokenizer when embedding with BERT, as this is what the BERT model was trained with. WordPiece is another sub-unit tokenization algorithm similar to BPE that evaluates the lost benefit before merging two symbols, ensuring that all mergers are beneficial.

3.2. Embedding

After tokenization, the input sequence x is then embedded by projecting the sequence into a continuous space (Mikolov et al., 2013a). The goal of embedding is to minimise the Euclidean distance between words with similar meanings. The most common embedding is a single linear layer, which takes an input sequence $x = (x_1, x_2, ..., x_W)$ with W words and turns it into a matrix of $[W \times E]$ where E is the models embedding width. In models such as BERT and Word2Vec, embeddings are learnt via training on a large corpus of spoken language data. To maximise the benefit from using BERT we fine tune the pre-trained model on the mineDGS dataset using masked-language modeling.

When using a BERT model, we define the transformation as follows. Given an input sequence x we first apply WordPiece tokenization.

$$X_{WP} = WordPiece(x) \quad (1)$$

Then apply the BERT embeddings as:

$$X_{BERT} = BERT(X_{WP}) \quad (2)$$

Note that we take the embedding from the last layer of BERT. We define the Word2Vec transformation as:

$$X_{W2V} = Word2Vec(x) \quad (3)$$

Additionally, we experiment with concatenating or fusing contextual information into the input x. We define the contextual information as x_{ave} and the scaling factor as S, used to place additional emphasis on the contextual information. In the case of Word2Vec we take a mean average of each word's embedding in the sentence and treat this as a vector that contains information about the whole sentence. For BERT we use the embedding of the classification token ([CLS]), which contains contextual information about the sentence (Devlin et al., 2019). We either concatenate the information to the beginning of a sequence $x = (x_{ave} * S, x_1, x_2, ..., x_W)$ (CON), or we fuse it into each step of the sequence $x = ((x_{ave} * S) + x_1, (x_{ave} * S) + x_2, ..., (x_{ave} * S) + x_W)$ (ADD).

3.3. Supervision

In sign language, there exists a strong correlation between hand shape and meaning (Stokoe, 1980). Therefore, we investigate forcing the transformer to predict the hand shape alongside the gloss or HamNoSys sequences, to enrich the learnt representation. We scale the loss from the hand shape prediction $\mathcal{L}_{\mathcal{H}}$ by factor F. We combine both losses from the translation $\mathcal{L}_{\mathcal{T}}$ and hand shape prediction $\mathcal{L}_{\mathcal{H}}$ to create L_{total} as:

$$L_{total} = L_T + (L_H * F) \quad (4)$$

In this setup, the model learns the joint conditional probability of

$$p(y|x) * p(H|x) \quad (5)$$

where H is the sequence of hand shape symbols:

$$H = (h_1, h_2, ..., h_G) \quad (6)$$

and G is the number of glosses in the sequence. Overall this forces that model to focus on hand shape during training. We show that by forcing the model to predict hand shape we improve the performance on T2H.

4. Experiments

In this section we test the translation performance of our models in both the T2G and T2H setups. We first explain the experimental setup of our models. Next, we compare quantitative results against previous state-of-the-art and our own baselines. Finally we provide qualitative results.

4.1. Experimental Setup

When training our T2G model, we experiment with different embedding sizes, number of layers and heads. We observe a large change in performance based on these three parameters, and search for the best configurations for further tests. Our transformer uses a xavier initializer (Glorot and Bengio, 2010) with zero bias and Adam optimization (Kingma and Ba, 2014) with a learning rate of 10^{-4}. We also employ dropout connections with a probability of 0.2 (Srivastava et al., 2014). When decoding, we use a beam search with a search size of 5.

Our code base comes from Kreutzer et al. (2019) NMT toolkit, JoeyNMT (Kreutzer et al., 2019) and is implemented using Pytorch. While our BPE and word piece tokenizers come from Huggingface's python library transformers (Wolf et al., 2019). When embedding with BERT, we use an open source pre-trained model from Deepset (Chan et al., 2020). Finally we used fasttext's implementation of Word2Vec for word level embedding (Mikolov et al., 2013b).

The publicly available mDGS dataset contains aligned spoken German sentences and their gloss counter parts, from unconstrained dialogue between two native deaf signers (Kaur and Kumar, 2014). The providers of this dataset also have a dictionary for all glosses in the corpus, of which some contain HamNoSys descriptions. Following the translation protocols set in Saunders et al. (2022), we created a subset of the mDGS dataset with aligned sentences, glosses and HamNoSys. mDGS is a larger dataset compared to PHOENIX14T (7.5 times more parallel examples, with a source vocabulary of 18,457) with 330 deaf participants performing free form signing. The size of mDGS overcomes some of the limitation of PHOENIX2014T. Note we remove the gloss variant numbers to reduce singletons.

We use the PHOENIX14T (Camgoz et al., 2018) dataset to compare our best model to previous NMT baseline results (Saunders et al., 2020; Stoll et al., 2018; Moryossef et al., 2021; Li et al., 2021). PHOENIX14T contains parallel monolingual German data, with approximately 7000 examples of aligned gloss and text.

4.2. Quantitative Evaluation

In this section, we evaluate our models on both mDGS and PHOENIX14T using BLEU (BLEU-1,2,3 and 4) and Rouge (F1-score) scores for both dev and test sets. We group our experiments in five sections:

1. Baseline T2G, T2H and Text to Gloss to HamNoSys (T2G2H) with a standard transformer.
2. T2G and T2H with different embedding layers and sentence averaging.
3. T2G and T2H with different tokenizers (BPE, Word, and Character).
4. T2G and T2H with additional supervision.
5. Comparison of our approach on PHOENIX14T and mDGS.

Approach:	DEV SET BLEU-4	DEV SET BLEU-3	DEV SET BLEU-2	DEV SET BLEU-1	DEV SET ROUGE	TEST SET BLEU-4	TEST SET BLEU-3	TEST SET BLEU-2	TEST SET BLEU-1	TEST SET ROUGE
Linear Layer	**16.26**	**24.14**	**32.83**	**43.05**	**42.02**	**16.47**	**24.51**	**33.27**	**43.58**	**41.53**
BERT	14.69	21.51	29.39	38.66	30.87	14.2	21.19	29.09	38.33	30.31
BERT SA ADD	13.23	19.41	26.43	34.75	32.38	13.43	19.47	26.31	34.3	32.34
BERT SA CON	14.89	21.45	28.73	36.85	34.73	15.14	21.57	28.79	36.91	34.44
Word2Vec	11.47	17.59	24.68	34.21	29.45	11.73	17.83	25.14	34.90	30.22
Word2Vec SA ADD	13.8	21.07	29.72	42.29	30.65	13.31	20.56	29.31	42.13	30.67
Word2Vec SA CON	0.03	0.05	0.06	0.04	9.44	0.03	0.06	0.06	0.04	9.32

(a) MineDGS (mDGS) on Text to Gloss to HamNoSys (T2G2H)

Approach:	DEV SET BLEU-4	DEV SET BLEU-3	DEV SET BLEU-2	DEV SET BLEU-1	DEV SET ROUGE	TEST SET BLEU-4	TEST SET BLEU-3	TEST SET BLEU-2	TEST SET BLEU-1	TEST SET ROUGE
Linear Layer	14.46	23.27	32.62	47.44	50.85	14.80	23.54	32.89	47.36	50.87
BERT	**20.26**	**29.14**	**38.01**	**48.92**	**53.67**	**21.03**	**29.87**	**38.79**	**49.77**	**53.93**
BERT SA ADD	14.64	22.33	30.91	43.99	50.30	15.16	22.92	31.41	44.21	50.33
BERT SA CON	11.82	19.2	27.39	40.58	53.36	12.21	19.39	27.44	40.48	53.67
Word2Vec	16.43	24.77	33.71	46.62	51.14	17.09	25.23	34.22	47.31	51.52
Word2Vec SA ADD	16.72	25.14	34.39	48.00	51.28	16.98	25.31	34.59	48.08	51.12
Word2Vec SA CON	14.98	22.49	30.65	42.42	51.11	15.18	22.65	30.80	42.75	50.10

(b) MineDGS (mDGS) on Text to HamNoSys (T2H)

Table 1: Embedding transformer results for Text to Gloss (T2G) and Text to HamNoSys (T2H) translation.

Tokenizer Input	Tokenizer Output	DEV SET BLEU-4	DEV SET BLEU-3	DEV SET BLEU-2	DEV SET BLEU-1	DEV SET ROUGE	TEST SET BLEU-4	TEST SET BLEU-3	TEST SET BLEU-2	TEST SET BLEU-1	TEST SET ROUGE
Word	Word	16.47	24.35	33.06	43.41	36.32	16.55	24.45	33.14	43.54	36.34
Word	BPE	**22.06**	**28.53**	**36.32**	**47.55**	36.20	**21.87**	**28.31**	**36.02**	**47.08**	35.74
Word	Char	16.47	24.35	33.06	43.41	36.32	16.55	24.45	33.14	43.54	36.34
BPE	Word	20.84	26.77	34.02	44.77	35.31	20.84	26.80	34.12	44.97	35.35
BPE	BPE	21.39	27.28	34.31	43.86	**36.61**	21.28	27.25	34.34	43.86	**36.86**
BPE	Char	1.99	5.5	10.35	30.01	2.61	1.46	5.18	10.0	29.77	2.61

(a) MineDGS (mDGS) on Text to Gloss to HamNoSys (T2G2H)

Tokenizer Input	Tokenizer Output	DEV SET BLEU-4	DEV SET BLEU-3	DEV SET BLEU-2	DEV SET BLEU-1	DEV SET ROUGE	TEST SET BLEU-4	TEST SET BLEU-3	TEST SET BLEU-2	TEST SET BLEU-1	TEST SET ROUGE
Word	Word	21.81	**31.86**	**42.05**	**54.88**	**55.39**	21.89	**31.92**	**42.16**	**55.04**	**55.23**
Word	BPE	25.41	29.28	34.11	41.25	48.03	25.54	29.39	34.25	41.35	48.09
Word	Char	21.63	31.76	41.99	54.94	55.3	21.59	31.79	42.09	55.01	55.14
BPE	Word	20.98	30.29	39.38	50.04	55.24	21.18	30.37	39.4	49.84	55.04
BPE	BPE	**26.14**	30.83	36.47	44.35	49.95	**26.21**	30.84	36.43	44.14	50.05
BPE	Char	1.91	6.01	11.72	37.56	37.22	1.92	5.88	11.59	37.63	37.31

(b) MineDGS (mDGS) on Text to HamNoSys (T2H)

Table 2: Tokenizer transformer results for Text to Gloss (T2G) and Text to HamNoSys (T2H) translation.

Note we expect the performance to be lower than 100 BLEU. As this is a translation problem there are several valid answers for a given input, thus human evaluation is still necessary. We are also unable to provide T2H results on PHOENIX14**T**, as HamNoSys is not available for some words in its vocabulary.

4.2.1. Baseline Results

Our baseline models achieved a BLEU-4 score of 2.86 (T2G), 16.26 (T2G2H) and 14.46 (T2H) on the mDGS dev set. Our baseline setup uses a word level tokenizer on both the input and output, providing a baseline to ablate our proposed techniques in the next three sections. We perform a hyper-parameter search and make modification to the model architecture (number of heads, layers and embedding size) to find the best performance.

In general, a sequence of HamNoSys is significantly longer than it's gloss counter part, ($H >> G$). As a result our T2H performance is artificially higher than our T2G. Therefore, in order to make our T2G and T2H results comparable, we perform a dictionary lookup to convert the gloss to HamNoSys (T2G2H) before calculating the BLEU score. Given these results, we conclude a transformer architecture is the best baseline approach and continue with this setup for all future experiments.

4.2.2. Embedding

Next we experiment with using different embedding techniques for the T2G and T2H tasks. As discussed in Section 3.1 we use a linear layer, BERT and Word2Vec in combination with sentence averaging. From the results in Table 1 we make several observations. Firstly, using a language model improves the translation performance on the T2H task (Tab. 1a). While on the T2G task, using language models was detrimental to the translation performance (Tab. 1b). We assume this is due to the reduced information within the gloss and smaller sequence length. Secondly, we observe that applying sentence averaging to the BERT embedding has a negative effect on the scores, independent of what type of average was used (adding or concatenating). On the other hand, adding the sentence averaging to the Word2Vec embedding marginally improved performance compared to the stand alone Word2Vec embeddings on T2H. But note

Approach:	Supervision	DEV SET BLEU-4	BLEU-3	BLEU-2	BLEU-1	ROUGE	TEST SET BLEU-4	BLEU-3	BLEU-2	BLEU-1	ROUGE
T2G2H	✗	**22.06**	**28.53**	**36.32**	**47.55**	**36.20**	**21.87**	**28.31**	**36.02**	**47.08**	35.74
T2G2H	✓	21.79	27.98	35.45	46.21	35.79	21.49	27.76	35.27	46.11	35.99
T2H	✗	26.14	30.83	**36.47**	**44.35**	**49.95**	26.21	30.84	**36.43**	**44.14**	**50.05**
T2H	✓	**26.99**	**31.07**	35.99	42.73	48.89	**27.37**	**31.42**	36.3	42.92	48.85

Table 3: HamNoSys hand shape supervision results for Text to Gloss to HamNoSys (T2G2H) and Text to HamNoSys (T2H) translation.

that Word2Vec plus sentence averaging still has lower performance than just using a linear layer. Overall, we find the best performing embedding to come from using BERT, which scored 5.8 BLEU-4 higher than using a linear layer. This demonstrates that using a pre-trained language model can enhance translation.

4.2.3. Tokenizer

We next experiment with using different tokenizers, as described in Section 3.2. We performed a parameter search to find the best vocabulary size for the BPE algorithm, which we find to be 2250 and 7000 on the input and output respectively. The result of our experiments are shown in Table 2.

When using a character level tokenizer each input contains a minimal amount of information (one letter). As expected this increases the difficulty of the problem, and reduces performance. When applied to the input it was extremely detrimental for the performance on both T2G2H and T2H, independent of which output tokenizer was used. Therefore to save space, we do not present the input character level results. Using a word level tokenizer achieved very reasonable results, supporting our theory that using larger units of language that contains more information is beneficial for translation. But as BPE outperformed the word level tokenizer on the BLEU-4 score, we assume that by using whole words we create a harder problem, as the dataset contains several word inflections. We conclude that BPE is the best algorithm to use when translating from T2H. This is due to the algorithms ability to reduce inflections and reduce the vocabulary size which simplifies the networks task. Our results also show that the biggest impact comes from having BPE on the output, suggesting that most of the challenge comes from the decoding section of the network. Similarly, the best T2G result came from using a word level and BPE tokenizers on the input and output respectively.

4.2.4. Supervision

Our final ablation study investigates an additional loss explained in Section 3.3. This had a positive effect on the translation performance for T2H. As can be seen from Table 3, the use of supervision increased the BLEU-4 scores by 0.85. We conclude supervision enriches the learnt sign language representation due to the correlation between hand shape and context. Supervision forces the model to focus more on hand shape, allowing the model to group signs and find better trends in the data. Although the use of supervision marginally decreased the T2G2H BLEU score, we suggest this is due to reduced information in the target gloss.

4.3. State-of-the-art Comparisons

Finally, in Table 4 (PHOENIX14**T**) and 5 (mDGS) we compare our best performing models to state-of-the-art work. Note in Table 4 our baseline is marginally higher than (Saunders et al., 2020), we assume this is due to a larger hyper-parameter search. On both datasets, our best model for T2G and T2G2H uses a word level and BPE tokenizer on the input and output respectively. While our best T2H result comes from adding additional supervision on to this setup. As can be seen from Table 4 and 5 our models outperformed all other methods (Moryossef et al., 2021; Li et al., 2021; Saunders et al., 2020; Saunders et al., 2022; Stoll et al., 2018), setting a new state-of-the-art on PHOENIX14**T** and mDGS. Note we can only compare scores that are publicly available, therefore '-' denotes where the authors did not provide results.

4.4. Qualitative Evaluation

For qualitative evaluation, we share translation examples from our best models and our baseline model in Fig. 4, to allow the reader to better interpret the results. Note, we add a vertical black line after each word of HamNoSys to mark the end of a given sign. These results show how our BPE model has learnt richer translations than our baseline model.

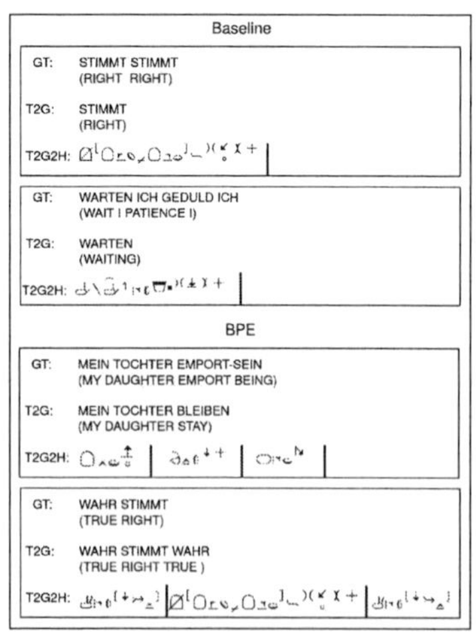

Figure 4: Translation examples from our baseline and best model.

	DEV SET					TEST SET				
Approach:	BLEU-4	BLEU-3	BLEU-2	BLEU-1	ROUGE	BLEU-4	BLEU-3	BLEU-2	BLEU-1	ROUGE
T2G (Stoll et al., 2018)	16.34	22.30	32.47	50.15	48.42	15.26	21.54	32.25	50.67	48.10
T2G (Saunders et al., 2020)	20.23	27.36	38.21	55.65	55.41	19.10	26.24	37.10	55.18	54.55
T2G (Li et al., 2021)	18.89	25.51	-	-	49.91	-	-	-	-	-
T2G (Moryossef et al., 2021)	23.17	-	-	-	-	-	-	-	-	-
T2G Baseline (ours)	22.47	30.03	41.54	58.98	57.96	20.95	28.50	39.99	58.32	57.28
T2G Best Model (ours)	**25.09**	**32.18**	**42.85**	**60.04**	**58.82**	**23.19**	**30.24**	**40.86**	**58.74**	**56.55**

Table 4: Baseline comparison results for Text to Gloss (T2G) translation on PHOENIX14**T**.

	DEV SET					TEST SET				
Approach:	BLEU-4	BLEU-3	BLEU-2	BLEU-1	ROUGE	BLEU-4	BLEU-3	BLEU-2	BLEU-1	ROUGE
T2G (Saunders et al., 2022)	3.17	-	-	-	32.93	3.08	-	-	-	32.52
T2G Our best	10.5	14.35	20.43	33.56	35.79	10.4	14.21	20.2	33.59	35.99
T2G2H Our best	22.06	28.53	36.32	47.55	36.20	21.87	28.31	36.02	47.08	35.74
T2H Our best	**26.99**	**31.07**	**35.99**	**42.73**	**48.89**	**27.37**	**31.42**	**36.3**	**42.92**	**48.85**

Table 5: Baseline comparison results for Text to Gloss (T2G), Text to Gloss to HamNoSys (T2G2H) and Text to HamNoSys (T2H) translation on mDGS.

5. Conclusion

In this paper, we employed a transformer to translate from spoken language sentences to a sequence of gloss or HamNoSys. We introduced T2H translation, showing the advantages of translating to HamNoSys instead of just gloss, and set baseline results for future work on mDGS. We showed that language models can be used to improve translation performance, but using more advanced tokenization algorithms like BPE gives a larger performance gain. Additionally, we have shown that translation can be improved by training the model to jointly predict hand shape and HamNoSys. We achieved a BLEU-4 score of 26.99 and 25.09, a new state-of-the-arts for SLT on the mDGS and PHOENIX14**T** datasets.

As future work, it would be interesting to create a representation, gloss++. This could combine the benefits of gloss and HamNoSys, including non-manual features as well as hand shape information, as this has been shown to be useful for translation. Furthermore, this could be beneficial for down stream tasks in the SLP pipeline.

6. Acknowledgements

We thank Adam Munder, Mariam Rahmani and Marina Lovell from OmniBridge, an Intel Venture, for supporting this project. We also thank Thomas Hanke and University of Hamburg for use of the mDGS data. We also thank the SNSF Sinergia project 'SMILE II' (CRSII5 193686), the European Union's Horizon2020 research project EASIER (101016982) and the EPSRC project 'ExTOL' (EP/R03298X/1). This work reflects only the authors view and the Commission is not responsible for any use that may be made of the information it contains.

7. Bibliographical References

Bahdanau, D., Cho, K., and Bengio, Y. (2014). Neural machine translation by jointly learning to align and translate. *arXiv preprint arXiv:1409.0473*.

Camgoz, N. C., Hadfield, S., Koller, O., Ney, H., and Bowden, R. (2018). Neural sign language translation. In *Proceedings of the IEEE Conference on Computer Vision and Pattern Recognition*.

Chan, B., Schweter, S., and Möller, T. (2020). German's next language model. In *Proceedings of the 28th International Conference on Computational Linguistics*.

Clinchant, S., Jung, K. W., and Nikoulina, V. (2019). On the use of bert for neural machine translation. *arXiv preprint arXiv:1909.12744*.

Devlin, J., Chang, M.-W., Lee, K., and Toutanova, K. (2018). Bert: Pre-training of deep bidirectional transformers for language understanding. *arXiv:1810.04805*.

Devlin, J., Chang, M.-W., Lee, K., and Toutanova, K. (2019). BERT: Pre-training of deep bidirectional transformers for language understanding. In *Proceedings of the 2019 Conference of the North*.

Efthimiou, E., Fotinea, S.-E., Vogler, C., Hanke, T., Glauert, J., Bowden, R., Braffort, A., Collet, C., Maragos, P., and Segouat, J. (2009). Sign language recognition, generation, and modelling: A research effort with applications in deaf communication. In *International Conference on Universal Access in Human-Computer Interaction*.

Efthimiou, E., Fontinea, S.-E., Hanke, T., Glauert, J., Bowden, R., Braffort, A., Collet, C., Maragos, P., and Goudenove, F. (2010). Dicta-sign–sign language recognition, generation and modelling: A research effort with applications in deaf communication. In *Proceedings of the 4th Workshop on the Representation and Processing of Sign Languages: Corpora and Sign Language Technologies*.

Elliott, R., Glauert, J. R., Kennaway, J., Marshall, I., and Safar, E. (2008). Linguistic modelling and language-processing technologies for avatar-based sign language presentation. *Universal Access in the Information Society*.

Glorot, X. and Bengio, Y. (2010). Understanding the difficulty of training deep feedforward neural networks. In *Proceedings of the 13th International Conference on Artificial Intelligence and Statistics*.

Hanke, T. (2004). Hamnosys-representing sign language data in language resources and language processing contexts. In *LREC*.

Kalchbrenner, N. and Blunsom, P. (2013). Recurrent continuous translation models. In *Proceedings of the 2013 Conference on Empirical Methods in Natural Language Processing*.

Kaur, R. and Kumar, P. (2014). Hamnosys generation system for sign language. In *2014 International Conference on Advances in Computing, Communications and Informatics (ICACCI)*.

Kaur, K. and Kumar, P. (2016). Hamnosys to sigml conversion system for sign language automation. *Procedia Computer Science*.

Kingma, D. P. and Ba, J. (2014). Adam: A method for stochastic optimization. *arXiv:1412.6980*.

Kreutzer, J., Bastings, J., and Riezler, S. (2019). Joey nmt: A minimalist nmt toolkit for novices. *arXiv:1907.12484*.

Lecun, Y., Bottou, L., Bengio, Y., and Haffner, P. (1998). Gradient-based learning applied to document recognition. *Proceedings of the IEEE*.

Li, D., Xu, C., Liu, L., Zhong, Y., Wang, R., Petersson, L., and Li, H. (2021). Transcribing natural languages for the deaf via neural editing programs. *arXiv preprint arXiv:2112.09600*.

Mikolov, T., Chen, K., Corrado, G., and Dean, J. (2013a). Efficient estimation of word representations in vector space. *arXiv preprint arXiv:1301.3781*.

Mikolov, T., Sutskever, I., Chen, K., Corrado, G. S., and Dean, J. (2013b). Distributed representations of words and phrases and their compositionality. *Advances in Neural Information Processing Systems*.

Moryossef, A., Yin, K., Neubig, G., and Goldberg, Y. (2021). Data augmentation for sign language gloss translation. *arXiv:2105.07476*.

Radford, A., Wu, J., Child, R., Luan, D., Amodei, D., Sutskever, I., et al. (2019). Language models are unsupervised multitask learners. *OpenAI blog*.

Saunders, B., Camgoz, N. C., and Bowden, R. (2020). Progressive transformers for end-to-end sign language production. In *European Conference on Computer Vision*.

Saunders, B., Camgoz, N. C., and Bowden, R. (2021a). Anonysign: Novel human appearance synthesis for sign language video anonymisation. In *2021 16th IEEE International Conference on Automatic Face and Gesture Recognition (FG 2021)*.

Saunders, B., Camgoz, N. C., and Bowden, R. (2021b). Mixed signals: Sign language production via a mixture of motion primitives. In *Proceedings of the IEEE/CVF International Conference on Computer Vision*.

Saunders, B., Camgoz, N. C., and Bowden, R. (2022). Signing at Scale: Learning to Co-Articulate Signs for Large-Scale Photo-Realistic Sign Language Production. In *Proceedings of the IEEE Conference on Computer Vision and Pattern Recognition (CVPR)*.

Schuster, M. and Nakajima, K. (2012). Japanese and korean voice search. In *2012 IEEE International Conference on Acoustics, Speech and Signal processing (ICASSP)*.

Sennrich, R., Haddow, B., and Birch, A. (2015). Neural machine translation of rare words with subword units. *CoRR*.

Srivastava, N., Hinton, G., Krizhevsky, A., Sutskever, I., and Salakhutdinov, R. (2014). Dropout: A simple way to prevent neural networks from overfitting. *The Journal of Machine Learning Research*.

Stokoe, W. C. (1980). Sign language structure. *Annual Review of Anthropology*.

Stoll, S., Camgöz, N. C., Hadfield, S., and Bowden, R. (2018). Sign language production using neural machine translation and generative adversarial networks. In *Proceedings of the 29th British Machine Vision Conference*.

Tamura, S. and Kawasaki, S. (1988). Recognition of sign language motion images. *Pattern Recognition*.

Vaswani, A., Shazeer, N., Parmar, N., Uszkoreit, J., Jones, L., Gomez, A. N., Kaiser, Ł., and Polosukhin, I. (2017). Attention is all you need. *Advances in Neural Information Processing Systems*.

Vrandečić, D. and Krötzsch, M. (2014). Wikidata: a free collaborative knowledgebase. *Communications of the ACM*.

WHO. (2021). Deafness and hearing loss.

Wolf, T., Debut, L., Sanh, V., Chaumond, J., Delangue, C., Moi, A., Cistac, P., Rault, T., Louf, R., Funtowicz, M., et al. (2019). Huggingface's transformers: State-of-the-art natural language processing. *arXiv preprint arXiv:1910.03771*.

Wu, Y., Schuster, M., Chen, Z., Le, Q. V., Norouzi, M., Macherey, W., Krikun, M., Cao, Y., Gao, Q., Macherey, K., et al. (2016). Google's neural machine translation system: Bridging the gap between human and machine translation. *arXiv preprint arXiv:1609.08144*.

Zhu, J., Xia, Y., Wu, L., He, D., Qin, T., Zhou, W., Li, H., and Liu, T.-Y. (2020). Incorporating bert into neural machine translation. *arXiv preprint arXiv:2002.06823*.

8. Language Resource References

Hanke, T., Schulder, M., Konrad, R., and Jahn, E. (2020). Extending the Public DGS Corpus in size and depth. In Eleni Efthimiou, et al., editors, *Proceedings of the LREC2020 9th Workshop on the Representation and Processing of Sign Languages*, pages 75–82, Marseille, France, May. ELRA.

Koller, O., Forster, J., and Ney, H. (2015). Continuous sign language recognition: Towards large vocabulary statistical recognition systems handling multiple signers. *Computer Vision and Image Understanding*, 141:108–125. Pose Gesture.

Proceedings of the 7th International Workshop on Sign Language Translation and Avatar Technology (SLTAT 7), pages 125–130
Language Resources and Evaluation Conference (LREC 2022), Marseille, 20-25 June 2022

Supporting Mouthing in Signed Languages: New innovations and a proposal for future corpus building

Rosalee Wolfe[1], John McDonald[2], Ronan Johnson[2], Ben Sturr[2], Syd Klinghoffer[2], Anthony Bonzani[2], Andrew Alexander[2], Nicole Barnekow[2]
[1]Institute for Language and Speech Processing, Athens Greece
[2]DePaul University, Chicago USA
Rosalee.Wolfe@athenarc.gr,
jmcdonald@cs.depaul.edu, {sjohn165, bsturr, sklingho, abonzan1, aalexa47, nbarneko}@depaul.edu

Abstract

A recurring concern, oft repeated, regarding the quality of signing avatars is the lack of proper facial movements, particularly in actions that involve mouthing. An analysis uncovered three challenges contributing to the problem. The first is a difficulty in devising an algorithmic strategy for generating mouthing due to the rich variety of mouthings in sign language. For example, part or all of a spoken word may be mouthed depending on the sign language, the syllabic structure of the mouthed word, as well as the register of address and discourse setting. The second challenge was technological. Previous efforts to create avatar mouthing have failed to model the timing present in mouthing or have failed to properly model the mouth's appearance. The third challenge is one of usability. Previous editing systems, when they existed, were time-consuming to use. This paper describes efforts to improve avatar mouthing by addressing these challenges, resulting in a new approach for mouthing animation. The paper concludes by proposing an experiment in corpus building using the new approach.

Keywords: sign language avatar, sign language display, computer animation, sign language linguistics, sign language translation, mouthing

1. Introduction

For nearly 25 years, researchers have been working toward the goal of an avatar that can produce grammatically correct signing that is easy to read. In the late 1990s Kuroda et al. (Kuroda, Sato, & Chihara, 1998) reported on an avatar-based system for Japanese Sign Language, and shortly thereafter, the ViSiCAST project began in Europe (Elliott, Glauert, Kennaway, & Marshall, 2000). A vital component of the project was evaluation by user communities, and Verlinden (2001) reported on avatar signing quality. The conclusion was "The main aspects that need further attention are the mouthing and to a lesser extent the mimicry."

In a subsequent evaluation ten years later, researchers organized two focus groups comprised of members from deaf communities in Germany to assess the potential use of signing avatars. They examined and evaluated videos of existing avatars. The researchers reported, "The absence of mouth patterns, especially mouthings (i.e., mouth patterns derived from the spoken language), seemed to be one of the most disturbing factors for the participants since this is an important element of DGS [German Sign Language]" (Kipp, Nguyen, Heloir, & Matthes, 2011). Even with an improved avatar, the same researchers noted, "In many cases, the lack of mouthing simply introduces irritation (Kipp, Heloir, & Nguyen, 2011) ."

In 2016 (Ebling & Glauert) and again in 2019 (Brumm, Johnson, Hanke, Grigat, & Wolfe) feedback indicated that mouthing on signing avatars is an aspect that still requires improvement. This paper analyses the causes for this deficit and presents an innovative strategy that incorporates important, but previously neglected considerations and proposes a methodology that capitalizes on these considerations to provide an additional tool for corpus building.

2. Related work

Of the myriad challenges to creating convincing mouthing on an avatar, we found three to be quite substantive. The first is the linguistic consideration of the diversity of mouthing within a sign language, and the second consideration entails the exacting requirements of mouth animation. The third consideration is a lack of usability in the current editing tools.

2.1 Linguistic considerations

"Mouthings," quoting Pfau, (2010) "are silent articulations of (a part of) a corresponding spoken word of the surrounding language." The usage of mouthing varies by language, ranging from occurring on virtually every sign, as in DGS, (Ebbinghaus & Heßmann, 1996) to virtually none at all as in Kata Kolok (De Vos & Zeshan, 2012). Within a single sign language, mouthing the whole word or part of a word also varies. In NGT (Sign Language of the Netherlands), signs can be accompanied by full or partial mouthing, but in the partial case, it is usually the stressed syllable (Bank, Crasborn, & Van Hout, 2011). However, the temporal reduction in a mouthed word may be even more extreme, up to the "mere onset consonant of the stressed syllable." Further, for a particular sign within a specified language, mouthing variations can occur based on register and the discourse setting.

Such rich diversity is intrinsic to natural language; however, from the standpoint of a software developer, this diversity renders it difficult to find a reliable pattern to automate. Previous efforts to create avatar mouthing have either relied on SAMPA or a speech generator to create complete mouthings. SAMPA is a set of computer-readable characters based on the International Phonetic Alphabet and is part of the SiGML standard (Jennings, Elliott, Kennaway, & Glauert, 2010). It was used in several projects, including ViSiCAST (Zwitserlood, 2005), eSIGN

(Hanke, Popescu, & Schmaling, 2003), DICTA-SIGN (Efthimiou, et al., 2012) and Trainslate (Ebling, 2013). Efforts utilizing speech generators included an extension to the EMBR (Kipp, Heloir, & Nguyen, 2011) and Paula avatars (Wolfe, et al., 2018).

2.2 Animation considerations

By stepping back from the challenge of mouthing in sign language to examine the closely related process of *lip sync* (lip synchronization) in animation (Williams, 2009), we (temporarily) remove the issue of choosing partial or full mouthing, and we focus on the basic steps:

1. Generate the phonemes corresponding to a spoken word.
2. Map each phoneme to a viseme, which is the visual appearance of the phoneme. There is a reasonable amount of consensus for the mappings, but the visemes are language dependent.
3. Retrieve the visemes from a library of facial poses.
4. Apply the viseme poses to the avatar as animation keys.

Previous avatars suffered from either a lack of realism in their visemes, a lack of realistic timing, or a combination of both. They relied on the MPEG4 H-Anim standard which did not allow for sufficient precision for naturally appearing visemes, but recent developments (Johnson, 2022), (McDonald, Wolfe, & Johnson, 2022) have created more responsive rigs that facilitate better realism.

In the end, visemes are simply poses. How effective they are in conveying mouthing depends on the timing and intensity of their appearance. A string of equally spaced visemes at equal intensities will not correspond to speech production – vowels and consonants have different durations, and these vary based on their location within a word. Therefore, the use of text-to-speech software is preferred to relying solely on SAMPA. Such software will produce timing information that an avatar can utilize for placing visemes as animation keys. Although the EMBR and Paula projects did use text-to-speech software, the EMBR project did not make use of any timing information for individual visemes, and the Paula project's visemes were not adequate for mouthing beyond American Sign Language and exhibited a curious 'lip snap', where the mouth occasionally moved too abruptly from one viseme to the next.

2.3 Usability considerations in editing

Several software packages offer tiers for annotation, (Neidle, Opoku, Dimitriadis, & Metaxas, 2018), (Max Planck Institute for Psycholinguistics, 2022), (Hanke, 2002) but there are only two systems that offer editing capabilities for mouthing, namely iLex/eSIGN (Hanke, 2014) and Paula. The interface in iLex supports three conventions for storing mouthings as text: orthography, IPA and SAMPA. The pronunciation data in iLex allows for the generation of visemes from orthography (Figure 1). iLex does not include functionality for adding timing or intensity to individual visemes.

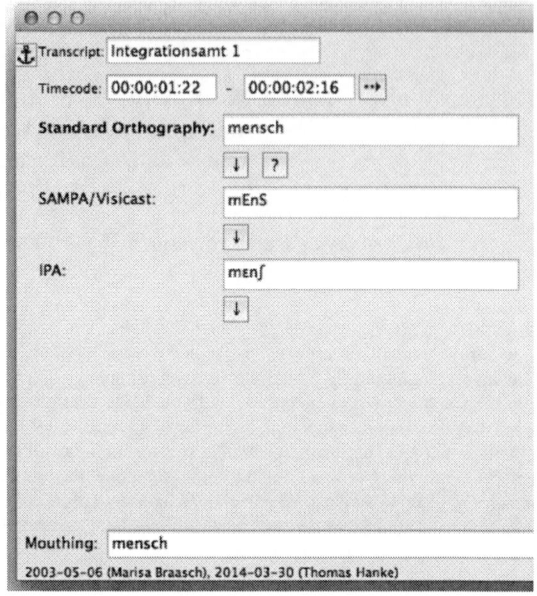

Figure 1: Mouthing dialog from iLex

The previous Paula mouthing interface did provide a rudimentary interface to edit mouthing. After the system generated the visemes via a speech generator, a user could edit the results if the animation was not convincing, or it contained an error such as a lip snap. However, the editing dialog was primitive, consisting of a data grid where each row contained a viseme, its start time relative to the beginning of the word, and its intensity (Figure 2). The editing process was cumbersome, as the user was forced to use the mouse to change the input focus to the cell needing modification before typing a new value and was required to rely on a sequence of numbers rather than a graphical interface for timing; a mode of interaction that is not artist friendly. This required continual switching from keyboard to mouse, when the preference is to use the mouse exclusively. Further, if a user wanted to increase the duration of a viseme, it was necessary to modify the starting times of all subsequent visemes. The editing experience proved sufficiently awkward that it was rarely used.

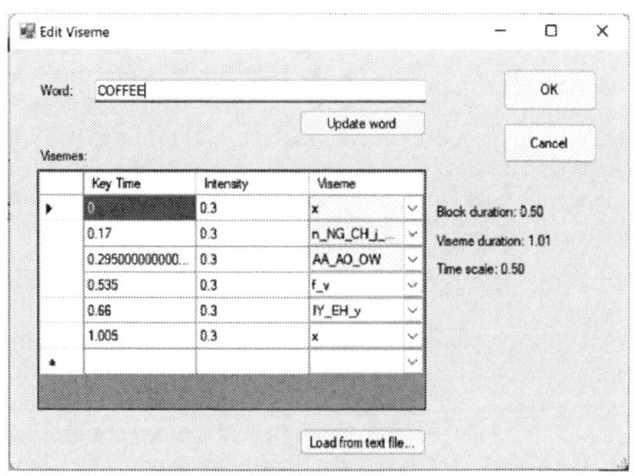

Figure 2: Mouthing dialog from circa 2019 Paula.

3. An improved approach

We introduce a new approach which consists of an improved set of automation heuristics for mouthing animation combined with a more artist friendly interface. The new approach produces better mouthing without lip snap errors through an integrated interface that combines better timing strategies informed by linguistics and offers an editing dialog that facilitates quicker, easier modifications. Additionally, it supports the fine-tuning of mouthing on a case-by-case basis depending on the context of the utterance being produced.

Animators can choose one of four automation hyperparameters: mouthing an entire word, mouthing the first syllable, mouthing the first viseme, or no mouthing, and then view the resulting animation. The new automation incorporates several strategies from traditional character animation, most notably that visemes need to be at least two frames long to avoid the dreaded lip snap. This is a duration of 0.083 seconds in conventional 24 frames-per-second movie technology. When using a frame rate of 30 frames-per-second, a duration of 0.083 seconds is the equivalent of a duration of 2.5 frames. In our experience, using a minimum of three frames works well when displaying on video playing at 30 fps.

Although this approach is working well, particularly for one- and two-syllable words, there will always be a need for possible revisions. The new mouthing dialog (Figure 3) offers multiple modification options, some at the word level, and some at the viseme level.

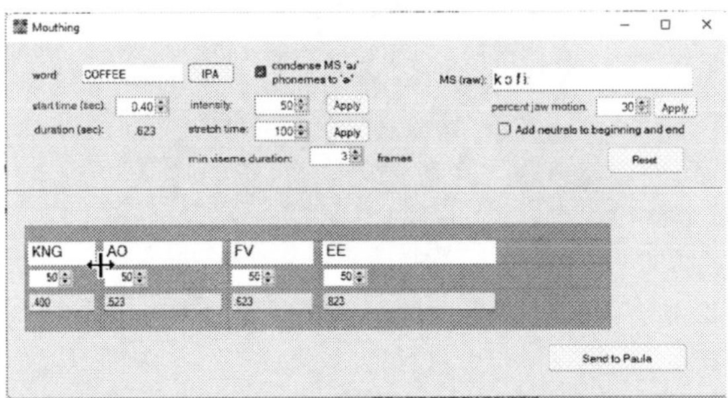

Figure 3: An improved editing interface. The animator is currently adjusting the duration of the initial viseme.

Animators can change the overall intensity, duration, and the start time relative to the manual channel[1]. They have two ways to change visemes – they can either edit the IPA characters in the upper right text box, or they can use the viseme editor. The viseme editor is contained in the blue rectangle in the lower half of the dialog. Each viseme has its own block whose width corresponds to the duration of the viseme. An animator can change the duration of the viseme by using the mouse to change the width of the block. All subsequent blocks are automatically realigned to visualize the new timing. Further, animators can add or delete visemes, change their individual intensities as well as modify the viseme selection through a context menu, as demonstrated in Figure 4. After making changes through the interface, an animator can tell Paula to display the modified animation through the "Send to Paula" button.

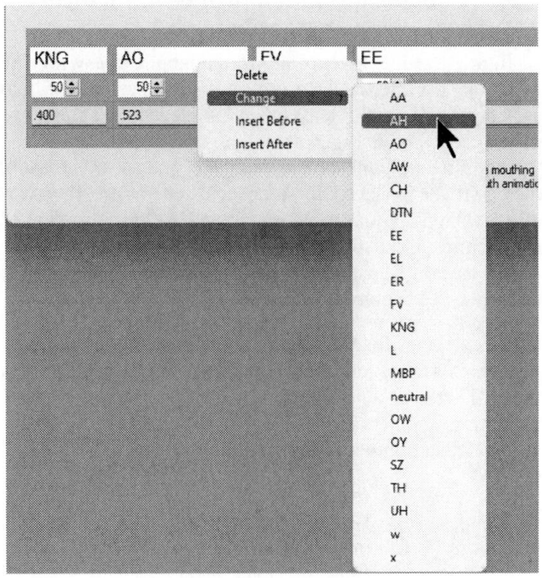

Figure 4: Context menu for adding, deleting, or changing a viseme.

Although there are still options for text input, our animators use mouse gestures exclusively, obviating the need to switch from mouse to keyboard. The result is quicker and more intuitive editing, particularly for visually oriented animation artists.

Although there are options to create complete or partial mouthing at the lexical level in our Sign Transcriber, the proclivity is towards recording complete mouthing for individual signs, because there are also mouthing options available when building complete sentences.

Our Sentence Generator builds sentences by retrieving lexical items from a database and applying modifications to them. In a mouthing track (tier) separate from the gloss, or lexical item track, an animator has the option to do nothing and use the mouthing associated with the basic lexical item, or to activate the same mouthing dialog as seen in Figure 3. Changes made to the mouthing in a sentence do not change the mouthings of a basic lexical item but are stored separately.

4. Results

The new interface supports multiple languages, including LSF, GSL, DGS, DSGS and ASL. For examples demonstrating the different styles of mouthing, including complete words, partial words and single viseme, please refer to Table 1. Although Figure 5 includes several sample images from the mouthings, the reader is encouraged to

[1] In our Sign Transcriber, a preparatory stroke precedes the sign, and the sign starts at 0.5 seconds. Thus, a start time in the mouthing editor of 0.4 seconds means that the mouth will begin moving 0.1 seconds before the start of the manual portion of the sign.

view the full animations via the link http://asl.cs.depaul.edu/video/wolfe2022/Mouthing.mp4 .

5. Conclusions and a proposal for future work

A future avenue to explore is the applicability of the methods described here to portray mouth gestures, which are commonly found across sign languages. In contrast to mouthings, mouth gestures do not arise from the surrounding ambient spoken language, and for this reason, there will be no need for a speech generator. However, effective application would require careful investigation of the postures of the lower face that are created when a signer produces mouth gestures. What descriptive/corpus work is needed to feed such an extension?

However, even for the case of mouthing, there are many refinements and questions remaining, because there is a tradeoff between automated and manual animation. Manual animation quality is superior but expensive, whereas automated animation is awkward but cheap.

We propose an experiment in corpus acquisition for mouthing. This would involve using the automatic generation of full mouthing for all lexical items. Then, to create sentences, apply the hyperparameter (full, partial, single viseme, none) most appropriate for the sign language being produced. Then, in consultation with deaf communities, we customize those mouthings that are not acceptable via the new editing options and store those modifications. We anticipate that this will provide a promising resource for future study of mouthing synthesis.

English translation	Language mouthed	Mouthing type
EASIER project (name sign)	English	full
Hello, I'm ready to begin.	Swiss German	full
Please wait – response is pending	Greek	viseme
Thank you for using our service. Goodbye!	French	partial

Table 1: Examples of avatar mouthing found in http://asl.cs.depaul.edu/video/wolfe2022/Mouthing.mp4

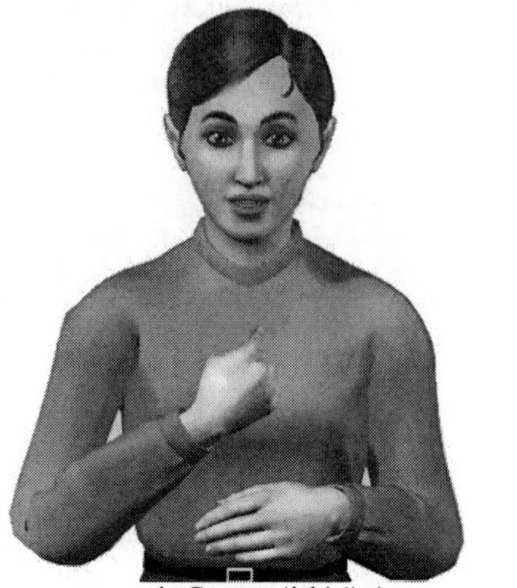
ɪ in German 'ich' ('ɪç)

i in English 'easier' ('i:zi:ɚ)

i in French 'merci' (mɛʁsi)

Figure 5: Mouthing samples from various languages.

6. Acknowledgements

The authors are grateful to Rebecca Shaftman and Kathryn Willis Wolfe for sharing their linguistic knowledge, for their keen observational skills and for their articulate, constructive feedback.

This work is supported in part by the EASIER (Intelligent Automatic Sign Language Translation) Project. EASIER has received funding from the European Union's Horizon 2020 research and innovation programme, grant agreement n° 101016982.

7. Bibliographical References

Bank, R., Crasborn, O. A., & Van Hout, R. (2011). Variation in mouth actions with manual signs in Sign Language of the Netherlands (NGT). *Sign Language & Linguistics, 14*, 248–270.

Brumm, M., Johnson, R., Hanke, T., Grigat, R. R., & Wolfe, R. (2019). Use of avatar technology for automatic mouth gesture recognition. *SignNonmanuals Workshop, 2.*

De Vos, C., & Zeshan, U. (2012). Introduction: Demographic, sociocultural, and linguistic variation across rural signing communities. *Sign languages in village communities: Anthropological and linguistic insights*, 2–23.

Ebbinghaus, H., & Heßmann, J. E. (1996). Signs and words: Accounting for spoken language elements in German Sign Language. *International review of sign linguistics, 1*, 23–56.

Ebling, S. (2013). Evaluating a swiss german sign language avatar among the deaf community.

Ebling, S., & Glauert, J. (2016). Building a Swiss German Sign Language avatar with JASigning and evaluating it among the Deaf community. *Universal Access in the Information Society, 15*, 577–587.

Efthimiou, E., Fotinea, S.-E., Hanke, T., Glauert, J., Bowden, R., Braffort, A., . . . Lefebvre-Albaret, F. (2012). The dicta-sign wiki: Enabling web communication for the deaf. *International Conference on Computers for Handicapped Persons*, (pp. 205–212).

Elliott, R., Glauert, J. R., Kennaway, J. R., & Marshall, I. (2000). The development of language processing support for the ViSiCAST project. *Proceedings of the fourth international ACM conference on Assistive technologies*, (pp. 101–108).

Hanke, T. (2002). iLex-A tool for Sign Language Lexicography and Corpus Analysis. *LREC 3rd Workshop on the Representation and Processing of Sign Languages: Construction and Exploitation of Sign Language Corpora.*

Hanke, T. (2014). Annotation of Mouth Activities with iLex. *6 th Workshop on the Representation and Processing of Sign Languages: Beyond the Manual Channel Language Resources and Evaluation Conference (LREC)* (pp. 67-70). Reykjavik, Iceland: ELRA.

Hanke, T., Popescu, H., & Schmaling, C. (2003). eSIGN–HPSG-assisted Sign Language Composition. *Gesture Workshop.*

Jennings, V., Elliott, R., Kennaway, R., & Glauert, J. (2010). Requirements for a signing avatar. *sign-lang@ LREC 2010*, (pp. 133–136).

Johnson, R. (2022). Improved facial realism through an enhanced representation of anatomical behavior for signing avatars (submitted). *SLTAT@ LREC 2022.*

Kipp, M., Heloir, A., & Nguyen, Q. (2011). Sign language avatars: Animation and comprehensibility. *International Workshop on Intelligent Virtual Agents*, (pp. 113–126).

Kipp, M., Nguyen, Q., Heloir, A., & Matthes, S. (2011). Assessing the deaf user perspective on sign language avatars. *The proceedings of the 13th international ACM SIGACCESS conference on Computers and accessibility*, (pp. 107–114).

Kuroda, T., Sato, K., & Chihara, K. (1998). S-TEL: An avatar based sign language telecommunication system. *International journal of virtual reality, 3*, 20–26.

Max Planck Institute for Psycholinguistics. (2022). ELAN (Version 6.3) [Computer software]. The Language Archive. Retrieved from https://archive.mpi.nl/tla/elan

McDonald, J., Wolfe, R., & Johnson, R. (2022). A novel approach to managing the complexity of the lower face in signing avatars (submitted). *SLTAT @ LREC 2022.*

Neidle, C., Opoku, A., Dimitriadis, G., & Metaxas, D. (2018). New shared & interconnected asl resources: Signstream® 3 software; dai 2 for web access to linguistically annotated video corpora; and a sign bank. *8th Workshop on the Representation and Processing of Sign Languages: Involving the Language Community, Miyazaki, Language Resources and Evaluation Conference 2018.*

Pfau, R., & Quer, J. (2010). Nonmanuals: Their prosodic and grammatical roles. *Sign languages*, 381–402.

Verlinden, M., Tijsseling, C., & Frowein, H. (2001). Sign language on the WWW. *Proceedings of 18th Int. Symposium on Human Factors in Telecommunication.*

Williams, R. (2009). *The animator's survival kit.* Farrar, Strauss and Giroux.

Wolfe, R., Hanke, T., Langer, G., Jahn, E., Worseck, S., Bleicken, J., . . . Johnson, S. (2018). Exploring Localization for Mouthings in Sign Language Avatars. *sign-lang@ LREC 2018*, (pp. 207–212).

Zwitserlood, I. (2005). Synthetic signing. *The World of Content Creation, Management, and Delivery*, 352–357.

Author Index

Association for Computational Linguistics
209 N. Eighth Street
Stroudsburg, Pennsylvania 18360

CURRAN ASSOCIATES INC. proceedings.com

ISBN 978-1-7138-6139-3

9 781713 861393